WITNESSING AUSTRALIAN STORIES

WITNESSING AUSTRALIAN STORIES

HISTORY, TESTIMONY, AND MEMORY IN CONTEMPORARY CULTURE

KELLY JEAN BUTLER

Transaction Publishers

New Brunswick (U.S.A.) and London (U.K.)

This book is printed on acid-free paper that meets the American National Standard for Permanence of Paper for Printed Library Materials.

Library of Congress Catalog Number: 2012032347
ISBN: 978-1-4128-5158-9
Printed in the United States of America

Library of Congress Cataloging-in-Publication Data

Butler, Kelly Jean.
    Witnessing Australian stories : history, testimony, and memory in contemporary culture / Kelly Jean Butler.
        pages cm
    Includes bibliographical references and index.
    ISBN 978-1-4128-5158-9 (acid-free paper)
    1. Australia—Historiography. 2. Australia—Social conditions. 3. Historiography—Social aspects—Australia. 4. Public history—Social aspects—Australia. 5. Collective memory—Australia. 6. Witnesses—Australia. 7. Marginality, Social—Australia—Historiography. 8. Indigenous peoples—Australia—Historiography. 9. Immigrants—Australia—Historiography. 10. Political refugees—Australia—Historiography. I. Title.
    DU108.B88 2013
    994.0049'915—dc23
                                                                      2012032347

Contents

Acknowledgments

This book started life as a PhD thesis, written while based at The Australian Centre, School of Historical and Philosophical Studies, University of Melbourne. I feel enormously privileged to have been part of the Centre's intellectual community, especially at a time when the value of "national" studies is under threat from both within and outside the academy. I am thankful to my fellow postgrads and colleagues—Pamie Fung, Penny Duckworth, Dr. Damien Williams and Dr. Jess Carniel—and especially to Dr. Caitlin Nunn, for always reminding me of the responsibility that we owe to our communities and readers.

This project would simply not exist without the unstinting support of my supervisor—Professor Kate Darian-Smith. I have been touched by her generosity and fortitude, and am thankful for her ongoing friendship. I also thank my associate supervisor, Dr. Sara Wills, for her kindness and rigor.

A number of people have assisted me on the journey from thesis to book. I thank my examiners Professor Susannah Radstone and Professor Gay Hawkins for their critical engagement with my work and their encouragement for publication. I owe a special thanks to Dr. Rick Crownshaw—formerly of Transaction's Memory and Narrative Editorial Board—for supporting my manuscript and wrangling with reader's reports.

At Transaction, I am especially thankful to my editor, Andrew McIntosh, for his patience and for guiding me through the complexities of publication.

Lastly, I thank my parents, Julie Hevey and Michael Butler, my brother Simon, and my partner Glenn Anderson, for their faith and support, and for putting up with me throughout the whole project.

Introduction: Public Histories, Personal Stories

Simply to listen is to be drawn into a world of ethical encounter: to hear is to witness; to witness is to become entangled.
—Deborah Bird Rose[1]

The problem has always been our ears, not their voices.
—Breyten Breytenbach[2]

On February 13, 2008, the first day of the forty-second parliament, then Prime Minister Kevin Rudd (2007–2010) delivered an apology to Australia's Indigenous peoples. The need to listen to the stories of Indigenous people lay at the heart of Rudd's speech. Throughout the apology, Rudd considered the testimonies contained in *Bringing them Home*, the 1997 report of the Human Rights and Equal Opportunity Commission (HREOC) Inquiry into the Separation of Aboriginal and Torres Strait Islander Children from their Families.[3] Reflecting on the stories contained in the report, Rudd declared that

> there is something terribly primal about these firsthand accounts. The pain is searing; it screams from the pages. The hurt, the humiliation, the degradation and the sheer brutality of the act of physically separating a mother from her children is a deep assault on our senses and on our most elemental humanity.[4]

Reading testimonies of child removal, Rudd argued, was a profoundly moving experience and, as such, one that demanded a reply

1

from the reader. "These stories cry out to be heard," he asserted, "they cry out for an apology."[5]

Rudd's speech was designed as a response to the affective power of Indigenous testimony—an attempt to acknowledge and affirm the truth of Indigenous voices. In particular, Rudd used the apology to highlight the testimony of Nungal or "Nanna" Fejo, an Aboriginal woman who had been removed from her family as a child. Rudd's emphasis on Fejo's testimony performed a crucial rhetorical move by personalizing Australia's history of dispossession and child removal. In focusing on the experience of one individual, among thousands, Rudd drew attention to the conjunction of intimate, personal stories with national history.

In the apology, Rudd positioned his reaction to Fejo's story as a collective testimonial exchange. In responding empathetically to Fejo's individual story—in hearing and validating her words—Rudd witnessed to the testimony of all members of the stolen generation. In this way, the apology was an act of collective witnessing, a national response to Indigenous testimony and its "cry" for recognition.[6]

Throughout his speech, Rudd drew on an understanding of Australian values to emphasize the need to say sorry. "Reconciliation is in fact," he argued, "an expression of a core value of our nation—and that value is a fair go for all."[7] He was motivated by a "pretty basic Aussie belief."[8] For Rudd, saying sorry was not simply the right thing to do; it was the right thing to do as an Australian. Witnessing was, thus, yoked to notions of good citizenship. To listen to the stories of Indigenous dispossession and to respond appropriately—in this instance, with an apology—was to act in the spirit of that most fundamental Australian ethic: a "fair go."

Sixteen years earlier, in the Sydney suburb of Redfern, the then Labor Prime Minister Paul Keating (1991–1996) also drew on the concept of the "fair go" in a speech delivered to mark the Australian launch for the International Year of Indigenous People. In a move that prefigured Rudd's apology, Keating argued that it was time to embrace Aboriginal Australians to demonstrate "that Australia *is* a first rate social democracy, that we are what we should be—*truly* the land of the fair go and the better chance."[9]

In calling for a new era in the relationship between Indigenous and non-Indigenous Australians, Keating asserted that

> The Report of the Royal Commission into Aboriginal Deaths in Custody showed with devastating clarity that the past lives

on in inequality, racism and injustice in the prejudice and ignorance of non-Aboriginal Australians, and in the demoralisation and desperation, the fractured identity, of so many Aborigines and Torres Strait Islanders.[10]

The Royal Commission into Aboriginal Deaths in Custody (1987–1991), similar to the HREOC inquiry (1995–1997) that followed, sent investigators throughout Australia to gather evidence and collect the oral and written testimonies of Australian Indigenous peoples. Both inquiries developed a process of listening to the stories of Aboriginal people as both a form of historical evidence and a testimony of the present effects of colonialism.

Central to Keating's "Redfern speech" was the call for settler Australians to recognize Indigenous testimony as truthful, as "historical fact." The future, he urged,

> begins, I think, with the act of recognition. Recognition that it was we who did the dispossessing. We took the traditional lands and smashed the traditional way of life. We brought the disasters. The alcohol. We committed the murders. We took the children from their mothers. We practised discrimination and exclusion.[11]

It was a startling and unprecedented admission from the elected leader of the nation. Keating urged settler Australians—his "we"—to witness to the devastation that their actions, and the actions of their ancestors, had caused Indigenous peoples. Empathy was at the heart of this witnessing. His speech called on non-Indigenous Australians to "open our hearts a bit" and establish an empathetic identification with Aboriginal peoples: to "imagine" the pain they have suffered.[12]

Both Keating and Rudd used their speeches as acts of collective witnessing. In doing so, both positioned the act of witnessing as a demonstration of ethical Australian citizenship, signaling the birth of a new national community forged through an acceptance of the truth of Indigenous peoples' testimony. More than this, both viewed their acts as interventions in national storytelling—"an historic *turning point*" in public history—and a challenge to those Australians who had denied the truth of Indigenous testimony.[13] For Rudd, the acceptance of the validity of *Bringing them Home* "is not, as some would argue, a black-armband view of history; it is just the truth: the cold, confronting, uncomfortable truth."[14] Here, Rudd was explicit in dismissing the views

3

of former Liberal Coalition Prime Minister John Howard (1996–2007), who was highly skeptical of the value of Aboriginal testimony and suspicious, more generally, of attempts to acknowledge the violence of the past. The apology marked a symbolic break in Australian history: a self-conscious end to the "history wars"; an end to Howard's denial; and, in Rudd's words, an end to the parliament's "stony and stubborn and deafening silence for more than a decade" on the issue of reconciliation between Indigenous and non-Indigenous Australians.[15] The aim of this book is to explore the forms of witnessing that punctured the "deafening silence" of the Howard era, forms of public action and protest which challenged the government's rejection of testimony and resistance to reconciliation.

*****

While I have begun by reflecting on two public occasions in which the nation "officially" responded to the truth of Indigenous testimony—Keating's Redfern speech (1992) and Rudd's Apology (2008)—this book examines the period between these two symbolic events, a period dominated by the historical denial of the Howard-led Liberal Coalition Government. If Keating was instrumental in articulating a mode of "being Australian" that was orientated to an acceptance of the truth of Indigenous testimony, and marked by openness to the stories of migrants and non-Anglo Australians, Howard worked to discredit the truth value of "other" voices in the public sphere. As Meaghan Morris, writing against the new cultural agenda of the Howard Government, lamented, "we are being asked to forget about the past few years of remembering."[16] What follows, then, is a cultural history of a particular kind of contemporary memory work: witnessing.

At its heart, this book is concerned with how Australians have responded to stories about suffering and historic injustice. In particular, I am interested in how the testimony of Indigenous peoples and asylum seekers has been received by the settler majority. Theorists have named this process of listening and responding to the stories of others as "witnessing." This book focuses on acts of witnessing that occurred between the release of *Bringing them Home* in 1997 and Rudd's apology in 2008. During this period, the voices of Australian Indigenous peoples; migrants; and, more recently, asylum seekers received unprecedented attention in the public sphere, disrupting comfortable stories of belonging and national identity. As these "liminal" voices became unavoidably public, they posed a challenge not only to historians, critics, and politicians, but also to ordinary citizens. The challenge of testimony has been to reimagine a vision of good citizenship against the revelation that Australia is not only a nation founded on dispossession, but also one which actively perpetuates the disadvantage of a range of sociocultural groups.

It is my contention that parallel to the official "silence" of the Howard Government, a widespread, diverse, and popular public discourse on witnessing developed during the 1990s. In responding to the testimony of Indigenous peoples and other socially marginalized groups, such as asylum seekers, this discourse considered the past as personal, and linked intimate, individual stories—of suffering, loss, and dispossession—with broader, national histories. Recently, historian Bain Attwood has referred to the "last few decades" as "the Age of Testimony," and has decried "the privileging of testimony [that] has blurred the relationship between the personal and the collective and between the particular and the general."[17] Similarly, Nancy Miller and Jason Tougaw have written that the process of witnessing to testimony "records a movement from individual experience to the collective archive, from personal trauma to public memory."[18] I examined how different forms of witnessing probed this nexus between the private and public spheres and, in doing so, reconfigured national history in highly personalized, emotive forms. It is my aim to map the multiplicity of ways that settler Australians witnessed to the testimony of the socially and politically marginalized during the tenure of the Howard Government. Through the conjunction of personal stories and public histories, witnessing has served to articulate ideas about nation and citizenship, challenging what it meant to be a "good" Australian. In between the public acts of Keating and Rudd, witnessing came to represent, for a large and diverse group of settler Australians, the apotheosis of a "fair go."

All of "Us": History and Nation under Howard

To begin by reflecting on the contributions of three prime ministers to public discourses on history and testimony is to emphasize, as Elazar Barkan and Alexander Karn have done, that "individual personalities and leadership make an important difference; . . . apology discourse cannot be understood properly if it is treated as an impersonal phenomenon."[19] Yet if Rudd and Keating have been instrumental in promoting openness to the stories of Aboriginal and non-Anglo Australians, Howard's leadership style and personality have been equally important in the production of a climate of historical denial and resistance to testimony. During the tenure of the Howard Government, from 1996 to 2007, the need to listen to the voices of the socially and politically marginalized was officially and repeatedly rejected. Winning government on the back of the slogan "For All of Us," Howard was quick to assert his disdain for Keating's policies and future vision, promising to eschew the needs of "elites" to serve the interests of the "majority." In an interview on the Australian Broadcasting Commission's (ABC) television program *Four Corners* during the lead-up to his 1996 election victory, Howard declared that by the year 2000, he "would like to see an Australian nation that feels comfortable and relaxed about . . . their history."[20] Yet, as historians Stuart Macintyre and Anna Clark have demonstrated, the period of the Howard Government saw an intensification of debate surrounding the nation's history, which became a site of vigorous contestation rather than "relaxed" contemplation.[21]

In particular, the founding violence of colonial Australia and the enduring issue of the stolen generations were matters of concern for Howard and his supporters. They were alarmed by the prevalence of what they dubbed the "black-armband view of Australian history": history that sought to emphasize the "guilt" of settler Australians vis-à-vis the colonial past and the present social disadvantage of Aboriginal peoples.[22] In contrast, Howard and his supporters in the conservative media maintained that Australians should feel nothing but pride in their national history, and should honor, not repudiate, their British heritage.

Many politicians and public figures called for a collective recognition of the role of Anglo-Australians and their ancestors in the dispossession of Aboriginal peoples, whereas Howard insisted that present-day Australians could not be held responsible for the actions of their forebears, and, as such, should not feel undue guilt or shame about the past. Howard's unwillingness to engage with notions of collective responsibility was not simply a denial of aspects of Australian history, but rather constituted a refusal to witness and acknowledge the validity of Indigenous testimony as a form of truthful evidence about the past. This inability to listen to testimony as history was perhaps most stark in his now infamous opening address to the 1997 Reconciliation Convention. Timed to coincide with the tabling of *Bringing them Home* in parliament, the Reconciliation Convention brought together Indigenous and non-Indigenous politicians, historians, and activists to discuss the future of reconciliation in the wider community. In his opening speech, Howard expressed his "deep sorrow for those of my fellow Australians who suffered injustices under the practices of past generations towards indigenous people."[23] However, he refused to extend this personal apology to a formal apology on behalf of the parliament in recognition of its historical role in the forced removal of children from their families. The response of the convention's Indigenous delegates, many of whom turned their backs and jeered at the prime minister, at once mirrored Howard's refusal to listen and sought to shame the nation's leader.[24]

Instead of using his speech to witness to the truth of *Bringing them Home* and, in doing so, affirming the relationship between Indigenous testimony and national history, Howard took the opportunity to attack those who, he believed, focused inappropriately on the "negative" aspects of the past. Howard argued that

> in facing the realities of the past, however, we must not join those who would portray Australia's history since 1788 as little more than a disgraceful record of imperialism, exploitation and racism.
>
> Such a portrayal is a gross distortion and deliberately neglects the overall story of great Australian achievement that is there in our history to be told, and such an approach will be repudiated by the overwhelming majority of Australians who are proud of what this country has achieved although inevitably acknowledging the blemishes in its past history.[25]

For Howard, too much emphasis on Australia's history of dispossession only served as a morbid distraction from the nation's more positive history of "achievement."

Howard's desire to return a "sense of balance" to public discussions about history became a key feature of his government's cultural agenda.[26] He criticized those public institutions and figures who he believed did not support a "balanced" view of the past.[27] Moreover, Howard lent public and political favor to the individuals and institutions who endorsed his version of Australian history. Most notably, Howard supported Keith Windschuttle—a key figure in the history wars and conservative author of the contentious frontier history *The Fabrication of Aboriginal History*—by appointing him to the board of the nation's public broadcaster, the ABC.[28] While denying the importance of Indigenous testimony was a key focus of Howard's attempts to reconfigure Australian history, his government also sought to limit the effects of "other" non-Anglo voices. This was particularly so in the latter period of his government after the 9/11 attacks and the 2002 Bali bombings, in which members of the Indonesian terrorist group Jemaah Islamiyah targeted Australians who were working and holidaying in Bali. In response to a range of regional and global political events, including an upsurge in asylum seekers attempting to enter Australia by sea, Howard became preoccupied with issues of immigration, terrorism, and border control.

During the asylum seeker crises of 2001—in which the government controversially prevented the *Tampa*, a boat overloaded with asylum seekers, from landing in Australia—Howard and his ministers sought to prevent asylum seeker testimony from reaching the public, and worked hard to discredit the refuge claims of so-called "illegals."[29] As with their attacks on "black-armband" history, government ministers rejected testimony on moral grounds, arguing that the country's intake of refugees should be limited in order to maintain border security. Against criticism of their immigration policy, the government maintained that ignoring the claims of asylum seekers served to preserve the sovereignty and integrity of the settler nation. Through this discourse, Howard positioned asylum seekers as a nefarious group who tried to prey on the innate goodness of the Australian people: "we are a humane people," he argued, "and others know that and they sometimes . . . try and intimidate us with our own decency."[30] In this way, the Howard Government presented its rejection of both asylum seeker and Indigenous testimony as a moral imperative. In doing so, it supported the emergence of a conservative denial of testimony within the media and sections of the academy, and fueled broader hostility to asylum seekers and Indigenous peoples within the public sphere.

Yet, during this same period, a diverse public discourse on witnessing thrived. Many of Australia's most noted historians and public intellectuals called for settler Australians to confront the violence and dispossession of the past, to acknowledge and make amends for the destruction wrought on the nation's first peoples. Some, such as philosopher and public intellectual Raimond Gaita, argued that settler Australians were struggling under the burden of "national shame" and, as such, were "called to communal responsiveness to those who are the victims of our wrongdoing or the wrongdoing of those who preceded us."[31] The Howard Government, some intellectuals, and the conservative media worked tirelessly to foreclose discussion of the violent aspects of Australia's past; whereas numerous historians, artists, novelists, and public figures challenged their government in their efforts to respond to the voices of the marginalized. Some defied the government through their creative or scholarly work, whereas others engaged in forms of public political protest and advocacy for Indigenous peoples and asylum seekers. In the year 2000, hundreds of thousands of "ordinary" citizens marched in support of reconciliation between Indigenous and non-Indigenous Australians. A year later, in the wake of the so-called *Tampa* crisis, a broad range of people marched again in protest against the government's border protection policy and wrote letters in support of the claims of asylum seekers. Howard had reconfigured public debates about Indigenous people and asylum seekers as contests over Australian values, whereas many settler Australians resisted their government through their efforts to witness. In doing so, they attempted to recuperate the notion of a fair go and to forge a national community founded on respect for and attentiveness to the testimony of the socially and politically marginalized.

It is my contention that over this period, witnessing—that is, not only listening to the voices of others, but also acting on their behalf— has come to form a key tenet of ethical citizenship in contemporary Australian culture. This book not only demonstrates the emergence of this culture, but also emphasizes the extent to which not all Australians responded to the persuasion of testimony. In fact, as Howard's attitude of skepticism and denial demonstrated, witnessing has not been "officially" endorsed by the federal government for much of the past two decades. As such, I understand witnessing as an unstable, ambivalent discourse, a kind of "minor" nationalism. This notion recalls the concept of a minor literature that was developed by Gilles Deleuze and Felix Guattari; however, the usage is not wholly apposite given that I am concerned with a discourse produced by majority subjects: settler Australians.[32] Nevertheless, I find the phrase useful in evoking the sense that witnessing is both mainstream and counter-hegemonic. Speaking through the "major language" of Australian nationalism, witnessing as a minor practice seeks to remake what it means to be a "good" national subject by employing foundational national concepts, such as the fair go. In this way, I underscore the extent to which witnessing has emerged as a way of being Australian that, though prominent and widespread, was not shared by the overwhelming majority of national citizens.

9

Witnessing the National Story: Colonialism and Migration

This book not only pays particular attention to the way that Aboriginal voices have been listened to by settler Australians, but also investigates how the testimony of asylum seekers has been understood within contemporary Australian culture. Indigenous peoples and asylum seekers occupy radically different structural relationships within the settler nation and its institutions of power and influence. Indeed, if asylum seekers have been routinely figured as extranational or an "external" threat, Indigenous peoples have frequently been consigned as prenational, a prelude to the establishment of the settler-colonial state. Yet, crucially, both groups have been produced as "other" to the dominant settler culture and, as such, have posed distinct challenges to the authority and stability of the (white) nation. As Ann Curthoys has argued, colonialism and migration form the two central narratives within Anglo-Australian history, and, subsequently, "can neither be conceptualised together nor maintained as fully distinct."[33] Curthoys has traced what she terms the "uneasy conversation" between the Indigenous and the multicultural, and sought to untangle the distinct, yet linked, ways in which Aboriginal peoples and non-Anglo migrants have been othered by white Australian culture. At the same time, Curthoys has been concerned to emphasize the priority of Indigenous Australians as sovereign within the migrant nation. "All non-indigenous people," she has noted, "share the situation of living on someone else's land."[34]

Similarly, I examine the specificities of practices of witnessing to Indigenous peoples and asylum seekers as distinct phenomena, but have come to understand these discourses as complexly interlinked. First, both Indigenous and asylum seeker testimony are culturally marginalized modes of expression that have tested the boundaries of the settler nation, bringing into crisis taken-for-granted concepts of history, identity, and citizenship. In particular, "minority" testimony challenges the position of the Anglo subject as the center of the Australian national imaginary.

Second, witnessing to both forms of testimony was crucial in the performance of resistance to the Howard federal government. It should not be a surprise that many of the public intellectuals and prominent figures associated with Aboriginal reconciliation—such as academic Robert Manne and philosopher Raimond Gaita—have also been involved in advocacy for asylum seekers, and have argued vehemently for settler Australians to witness to testimony.

Third, and most importantly for my interests, acts of witnessing to the voices of asylum seekers and Indigenous peoples have made appeals to so-called "Australian values," and in doing so, have been crucial in the formation of self-consciously ethical communities. That is, discourses on witnessing to both Indigenous peoples and asylum seekers have sought to interpellate settler Australians as "good" citizens through a common focus on listening as a civic virtue. As such, witnessing has functioned as a form of nation building, drawing together both the Indigenous and the multicultural in a narrative that affirms the benevolent "goodness" of settler Australians.

In writing about the contours of settler Australian culture, I have chosen to use the terms "settlers" and "settler Australians" to refer to all non-Indigenous Australians. I do so, however, with an awareness of the diversity of experiences and subject positions glossed by these terms.[35] As such, I augment my discussion of settler culture with specific comments on what I term "white" or "Anglo-Australians," terms I employ to refer to non-Indigenous Australians of British and Irish descent, a group that comprises the Australian "mainstream." Similar to migration historian James Jupp, I find the terms "European," "Anglo-Celtic," and "Anglo-Saxon" somewhat wanting in attempting to describe not simply a racial or ethnic identity, but also a cultural group.[36] This emphasis on the cultural specificity of non-Indigenous Australians has been particularly useful in analyzing not only how Anglo-Australians have witnessed to Indigenous peoples and asylum seekers, but also to their own experiences.

Key Concepts: Witnessing and Testimony

Central to this book is an understanding of the twinned concepts of "testimony" and "witnessing." There is an extremely large body of work that theorizes testimony, particularly in relation to the Holocaust.[37] More recently, concepts of testimony and witnessing have been used in studies of national processes of forgiveness and apology, and in discussions of South Africa's Truth and Reconciliation Commission.[38] Most relevant to this book, however, have been the pioneering work of Shoshana Felman and Dori Laub, American feminist philosopher Kelly Oliver, and the important contributions of Gillian Whitlock and Rosanne Kennedy, who have drawn on theories of witnessing to address the specificities of Australian culture.[39]

Stripped to its most fundamental meaning, to testify "is to produce one's own speech as material evidence for truth."[40] Someone who gives testimony may be variously referred to as a "testifier," a "witness," or an "eyewitness." Yet, theorists of witnessing—including Felman, Laub, Oliver, Whitlock, and Kennedy—have written of testimony as a process that actually involves two witnesses.[41] The primary eyewitness, the one who testifies, is paired with the so-called "second person," the listener or secondary witness who is called on to complete the testimonial exchange.[42] In this way, the concepts of "testimony" and "witnessing" are inextricably linked. The presence of a secondary witness—the availability of an audience to hear—is a necessary condition of the production of testimony. As Laub has contended, "the absence of an empathic listener, or more radically, the absence of an *addressable other*, an other who can hear the anguish of one's memories and thus affirm and recognize their realness, annihilates the story."[43] Following Whitlock, I focus on the role of this "second person," and in particular on the way settler Australians have performed this role.[44]

Witnessing in these terms is an intersubjective process that is productive of a specific set of relations between others. It is an exchange that bonds individuals and collectives through the telling and hearing of testimony. To be sure, this is a fundamentally unequal relationship. As Gayatri Chakravorty Spivak has noted, "testimony is the genre of the subaltern giving witness to oppression, to a less oppressed other."[45] It is a process founded on a power differential that produces what Deborah Bird Rose has described as "an ethical encounter."[46] Through the testimonial exchange, the secondary witness becomes "entangled" with the other, and bonded to others through modes of empathy, identification, and subjectification.

For Oliver, the process of witnessing not only draws together the subject and the other, but also acts as a process of subjectification whereby the subject is differentiated and produced as a social agent only through their encounter with otherness. Oliver's project has been to rethink the relationship between the self and the other by rejecting "recognition" as assimilative and inherently destructive, and by developing a notion of witnessing as the key to "a more humane and ethical future beyond violence."[47] Accordingly, "if we are selves, subject, and have subjectivity and agency by virtue of our dialogical relationships with others, then we are not opposed to others. We are by virtue of others."[48] However, more than this, since the subject position of the secondary witness usually affords them a cultural and political authority which is disproportionate to that of the testifier, the witness should bear what Oliver calls a "response-ability" to listen and act appropriately.[49]

At the same time, the role of the secondary witness is multiple, entailing a primary responsibility to the other, as well as a focused attention on the self. As Laub has outlined, the secondary witness or "listener"

> has to be at the same time a witness to the trauma witness and a witness to himself. It is only in this way, through his simultaneous awareness of the continuous flow of those inner hazards both in the trauma witness and in himself, that he can become the enabler of the testimony.[50]

Thus, although witnessing is dependent on the ability of the secondary witness to forge an empathetic identification with the testifier (or in Laub's terminology the "trauma witness"), and, in some sense, vicariously experience "trauma" alongside the testifier, witnessing is risky and fraught with "inner hazards," including the perils of unexamined transference.[51] Witnessing, thus, involves a double move: the need to witness to the other, while at the same time, witnessing to the self in the act of witnessing. In this way, witnessing is simultaneously a process of self-fashioning, of articulating different forms of selfhood, and of forging new kinds of communities among witnesses.

The forms of expression and kinds of texts that constitute testimony are diverse. Throughout the twentieth century, Australian Indigenous people have given testimony in a variety of forms and contexts: through poetry, social realist novels, life writing, and legal evidence; during Royal Commissions, land rights cases, and within the context of literary and artistic production. Similarly, asylum seekers have provided testimony in letters, interviews, and, most contentiously, through physical acts of bodily harm. As Rosanne Kennedy has warned, testimony "should not be treated as a monolithic category."[52] Testimony is a broad and at times amorphous label, encompassing a wide range of texts and events, expressed within a range of contexts: judicial, political, cultural, and literary. However, at their core, all instances of testimony are moments of "truth," anchored by both personal and collective experience.

Likewise, actions that may constitute an act of witnessing are diverse. Political speeches, similar to those of Keating and Rudd, are acts of witnessing. So too are works of history, art, and literature that attempt to engage with testimonial expression. Moreover, many forms of witnessing respond to the testimony of specific individuals—or particular groups of individuals as is the case with *Bringing them Home*—whereas some attempts to witness work to engage more broadly with histories of suffering, injustice, or dispossession. The imperatives of testimony may differ between contexts and situations, and may be expressed in a variety of ways—from political or social protest to critical or creative work—whereas the need to respond remains the core responsibility of the secondary witness. It is an exchange that entangles the secondary witness in a web of obligation, care, and responsibility. Witnessing names a specific relationship between individuals or groups, in which a subaltern or marginalized testimony seeks the response of a more dominant audience.

Witnessing the Holocaust

Historically, the concept of witnessing has been closely allied with efforts to respond to Holocaust testimony. The paradigms of testimony and trauma that have emerged from the Holocaust have been so influential that, as Gillian Whitlock has written, "almost all that we know about the cultural processes of traumatic memory has been transferred from Holocaust related issues, insights, vocabularies, and therapeutic paradigms."[53] Although I have drawn extensively from Holocaust-related literature in order to conceptualize witnessing, I maintain several reservations. First, the forms of witnessing that occur within the ambit of a truth and reconciliation commission—or in the case of Australia, a broad effort to engage with the effects of the past—often call on the witness to acknowledge a form of complicity with acts of violence or dispossession. As Whitlock has argued, the Australian context is marked by the absence of an abhorrent "Nazi" figure: the evil other onto which blame may be projected and contained.[54] If the paradigm of witnessing centered on the Holocaust works to collapse the distance between the secondary witness and testifier, through a communal rejection of the figure of the Nazi perpetrator, in postcolonial arenas, a similar identification with the testifier would risk ignoring the centrality of race as a structuring category, not only in historical abuse but also in ongoing suffering. Thus, in postcolonial contexts, the witness is "called upon to witness her own complicity and implication in the loss and suffering which is finally being spoken."[55] Even if, as in the case of some discussions about colonial violence, blame can be conferred on "the British," Anglo-Australians are, nevertheless, drawn to consider their ancestral links to the past. In response to stolen generations' testimony, then, the settler witness is drawn to engage in a self-reflexive analysis of how the settler self is complicit in forms of colonial dominance that are ongoing. In the case of asylum seekers, this sense of complicity is even more acute, as the witness is called on to witness the unfolding of injustice in the present. In this way, the specifities of an Australian context reconfigure the responsibilities and affects of witnessing.

Another crucial complication is the extent to which critics should follow the Holocaust paradigm and read testimony psychoanalytically. As Rosanne Kennedy and Tikka Jan Wilson have argued, "psychoanalysis favours testimony that is inaccessible to cognition and to being spoken . . . it therefore neglects, and calls into question the value and validity of acts of testimony in which the narrator claims to speak as an 'expert' about her own condition or experience."[56] It is necessary to note here that psychoanalysis does not offer only one way to understand the process of witnessing, as Susannah Radstone has emphasized in her use of Jean Laplanche.[57] However, psychoanalytic approaches are linked through their common insistence on the impossibility or unspeakability of traumatic testimony.

This sense of impossibility and unrepresentability is a core feature of the paradigms of testimony developed in response to the Holocaust and, in particular, to the seminal work of Felman and Laub.[58] For Felman, testimony should be read as an inchoate expression of trauma, rather than as a form of knowledge or a representation of actual events. Accordingly, she has suggested that testimony

> seems to be composed of bits and pieces of a memory that has been overwhelmed by occurrences that have not settled into understanding or remembrance, acts that cannot be constructed as knowledge nor assimilated into full cognition . . . What testimony does not offer is . . . a completed statement, a totalizable account of those events.[59]

Similarly, Giorgio Agamben has written that Holocaust "testimony contained at its core an essential lacuna; in other words, the survivors bore witness to something it is impossible to bear witness to."[60] In this way, testimony has been figured as impossibility: a form of speech that through its fragmentation witnesses to the inability of representing traumatic experience.

As such, theories of witnessing have tended to favor highly aestheticized forms of testimony, such as modernist film and literature, which have been read as stylistically expressive of the process of traumatic cognition. Though this mode of expression has been popular within the literature of the Holocaust, in other contexts, testimony has often been expressed in less literary forms. In particular, the bulk of stolen generations' testimony has occurred in what Kennedy and Wilson have described as "vernacular forms."[61] As such, they have argued that "a performative conception of testimony as an address to a community, which has been neglected in trauma studies, provides a more appropriate model for analyzing Stolen Generations testimony."[62] This movement shifts critical emphasis away from the role of the secondary witness as translator or analyst, interpreting the other's experience, to an acknowledgment that it is the process of intersubjective exchange which produces testimonial truth.

The emphasis placed on absence and "unspeakability" in trauma studies poses a considerable obstacle in reading forms of testimony that stake a claim to truth and individual agency, as well as modes of sociopolitical protest. Rather than persist with the Holocaust framework, within an Australian context we can look to the work of Penny van Toorn, who, following Michel de Certeau, has conceptualized testimony as "tactical."[63] In doing so, we should recognize that testimony is always elicited by a dominant audience and that the decision of the "subaltern" to provide testimony maintains a complex relationship to resistance.[64] Testimony is always subject to editorial selection and framing, and should be articulated and received within specific institutional and generic frameworks.[65] Yet, while the testifier cannot exert total control over the meaning of their words, they, nevertheless, display their agency in the decision to respond, and in what ways, to the demands of their audience. To insist on this type of reading is to acknowledge the extent to which testimony is both individual and psychic and enmeshed in the political and cultural scene of its expression.

Methodology and Sources

Throughout this book, I use the term "witnessing" to refer specifically to the actions of the secondary witness. In order to explore how the concept of witnessing has developed in contemporary public culture, I undertake a discourse analysis of a range of cultural texts, including academic histories, autobiographies, political speeches, novels, royal commission and enquiry reports, films, and television programs. All the texts examined have circulated widely within public culture, with the exception of a few of the more "academic" histories, such as Katrina Schlunke's *Bluff Rock* (2005), a work that has been surprisingly little discussed even in academic circles. Kate Grenville's 2005 novel *The Secret River,* for example, has been a popular and critical success, and has been promoted widely on television as well as in the online and print media.[66] The 2007 documentary *Bra Boys,* discussed in Chapter 6, was an extraordinary success and is currently the highest grossing Australian documentary ever.[67] By analyzing these popular texts alongside more marginal academic works such as Schlunke's, I seek to emphasize both the diversity of practices of witnessing and the extent to which witnessing has permeated both public and academic contexts.

A focus on texts and events within the ambit of the public sphere has enabled a consideration of the visibility and pervasiveness of witnessing discourses in contemporary Australian culture. Witnessing is not simply an academic concern, nor has it been only the preserve of isolated, individual relationships. It has developed as a widespread, albeit diverse, practice that has been enacted through a range of texts, public institutions, and government bodies. This focus on texts—as not simply expressive of witnessing, but as shaping and producing different modes or genres of witnessing—draws attention to testimony's "articulation" through a range of institutions, genres, and contexts.[68] As Radstone has reminded us, "texts and their meanings are complexly related to the broader social formation in which their meanings are forged."[69]

Drawing on the work of Jill Bennett and Rosanne Kennedy, I place "aesthetic texts into dialogue with non-aesthetic texts" or "vernacular texts" in order to underscore both the pervasiveness of witnessing as a form of public memory work and the generic and formal diversity of acts of witnessing.[70] In their work on trauma and memory, Bennett and Kennedy employ the notion of "languages" of trauma in order to bring literary and vernacular forms of trauma into conversation. To adopt a similar approach to witnessing is to recognize that witnessing, at its essence, names a particular relationship between the self and the other, a relationship that can be spoken and negotiated through a variety of different "languages," encompassing the literary, the historical, the political, and the vernacular or "everyday."

Similarly, the diversity of the contexts within which witnessing may occur has been explored by Sara Ahmed and Jackie Stacey. "Just as testimony does not have a singular form," they argue, "neither does it have a singular politics or ethics."[71] More than this, Ahmed and Stacey argue that testimony is generative of its own context of reception:

> it does not reflect some already existent truth, politics or ethics, but . . . creates the conditions for its own existence and reception, by constituting different configurations of self, space and community.[72]

In this way, we can speak of "testimonial cultures" that through their discourses produce diverse audiences and spaces of reception. These spaces can be usefully conceived of as counter-publics or "sphericules."

The notion of public "sphericules" has developed to complicate the "classical" notion of the public sphere. Some critics have emphasized the "dissolution" or mediatization of this sphere, whereas others have been concerned with mapping the emergence of "public sphericules" or counter-publics. These smaller public spheres have been described as subsets of the nationally oriented public sphere, though John Hartley and Alan McKee have understood them as local, transnational or global spaces for the expression of "other 'virtual' or nonterritorially defined communities, such as ethnic groups, people of particular sexual orientation, environmentalists, peace and human rights activists, children, even taste constituencies of various kinds."[73]

In the field of social theory, the notion of the "dissolution" of the public sphere has been particularly resonant, especially in the influential work of Paul Antze and Michael Lambek, and Lauren Berlant who, separately, have decried the personalization of politics and the erosion of any comprehensively communal public space.[74] This view is interested in how the proliferation of testimony is implicated in a personalization of public debate, whereas I am concerned with the critical tendency to view this shift as an a priori negative or indicative of a contraction of political space. By mobilizing the notion of couterpublics, it is possible to view the rise of testimony as a force in the formation of discrete ethical and political communities or publics. Witnessing, as a minor or counter-hegemonic practice, may be said to produce a counter-public concerned with listening to the voices of others. Yet this is not to argue that witnessing forms any homogenous community, or group. Rather, as Ahmed and Stacey have insisted, "the effects of testimonial forms are dependent on the context in which they are used, even if the contexts themselves are unstable."[75]

The proliferation of testimony is a global and transnational phenomena, yet close attention should be paid to the relationship between specific instances of testimony and the particular cultures that develop to sustain its circulation and reception.[76] Within an Australian context, the concept of witnessing has been crucial to both contemporary reconciliation politics and campaigns to end the detention of asylum seekers. A sizeable body of critical work has emerged to examine the way in which settler Australians have listened to and responded to the testimonies associated with *Bringing them Home.*[77] Although there have been a number of studies which place Indigenous testimony within a global context, such as Kay Schaffer and Sidonie Smith's important *Human Rights and Narrated Lives: The Ethics of Recognition* (2004), there has hitherto been a reluctance to consider Aboriginal testimony alongside the other forms of testimony that circulate within the Australian public sphere.[78] Though I acknowledge that there is much to gain from a global or transnational approach to testimony, here I reaffirm the importance of a national frame of analysis. I do this in order to underscore how witnessing has developed within and responded to the specifities of an Australian social, political, and historical context.

In doing so, I emphasize the extent to which the exchange between testifier and witness is crucial in the production of national affective communities. As Felicity Collins and Therese Davies have argued in *Australian Cinema after Mabo* (2004), "while memory discourse[s] appear to be global in one register, in their core they remain tied to the histories of specific nations and states."[79] Acts of witnessing to both Indigenous and asylum seeker testimony have drawn on globalized notions of human rights and postcolonialism. However, they have also drawn on peculiarly Australian experiences and histories and, as such, have sought to engage with and reconfigure so-called "Australian values." In this way, witnessing is not simply concerned with responding to testimony. It is a mode of self-fashioning and community formation—a way of producing affective bonds with other national citizens and, at the same time, a way of reshaping a specifically national imaginary. Thus, my archive is comprised primarily of texts and events that exist within a national framework.

Testimony, History, and Memory

This book understands witnessing as a form of public memory work and, as such, aims to draw on and expand studies of memory in Australia. Memory studies has proliferated globally as an interdisciplinary field, whereas the literature based on Australia is alarmingly slight.[80] This lack of engagement with "memory" as a category of analysis is despite the fact that, as Paula Hamilton has suggested, "a memorial culture has come to dominate the national consciousness."[81] This sense of disconnection between history and memory studies has been noted by Katharine Hodgkin and Susannah Radstone as a feature of memory studies more generally. They have asserted that memory studies has tended to reject history to forge close relationships with those disciplines centered on the study of representation: literature, cinema, and media studies.[82]

As a work of cultural history, this book sits at the interface between memory studies, cultural studies, and history, fields that have had a notably fraught relationship both to each other, and to "memory" as a useful category of analysis.[83] I seek to navigate this terrain by understanding the process of witnessing as a space of negotiation between the individual and the collective. As such, the book pays close attention to the expression of testimony through specific textual genres; its circulation across particular institutional contexts; and its broader reception within the arenas of public life. As Whitlock has indicated, witnessing entails the exchange of "acts of memory," and, thus, plays a crucial role in the way historical events are remembered and linked with contemporary publics.[84] As a form of memory, witnessing, in the first instance, involves an exchange of personal or individual recollection. However, this exchange contributes to the formation of wider or "collective" memories about specific historical events. This is not to suggest that cultures or nations can remember, but that memory's articulation and mediation through public texts and institutions produces "cultural memory" as "a field of cultural negotiation through which different stories vie for a place in history."[85] My focus on the exchange of testimony, an exchange at once personal and public, highlights the way that memory texts register "the collective nature of the activity of remembering."[86]

As a form of memory work, witnessing has impacted both public and professional understandings of history. Storytelling lies at the heart of history-making, and the transmission of memories about the past—through oral history, television programs, films, and museum exhibits—has been crucial to changing understandings about which stories, and whose experiences, count as "Australian." As this book demonstrates, testimony has been central to shifting understandings about Australian history, especially in relation to debates about the significance of settler violence to the present.

Despite testimony's influence within public culture as a vehicle for the dissemination of hitherto ignored or marginalized stories, it has been a focus of concern for some historians who have lamented the role of testimony as a "substitute" for history.[87] In particular, Bain Attwood has been an outspoken critic of the role of Indigenous testimony in the popularization of a "stolen generations narrative" within contemporary Australian historical culture.[88] According to Attwood, the danger of personal testimony being received as history lies in the inability of testimony to explain the past. Rather than maintain a temporal distance from the past—as professional history does—testimony privileges a personal connection to the past that is sustained by proximity.[89]

Although I do not share Attwood's belief that historians need to work to "check the influence"[90] of testimony, I do contend that the increased importance of testimonial speech signals "a new kind of cultural politics."[91] The rise of testimony and memory, more generally, has signaled the erosion of the authority of the historian and the democratization of practices of history-making and remembrance, and it has also marked a reconfiguration of the relationship between history, politics, and public culture. As Andreas Huyssen, a key figure in memory studies has argued, questions regarding the representation of national, local, or regional memories are "fundamentally political question[s] about the nature of the public sphere, about democracy and its future, about the changing shape of nationhood, citizenship, and identity."[92] Most importantly, the contemporary importance of testimony signals how "forms of intimate attachment . . . are increasingly replacing and transforming former relations between the public sphere and the private."[93]

The rise of testimony has heralded a new emphasis on personal experience within public culture. This has been accompanied by a valorization of victimhood and a reification of "the evidence of experience."[94] Hamilton has drawn attention to the potential problems of the desirability of victimhood, particularly its tendency to underwrite the formation of constituencies of suffering.[95] Yet, the omnipresence of testimony does not necessarily mark an erosion of political or

21

public space, nor does it prevent critical comments on testimony's meanings and affects. Moreover, I am less concerned with how the rise of testimony has, pace Attwood, impacted the authority of "History" and historians, though I do address this in Chapter 3. Rather, I am interested in how witnessing, as a public mode of memory work, has reshaped notions about what it means to be a "good" Australian in the twenty-first century. That is, I am concerned with exploring the political and cultural work performed by testimony. To do so is to consider witnessing as productive, rather than destructive, of public culture.

Although witnessing is a form of remembering—and, as such, an intervention into historical culture—it is also a privileged mode of (re)producing subjectivity in the present. During the latter half of the twentieth century, autobiographical speech, particularly in the form of testimony, became the preeminent mode of speaking, and writing, about the past in the present.[96] I am concerned with probing the constellation of truth, testimony, and civic virtue that has come not only to structure contemporary historical debate, but also to determine what kinds of stories about our past can be narrated within the public sphere. To do so is to examine how personal testimony and forms of self-representation such as life writing, memoir, and autobiography have come to play a central role in debates about history and the nation.[97] For Leigh Gilmore, it is testimony and autobiography's "investment in the representative person" that "allies it to the project of lending substance to the national fantasy of belonging."[98] That is, testimony exists at "the interface of singular and shareable," invoking collective understandings of belonging, nation, and truth.[99] It is both an individual technology of the self and a form of representative expression that is able to unite particular communities through its claims to truth, authenticity, and victimhood.

This book aims at demonstrating how a discourse on witnessing to testimony has come not only to dominate debates regarding the past, but also to regulate how we can speak the truth, and be believed, in the present. The pervasive and obsessive focus on truth-telling that has been a feature of recent Australian history has signaled a destabilization of notions of truth, authenticity, and authority which is at once the legacy of a popular encounter with postmodernism, as well as the specific manifestation of a series of disruptions within dominant conceptions of Australian nationhood. This fracturing of historical certainty is, thus, both an expression of the "cultural logic" of the present—to borrow from Fredric Jameson—and a response to the presence of alternative, subaltern voices within a nationally oriented conscious-ness. As Shoshana Felman has contended, "testimony is called for in a situation where the truth is not clear, where there is already a 'crisis of truth.'"[100] Indeed, as Ahmed and Stacey have argued:

> if testimony is bound up with truth and justice, then it's coming into being also registers the crisis in both of these concepts; for one testifies when the truth is in doubt (when it has yet to be decided) and when an injustice has occurred. If there has indeed been a proliferation of testimonial forms, and a collapse of boundaries between the legal, the political and the cultural, then it might be precisely because "truth" itself has become subject to appeal.[101]

However, if uncertainty, postmodern ennui, and conservative "backlash" are omnipresent global phenomena—the *raison d'être* of the now—this book returns to the specificities of an Australian national consciousness as the site of particularly local historical discourses. In examining an Australian national imaginary, this book argues that national memory has become the ground of key political and ethical debates in which witnessing and truth-telling have become tied to the production of civic virtue.

Structural Overview

What follows is a study of how other or "subaltern" voices have been heard in Australian public culture. The book charts the emergence of settler witnessing from the late 1980s to its zenith in *fin-de-siècle* discourses on national maturity. Though I trace the diversity and prevalence of practices of witnessing, I also examine its limits as a liberal cultural politics of recognition. I argue that dominant modes of witnessing actually work to recuperate the authority of settler Australians, at the same time as they attempt to expose settlers to disruptive testimonies. Thus, though witnessing seeks to recognize the testimony of others, as a practice of nation building, witnessing firmly positions settler Australians as national "gatekeepers" who witness to demonstrate their benevolent civic mindedness.

Indigenous peoples, migrants, and asylum seekers have been his-torically positioned within broader national discourses on hospitality and paternalism, from the mid-1990s whereas witnessing came to be associated quite explicitly with national renewal. Here, witnessing to

23

Indigenous peoples and asylum seekers became linked to the recovery of core Australian values that had supposedly been "lost" in the latter half of the twentieth century. This sense of national recuperation—of trying to recapture some kind of prelapsarian fair go—intensified during the Howard period, in which a diverse range of individuals and groups sought to challenge the government's official "deafness" to testimony. To be clear, I am concerned with the cultural space in between the public acts of witnessing of two Labor prime ministers. This book does not, however, contribute to Manichean debates that align Howard with the degeneration of Australian social values, and the Australian Labor Party with the perpetuation of liberal multiculturalism or a "working-class" ethic of egalitarianism. Nor is it concerned simply with an analysis of history and public culture under Howard. Though framed by the historiographical turmoil that marked the Howard era, I am not interested in the "truth" or validity of testimony for history. Rather, I am drawn to consider how processes of remembering and history making have become entangled with what Gilmore has termed "discourses of self-representation."[102]

In tracing the emergence of witnessing in public culture, I am particularly concerned with its limitations as a politics of "goodness," and its imbrication with a polarized domestic politics of "resistance" to Howard. In my analysis of settler witnessing as a liberal-multicultural practice, I am concerned with probing the pleasures of witnessing for the second person and the way that witnessing may work to consolidate the virtue of white Australians. In this focus on the settler Australian as witness, I draw on the work of Sara Ahmed, Elizabeth Povinelli, and Jennifer Rutherford, who have, separately, explored the mechanics of shame and goodness, and the politics of recognition within Australian public culture.[103] To investigate feelings of shame, and the notion of goodness, is to think about how people are moved to feel for each other. It is also to consider how feelings shape different kinds of community and, in doing so, examine what Ahmed describes as the "cultural politics of emotion": how "feelings may stick to some objects and slide over others."[104] Yet, to consider feelings as a subject of inquiry is not to question their authenticity or genuineness as expressions of personal attachment. As Shane McGrath has suggested, we may "recognise and affirm *feelings* of compassion while questioning the *politics* that seem to emanate from those feelings."[105]

In exploring the figure of the settler witness, my concerns have overlapped with and built on those of the emergent interdisciplinary

24

field of whiteness studies.[106] In particular, the work of Fiona Nicoll, Anne Brewster, Fiona Probyn-Rapsey, and Robyn Westcott has been instructive in exploring witnessing as a key process in the production of the contemporary white liberal subject.[107] Their insights have been useful not only in considering how whiteness has shaped understandings of settler selfhood and its potential transformation through witnessing, but also in thinking through how Anglo-Australians exchange their own testimonial narratives. Though I understand settler Australians to be a heterogeneous group, shaped by the specificities of class, race, and gender, I have found the concept of whiteness useful in thinking through the endurance of Anglo-Australian victim narratives and the pleasures of particular kinds of testimony for white Australians.

Though this book argues that witnessing has opened space for the validation of marginalized stories within cultural memory, it has also had the effect of strengthening the speaking positions of settler Australians. What is at stake here is not simply the access of Indigenous peoples and non-Anglo Australians to forms of cultural and political representation. Rather witnessing, as a form of nation building, positions Indigenous peoples; asylum seekers; and, to some extent, recent migrants as objects, rather than subjects of feeling. As such, it precludes their participation in the performance of ethical citizenship that witnessing offers. As an intervention into the national imaginary, witnessing too often works to reaffirm the position of settler Australians and solidify their affective ties to foundational myths of Australianness, such as the fair go. This book examines this dominant form of witnessing—a mode I describe as "liberal-multicultural"—and juxtaposes it with alternative practices that envisage witnessing as a project fraught with ambiguity and risk. To open the self, and by extension the settler nation, to testimony may be productive of new iterations of Australianness—iterations that sustain difference and eschew settler "goodness" in the service of developing more just, and cosmopolitan, ways of being Australian.

Through the conjunction of personal stories and public histories, witnessing has, since the late 1980s, articulated ideas about nation and citizenship, reconfiguring what it means to be a "good" Australian. In this sense, it is a form of nation building that has sought to reimagine a national community which is grounded in witnessing.[108] Although this discourse has fueled a range of real-world activism that has brought material benefits to some disadvantaged groups, particularly asylum seekers, this book traces the symbolic and imaginary power of witnessing more broadly. Accordingly, this book performs a connected reading of a range of resonant texts that does not intend to be comprehensive. Rather, each chapter focuses on several key moments of witnessing in public culture, moments that are frequently points of disruption in the public economy of history, truth, and authenticity. Chapter 1 begins by outlining the emergence of Indigenous testimony as a force within Australian public culture. It focuses on the period between 1997 and 2000, which formed the zenith of Australia's popular reconciliation movement. Here, I contextualize the *Bringing them Home* testimonies within a long history of tactical testimonial expression, tracing the relationship between Indigenous testimonies and white audiences. Chiefly, the chapter examines responses to *Bringing them Home*, from the work of public intellectuals to the actions of "ordinary" Australians. The Howard Government refused to witness to testimony, whereas hundreds of thousands of "ordinary" Australians sought to express their own apologies to the stolen generations through numerous acts of public witnessing. In particular, the chapter considers the figures of Robert Manne and Raimond Gaita, and the People's Walk for Reconciliation, as case studies in the development of settler witnessing.

Chapter 1 understands settler responses to Indigenous testimony as a part of a broader contestation over the place of history within the nation, and argues that discourses on settler witnessing have worked to produce a loose community of Australians committed to national renewal. Here, I develop the idea that from the mid-1990s, and for a large minority of Australians, witnessing to the testimony of others came to be understood as a mode of being a "good" Australian. In this way, witnessing to Indigenous testimony became linked to *fin-de-siècle* ideas about national maturity, ideas that were particularly prominent in discussions of the Sydney 2000 Olympic Games, the Centenary of Federation, and the republic debates. In this way, witnessing developed not only as a response to the claims of Indigenous testimony, and its call to acknowledge the impact of the past in the present. It also articulated with discourses on citizenship and nation building that were suffused with anxiety over the "maturity" of the hundred-year-old nation.

In Chapter 2, I augment this focus on the place of witnessing in public culture, with an exploration of more focused, creative responses to Indigenous testimony. Although witnessing is most often conceived as a mode of political or interpersonal interaction, this chapter extends this framework to consider the contribution of creative work to

Australian cultural memory. Focusing primarily on the work of novelist Kate Grenville, the chapter draws attention to the role of creative witnessing within Australian public culture. I argue that creative works not only form a part of the artist's own expression of witnessing, but also serve as a space for readers and audiences to be drawn to consider the imperatives of witnessing. Though focused primarily on the work of Grenville—examining how her novel and memoir construct her as a self-consciously apologetic witness—the chapter contextualizes her work alongside other recent "frontier" fictions, including texts by Gail Jones, Andrew McGahan, and Richard Flanagan. In doing so, the chapter draws attention to the role of the frontier as a key site within the settler imaginary, a site that serves both as the ground for a confrontation with settler violence, and as a reconfiguration of settler authority. Alongside this, the chapter examines films as a medium of witnessing. Through a twinned reading of *Rabbit-Proof Fence* (2002) and *Australia* (2008), the chapter considers witnessing as a mode of spectatorship that offers a space for identification, attachment, and recognition within Australian historical consciousness.

Chapter 3 explores the impact of Indigenous testimonial expression on the writing of Australian history through two case studies: Inga Clendinnen's "Australian" work, especially her monograph *Dancing with Strangers* (2003), and Katrina Schlunke's *Bluff Rock* (2005). In doing so, I examine the role of autobiography, empathy, and the imagination in contemporary settler histories. The chapter compares Clendinnen's approach to witnessing with Schlunke's and suggests that Schlunke's work serves to challenge the liberal-multicultural mode of witnessing championed by Clendinnen. Schlunke's emphasis on the dissolution of the white self questions the tendency of witnessing to function as a way of recuperating settler authority, and serves as one model of a more ambivalent form of witnessing. This chapter ends with a brief consideration of the recent SBS television history *First Australians* (2008). By juxtaposing academic and popular forms of history making—and the responses of these practices to the challenge of Indigenous testimony—it considers how the program links academic and popular genres of history making to perform a collaborative, dialogic form of witnessing to the past.

In Chapter 4, I shift focus to consider how settler Australians have responded to the suffering of asylum seekers. The chapter examines the explosion in asylum-seeker advocacy that followed the 2001 border "crises": *Tampa*, the children overboard "affair," and the sinking of the Suspected Illegal Entry Vessel X (SIEV X). The chapter details the complex ways in which asylum-seeker testimony was made public, emphasizing that many of the stories of asylum seekers were only made audible through the collaborative and mediating efforts of advocates. Many advocates understood the dissemination of testimony as central to their role as witnesses, and worked to make asylum-seeker stories public through letter writing and online forums. For many, the preservation of testimony functioned as a way of archiving the present for future generations.

This chapter argues that witnessing to asylum seekers became central to popular discourses on political dissent and served as a way of defying the Howard Government and its policy of mandatory detention. At the same time, I argue that asylum-seeker advocacy is linked with practices of witnessing to Indigenous people, through a common focus on national renewal. Through an examination of two case studies—the People's Inquiry into Detention and a collection of the stories of asylum-seeker advocates, *Acting From the Heart* (2007)—the chapter explores the way witnesses understood their work as a way of recovering the "national" values of decency and a fair go.

Chapter 5 pauses to consider the attitudes of those who refused to witness to the stories of Indigenous peoples and asylum seekers, those who denied the "truth" and the affective power of testimony. Here, I unravel two twinned phenomena: the specter of the false witness and the refusal to witness. The chapter uses the documentary *Forbidden Lie$* (2007), based on the Norma Khouri literary hoax, as a starting place to reflect on the place of false witnessing within Australian culture. The chapter argues that the fear of the false witness—a fear "proven" correct in the case of Norma Khouri—lies at the heart of the refusal to witness. The chapter further considers the conjunction of truth, lies, and testimony in public culture through a brief focus on the events surrounding the Hindmarsh Island Royal Commission (1995) and tabloid journalist Andrew Bolt's "exposé" of the Indigenous leader Lowitja O'Donoghue (2001). While writing against conservative practices of denial, this chapter seeks to probe the fear of the false witness and consider its place within contemporary cultures of history and memory. Although this book works to analyze witnessing as a distinct phenomenon, at the same time, it acknowledges its status as a counter-hegemonic, or "minor" mode of relating both to the past and to experiences of suffering. This chapter takes seriously the concerns of the "silent" majority who nurtured suspicion about the validity of testimony, while also considering their role in underwriting a climate of historical denial.

My final chapter uses the 2007 surf-documentary *Bra Boys* (2007) as a way of opening a discussion of the ways settler Australians have witnessed to their own experiences. This constitutes a form of witnessing oriented not toward the other, but to the concerns of the dominant cultural group. This chapter explores the way *Bra Boys* uses the battler trope to witness to an old story of Anglo-Australian victimhood. It examines the persistence of the battler trope—and the potential pleasures this narrative holds for settler Australians—in the context of the contemporary explosion of "minority" testimony. In doing so, I consider the role of testimony as the preeminent genre of contemporary identity politics, and the ambivalence of witnessing as a liberal practice of recognition and social justice.

Chapter 6 also discusses the relationship between testimonies of suffering and trauma, and positive stories of battler triumph, by examining the long-running ABC television program *Australian Story* (1996–). It focuses on the program as a vehicle of "positive" testimony, contextualizing it with reference to broader questions concerning the proliferation of "ordinary" voices within the public sphere. I argue that *Australian Story* highlights the desire of Australians to connect with each other through the sharing of testimony. At the same time, it affirms the power of dominant cultural narratives to shape the kinds of stories "we" tell each other. By spotlighting the continued valency of battler narratives, I emphasize the ambivalence of witnessing as a mode of recognition and a vehicle for achieving social justice. Through a consideration of the way understandings of class and race have shaped the reception of testimony, the chapter considers the centrality of testimony in the production of both local and national affective communities.

As Kate Douglas has argued, "the past two decades have been notable for the emergence of life narratives that challenge dominant histories, engage in political debates and attempt to insert counter-narratives and new voices into mainstream culture."[109] Witnessing to these life narratives and testimonies, as expressed in a range of texts, has become central to understandings of Australianness for a large minority of Australians. The emergence of a counter-public dedicated to listening and responding to marginalized peoples represents a significant change in contemporary public culture, marking a new relationship between history, testimony, and memory. Though I find witnessing to be, ultimately, an ambivalent cultural politics, I emphasize that it has also performed vital public memory work, challenging established notions about whose pasts are important, whose testimonies we should listen to, and whose stories we should remember.

Notes

1. Deborah Bird Rose, *Reports from a Wild Country: Ethics for Decolonisation* (Sydney: UNSW Press, 2004), 213.
2. Breyten Breytenbach cited in Stevan Weine, *Testimony after Catastrophe: Narrating the Traumas of Political Violence* (Evanston, I.L.: Northwestern University Press, 2006).
3. Human Rights and Equal Opportunity Commission (HREOC), *Bringing Them Home: Report of the National Inquiry into the Separation of Aboriginal and Torres Strait Islander Children from Their Families* (Sydney: Human Rights and Equal Opportunity Commission, 1997).
4. Kevin Rudd, "Apology to Australia's Indigenous Peoples," February 13, 2008, Parliament House, Canberra, *Prime Minister of Australia: Speeches*, http://www.pm.gov.au/ node/5952 (accessed January 23, 2010).
5. Ibid.
6. For an individual witnessing of this event, see Juno Gemes, "Witnessing the Apology," *Australian Aboriginal Studies*, no. 1 (2008): 115–23.
7. Rudd, "Apology to Australia's Indigenous Peoples."
8. Ibid.
9. Italics in original. Paul Keating, "The Redfern Address, 1992," in *Stirring Australian Speeches: The Definitive Collection from Botany to Bali*, ed. Michael Cathcart and Kate Darian-Smith (Melbourne: Melbourne University Press, 2004), 318.
10. Ibid., 319.
11. Ibid.
12. Ibid., 319, 320.
13. Italics in original. Ibid., 320.
14. Rudd, "Apology to Australia's Indigenous Peoples."
15. Ibid.
16. Meaghan Morris, *Identity Anecdotes: Translation and Mass Culture* (London: Sage, 2006), 120.
17. Bain Attwood, "In the Age of Testimony: The Stolen Generations Narrative, 'Distance,' and Public History," *Public Culture* 20, no. 1 (2008): 75, 89.
18. Nancy K. Miller and Jason Tougaw, "Introduction: Extremities," in *Extremities: Trauma, Testimony, and Community*, ed. Nancy K. Miller and Jason Tougaw (Urbana and Chicago: University of Illinois Press, 2002), 13.
19. Elazar Barkan and Alexander Karn, eds., *Taking Wrongs Seriously: Apologies and Reconciliation* (Stanford, C.A.: Stanford University Press, 2006), 23.
20. John Howard cited in Liz Jackson, "Interview with John Howard, 19 February 1996," *Four Corners*, ABC, [Transcript], http://www.abc.net. au/4corners/content/2004/ s1212701.htm (accessed January 28, 2009). On Howard's view of the incommensurability of Indigenous rights and a unified Australian nation, see Jane Robbins, "The Howard Government and Indigenous Rights: An Imposed National Unity?," *Australian Journal of Political Science* 42, no. 2 (June 2007): 115–28.

21. Stuart Macintyre and Anna Clark, *The History Wars* (Melbourne: Melbourne University Press, 2003). A large critical literature has developed around the so-called "history wars" in Australia. See especially Tony Birch, "'History Is Never Bloodless': Getting It Wrong after One Hundred Years of Federation," *Australian Historical Studies* 33, no. 118 (2002): 42–53; Adi Wimmer, "Why We Need Black Armbands," *Journal of Australian Studies* 75 (2002): 13–16; Julia Yonetani, "The 'History Wars' in Comparative Perspective," *Cultural Studies Review* 10, no. 2 (September 2004): 33–50; Mark McKenna, "Metaphors of Lights and Darkness: The Politics of 'Black Armband' History," *Melbourne Journal of Politics* 25 (1998): 67–84; John Lewis, "The History Wars from a Logical Perspective," *Quadrant* 48, no. 1–2 (January–February 2004): 54–57; Janet Albrechsten, "The History Wars," *Sydney Papers* 15, no. 3/4 (Winter/Spring 2003): 84–92; Keith Windschuttle, *The Fabrication of Aboriginal History Volume 1: Van Dieman's Land 1803-1847*, vol. 1 (Sydney: Macleay Press, 2002); Robert Manne, ed., *Whitewash: On Keith Windschuttle's Fabrication of Aboriginal History* (Melbourne: Black Inc. Agenda, 2003); Aileen Moreton-Robinson, "Indigenous History Wars and the Virtue of the White Nation," in *The Ideas Market: An Alternative Take on Australia's Intellectual Life*, ed. David Carter (Melbourne: Melbourne University Press, 2004), 219–35; Mark Davis, *The Land of Plenty: Australia in the 2000s* (Melbourne: Melbourne University Press, 2008).
22. The term "black-armband" was first used to describe a particular view of Australian history by historian Geoffrey Blainey in his 1993 John Latham Memorial Lecture. It was quickly adopted by John Howard and conservative commentators as a derisive term for historians who were concerned about discussing Australia's treatment of Indigenous peoples. Macintyre and Clark, *History Wars*, 128–33.
23. John Howard, "Opening Address to the Australian Reconciliation Convention—Melbourne, 1997," *Australian Legal Information Institute*, http://www.austlii.edu.au/ au/other/IndigLRes/car/1997/4/pmspoken.html (accessed January 25, 2009).
24. Cameron Forbes, "I'm Sorry, PM Tells Aborigines / But Leaders Seek National Apology," *Australian*, May 27, 1997, 1.
25. Howard, "Opening Address to the Australian Reconciliation Convention."
26. John Howard, "Address to the National Press Club," Great Hall, Parliament House, January 25, 2006, http://pandora.nla.gov.au/pan/10052/20060321-0000/; http://www.pm.gov.au/news/speeches/speech1754.html (accessed January 30, 2009).
27. Most notably, he attacked the new National Museum of Australia for its limited portrayal of Australia's British heritage, and instigated a "root and branch renewal" of school history teaching. On the controversy surrounding the National Museum of Australia see James Gore, "The Idea of a National Museum for Australia," *Museum History Journal* 1, no. 1 (2008): 75–102; Catriona Elder, *Being Australian: Narratives of National Identity* (Sydney: Allen & Unwin, 2007), 320–51; Dawn Casey, "Culture Wars: Museums, Politics and Controversy," *Open Museum Journal* 6 (September 2003): 1–23; Bain Attwood, "Whose Dreaming? Reviewing the *Review of the National Museum of Australia*," *History Australia* 1, no. 2 (July 2004): 279–94; Guy

Hansen, "White Hot History: The Review of the National Museum of Australia," *Public History Review* 11 (2004): 39–50. On Howard's school history summit see Jenny Gregory, "At the Australian History Summit," *History Australia* 4, no. 1 (June 2007): 10.1–10.5. DEST, "The Australian History Summit: Transcript of Proceedings" (Canberra: Department of Education, Science and Training, 2006).

28.   See Michelle Grattan, "ABC Gets a Culture Warrior," *Age*, June 16, 2006, 1.

29.   See especially David Marr and Marian Wilkinson, *Dark Victory* (Sydney: Allen & Unwin, 2003).

30.   John Howard cited in Linda Briskman, Susie Latham, and Chris Goddard, *Human Rights Overboard: Seeking Asylum in Australia* (Carlton North: Scribe, 2008), 270. For a comprehensive analysis of Howard's understanding of national "values," see Carol Johnson, "John Howard's 'Values' and Australian Identity," *Australian Journal of Political Science* 42, no. 2 (June 2007): 195–209.

31.   Raimond Gaita, "Guilt, Shame and Collective Responsibility," in *Reconciliation: Essays on Australian Reconciliation*, ed. Michelle Grattan (Melbourne: Black, 2000), 275.

32.   Gilles Deleuze and Felix Guattari, *Kafka: Toward a Minor Literature*, trans. Dana Polan (Minneapolis: University of Minnesota Press, 1986).

33.   Ann Curthoys, "An Uneasy Conversation: The Multicultural and the Indigenous," in *Race, Colour and Identity in Australia and New Zealand*, ed. John Docker and Gerhard Fischer (Sydney: UNSW Press, 2000), 21–36. See also Bob Hodge and John O'Carroll, *Borderwork in Multicultural Australia* (Sydney: Allen & Unwin, 2006); Tony Birch, "'The Invisible Fire': Indigenous Sovereignty, History and Responsibility," in *Sovereign Subjects: Indigenous Sovereignty Matters*, ed. Aileen Moreton-Robinson (Crows Nest, NSW: Allen & Unwin, 2007), 105–17; Ghassan Hage, *Against Paranoid Nationalism: Searching for Hope in a Shrinking Society* (Annandale, NSW: Pluto Press, 2003); Suvendrini Perera, ed., *Our Patch: Enacting Australian Sovereignty Post-2001* (Perth: API Network, 2007); John Docker and Gerhard Fischer, *Race, Colour and Identity in Australia and New Zealand* (Sydney: UNSW Press, 2000); Sneja Gunew, *Haunted Nations: The Colonial Dimensions of Multiculturalisms* (London: Routledge, 2004).

34.   Curthoys, "An Uneasy Conversation: The Multicultural and the Indigenous," 32.

35.   See Anthony Moran, "What Settler Australians Talk About When They Talk About Aborigines: Reflections on an In-Depth Interview Study," *Ethnic and Racial Studies* 32, no. 5 (2009): 782.

36.   James Jupp, *From White Australia to Woomera: The Story of Australian Immigration*, 2nd ed. (Melbourne: Cambridge University Press, 2007), 3.

37.   See especially Dominick LaCapra, *History and Memory after Auschwitz* (Ithaca, N.Y. and London: Cornell University Press, 1998); *Writing History, Writing Trauma* (Balitmore, M.D. and London: The John Hopkins Press, 2001); *History in Transit: Experience, Identity, Critical Theory* (Ithaca, N.Y. and London: Cornell University Press, 2004); "Resisting Apocalypse and Rethinking History," in *Manifestos for History*, ed. Keith Jenkins, Sue Morgan, and Alun Munslow (London and New York: Routledge, 2007);

Cathy Caruth, ed., *Trauma: Explorations in Memory* (Baltimore, M.D.: John Hopkins University Press, 1995); *Unclaimed Experience: Trauma, Narrative, and History* (Baltimore, M.D.: John Hopkins University Press, 1996). See also Saul Friedlander, ed., *Probing the Limits of Representation: Nazism and the "Final Solution"* (Cambridge, M.A. and London: Harvard University Press, 1992); Vivian Sobchack, ed., *The Persistence of History: Cinema, Television, and the Modern Event* (New York and London: Routledge, 1996); Giorgio Agamben, *Remnants of Auschwitz: The Witness and the Archive* (New York: Zone Books, 1999); Dora Apel, *Memory Effects: The Holocaust and the Art of Secondary Witnessing* (New Brunswick, N.J. and London: Rutgers University Press, 2002); Weine, *Testimony after Catastrophe: Narrating the Traumas of Political Violence*. Annette Wieviorka, *The Era of the Witness*, trans. Jared Stark (Ithaca, N.Y.: Cornell University Press, 2006); Barkan and Karn, eds., *Taking Wrongs Seriously*; Libby Saxton, *Haunted Images: Film, Ethics, Testimony and the Holocaust* (London and New York: Wallflower Press, 2008). For work on testimony that predates the impact of Felman and Laub, see Lawrence L. Langer, *Holocaust Testimonies: The Ruins of Memory* (New Haven, C.T.: Yale University Press, 1991).

38. On South Africa's Truth and Reconciliation Commission, see especially Sarah Nuttall and Carli Coetzee, eds., *Negotiating the Past: The Making of Memory in South Africa* (Oxford: Oxford University Press, 1998); Wilmot James and Linda van de Vijver, eds., *After the TRC: Reflections on Truth and Reconciliation in South Africa* (Cape Town: David Philip Publishers, 2000); Christopher J. Colvin, "'Brothers and Sisters, Do Not Be Afraid of Me': Trauma, History and the Therapeutic Imagination in the New South Africa," in *Contested Pasts: The Politics of Memory*, ed. Katharine Hodgkin and Susannah Radstone (London: Routledge, 2003). On political forgiveness and apology, see Martha L. Minow, *Between Vengeance and Forgiveness: Facing History after Genocide and Mass Violence* (Boston, M.A.: Beacon Press, 1998); James Hatley, *Suffering Witness: The Quandary of Responsibility after the Irreparable* (Albany, N.Y.: State University of New York Press, 2000); Janna Thompson, *Taking Responsibility for the Past: Reparation and Historical Injustice* (Cambridge: Polity Press, 2002); Barkan and Karn, eds., *Taking Wrongs Seriously*; Jeffrey K. Olick, *The Politics of Regret: Collective Memory in the Age of Atrocity* (New York: Routledge, 2007). Testimony has also been taken up within legal and philosophical circles. See, for example, C.A.J. Coady, *Testimony: A Philosophical Study* (Oxford: Clarendon Press, 1992); Jennifer Lackey and Ernest Sosa, eds., *The Epistemology of Testimony* (Oxford: Clarendon Press, 2006).

39. Shoshana Felman and Dori Laub, *Testimony: Crises of Witnessing in Literature, Psychoanalysis, and History* (New York and London: Routledge, 1992); Kelly Oliver, *Witnessing: Beyond Recognition* (Minneapolis and London: University of Minnesota Press, 2001); Gillian Whitlock, "In the Second Person: Narrative Transactions in Stolen Generations Testimony," *Biography* 21, no. 1 (Winter 2001): 197–214; Rosanne Kennedy, "Stolen Generations Testimony: Trauma, Historiography, and the Question of 'Truth,'" *Aboriginal History* 25 (2001): 116–31; Rosanne Kennedy and Tikka Jan Wilson, "Constructing Shared Histories: Stolen Generations Testimony, Narrative Therapy and Address," in *World Memory: Personal Trajectories in*

Global Time (London and New York: Palgrave Macmillan, 2003), 119–39; Jill Bennett and Rosanne Kennedy, eds., *World Memory: Personal Trajectories in Global Time* (London and New York: Palgrave Macmillan, 2003).

40. Shoshana Felman, "Introduction," in *Testimony: Crises of Witnessing in Literature, Psychoanalysis, and History*, ed. Shoshana Felman and Dori Laub (New York and London: Routledge, 1992), 5.

41. Sara Ahmed and Jackie Stacey, "Testimonial Cultures: An Introduction," *Cultural Values* 5, no. 1 (2001), 1–6.

42. See especially Whitlock, "In the Second Person."

43. Dori Laub, "Bearing Witness, or the Vicissitudes of Listening," in *Testimony*, 68.

44. Whitlock, "In the Second Person."

45. Gayatri Chakravorty Spivak, "Three Women's Texts and Circumfession," in *Postcolonialism & Autobiography*, ed. Alfred Hornung and Enrstpeter Ruhe (Amsterdam: Rodopi, 1998), 7.

46. Rose, *Reports from a Wild Country*, 213.

47. Oliver, *Witnessing*, 18.

48. Ibid.

49. Ibid., 7. Oliver's work can be contrasted with the recent emergence of a nebulous body of work on the idea of "listening." Though much of this material draws on the theories of Emmanuel Levinas and Hannah Ardent—key figures in the philosophy of testimony—it does not engage with the bulk of work on witnessing. As such, it remains a largely disconnected, ahistorical critical project. See Cate Thill, "Courageous Listening, Responsibility for the Other and the Northern Territory Intervention," *Continuum: Journal of Media & Cultural Studies* 23, no. 4 (2009): 537–48; Tanja Dreher, "Listening across Difference: Media and Multiculturalism Beyond the Politics of Voice," *Continuum: Journal of Media & Cultural Studies* 23, no. 4 (2009): 445–58; Mark Gibson, "Noel Pearson and the 'Cultural Left': Between Listening and Deaf Opposition," *Continuum: Journal of Media & Cultural Studies* 23, no. 4 (2009): 465–76. Charles Husband, "Between Listening and Understanding," *Continuum: Journal of Media & Cultural Studies* 23, no. 4 (2009): 441–43; Justin Lloyd, "The Listening Cure," *Continuum: Journal of Media & Cultural Studies* 23, no. 4 (2009): 447–87; John Tebbutt, "The Object of Listening," *Continuum: Journal of Media & Cultural Studies* 23, no. 4 (2009): 549–59. This work has drawn heavily on Susan Bickford, *The Dissonance of Democracy: Listening, Conflict, and Citizenship* (Ithaca, N.Y.: Cornell University Press, 1996). Notable exceptions, which have understood listening as more closely related to practices of witnessing, have included Les Back, *The Art of Listening* (London: Berg, 2007); Wendy Hui Kyong Chun, "Unbearable Witness: Toward a Politics of Listening," *Differences: A Journal of Feminist Cultural Studies* 11, no. 1 (1999): 112–49; Jennifer Jones, "Why Weren't We Listening? Oodgeroo and Judith Wright," *Overland* 171 (2003): 44–49.

50. Laub, "Bearing Witness, or the Vicissitudes of Listening," 58.

51. On transference, see especially LaCapra, *History and Memory after Auschwitz*, 11–12.

52. Kennedy, "Stolen Generations Testimony: Trauma, Historiography, and the Question of 'Truth,'" 128.

53. Whitlock, "In the Second Person," 204. The extent to which this has been the case is reinforced by the persistence of "comparative" discussions of genocide and trauma whereby the Holocaust has assumed the status of *ur*-event. For reflections on the centrality of the Holocaust, see, for example, Steven K. Baum, *The Psychology of Genocide: Perpetrators, Bystanders, and Rescuers* (Cambridge: Cambridge University Press, 2008); Colin Tatz, *With Intent to Destroy: Reflecting on Genocide* (London: Verso, 2003); Simone Gigliotti, "Unspeakable Pasts as Limit Events: The Holocaust, Genocide, and the Stolen Generations," *Australian Journal of Politics and History* 49, no. 2 (2003): 164–81.

54. Whitlock, "In the Second Person."

55. Ibid., 209.

56. Kennedy and Wilson, "Constructing Shared Histories," 123.

57. Susannah Radstone, "Social Bonds and Psychical Order: Testimonies," *Cultural Values* 5, no. 1 (2001); Susannah Radstone, *The Sexual Politics of Time: Confession, Nostalgia, Memory* (London and New York: Routledge, 2007).

58. Felman and Laub, *Testimony.*

59. Felman, "Introduction," 5.

60. Agamben, *Remnants of Auschwitz*, 13.

61. Kennedy and Wilson, "Constructing Shared Histories," 121.

62. Ibid.

63. Penny van Toorn, "Indigenous Australian Life Writing: Tactics and Transformations," in *Telling Stories: Indigenous History and Memory in Australia and New Zealand*, ed. Bain Attwood and Fiona Magowan (Sydney: Allen & Unwin, 2001), 2. See also Penny van Toorn, "Tactical History Business: The Ambivalent Politics of Commodifying the Stolen Generations Stories," *Southerly* (Spring–Summer 1999): 252–66.

64. Spivak, "Three Women's Texts and Circumfession," 8–9.

65. Paul Atkinson and Anna Poletti, "The Limits of Testimony," *Southern Review* 40, no. 3 (2008): 1–6.

66. *The Secret River* has achieved sales of more than 500,000 worldwide, and was short-listed for the Man Booker Prize and won the Commonwealth Writers' Prize.

67. "Bra Boys Breaks Box Office Record," *ABC Online*, March 27, 2007, http://www.abc.net.au/news/stories/2007/03/27/1882217.htm (accessed April 24, 2009).

68. Susannah Radstone, "Reconceiving Binaries: The Limits of Memory," *History Workshop Journal* 59 (2005): 134.

69. Ibid., 135.

70. Jill Bennett and Rosanne Kennedy, "Introduction," in *World Memory: Personal Trajectories in Global Time*, ed. Jill Bennett and Rosanne Kennedy (London and New York: Palgrave Macmillan, 2003), 11.

71. Ahmed and Stacey, "Testimonial Cultures," 5.

72. Ibid.

73. John Hartley and Alan McKee, *The Indigenous Public Sphere: The Reporting and Reception of Aboriginal Issues in the Australian Media* (Oxford: Oxford University Press, 2000), 3. See especially Jürgen Habermas, *The Structural Transformation of the Public Sphere: An Inquiry into a Category of Bourgeois*

Society, trans. Frederick Lawrence (Cambridge, M.A.: MIT Press, 1989); Nancy Fraser, "Rethinking the Public Sphere: A Contribution To the Critique of Actually Existing Democracy," in *Habermas and the Public Sphere,* ed. Craig Calhoun (Cambridge, M.A.: MIT Press, 1992), 109–42; Todd Gitlin, "Public Sphere or Public Sphericules?," in *Media, Ritual and Identity,* ed. Tamar Liebes and James Curran (London: Routledge, 1998), 175–202; Charles Husband, "Differentiated Citizenship and the Multi-Ethnic Public Sphere," *Journal of International Communication* 5, no. 1/2 (1998): 137–48; Stuart Cunningham, "Popular Media as Public 'Sphericules' for Diasporic Communities," *International Journal of Cultural Studies* 4 (2001): 131–47; and Michael Warner, "Publics and Counterpublics," *Public Culture* 14, no. 1 (2002): 49–90.

74. See Radstone, "Reconceiving Binaries," 140.

75. Ahmed and Stacey, "Testimonial Cultures," 5.

76. The extent to which testimony is productive of global or transnational counter-publics is particularly evident in the witnessing that has sprung up around AIDS. Sarah Brophy, *Witnessing AIDS: Writing, Testimony and the Work of Mourning* (Toronto: University of Toronto Press, 2004).

77. See especially Kay Schaffer, "Legitimating the Personal Voice: Shame and the Stolen Generation Testimony," in *Resistance and Reconciliations: Writing in the Commonwealth,* ed. Bruce Bennett et al. (Canberra: The Association for Commonwealth Literature and Language Studies, 2003); John Frow, "A Politics of Stolen Time," *Australian Humanities Review,* February 1998, http://www.australianhumanitiesreview.org/archive/Issue-February-1998/frow1.html (accessed May 5, 2007); Haydie Gooder and Jane M. Jacobs, "'On the Border of the Unsayable': The Apology in Postcolonizing Australia," *Interventions* 2, no. 2 (2000): 229–47; Brigitta Olubas and Lisa Grenwell, "Re-Membering and Taking up an Ethics of Listening: A Response to Loss and the Maternal in 'the Stolen Children,'" *Australian Humanities Review,* July 1999, http://www.lib.latrobe.edu.au/AHR/archive/Issue-July-1999/olubas.html (accessed April 20, 2007); Cath Ellis, "A Strange Case of Double Vision: Reading Carmel Bird's *Stolen Children: Their Stories,*" *Overland* 158 (2000): 75–79.

78. Kay Schaffer and Sidonie Smith, *Human Rights and Narrated Lives: The Ethics of Recognition* (New York: Palgrave Macmillan, 2004). For another study of testimony within a transnational context, see Gillian Whitlock, *Soft Weapons: Autobiography in Transit* (Chicago, I.L.: Chicago University Press, 2007).

79. Felicity Collins and Therese Davis, *Australian Cinema after Mabo* (Cambridge: Cambridge University Press, 2004), 5.

80. It does, however, include the innovative work of Chris Healy, Paula Hamilton, Kate Darian-Smith, and Maria Tumarkin. See Chris Healy, *From the Ruins of Colonialism: History as Social Memory* (Cambridge: Cambridge University Press, 1997); *Forgetting Aborigines* (Sydney: UNSW Press, 2008); Paula Hamilton, "Sale of the Century?: Memory and Historical Consciousness in Australia," in *Contested Pasts: The Politics of Memory,* ed. Katharine Hodgkin and Susannah Radstone (London: Routledge, 2003), 136–52; Kate Darian-Smith and Paula Hamilton, *Memory and History in Twentieth Century Australia* (Melbourne: Oxford University Press, 1994);

Maria Tumarkin, *Traumascapes: The Power and Fate of Places Transformed by Tragedy* (Carlton: Melbourne University Press, 2005). See also Annie Coombes' important transnational study of memory and history in settler societies. Annie E. Coombes, ed., *Rethinking Settler Colonialism: History and Memory in Australia, Canada, Aotearoa New Zealand and South Africa* (Manchester and New York: Manchester University Press, 2006). On memory studies as an emergent field, see Paul Antze and Michael Lambek, eds., *Tense Past: Cultural Essay in Trauma and Memory* (New York: Routledge, 1996); Alon Confino, "Collective Memory and Cultural History: Problems of Method," *American Historical Review* 102, no. 5 (December 1997): 1386–403; Andreas Huyssen, "Present Pasts: Media, Politics, Amnesia," in *Globalization*, ed. Arjun Appadurai (Durham, NC and London: Duke University Press, 2001), 55–77; Pierre Nora, "Reasons for the Current Upsurge in Memory," *Eurozine*, April 19, 2002, http://www.eurozine.com/articles/2002-04-19-nora-en.html (accessed August 3, 2007); Andreas Huyssen, "Trauma and Memory: A New Imaginary of Temporality," in *World Memory: Personal Trajectories in Global Time*, ed. Jill Bennett and Rosanne Kennedy (London and New York: Palgrave Macmillan, 2003), 16–29; Radstone, "Reconceiving Binaries: The Limits of Memory," 135–50; Susannah Radstone, "Memory Studies: For and Against," *Memory Studies* 1, no. 1 (2007): 27–35.

81. Paula Hamilton, "Memory Studies and Cultural History," in *Cultural History in Australia*, ed. Hsu-Ming Teo and Richard White (Sydney: UNSW Press, 2003), 88. It should be noted that though there are a few Australian scholars working with theories of memory, studies of oral history, public history, and commemoration have become central to the practice of academic history in Australia. A notable exception to the study of war and commemoration in Australia is the work of Joy Damousi, which does employ critical concepts of "memory." Joy Damousi, *The Labour of Loss: Mourning, Memory and Wartime Bereavement in Australia* (Cambridge and Melbourne: Cambridge University Press, 1999); *Living with the Aftermath: Trauma, Nostalgia and Grief in Post-War Australia* (Cambridge and Melbourne: Cambridge University Press, 2001).

82. Katharine Hodgkin and Susannah Radstone, eds., *Contested Pasts: The Politics of Memory* (London: Routledge, 2003), 2. For reflections on the relationship between history and memory, see Paula Hamilton and Linda Shopes, "Introduction: Building Partnerships between Oral History and Memory Studies," in *Oral History and Public Memories*, ed. Paula Hamilton and Linda Shopes (Philadelphia, P.A.: Temple University Press, 2008), vii–xvii. James Young, *The Texture of Memory: Holocaust Memorials and Meaning* (New Haven, C.T. and London: Yale University Press, 1993); Michael S. Roth, *The Ironist's Cage: Memory, Trauma and the Construction of History* (New York: Columbia University Press, 1995); J.M. Winter, *Sites of Memory, Sites of Mourning: The Great War in European Cultural History* (Cambridge and New York: Cambridge University Press, 1995); LaCapra, *History and Memory after Auschwitz*; Mieke Bal, Jonathan Crewe, and Leo Spitzer, eds., *Acts of Memory: Cultural Recall in the Present* (Hanover, N.H.: Dartmouth College & University Press of New England, 1999); Kerwin Lee Klein, "On the Emergence of Memory in Historical Discourse,"

Representations 69 (2000); Michael S. Roth and Charles G. Salas, eds., *Disturbing Remains: Memory, History and Crisis in the Twentieth Century* (Los Angeles, C.A.: Getty Research Institute, 2001); J.M. Winter, ed., *Remembering War: The Great War between Memory and History in the Twentieth Century* (New Haven, C.T.: Yale University Press, 2006).

83. On the relationship between history and cultural studies, see Graeme Turner, "Why Does Cultural Studies Want History," *Australian Historical Studies* 33, no. 118 (2002): 113–20.

84. Whitlock, "In the Second Person," 205.

85. Marita Sturken, *Tangled Memories: The Vietnam War, the Aids Epidemic, and the Politics of Remembering* (Berkeley: University of California Press, 1997), 1. On the articulation and mediation of memory, see Radstone, "Reconceiving Binaries," 134–50.

86. Annette Kuhn, *Family Secrets: Acts of Memory and Imagination* (London and New York: Verso, 2002), 6.

87. Attwood, "In the Age of Testimony," 75.

88. Bain Attwood, "'Learning About the Truth': The Stolen Generations Narrative," in *Telling Stories*, 181212. See also Bain Attwood, *Telling the Truth About Aboriginal History* (Sydney: Allen & Unwin, 2005).

89. Attwood, "In the Age of Testimony," 86–88. See also Hamilton, "Sale of the Century?"

90. Attwood, "In the Age of Testimony," 94.

91. Ahmed and Stacey, "Testimonial Cultures," 4.

92. Huyssen, "Present Pasts," 73.

93. Lauren Berlant, "The Subject of True Feeling: Pain, Privacy, and Politics," in *Cultural Pluralism, Identity Politics, and the Law*, ed. Austin Sarat and Thomas R. Kearns (Ann Arbor: University of Michigan Press, 1999), 61.

94. Joan W. Scott, "The Evidence of Experience," *Critical Inquiry* 17, no. 4 (Summer 1991): 773–97.

95. Hamilton, "Memory Studies and Cultural History," 96.

96. Though my focus throughout is on testimony, as distinct from confession, I note Susannah Radstone's view that testimony "may now be superseding confession's dominance in literature and other media." Susannah Radstone, "Cultures of Confession/Cultures of Testimony: Turning the Subject inside Out," in *Modern Confessional Writing: New Critical Essays*, ed. Jo Gill (London and New York: Routledge, 2006), 167.

97. On the multiplicity of forms of self and life expression, see Sidonie Smith and Julia Watson, *Reading Autobiography: A Guide for Interpreting Life Narratives* (Minneapolis and London: University of Minnesota Press, 2001).

98. Leigh Gilmore, *The Limits of Autobiography: Trauma and Testimony* (Ithaca, N.Y. and London: Cornell University Press, 2001), 12.

99. Ibid.

100. Shoshana Felman cited in Linda Anderson, *Autobiography* (London and New York: Routledge, 2001), 127.

101. Ahmed and Stacey, "Testimonial Cultures," 2.

102. Gilmore, *Limits of Autobiography*, 2.

103. Sara Ahmed, *The Cultural Politics of Emotion* (New York: Routledge, 2004); "The Politics of Bad Feeling," *Australian Critical Race and Whiteness Studies*

Association Journal 1 (2005): 72–85; Jennifer Rutherford, *The Gauche Intruder: Freud, Lacan and the White Australian Fantasy* (Melbourne: Melbourne University Press, 2000); Elizabeth A. Povinelli, *The Cunning of Recognition: Indigenous Alterities and the Making of Australian Multiculturalism* (Durham, N.C. and London: Duke University Press, 2002). On shame, see also Elspeth Probyn, *Blush: Faces of Shame* (Minneapolis and London: University of Minnesota Press, 2005); Gaita, "Guilt, Shame and Collective Responsibility."

104. Ahmed, *Cultural Politics of Emotion*, 8. Though the concepts of emotion and affect can be used interchangeably in discussions of "feeling," the recent explosion of work on affect within cultural studies employs the term "affect," following the work of Eve Kosofsky Sedgwick and Adam Frank, in order to draw attention to both the multiplicity of felt emotion and its embodiment Eve Kosofsky Sedgwick and Adam Frank, eds., *Shame and Its Sisters: A Silvan Tomkins Reader* (Durham, N.C. and London: Duke University Press, 1995); Ahmed, *Cultural Politics of Emotion*; Lauren Berlant, ed., *Compassion: The Culture and Politics of an Emotion* (London: Routledge, 2004); Probyn, *Blush: Faces of Shame*; Melissa Gregg, "Affect," *M/C Journal* 8, no. 6 (2005): 1–13; Elspeth Probyn, "A-Ffect: Let Her Rip," *M/C Journal* 8, no. 6 (2005): 1–18; Melissa Gregg, *Cultural Studies' Affective Voices* (London: Palgrave Macmillan, 2006).

105. Italics in original. Shane McGrath, "Compassionate Refugee Politics," *M/C Journal* 8, no. 6 (2005): 7.

106. Though whiteness studies developed as a largely American concern, it has been enthusiastically adopted and extended by Australian scholars who are keen to trace the specificities of whiteness within Australian history and culture. See especially Aileen Moreton-Robinson, ed., *Whitening Race: Essays in Social and Cultural Criticism* (Canberra: Aboriginal Studies Press, 2004); Ghassan Hage, *White Nation: Fantasies of White Supremacy in a Multicultural Society* (Annandale, NSW: Pluto Press, 2000); Leigh Boucher, Jane Carey, and Katherine Ellinghaus, eds., *Historicising Whiteness: Transnational Perspectives on the Construction of an Identity* (Melbourne: RMIT Publishing in association with the School of Historical Studies, University of Melbourne, 2007); Jane Carey and Claire McLisky, eds., *Creating White Australia* (Sydney: Sydney University Press, 2009).

107. See especially Fiona Nicoll, "Indigenous Sovereignty and the Violence of Perspective: A White Woman's Coming out Story," *Australian Feminist Studies* 15, no. 33 (2000): 369–85; Fiona Nicoll, "Pseudo-Hyphens and Barbaric/Binaries: Anglo-Celticity and the Cultural Politics of Tolerance," *Queensland Review* 6, no. 1 (1999): 77–84l; Anne Brewster, "Writing Whiteness: The Personal Turn," *Australian Humanities Review*, no. 35 (June 2005), http://www.lib.latrobe.edu.au/AHR/archive/Issue-June-2005/brewster.html (accessed April 13, 2008); Anne Brewster and Hazel Smith, "Affections: Friendship, Community, Bodies," *TEXT* 7, no. 2 (2003), http://www.textjournal.com.au/oct03/brewstersmith.htm (accessed April 13, 2008); Fiona Probyn, "A Poetics of Failure Is No Bad Thing: Stephen Muecke and Margaret Somerville's White Writing," *Journal of Australian Studies* 75 (2002): 17–26; Fiona Probyn, "Playing Chicken at the Intersection: The White Critic in/of Critical Whiteness Studies," *Borderlands ejournal* 13, no. 2

(2004), http://www.borderlands.net.au/ vol3no2_2004/probyn_playing. htm (accessed April 4, 2009); Fiona Probyn-Rapsey, "Complicity, Critique, and Methodology," *ARIEL: A Review of International English Literature* 38, no. 2 (2008): 65–82; Robyn Westcott, "Witnessing Whiteness: Articulating Race and the 'Politics of Style,'" *Borderlands ejournal* 3, no. 2 (2004), http://www.borderlands.net.au/ vol3no2_2004/westcott_witnessing.html (accessed June 6, 2009).

108. On the "imaginary" nature of national communities, see Benedict Anderson, *Imagined Communities: Reflections on the Origin and Spread of Nationalism* (London: Verso, 1983).

109. Kate Douglas, "'Lost and Found': The Life Narratives of Child Asylum," *Life Writing* 3, no. 1 (2006): 41.

1

Witnessing the Stolen Generations

When *Bringing them Home*, the report of the Human Rights and Equal Opportunity Commission (HREOC) National Inquiry into the Separation of Aboriginal and Torres Strait Islander Children from Their Families, was released in May 1997, its findings were circulated widely in the Australian media. The press, in particular, played a crucial role in communicating the effects of child removal to the public. Typically, this was achieved through the publication of extracts of testimony included in the report and summaries of its recommendations. However, beyond simply reporting the HREOC's findings, commentary in major newspapers sought to encourage settler Australians to witness to *Bringing them Home*. To do so, numerous journalists and opinion columnists promoted reconciliation as central to *fin-de-siècle* national renewal. In a paradigmatic editorial, the *Age* wrote that

> the removal of Aboriginal children constituted one of the most tragic and traumatic episodes in our history. As a nation, we must own it. We must acknowledge that it was a terrible error, we must recognise the damage it has done, and we must apologise. We claim, with good reason, to be a more sophisticated society now than when we implemented these policies. A sign of that maturity would be to face up to this issue and to try to make amends as best we can . . . It is about helping to clear the national slate of this century's mistakes so that we might face the next together, rather than from across a great divide.[1]

For the Melbourne-based *Age,* witnessing to *Bringing them Home* was tied explicitly to the end of the century. As an historical "turning point," the *Fin de siècle,* and the concomitant centenary of federation, provided a symbolic opportunity for the nation to demonstrate its "maturity." The need to witness to the stolen generations was central to this expression of cultural and political "sophistication." Here, the stolen generations figured as a "traumatic episode" that should be worked through, collectively, to clear "the national slate of this century's mistakes". Within this national teleology, progression was dependent on the willingness of settler Australians to "recognize" the suffering of Indigenous Australians and take responsibility, on behalf of previous generations, for the policies of child removal.

Reflecting on the 1901 federation of Australian states, Helen Irving wrote of "the strange, almost surreal optimism that accompanies the end of one century and the anticipation of another".[2] "As with other great temporal milestones," she argued, ". . . a new century is experienced by many as a time when change is both possible and expected, when the routine and predictable may be set aside".[3] For Irving, the *Fin de siècle* was not the cause of federation per se. Rather, "it encouraged the will to achieve Federation to emerge."[4] Similarly, for many Australians, the turn of the twenty-first century provided an opportunity to take stock of the nation and consider both the legacies of the past and the possibilities of the future.

The moment between 1997 and 2001 was, undoubtedly, the zenith of Australia's popular reconciliation movement. Alongside the release of *Bringing them Home*, a series of major events clustered around this period, including, in 1999, the Australian republic referendum; in 2000, the Sydney Olympic Games and the winding up of the Council for Aboriginal Reconciliation (CAR), the end of the "official" reconciliation process; and in 2001, the centenary of federation. As key moments within the "narrative" of Australian nationalism, all drew on the symbolic power of the end of the century, whether to celebrate the achievements of the nation or to propose change.[5] The imperative to advance reconciliation between Indigenous and non-Indigenous Australians was common to calls for change, and hinged on the need for settler Australians to witness to Aboriginal testimony.

Though this time was marked by fierce public debate over the meanings of Indigenous stories, it was a period that also saw hundreds of thousands of individuals express their own apologies to the stolen generations through numerous acts of public witnessing. Signing "Sorry Books" and attending reconciliation walks were two of the most popular and publicly visible ways "ordinary" settler Australians chose to witness to the nation's history of Indigenous dispossession. Similarly, many of Australia's prominent public intellectuals, artists, and critics spoke out in favor of reconciliation and an apology. In a direct challenge to the Howard Federal Government, a large minority of settler Australians understood witnessing not simply as a personal act, but also as a contribution to a collective, national process of confronting the past.

In this way, *Bringing them Home* became a site for the contestation of broader, collective truths, irrevocably changing the present ground of history making. Indeed, no other event in contemporary Australian sociopolitical life has necessitated such a profound reorientation of national history. The *Mabo* case was a landmark legal achievement, and, as such, has been oft cited as a turning point in the reconsideration of Australian history; whereas *Bringing them Home* captured the attention of "ordinary" Australians in a far more direct fashion.[6] It did this precisely, because it invited the attention—and, more importantly, the response—of settler Australians. The report collated and mediated stolen generations' testimony in such a way that it worked to elicit an empathetic response in its implied audience: Settler Australians signed Sorry Books and participated in reconciliation marches as a part of their own response and apology. Unlike the *Mabo* (1992) proceedings, which aroused the interest and criticism of many Australians but did not require their participation or assent, the reconciliation discourse centered on *Bringing them Home* produced a participatory occasion. The significance of *Bringing them Home*, then, lay in the way that it precipitated the development of a community of witnesses—a community bound by a shared commitment to recognizing the broader historical and cultural implications of stolen generations' testimony.

Although the discourse of reconciliation has been widely critiqued for its vagueness, I argue that the concept of witnessing was central to the way it functioned during the late 1990s.[7] The authors of *Bringing them Home* explicitly positioned witnessing as the core imperative of reading Indigenous testimony. To this end, the report promoted witnessing as a process that involved both recognition of the pain of the stolen generations and a broader engagement with the legacies of child removal. The report argued that

> in no sense has the Inquiry been "raking over the past" for its own sake. The truth is that the past is very much with us today, in the continuing devastation of the lives of Indigenous Australians. That devastation cannot be addressed unless the whole community listens with an open heart and mind to the

stories of what has happened in the past and, having listened and understood, commits itself to reconciliation.[8]

Here, witnessing was established as the starting place for reconciliation. In order for Indigenous and non-Indigenous Australians to come to terms with the past, the testimony of the stolen generations needed to be affirmed thorough a process of empathetic witnessing. To hear, and respond, was to contribute to historical change in the present; to play a pivotal role in "healing and reconciliation for the benefit of all Australians".[9]

Although the report stressed that this was the responsibility of the "whole community," the implication was that witnessing was, in fact, the task of settler Australians, as it was this community who had not previously "listened and understood" the history of child removal. In its "Australian Declaration Towards Reconciliation," the Council for Aboriginal Reconciliation (CAR)—the government body charged with advancing reconciliation between 1991 and 2000—figured reconciliation as a process that was grounded in witnessing.[10] CAR understood reconciliation as a dialogic process fueled by an exchange between the Indigenous testifier and the settler witness: "one part of the nation apologises and expresses its sorrow and sincere regret for the injustices of the past, so the other part accepts the apology and forgives".[11] The decision to "own the truth" of the stolen generations through witnessing would pave the way for a future in which all Australians could overcome the past and "move on together at peace with ourselves".[12] For CAR, the architects of popular reconciliation, witnessing was the key to healing for both individuals and the nation.

Accordingly, this chapter focuses on the actions of those settler Australians who adopted the challenge of reconciliation and worked to listen to Indigenous testimony "with an open heart and mind." It builds on the now extensive critical response to *Bringing them Home* to explore the diversity of settler Australians' public responses to stolen generations' testimony. It examines both collective events, such as CAR's year 2000 Sydney Bridge walk for reconciliation, and the acts of witnessing performed by prominent individuals, such as Robert Manne and Raimond Gaita. Broadly, I consider how a culture of witnessing to Aboriginal experience developed to produce a counter-public of settler Australians committed to reconciliation. To be clear, my focus is on the development of a settler audience for stolen generations' testimony. My suggestion is that *Bringing them Home* served as a moment of coalescence, building on earlier responses to Aboriginal testimony to figure witnessing as a preeminent mode of ethical citizenship.

Bringing them Home was ostensibly a vehicle for the voices of the stolen generations to be heard publicly, and it was also crucial in the development of a contemporary discourse on settler virtue. In witnessing to the dispossession and violence of the past, settler Australians—through their expressions of shame, contrition, and complicity—were, in fact, engaged in a performance of ethical citizenship in the present. By recognizing and taking steps to ameliorate the "mistakes" of the past, many forms of public witnessing provided a way for settler Australians to reaffirm the supposedly core national values of egalitarianism and a fair go. Thus, *Bringing them Home* not only posed a challenge to the settler nation by exposing the violence committed against Aboriginal children, but also, somewhat paradoxically, provided the grounds for the recuperation of that national community.

Accordingly, in examining the role of witnessing in the reproduction of settler identity, I also explore its ambivalence. Although witnessing has been understood by theorists of testimony as a vital component of the testimonial process, there exist a variety of ways in which witnessing may actually be performed.[13] Witnessing is often figured as a dialogic exchange, and it has also frequently contributed to individual and collective action that actually works to foreclose, rather than enhance, intersubjective dialogue. Indeed, if witnessing is, as a process, oriented toward an engagement with the demands of the other, the desire to witness to Aboriginal testimony has also provoked an inward turn, and a great deal of "soul searching" on the part of many settler Australians.

As a result, I address the way that stolen generations' testimony has fueled a broad, somewhat diffuse phenomenon of settler witnessing that has, largely, become estranged from any engagement with the imperatives of Aboriginal testimony. In addressing the ambiguous value of witnessing as a response to stolen generations' testimony, this chapter considers the core role that witnessing has played in the formation of a left-liberal multicultural public. Since the late 1990s, witnessing to Indigenous testimony has functioned as a pervasive mode of community formation, producing and sustaining loose groups of settler Australians who have come to understand witnessing as a performance of ethical Australian identity. In tracing the imbrication of settler witnessing with discourses on citizenship, virtue, and belonging, I consider what is at stake in grounding national renewal and historical change in the "good" white subject.

The Road to *Bringing them Home*

As elaborated in the Introduction, throughout this book I understand testimony in its widest sense, as a form of evidence or truth.[14] In this way, we can consider the interconnections between the *Bringing them Home* testimonies—elicited within a quasi-judicial context—alongside other genres of personalized truth telling such as autobiography or life writing, even drama or art, which circulate within literary and cultural domains. Although psychoanalytic models of testimony that emphasize a therapeutic paradigm have been popular within memory studies, some critics, including Jill Bennett and Roseanne Kennedy, have worked to signal the heterogeneous nature of contemporary testimony. Bennett and Kennedy have mobilized the concept of "testimonial languages" or "testimonial expressions" to encompass "both aesthetic and vernacular representational practices," and to include both the "verbal and non-verbal, and literary and non-literary" in their studies of trauma.[15] In similar critical moves, Susannah Radstone has employed the term "testimonial scenarios" in her work on Holocaust testimony; whereas Sara Ahmed and Jackie Stacey have articulated a concept of "testimonial cultures."[16]

Bennett and Kennedy's notion of "testimonial languages" underscores the diverse communicative, generic, and aesthetic modes of testimony; whereas Radstone, Ahmed, and Stacey have emphasized the operation of testimony as a dialogic, situated process. This shifts the focus from testimony as a mode of expression to testimony as a dynamic cultural event. In this way, testimony is not simply the words spoken or written (or the images painted or filmed); rather, it is inextricable from the arenas in which those words are produced, circulated, and heard. By extension, the truth value of testimony is not merely "announced" by the author or speaker, but it is also registered and affirmed by particular audiences within specific contexts. In this sense, the history of the emergence of Indigenous testimony within Australian public culture is also, necessarily, a history of the development of a culture of settler witnessing.

This chapter focuses on modes of settler witnessing inaugurated by *Bringing them Home*; whereas the report, and the witnessing it elicited, should be read as a part of a longer process of testimonial proliferation. Here, I follow Heather Goodall in emphasizing that the HREOC report should be considered as a part of the long history of Indigenous peoples' struggles for rights and recognition. Broadly, the circulation of Indigenous testimonies has functioned throughout the twentieth century as one element within wider sociopolitical campaigns for Aboriginal rights. This history encompasses the grassroots campaigns against child removal and "land dispossession" that stemmed from the 1920s; through to the efforts against rural segregation and the organized land rights campaigns of the 1960s and 1970s; and beyond that, the agitation around the effects of British nuclear testing and deaths in custody during the 1980s.[17]

In this way, earlier proliferations of Indigenous testimony actively elicited the response of a "mainstream" white audience, nurturing an empathetic community receptive to the affective pull of testimony. For Goodall, the willingness of settler Australians to respond to *Bringing them Home* had been developed through the "widespread and multifaceted set of interactions and alliances" that these earlier protests and movements had nurtured.[18] These prior events and campaigns were significant for the way they foregrounded the pivotal role of personal testimony in the fight to secure broader sociopolitical change. The decade of the 1980s was particularly important in the history of Indigenous testimony, as it saw an explosion in Aboriginal women's life writing, two royal commissions centered on Indigenous oral evidence, and a broader reconsideration of Australia's "black history" during the bicentenary.

Published a decade before the release of the *Bringing them Home* report Morgan's 1987 memoir, *My Place*, was, for many non-Indigenous Australians, their first encounter with Australia's history of assimilation and child removal.[19] Despite a largely positive popular reception, Morgan's work incited a divisive critical debate that focused on the nature and "appropriateness" of her Aboriginal identity.[20] *My Place* paved the way for a sudden increase in the publication of Indigenous women's life writing. Her text was, according to Indigenous author Ruby Langford Ginibi, "the first to open this country up".[21] Part of the popularity of Morgan's work can be explained by the way it tapped into the contemporary family history "boom," resonating with other Australians, particularly non-Indigenous Australians, who were devoting their time in increasing numbers in order to explore their personal links with history through genealogy.[22] *My Place* focused on family experience and included the oral histories of three of Morgan's family members. The narrative traced a movement toward Aboriginality in which Morgan gradually discovered, and embraced, her hitherto suppressed Aboriginal heritage. For Rosamund Dalziell, Morgan's genealogical quest actively engaged readers who were "provoked to reassess their own genealogies in the light of Morgan's narrative."[23]

In this way, Morgan's life narrative functioned as a form of testimony designed to elicit the witnessing of white readers. *My Place* was initially interpreted by critics as a form of autobiography—a Western, individualistic genre—whereas Kennedy has argued that the text is instead a form of testimony and, as such, functions not as a straightforward expression of "truth," but as a "representative story" of child removal.[24] Kennedy has drawn particularly on the South American notion of *testimonio* to figure Morgan's work as both a personal record of her own family experiences and a representative testimonial act that expresses a collective truth about Indigenous suffering. Accordingly, Schaffer has argued that Morgan's work formed a "presage" to the HREOC "stolen generations" inquiry and, alongside other Indigenous life narratives "confront[ed] white listeners and readers with new awareness, not just of past suffering and abuse, but of the effects experienced by generations of indigenous people, not in the past, but in the present."[25] As a testimonial life narrative, *My Place* claimed a specific authority as a form of truth telling that engaged readers to reflect on their own place within Australia's history of Aboriginal dispossession.

The year 1987 also saw the establishment of the Hawke Labor Government's Royal Commission into Aboriginal Deaths in Custody (RCADIC), which was designed to investigate the deaths of ninety-nine Aboriginal and Torres Strait Islander men and women who had died in custody between January 1, 1980 and April 30, 1989.[26] The RCADIC, led by Elliott Johnston, QC, followed a 1984 Royal Commission into British Nuclear Testing in Australia.[27] Both royal commissions called on Indigenous testimony as a form of evidence and were the result of concerted lobbying on the part of Indigenous peoples, who worked to secure appropriate forums to deliver their testimony.[28] Yet, in the RCADIC, testimony was not simply a form of evidence. Instead, it served as a prompt to a broader engagement with Australia's history of Indigenous dispossession.

To this end, Johnston included in his final report a history of "contact" between Indigenous and non-Indigenous peoples that acknowledged explicitly that Indigenous people had been "dispossessed of their land" by the British. Foreshadowing the work of *Bringing them Home*, the report also outlined the broad programs of assimilation and child removal instigated by state and territory governments throughout the nineteenth and twentieth centuries.[29] In this sense, the RCADIC positioned the reconsideration of Australian history as a form of witnessing to Aboriginal testimony. Not only did the Commission look to history in order to contextualize the incidence of Aboriginal deaths in custody, but also figured the exploration of history as a way of responding to the claims made by Indigenous testimony to injustice and suffering. Thus, the RCADIC sought to adequately explain the deaths of a group of specific individuals, and it was "equally important," Johnston argued, "to understand the experience of the whole Aboriginal community throughout their two hundred years of contact with non-Aboriginal society."[30]

Notwithstanding the criticism leveled at the RCADIC, both during and after its operation, the Commission had the effect of amplifying Indigenous voices. Although the Commission—and its core finding that Aboriginal people were not the victims of targeted institutional brutality—was the subject of heated debate, it, nevertheless, drew attention to Indigenous testimony as a powerful force of critique and protest.[31] The authority that Aboriginal voices had accrued during the Commission paved the way for Indigenous testimony to form the basis of a reevaluation of Australian history during the late 1990s.

The cultural and political power of Aboriginal testimony had developed during the 1980s in relation to Indigenous life writing and the two royal commissions, but the power of Indigenous words to disrupt the national imaginary was most evident during the bicentennial year. The year 1988 saw significant protests and a boycott of bicentennial events by Indigenous people and their allies, often under the slogan "White Australia has a Black History—Don't Celebrate 88."[32] The efforts of Aboriginal people to testify to their experiences of dispossession and discrimination radically undercut the event's celebratory mood, attracting widespread mainstream media attention and emphasizing the need for settler Australians to reappraise national history.[33]

The need to respond to Aboriginal testimony with a reconsideration of national history was again affirmed in key moments throughout the early to mid-1990s, including Keating's Redfern speech (1992), and the landmark *Mabo* (1992) and *Wik* (1996) land rights decisions. Despite the fact that the 1980s were, in Richard Broome's estimation, "ambivalent times" for Indigenous peoples, during this period, testimony came to the fore as a powerful expression of sociopolitical agency.[34] This was due to the political agitation of Indigenous peoples, who deployed their testimony tactically to engage the interest of settler Australians. Thus, if the 1980s heralded the arrival of Indigenous testimony within public culture, it also laid the groundwork for the emergence of the figure of the settler witness.

The Settler Witness

In the wake of *Bringing them Home*, some critics questioned the insistence of many settler Australians, including prominent figures such as historian Inga Clendinnen, who claimed that they were previously "unaware" of the practices of Indigenous child removal.[35] For historian Anna Haebich, these claims of "not knowing" were somewhat spurious, given that throughout the twentieth century "processes of removal were reported and discussed in a range of public domains and were observable in the wider community for those who cared to look."[36] As Penny van Toorn has argued, contemporary Indigenous testimony is a part of a long history of Aboriginal textual production in which *Bringing them Home* was far from the first occasion that Indigenous people had testified to child removal.[37] Indeed, as we have seen, the 1980s were marked by an explosion of Indigenous women's life writing about child removal, and also saw the publication of Carmel Bird and Peter Read's influential oral history of the stolen generations—*The Lost Children*.[38]

Haebich has accounted for the persistence of denial and white amnesia as, in fact, a core effect of the policies and practices of child removal. Individuals' participation in the process of child removal, including the non-Aboriginal practices of adoption and the employment of Indigenous housekeepers, was, for Haebich, contingent on a repression or "not knowing" of their "actual" effects.[39] Further underscoring the centrality of the mechanics of forgetting to child removal, Haebich quoted Jean Baudrillard on the Holocaust: "forgetting the extermination is part of the extermination itself."[40] Yet Haebich's insistence that the evidence was there for "those who cared" has foregrounded the extent to which public memory of child removal was dependent not only on the existence of Indigenous testimony, or even non-Indigenous historical documentation, but also on the willingness of a white audience to engage with this evidence.

In this sense, the development of a culture of settler witnessing is related to broader processes of remembering and forgetting within Australian culture. In his work on Aboriginality and cultural memory, Chris Healy has described remembering and forgetting as existing "in a state of dynamic tension."[41] Healy has argued that the "force of memory is ever present," whereas the workings of remembering and forgetting are complex and nonlinear.[42] There is no straight path between knowing and not knowing; within collective memory, "Aboriginal people and things appear and disappear as if by magic," shaped by the demands of white public culture.[43] The significance of *Bringing them Home*, then, lay not in its supposed uniqueness as a revelatory occasion, testifying for the "first time" to the fact of child removal, but as an event that succeeded in capturing and sustaining the interest of the "mainstream" settler community. Accordingly, Meaghan Morris has written that

> Only recently have we begun to develop a collective capacity to comprehend, to empathize, to imagine that trauma and disruption. This is a matter of a politics of remembering. It is important to clarify that many (I would guess most) white Australians "were not 'aware' of what was happening" *not* because we did not *know* it was happening (we did) but because we were unable or did not care to *understand* what we knew; we could not imagine how Aboriginal people felt. So we whites have not "just found out" about the lost children; rather, we are beginning to remember differently, to understand and care about what we knew.[44]

Here, Morris draws attention to the complex, symbiotic relationship between testimony and witnessing. *Bringing them Home* served as a profound intervention in cultural memory, not by highlighting the historical fact of child removal, but by interpellating and sustaining a community of settlers who are willing to respond to its core message of reconciliation. As Ahmed and Stacey have asserted, "testimony does not reflect some already existent truth, politics or ethics, but . . . creates the conditions for its own existence and reception, by constituting different configurations of self, space and community."[45] Thus, as a moment of "remembering," *Bringing them Home* was profoundly shaped by the expectations and memorial capacities of Anglo-Australians.

For historian Bain Attwood, the "capacity" for non-Indigenous Australians to respond to stolen generations" testimony was the result of a process of "narrative accrual" or "coalescence".[46] Inaugurated in the 1980s with the historical work of Peter Read and his coinage of the phrase "stolen generations," the frequent repetition of stories of child removal, chiefly through the proliferation of Aboriginal women's life narratives such as Morgan's *My Place,* began to combine and condense into an archetypal public "stolen generations narrative."[47] During the 1990s, this narrative became the focal point of Australian cultural politics and the lynchpin of the national reconciliation movement. Attwood's account is infused with a sense of anxiety regarding the displacement of professional history with Indigenous testimony, and he has succinctly described the process whereby stories of child removal became "central to Australian historical consciousness."[48]

Here, what Morris has described as the activation of the settler's "capacity" to understand, hinged on the development of a new interpretative framework for stolen generations' testimony. From the mid-1980s, through a commingling of testimonies and broader, nationally focused discourses on reconciliation, stories of child removal were slowly transformed from stories concerning Aboriginal people and their experiences, to testimonies that impacted how settlers saw both the nation and themselves. This process evinced the tension between testimony as a form of agency—in which a minority or subaltern community asserts the truth of their experience—and testimony as a highly mediated and constrained form of engagement with a dominant or "mainstream" community.

My focus on the development of a culture of settler witnessing has underscored the extent to which testimony is always already managed by the secondary witness. In her work on the history of Aboriginal writing, van Toorn has argued that, similar to earlier modes of Indigenous writing that were oriented to the demands of white missionaries, anthropologists, and bureaucrats, contemporary "Indigenous testimonies remain for the most part 'tactical' in Michel de Certeau's sense of being made and deployed in cultural territories predominately or officially under someone else's control."[49] This notion of testimony as "tactical" fittingly describes the conditions of production and reception of the testimonies associated with *Bringing them Home,* and draws attention to the shifting and ambivalent power relationship between the testifier and the secondary witness. On the one hand, subaltern testimony has been frequently elicited by a majority community, as was the case when the HREOC inquiry asked Indigenous people to testify to child removal. Yet, on the other hand, Australian Indigenous people have often deployed testimony tactically to interpellate the empathetic response, and action, of a secondary witness, as in the campaigns around Aboriginal deaths in custody and the bicentenary.[50]

The road to *Bringing them Home* was, thus, paved by a range of interactions between Indigenous peoples and settler witnesses in which, over time, the settler capacity to hear and respond to the suffering of Indigenous Australians slowly grew. This was not, to be sure, a linear process. As Healy has amply demonstrated, public culture has focused on a range of Aboriginal issues at different times throughout the twentieth century; issues that seem to have slipped from public view almost as quickly as they emerged.[51] Nevertheless, from the 1980s, a discourse on witnessing to Indigenous testimony slowly emerged that activated the interest of settler Australians who began to view the issue of child removal not as an "Aboriginal issue," but as an issue of urgent importance for the nation.

Bringing them Home

The extent to which testimony has been subtly and complexly employed by Australian Indigenous peoples is affirmed through an examination of the origins of the HREOC inquiry. If *Bringing them Home* formed a part of a general settler response to Aboriginal testimony—and a specific response by the Keating Government to the testimonial proliferation of the 1980s and early 1990s—it also had another genesis as a part of a campaign on the part of Indigenous legal and health organizations to provide better care for Indigenous peoples through an understanding of the history, and present impact, of policies of child removal. Such organizations included Link-Up (NSW) and the Secretariat of National Aboriginal and Islander Care (SNAICC), as well as those groups that participated in the influential *Going Home Conference* held in Darwin during 1994: a meeting of representatives from health organizations who were directly involved with the ongoing care of those effected by child removal.[52] As Linda Briskman has asserted in her study of the role of SNAICC in lobbying for the inquiry, *Bringing them Home* was "a huge success in the campaign for justice for Indigenous people," and "a clear example of Indigenous persistence and resilience."[53]

Yet if many of the Indigenous organizations involved in lobbying for the inquiry were focused on concrete change in the area of health-care provision, *Bringing them Home* became a hugely symbolic event within contemporary cultural memory. *Bringing them Home* not only began as a way of investigating the needs of those individuals and communities who had been affected by child removal, but it was also the product of the development of the settler "capacity to hear" testimony that had grown over the previous decade. *Bringing them Home* positioned settler witnessing as central to achieving reconciliation between Indigenous and non-Indigenous Australians. In doing so, it became the focal point of an end-of-the-century discourse on citizenship and moral virtue in which Indigenous testimony served as the ground for national renewal.

The HREOC Inquiry was established in 1995 by the then Keating Federal Government, and was overseen by Ronald Wilson, president of HREOC, and HREOC's Aboriginal and Torres Strait Islander Social Justice Commissioner Mick Dodson. The Inquiry set out to trace the history and the effects of forcible removal by drawing on the testimony of Indigenous peoples and their families. To this end, Wilson and Dodson conducted hearings in every Australian state and territory, with the assistance of a group of Indigenous women as co-commissioners.[54] During these hearings, the Inquiry collected evidence from Indigenous individuals and organizations, government representatives, representatives from church and nongovernment organizations, as well as from former mission and government employees, and other members of the public. The Inquiry also collected evidence confidentially from individuals and families affected directly by the forcible removals, including adoptive and foster parents.[55] Oral evidence was supplemented by invited written submissions from various Indigenous, government, and legal organizations, such as Link-Up (NSW), which had been prominent during the late 1980s and 1990s in working to unite Indigenous people who had been removed from their families.[56] In total, 535 Indigenous people provided testimony of their personal experiences of child removal.[57] Yet as the report has noted, the task of collecting testimonies was greatly hampered by a limited budget of $1.5 million.[58] On top of this, many Indigenous and legal organizations collected and submitted testimonies, greatly expanding the amount of testimony considered by the Inquiry. The WA Aboriginal Legal Service, for example, added more than 600.[59]

Testimony, then, lay at the heart of the Inquiry, and went on to form the foundation of *Bringing them Home*. Though the report drew on a range of documentary and academic sources, it centered on testimony. *Bringing them Home* quoted directly and copiously from extracted oral testimony, which was often employed in long block quotes to preface many of its chapters. Testimony is used throughout the report to personalize the subject of child removal, and to introduce or encapsulate a particular theme. However, it is also, crucially, threaded throughout the text as primary evidence for many of the report's key arguments, particularly in the state-by-state chapters detailing the removal process, and in those chapters that traced the psychological effects of removal.

Although the report acknowledged that the quasi-judicial nature of the Inquiry limited its ability to "test" evidence, "as thoroughly as would occur in a courtroom," *Bringing them Home*, nevertheless, asserted the truth value of Indigenous testimony by drawing on it as the primary evidence used to sustain its findings.[60] The Inquiry found that child removal was an integral part of Australia's history of Aboriginal dispossession. The core finding of the Inquiry was that the practices and policies of forcible removal conducted from the late nineteenth century constituted genocide, as defined by the United Nations.[61] The report concluded, "with confidence," that

> between one in three and one in ten Indigenous children were forcibly removed from their families and communities in the period from approximately 1910 until 1970. In certain regions and in certain periods the figure was undoubtedly much greater than one in ten. In that time not one Indigenous family has escaped the effects of forcible removal ... Most families have been affected, in one or more generations, by the forcible removal of one or more children.[62]

While *Bringing them Home* became the focus of conservative media and government criticism for its reliance on testimony as evidence, and for its understanding of child removal as a genocidal practice, it became, simultaneously, the lynchpin in a liberal public discourse on reconciliation.[63]

Bringing them Home employed Indigenous testimony in a way that foregrounded the role of the settler witness as addressee and listener. John Frow has argued that the report's juxtaposition of testimony with "third-person reporting and analysis ... is designed to allow these voices to have a space of effectivity, of answerability. It makes a claim for justice in relation to the voices of those who were removed from their families."[64] In this sense, *Bringing them Home* included testimony as a form of historical evidence, but it did so in a way that allowed testimony to speak to the reader, and to demand a response, in the present. Accordingly, the Report both gives its witnesses a hearing (which it relays), and takes their words up into a counter-speech which is *reporting-on* a system of government to which this Government is the legal successor. But this reporting-on is not being done for the sake of shaming; it is done as a claim that a kind of listening—a response, a taking-on of responsibility—must take place.[65]

What was at stake, the report suggested, was not simply recognition of injustice, but the responsibility of the settler witness.

As Kelly Oliver has argued, "the demand for recognition manifest in testimonies from those othered by dominant culture is transformed by the accompanying demands for retribution and compassion."[66] Recognition here was twofold: First, the need for settler Australians to recognize the truth of Indigenous testimony and second, the imperative that settler witnesses recognize their own responsibility to Indigenous testifiers.[67] *Bringing them Home* emphasized the need for the settler witness to respond to the demands of testimony by listening. For Frow, this listening emerged as "a form of ethical responsiveness which recognizes a duty to the story of the other."[68] In this way, *Bringing them Home* invoked a classic model of testimony in which the speech of a subordinated or traumatized other makes an affective claim—not simply for validation, but also for response—on a secondary witness.

Bringing them Home framed Indigenous testimony in a way that encouraged the settler reader to respond to its demands, and it figured this response as vital to national renewal. In its preface, the report explicitly positioned child removal as intimately connected to national history and, in doing so, linked Aboriginal experiences to the future of the Australian nation. For Wilson and Dodson, the "devastation" of Aboriginal Australians, "cannot be addressed unless the whole community listens with an open heart and mind to the stories of what has happened in the past and, having listened and understood, commits itself to reconciliation."[69] Listening here is conceived as integral to a broad process of reconciliation that is grounded in collective healing. Although the report focused closely on the effects of the policies and practices of forcible removal for Indigenous people, it explicitly framed child removal as an issue that was central not only to the Indigenous community, but also to the settler community. By linking reconciliation with communal settler responsiveness, the report, thus, "inaugurate[d] the release of these memories into the public sphere of the nation."[70]

Trauma and National Healing

In positioning the suffering of Indigenous people as the ground of national renewal, *Bringing them Home* adopted a psychotherapeutic approach to collective trauma that has been influential, globally, in the circulation of testimonies within the nation space.[71] On an individual level, the witnesses quoted by *Bringing them Home* are unambiguously positioned as traumatized. For example, in relaying the story of "Eric," the report quoted directly from a psychiatrist who had diagnosed Eric as suffering from Post Traumatic Stress Disorder, and who had suggested that his "symptomatology [was] obviously severe and chronic."[72] Within the report, the witnesses are portrayed as a traumatized group, and Wilson and Dodson describe the difficulties they faced in ensuring that the process of giving evidence to the Commission did not "re-traumatize" witnesses.[73] At the same time, the report presented the act of giving evidence as a mode of catharsis that was aimed at working through "unresolved trauma and grief."[74]

On a national level, *Bringing them Home* related the act of testifying to broader processes of collective remembrance. Drawing on the work of the Chilean National Commission for Truth and Reconciliation—established to investigate the Pinochet dictatorship—the report quoted Commission member José Zalaquett, who argued that

> society cannot simply block out a chapter of its history; it cannot deny the facts of its past, however differently these may be interpreted. Inevitably, the void would be filled with lies or with conflicting, confusing versions of the past. A nation's unity depends on a shared identity, which in turn depends largely on a shared memory. The truth also brings a measure of healthy social catharsis and helps to prevent the past from reoccurring.[75]

Within this schema, the giving of evidence related to past trauma is not only cathartic for the individuals involved, but also for society as a whole. As John Frow has suggested, *Bringing them Home* understood that "in the opening of memory and the restoration of a voice to the dispossessed, a kind of redemption can take place, a cathartic release from the pain of damaged lives."[76] Through witnessing, a nation could not only honor the words of the suffering, but might also guard against perpetuating this suffering in the present.

Witnessing, here, is the key to healing. However, the report called for a broad, collective response to stolen generations' testimony as a whole, rather than an engagement with the testimony of specific individuals. In this way, although *Bringing them Home* detailed the suffering of Indigenous individuals, it posited the healing of the Australian nation as the ultimate goal of witnessing. *Bringing them Home*, thus, transformed Indigenous suffering into the foundations of a reconciled (white) nation.

The HREOC's use of Indigenous testimony as a forum for a more general reconsideration of national history should be read as a part of a broader, global trend toward the use of testimony as counter-memory. Truth commissions aimed at reconciliation, rather than retribution, proliferated during the latter half of the twentieth century in countries struggling with the aftermath of colonialism and civil unrest.[77] Truth commissions have been convened by a diverse range of nations over the past three decades, including Afghanistan, Angola, Argentina, Bosnia, Burma, Burundi, Canada, Chad, Colombia, Congo, Cyprus, Fiji, Haiti, Indonesia, Kenya, Kosovo, Liberia, Malawi, Nigeria, Paraguay, Peru, Serbia, Sierra Leone, the Solomon Islands, Sri Lanka, South Africa, The Sudan, Uganda, Zambia, and Zimbabwe.[78] Crucially, *Bringing them Home* was released barely six months after Canada's Report of the Royal Commission on Aboriginal Peoples (1996), during a year in which South Africa's Truth and Reconciliation Commission (TRC; 1995–1998) was still ongoing. Similar to these other "truth commissions," *Bringing them Home* participated in a "public rehearsal of memory" that attempted to "recast the relation between the public and the private" by positioning testimony as a vehicle for national healing.[79] Typically, the imperative of confronting traumatic pasts through processes of testimony and collective witnessing has been emphasized through a psychoanalytically inflected language of trauma and healing. In this rubric past suffering and abuse figure as national trauma that appears to be pathological. As Mark Amstutz has suggested, "just as the failure to excise a cancer from the human body can lead to serious illnesses or even death, so too the failure to explicitly address collective offences can result in severe social and political pathologies."[80]

Psychoanalytic and psychotherapeutic concepts of trauma—particularly those developed in relation to the study of the Holocaust—have become a valuable currency within national processes of truth telling that are fueled by testimony.[81] Despite their dominance in structuring the aims of truth commissions, the efficacy of these paradigms of trauma and healing have been widely criticized.[82] In relation to the TRC, Christopher Colvin has questioned the confluence of discourses of trauma, testimony, and national history, and has decried the development of a so-called "psychotherapeutic culture."[83] For Colvin, the discourse on reconciliation that circulated during and after the TRC—driven by the pronouncements of prominent antiapartheid campaigner and Commission Chair Archbishop Desmond Tutu—employed a conception of history which was heavily influenced by the tenets of psychotherapy and trauma theory. In this discourse, the suffering of individuals was yoked to the healing of the nation and hinged on a collective confrontation with traumatic memory. In South Africa, Colvin has argued, the testimony and "suffering of victims acquire[d] historical meaning by highlighting the ways in which their suffering became part of the overall movement from oppression to freedom."[84] In this way, the meanings testifiers ascribed to their testimony, and the aims that they might have had for their words, become secondary to the ways in which their testimony could aid a broader national community to express its distance from past violence.

Witnessing for the Future

Bringing them Home enacted a process of witnessing to testimony that came to shape the way that the stolen generations' testimony was received in public culture. However, more than this, the report became the center of a popular discourse on reconciliation that figured witnessing—and an apology—as a necessary expression of Australian national maturity. Reconciliation had been an officially managed process since the promulgation of CAR in 1991, whereas the release of *Bringing them Home* galvanized the public and, for the first time, the concept of reconciliation "entered everyday discourse."[85] In particular, as Catriona Elder, Angela Pratt, and Cath Ellis have argued, "during the intense process of national introspection that preceded the Olympics it was an important concept in shaping stories the nation told about itself."[86]

The call for Australians to witness to the stolen generations intensified in the lead-up to the Sydney 2000 Olympic Games as Australia prepared to open itself to international scrutiny. Debate clustered around the need for an apology, and the possibility of Indigenous protests in its absence. One episode of the satirical television program *The Games* played on the confluence of the Olympics and discourses on nation and reconciliation. The mockumentary-style program, screened on the ABC between 1998 and 2000, focused on the Sydney Organizing Committee for the Olympic Games (SOCOG).

In the apology episode, first aired on July 3, 2000, SOCOG prepares a video message of the actor John Howard apologizing to the Aboriginal people of Australia. "We are sorry," Howard solemnly declared, "let the world know and understand, that it is with this sorrow, that we as a nation will grow and seek a better, a fairer and a wiser future."[87] Designed for the benefit of international audiences, the message was intended to deflect attention away from the prime minister's refusal to apologize and avoid media scrutiny in the lead-up to the Games. As a sly critique of the government's refusal to apologize to the stolen generations, the episode demonstrated the extent to which the need to apologize came to be viewed, by a large minority of Australians, as crucial to "a wiser future."

It was within this fraught context, Elder et al. have suggested, that "the Olympic Games provided a perfect means by which to represent stories of racial division as problems being overcome, and to reinforce ideas of non-Indigenous people's commitment to racial equality and unity".[88] As such, media coverage of the Olympics focused especially on the figure of Indigenous athlete Cathy Freeman.[89] Both her role as a flame lighter at the Opening Ceremony and her gold-winning run in the 400m event were understood in terms of symbolizing reconciliation. Most notably, then Labor opposition leader Kim Beazley conceived of her win as "400m of reconciliation."[90] In these terms, Freeman's "sporting victory could be understood as a reflection of Australia as a progressive and liberal nation."[91]

The themes of reconciliation and national unity were emphasized during the Opening Ceremony, through a centerpiece performance in which a young non-Indigenous girl, played by singer Nikki Webster, encountered Aboriginal dreaming. Though numerous critics have decried the conservative mode of reconciliation displayed in the opening ceremony, others have praised its "depiction of an Aboriginal cosmology enacted by Aboriginal performers."[92] The need to witness to the stolen generations was brought to the fore in the Closing Ceremony, during which several performers promoted their commitment to reconciliation through their clothing. In particular, Darren Hayes, a singer with pop group Savage Garden, wore a t-shirt that depicted the Aboriginal flag, and veteran rock group Midnight Oil sported shirts inscribed with the word "sorry." Though Elder et al. have criticized the version of reconciliation promoted by the Olympics as "conservative," the event served as a key site of debate over concepts of reconciliation, belonging, and nation. The small-scale protests of these musicians worked to intervene in the intended "script" for the Closing Ceremony and demonstrated—to both national and international media—a position of support for Indigenous Australians against "official" refusals to witness to their concerns.

The 2000 Olympics dovetailed with the centenary of the federation, another moment of national contemplation in the *fin-de-siècle* period. The centenary of the federation was also, crucially, the intended "end" date of Australia's politically mandated reconciliation process and, as such, became a moment of reflection about the future of the relationship between Indigenous and non-Indigenous Australians. In the print media, the federation was almost unanimously figured as a moment of national contemplation in which reconciliation was central. Much anxiety was expressed over the "end" of CAR, though the Olympics were understood to have expressed a pervasive popular "will" for reconciliation.[93] The general feeling was, as columnist James Grubel suggested, that 2000 was a year in which "the people claimed possession of the healing process."[94] The year saw the "mainstreaming" of the reconciliation process, through its association with the Olympics, and the success of CAR's Sydney Harbor Bridge walk. Even Prime Minister John Howard acknowledged that "as we approach the end of 2000, there can be no doubt that the mood of the Australian community is overwhelmingly in favor of reconciliation."[95]

It is difficult to quantify the extent of popular support for processes of reconciliation—however vaguely defined—and opinion polling throughout this period suggested that support for an apology fluctuated. Writing in 2000, journalist Michelle Grattan argued that though "eight out of ten people agree," reconciliation is important, "when the talk becomes specific—like embracing an apology, or acknowledging Aboriginal disadvantage—the nation has a long way to go."[96] Murray Goot and Tim Rowse have undertaken a comprehensive analysis of opinion polling on the issue of reconciliation. They found that an "examination of the data suggests that for Australians reconciliation was largely about non-Aboriginal Australians acknowledging the past and about Aboriginal Australians taking responsibility for their future."[97] Their work has demonstrated that support for reconciliation fluctuated widely depending on how questions were framed. For Goot and Rowse, these shifts illustrated how non-Indigenous Australians were often "divided" internally over what reconciliation should mean for the nation.[98] Yet the public witnessing of hundreds and thousands of "ordinary" Australians indicated that a large minority supported reconciliation. More than this, the mode of witnessing inaugurated by *Bringing them Home,* and articulated through events such as the Olympics and Federation, positioned settler witnessing as a performance of civic virtue. To confront Australia's history of Indigenous testimony was figured as a mode of being a "good" Australian.

I use the remainder of this chapter to focus on some of the ways settler witnessing developed in the aftermath of *Bringing them Home.* In particular, I discuss forms of witnessing modeled by prominent public intellectuals, as well as the collective activities of "ordinary" Australians, including the signing of Sorry Books and participation in reconciliation marches. Similar to the discourse on reconciliation itself, witnessing became a somewhat unwieldy practice that permeated the media, and became entangled with broader debates about Australian history, identity, and party politics. Nevertheless, it is possible to discern core features of a discourse on witnessing to Indigenous testimony. In particular, much of this witnessing adopted the paradigm of national healing set in motion by *Bringing them Home,* and, in doing so, was less concerned with reading testimony closely—and responding to the demands of the testifier—than with performing a diffuse, compassionate response to Aboriginal dispossession more broadly. At the same time, I argue that practices of witnessing to stolen generations' testimony were also forms of self-fashioning and community formation for settler Australians.

Public Intellectual Witnessing

In the absence of "official" support for the report and its reconciliation agenda, Australia's public intellectuals played a significant role in popularizing witnessing as a necessary response to the demands of stolen generations' testimony. Here, I follow David Carter in adopting a broad understanding of public intellectuals.[99] Public figures are often associated with a more specific field of achievement—such as history, science, or literature—whereas public intellectuals are those who address a broad public on issues of national concern. Public intellectual responses to *Bringing them Home* from settler Australians formed a part of a longer history of settler efforts to agitate both on behalf of, and in cooperation with, Indigenous peoples. This history includes the public work of A. P. Elkin, W.E.H. Stanner, Bernard Smith, and Judith Wright.[100] Much of this work was not figured as a direct response to Indigenous testimony, but rather was framed as a form of alliance and advocacy, designed to popularize so-called "Aboriginal issues" within the public sphere.

Gillian Whitlock has been pivotal in drawing attention to the relationship between Indigenous testimony and white autobiography in both contemporary Australian culture and that of other settler nations. Whitlock has written extensively on the recent phenomenon of Australian public intellectuals staging their own self-conscious confrontations with Australia's colonial past.[101] Whitlock has referred to the textual products of public intellectual witnessing—which have included works by historians Henry Reynolds, Peter Read, and Cassandra Pybus—as "becoming white" or "becoming migloo" narratives.[102] These are narratives that stage an ethical confrontation with Indigenous testimony as a part of the refashioning of white settler subjectivity. For the intellectuals who have produced these kinds of texts, a confrontation with Indigenous oral testimony and consequent engagement with Australia's history of Aboriginal dispossession has had complex implications for their self-perception as settler Australians.

The production of "becoming migloo" memoirs is just one of the ways settler public intellectuals have worked to engage with the implications of Indigenous testimony, and, in particular, the *Bringing them Home* testimonies. Public intellectuals were crucial in sustaining a culture of attentiveness to testimony against "official" refusals to hear. The public intellectuals who spoke out, in varying ways, in support of the report's recommendations were numerous, and included Robert Manne, Raimond Gaita, Inga Clendinnen, Germaine Greer, and Henry Reynolds. Some of these figures were authors of "migloo" memoirs, whereas many wrote more widely accessible essays and opinion pieces, and used their public and media appearances as forums to perform acts of witnessing to stolen generations' testimony. During the *fin-de-siècle* period, Robert Manne was particularly influential not only in modeling a form of settler witnessing to a broad audience, but also in using his work as a forum to discredit those Australians who had questioned the truth value of *Bringing them Home*.

Many of the public intellectuals who responded to *Bringing them Home* were associated with a broadly leftist political agenda, and Robert Manne has become well known for his shifting political allegiances. As a regular contributor to conservative political magazine *Quadrant*, and its editor from 1988 to 1997, Manne wrote numerous articles in support of reconciliation and *Mabo* and published similar work by philosopher and public intellectual Raimond Gaita. Manne resigned from *Quadrant* over the issue of *Bringing them Home*—inaugurating a personal turn to the political "left"—and went on to write in broad support of the report's finding in the broadsheet press and in 2001's inaugural *Quarterly Essay*, "In Denial: The Stolen Generations and the Right."[103]

Written several years after the release of *Bringing them Home*, one of Manne's chief aims in *In Denial* was to counter the conservative backlash that developed in the wake of the report. In particular, much of *In Denial* is geared toward attacking the conservative "think tank" the Institute of Public Affairs and *Quadrant*, which, Manne argued, had worked to "denigrate the moral meaning" of the HREOC report.[104] In order to challenge the conservative culture of denial that had emerged to question the ethical implications of *Bringing them Home*, Manne undertook a form of factual rebuttal—testing the claims of the report—while also modeling a way of reading and responding to testimony.[105]

For Manne, empathy was the key to witnessing the pain expressed by stolen generations' testimony. Manne described those who denied the existence of the stolen generations as people with "so little capacity for empathy that they genuinely cannot imagine the harm inflicted on a child taken from the warmth of a family to a loveless institution."[106] Here, Manne asked that settler Australians engage with testimony through forming an imaginative, empathetic identification with removed children and their families. In doing so, Manne encouraged his implied white audience to consider "what depth of grief and bitterness and powerlessness is experienced by mothers and families who are robbed of their children by welfare workers and police"?[107] In this way, Manne drew on a deracinated language of family to position stolen generations' testimonies within a "universal" emotional framework.[108]

Crucially, Manne did not lend his unequivocal support to *Bringing them Home*, and was careful to present himself as a considered reader. Manne argued that the report was "cobbled together" and viewed the historical chapters as being of an "uneven quality."[109] He also cautiously questioned *Bringing them Home's* estimation of the incidence of child removal and cast doubt on the report's understanding of genocide.[110] Nevertheless, he praised the report as a rare opportunity for "non-indigenous Australians to listen to cruelties they had never before understood."[111] Echoing Wilson and Dodson, Manne figured the report, and the need for settlers to witness to its testimonies, as being of fundamental national importance, comprising "the power to change forever the way they [white Australians] saw their country's history."[112]

Manne's work performed a vital role in countering conservative denial, and the form of witnessing it modeled has become the focus of criticism from some left-leaning critics. For Kay Schaeffer, the difficulties with *In Denial* rested on the modes of address established by Manne. Despite Manne's efforts to engage with some of the *Bringing them Home* testimonies, *In Denial* "maintains the [stolen generations] debate in hegemonic terms of the dominant white culture at odds with itself and, although Manne acknowledges the ongoing legacies of the past, his rebuttal maintains an historical focus on the rights and wrongs of the past."[113] That is, Manne is so focused on "speaking back" to those conservative settler Australians who had cast doubt on the report's findings that his work becomes entangled with issues of historiography, rather than with the urgent, present implications of Indigenous testimony. In this way, rather than witnessing to Indigenous Australians through a dialogic process of reading and responding to testimony, Manne's work was oriented to the concerns of settler Australians.[114]

Crucial to Manne's understanding of the importance of the report is the concept of national shame. Drawing on Raimond Gaita's understanding of guilt as distinct from shame, Manne positioned the stolen generations issue as a part of a collective "legacy of unutterable shame."[115] For Gaita, guilt can only stem from actions directly committed by an individual. Thus, in the case of the stolen generations, present-day Australians cannot feel "guilt" but are instead open to the collective effects of historical shame.[116] According to Manne, historical shame results from an individual's or group's allegiance to a nation: "to be an Australian is to be embedded or implicated in this country's history in a way outsiders or visitors cannot be."[117] Yet for Gaita, the experience of national or historical shame entails something more than basic citizenship, "perhaps a more *defining* attachment, to country."[118] In this sense, settler Australians can only feel a sense of shame when their attachment to the national imaginary—and its core value of egalitarianism—is interrupted.

Elspeth Probyn has theorized this sense of "attachment" as "interest," arguing that "only something or someone that has interested you can produce a flush of shame."[119] Following the work of Eve Kosofsky Sedgwick and Adam Frank, and their re-reading of Silvan Tomkins' notion of biological affects, Probyn understands interest as constitutive of "lines of connection between people and ideas. It describes a kind of affective investment we have in others. When, for different reasons, that investment is questioned and interest is interrupted, we feel deprived . . . Crucially, that is when we feel shame."[120]

Shame is not only dependent on the attachment of a community to a national imaginary, but Sara Ahmed has suggested that, at the same time, shame is also a productive mode of community formation and nation building. In her work on the cultural politics of "bad feeling," Ahmed has argued that "national shame can be a mechanism for reconciliation as self-reconciliation, in which the 'wrong' that is committed provides the grounds for claiming a national identity."[121] When settler Australians recognize the suffering of Indigenous peoples, their recognition and expression of sympathy or compassion serves to recuperate the nation in the present as a nation that "means well." The expression of shame—of disappointment in living up to the core national ethos of the fair go—simultaneously enacts the recovery of national ethics.

"Ordinary" Australians Witness

To illustrate her argument about national shame, Ahmed focused on one of the primary modes of witnessing "ordinary" settler Australians adopted after *Bringing them Home*: the signing of Sorry Books. Developed by the group Australians for Native Title (ANT), the books began to appear during 1997 as a forum for individuals to express their own messages of apology, in lieu of an official, national apology. The campaign was launched on Australia Day 1998 by two prominent settler Australians, Hazel Hawke—the ex-wife of former Labor Prime Minister Robert "Bob" Hawke (1983–1991)—and popular author Bryce Courtney, before 1,000 of the books were circulated throughout Australia. The books were promoted by a variety of public institutions, including local councils, museums, galleries, libraries, churches, and schools, that displayed the books for people to sign. Almost half of these Sorry Books were lodged with the Australian Institute of Aboriginal and Torres Strait Islander Studies (AIATSIS) in Canberra for permanent storage. In 2004, 461 Sorry Books were inscribed on the UNESCO Australian Memory of the World register, in formal recognition of their status as historically and culturally significant national artefacts.[122]

The kinds of messages recorded in the Sorry Books are diverse, ranging from simple statements of apology—"I'm sorry"—to longer reflections on the history of the stolen generations.[123] For Ahmed, these messages are typically performances of shame in which authors petition the government to make national shame "official." The mode of witnessing undertaken here is not to the trauma of Indigenous peoples, but of the (white) national subject "witnessing its own history of injustice towards others."[124] This witnessing entails a kind of erasure, in which the violence of the past is overcome and crucially "re-covered" through the expression of collective shame.[125] Here, witnessing is not a dialogic process that is designed to inaugurate a conversation between Indigenous and non-Indigenous Australians through a focus on Aboriginal testimony. Instead, witnessing as a performance of shame became a recuperative performance of civic virtue.

It is necessary to note here that the area of performance studies has recently become interested in the concept of witnessing and the way in which this might reconfigure conventional understandings of the relationship between audience and actor/performer.[126] However, the notion of performance here is useful not only in thinking through the relationship between theater and witnessing, but also in understanding the decision of Australians to participate in reconciliation activities as an act of citizenship; a performance of their relationship to the nation.[127]

Alongside the signing of Sorry Books, hundreds of thousands of "ordinary" Australians participated in a range of other activities designed to express their support for reconciliation. One popular initiative was the sea of hands project organized by Australians for Native Title and Reconciliation (ANTaR). This involved people signing their names to small plastic hands that were then arranged in a different formation in public places and outside government buildings.[128] Unlike the Sorry Book phenomenon, the sea of hands was not concerned with witnessing testimony, but rather functioned as a form of material petition in support of Aboriginal land rights.

During the year 2000, thousands of "ordinary" Australians also participated in reconciliation marches. Similar to the signing of Sorry Books, participation in reconciliation walks were, as Maryrose Casey suggests, "performances of public sentiment."[129] While reconciliation marches were held in other state capital cities, on May 28, 2000, the Council for Aboriginal Reconciliation (CAR) held the People's Walk for Reconciliation across Sydney Harbour Bridge, "one of the largest public demonstrations for a cause ever seen in Australia."[130] Though attendance estimates varied, at least 250,000 people participated in the walk, a number significantly greater than those who participated in Sydney's post–World War II Victory celebrations in 1945 and the anti-Vietnam War protests during the 1960s.[131] As a part of CAR's Corroboree 2000—a celebration of the release of Council's Declaration Toward Reconciliation, its blueprint for formal and legislative reconciliation—the high attendance figures elicited by the event were seen by many as evidence of strong "grassroots" support for a formalized expression of reconciliation, such as a treaty.[132] Yet as Casey has argued, despite the intentions of the various individuals who participated in the walks, the marches came to serve a largely symbolic function as "a salve to white consciences rather than an expression of commitment to change."[133]

As examples of collective witnessing, the Sorry Books and the Sydney Bridge walk demonstrate what Elizabeth Povinelli has identified as "the generation of a new national metaethics around multiculturalism," which she has termed "the cunning of recognition."[134] Although these two modes of witnessing are ostensibly presented as oriented toward the recognition of Indigenous trauma, they are, at the same time, acts of recognition "inflected by the conditional."[135] That is, expressions of national shame over the stolen generations proceed "as long as real economic resources are not at stake"; in this instance, compensation for removed children.[136] Indeed, many of the acts of witnessing discussed here pivot not around an engagement with difference—and with the imperatives of Indigenous testimony as agentic expression—but around "mourning a shared shameful past . . . [in order to] propel the nation into a new cleansed national form."[137] The idealized national imaginary that is recuperated through the performance of shame does not allow for the possible incommensurability of difference, nor can it hear the demands of testimony as an expression of enduring Indigenous sovereignty.

Shame, Complicity, and Ambiguity

If many of the public acts of witnessing and reconciliation performed by settler Australians have been criticized as modes of white virtue geared toward the recuperation and perpetuation of an idealized Australian nation, critics have also argued that shame may be productive of more ambiguous and attentive subject relations. As Probyn has suggested, an acknowledgement of ancestral or national shame may draw attention to "how we are forged in many different relations—those of kin but also those of geography and history."[138] In this way, shame can work to underscore the fundamental intersubjectivity of (post)colonial relations, and emphasize the need not merely to "recognize" the other, but also to appreciate a deeper mode of attachment. Oliver has extended this, arguing that "we are selves, subject, and have subjectivity and agency by virtue of our dialogical relationships with others."[139] For Oliver, being subject is "the process of witnessing sustained through response-ability."[140] To appreciate this is to understand that witnessing entails "an obligation not only to respond but also to respond in a way that opens up rather than closes off the possibility of response by others."[141]

This notion of response as crucial to witnessing has also been elaborated by Ahmed. Ahmed has not only been highly critical of public expressions of shame, but she has also argued that shame may be refigured as a "return address" which contains the possibility of opening up our relations with others. Accordingly,

> if we consider shame as a return address, rather than as a bad feeling that is about our relation to ourselves, then perhaps something else might occur. When others, who have been wronged, ask for signs of shame, then the expression of shame does not return ourselves to ourselves, but respond to demands that come from a place other than where we are.[142]

In Australia, shame in this mode would encourage engagement with Indigenous Australians as subjects, rather than objects, of feeling. Here, Ahmed echoes Oliver's understanding of witnessing as fundamentally dialogic, and dependent on a process of listening and response. Crucially, for expressions of shame to function dialogically, shame should not be thought of as a transitory emotion, as "we can only stay open to hearing the claims of others, only if we assume that the act of speaking one's shame does not undo the shame of what we speak."[143]

This need to appreciate the enduring nature of historical injustice—its contemporary presence—has been articulated by Fiona Probyn-Rapsey through the concept of complicity. For Probyn-Rapsey, complicity is "a practice and theory of ethical engagement with others and in relation to present encounters with the past."[144] Unlike guilt and shame, which, Probyn-Rapsey has argued, describe "vertical" relations through time, complicity connotes a contemporary embeddedness in history and "describes the network in which Australians are located: a settler colonial state."[145] Here, complicity names a structural relationship between others; it cannot simply be overcome. To conceive of settler Australians as "complicit" with colonialism, and with practices of Indigenous dispossession that are ongoing, is to refuse to view the past as "settled." To do so is to appreciate that "the future of shared histories and reconciliation . . . remains a question mark and a mark of questioning."[146] In terms of the imperative for settler Australians to witness to Indigenous testimony, an acceptance of complicity could enable modes of witnessing that are flexible and responsive, practices which refuse to use "bad feelings" as a road to national rejuvenation.

Conclusion

This chapter has examined the emergence of the figure of the settler witness in Australian public culture. While engaging with the sizeable literature about *Bringing them Home*, the chapter has extended existing analyses by drawing on the concept of witnessing to explore the responses of settler Australians to Indigenous testimony. Throughout, I have argued that the end of the twentieth century was marked by the confluence of discourses on witnessing, nation, and settler belonging. As such, witnessing to Indigenous testimony was figured as a performance of civic virtue in which national shame paved the way for a reconciled future.

On its release, *Bringing them Home* became a cultural phenomenon, a moment of coalescence that interpellated settler Australians as secondary witnesses. Rather than reading *Bringing them Home* as an opportunity to engage with the imperatives of Indigenous testimony, many settler Australians adopted witnessing as a way of being and performing a liberal, multicultural Australianness. These performances linked individuals together as a loose community who understood witnessing as key to demonstrating Australia's national maturity. In this way, witnessing came to describe a triangulated relationship between testifier, witness, and nation, rather than a dialogic, intersubjective relationship between testifying subject and secondary witness.

To be sure, although witnessing was a pervasive mode of relating to testimony, it was far from hegemonic. Yet, while there were many vocal critics of *Bringing them Home* and the process of reconciliation, more broadly, witnessing was a prominent way of working through the affects of the past. In the face of conservative denial, hundreds of thousands of "ordinary" Australians participated in collective and individual acts of witnessing as a way of "talking back" to Howard's official refusal to listen.

Notes

1. "Children Betrayed I," *Age*, May 22, 1997, 14.
2. Helen Irving, *To Constitute a Nation: A Cultural History of Australia's Constitution* (Melbourne: Cambridge University Press, 1999), 212.
3. Ibid.
4. Ibid.
5. Homi K. Bhabha, ed., *Nation and Narration* (London: Routledge, 1990).
6. On the historical significance of *Mabo*, see Bain Attwood, ed., *In the Age of Mabo: History, Aborigines and Australia* (Sydney: Allen & Unwin, 1996); Murray Goot and Tim Rowse, eds., *Make a Better Offer: The Politics of Mabo* (Leichhardt, NSW: Pluto Press, 1994); Tim Rowse, *After Mabo: Interpreting Indigenous Traditions* (Carlton: Melbourne University Press, 1993).
7. See especially Angela Pratt, *Practising Reconciliation?: The Politics of Reconciliation in the Australian Parliament, 1991–2000* (Canberra: Department of Parliamentary Services, 2005); Colin Tatz, "The Reconciliation Bargain," *Melbourne Journal of Politics* 25 (1998): 1–5.
8. HREOC, *Bringing Them Home*, 3.
9. Ibid., 4.
10. Council for Aboriginal Reconciliation, "Australian Declaration Towards Reconciliation," *Reconciliation Australia*, 2000, http://www.austlii.edu. au/au/other/ IndigLRes/car/2000/12/pg3.htm (accessed April 15, 2009).
11. Ibid.
12. Ibid.
13. The notion of testimony as dialogic is particularly strong in the Holocaust-based work of Shoshana Felman and Dori Laub, and in the philosophical contributions of Kelly Oliver. Felman and Laub, *Testimony*; Oliver, *Witnessing*.
14. Here, the expansive simplicity of the *Oxford English Dictionary* definition of testimony is useful: "personal or documentary evidence or attestation in support of a fact or statement; hence, any form of evidence or proof."
15. Bennett and Kennedy, "Introduction," 4, 11.
16. Radstone, "Social Bonds and Psychical Order," 73; Ahmed and Stacey, "Testimonial Cultures," 1–6.
17. Heather Goodall, "Challenging Voices: Tracing the Problematic Role of Testimony in Political Change," *Australian Literary Studies* 22, no. 4 (2006): 516.
18. Ibid.
19. Sally Morgan, *My Place* (Fremantle: Fremantle Arts Centre Press, 1987).
20. See Stephen Muecke, "Aboriginal Literature and the Repressive Hypothesis," *Southerly* 48, no. 4 (December 1988): 405–18; Bain Attwood, "Portrait of an Aboriginal as an Artist: Sally Morgan and the Construction of Aboriginality," *Australian Historical Studies* 25, no. 99 (1992): 302–18; Tony Birch, "'Half-Caste,'" *Australian Historical Studies* 25, no. 100 (1993): 458; Tim Rowse, "Sally Morgan's Kaftan," *Australian Historical Studies* 25, no. 100 (1993): 465–68; Jackie Huggins, "Always Was Always Will Be," *Australian Historical Studies* 25, no. 100 (1993): 459–64. Despite the furore over Morgan's identity, she remained the most visible Indigenous writer during the late 1980s and 1990s. See Mudrooroo, *The Indigenous Literature of*

Australia: Milli Milli Wangka (Melbourne: Hyland House, 1997), 192–95. It remains to be seen whether contemporary Indigenous writers such as Kim Scott and Alexis Wright—Miles Franklin Prize winners in 2000 and 2007, respectively—will come to eclipse Morgan's iconic status.

21. Anne Brewster, *Reading Aboriginal Women's Autobiography* (Sydney: Sydney University Press, 1996), 7. See also Tikka Wilson, "Racism, Moral Community, and Australian Aboriginal Testimony," *Biography* 27, no. 1 (Winter 2004): 84. For a representative account of Morgan's place within the history of Australian Indigenous literature, see Penny van Toorn, "Indigenous Texts and Narratives," in *The Cambridge Companion to Australian Literature*, ed. Elizabeth Webby (Cambridge: Cambridge University Press, 2000), 19–49.

22. Graeme Davison, *The Use and Abuse of Australian History* (Sydney: Allen & Unwin, 2000), 100.

23. Rosamund Dalziell, *Shameful Autobiographies: Shame in Contemporary Australian Autobiographies and Culture* (Melbourne: Melbourne University Press, 1999), 141. See also Susan Sheridan, "Different Lives: Two Aboriginal Women's Stories," *Antipodes* 2, no. 1 (1989): 20.

24. Rosanne Kennedy, "The Narrator as Witness: Testimony, Trauma and Narrative Form in *My Place*," *Meridian* 16, no. 2 (1997): 237. See also John Beverley, *Testimonio: On the Politics of Truth* (Minneapolis and London: University of Minnesota Press, 2004). For a discussion of how Aboriginal women's life narratives complicate the Western genres of autobiography and biography, see Gillian Whitlock, "From Biography to Autobiography," in *The Cambridge Companion to Australian Literature*, ed. Elizabeth Webby (Cambridge: Cambridge University Press, 2000), 232–57.

25. Schaffer, "Legitimating the Personal Voice," 56, 61. Compare with Joan Newman, "Race, Gender and Identity: *My Place* as Autobiography," in *Whose Place?: A Study of Sally Morgan's My Place*, ed. Delys Bird and Dennis Haskell (Sydney: Angus & Robertson, 1992), 73; Eva Rask Knudsen, *The Circle & the Spiral: A Study of Australian Aboriginal and New Zealand Maori Literature* (Amsterdam and New York: Rodopi, 2004), 110; and Christine Watson, "'Believe Me': Acts of Witnessing in Aboriginal Women's Autobiographical Narratives," *Journal of Australian Studies* 64 (2000): 142–52.

26. Royal Commission into Aboriginal Deaths in Custody, *National Report of the Royal Commission into Aboriginal Deaths in Custody*, vol. 1 (Canberra: Australian Government Publishing Service, 1991).

27. Royal Commission into British Nuclear Tests in Australia, *Report of the Royal Commission into British Nuclear Tests in Australia* (Canberra: Australian Government Publishing Service, 1985).

28. On the origins of the RCADIC, see Royal Commission into Aboriginal Deaths in Custody, *National Report of the Royal Commission into Aboriginal Deaths in Custody*, 1; Helen Corbett and Tony Vinson, "Black Deaths in Custody: Instigating the Royal Commission," in *Actions Speak: Strategies and Lessons from Australian Social and Community Action*, ed. Eileen Baldry and Tony Vinson (Melbourne: Longman Cheshire, 1991). On the efforts of the Pitjantijatjara Anangu and Yanykuntjatjara peoples in securing the Royal Commission into British Nuclear Testing, see Heather Goodall, "Colonialism and Catastrophe: Contested Memories of Nuclear

Testing and Measles Epidemics at Ernabella," in *Memory and History in Twentieth-Century Australia*, ed. Kate Darian-Smith and Paula Hamilton (Melbourne: Oxford University Press, 1994), 55–76.

29. Royal Commission into Aboriginal Deaths in Custody, *National Report of the Royal Commission into Aboriginal Deaths in Custody*, 7–11.

30. Ibid., 5.

31. For a summary of much of the criticism on the Commission and its after effects, see Elena Marchetti, "Critical Reflections Upon Australia's Royal Commission into Aboriginal Deaths in Custody," *Macquarie Law Journal* 5 (2005): 103–25. See also Jeannie Purdy, "Royal Commissions and Omissions: What Was Left out of the Report on the Death of John Pat," *Australian Journal of Law and Society* 10 (1994): 37–66. David McDonald and Chris Cunneen, "Aboriginal Incarceration and Deaths in Custody: Looking Back and Looking Forward," *Current Issues in Criminal Justice* 9, no. 1 (1997): 5–20; Elena Marchetti, "The Deep Colonizing Practices of the Australian Royal Commission into Aboriginal Deaths in Custody," *Journal of Law and Society* 33, no. 3 (2006): 451–74.

32. Richard Broome, *Aboriginal Australians* (Sydney: Allen & Unwin, 2001), 225. On the bicentenary, especially its invocation of competing versions of Australian nationalism, see Stephen Castles et al., *The Bicentenary and the Failure of Australian Nationalism* (Annandale, NSW: Common Ground, 1987); Susan Janson and Stuart Macintyre, eds., *Making the Bicentenary: Special Issue of Australian Historical Studies* (Parkville, VIC: University of Melbourne, 1988); Meaghan Morris, "Panorama: The Live, the Dead and the Living," in *Island in the Stream: Myths of Place in Australian Culture*, ed. Paul Foss (Pluto Press, 1988), 160–87; Tony Bennett et al., eds., *Celebrating the Nation: A Critical Study of Australia's Bicentenary* (Sydney: Allen and Unwin, 1992); Lyn Spillman, *Nation and Commemoration: Creating National Identities in the United States and Australia* (Cambridge and New York: Cambridge University Press, 1997).

33. It does need to be emphasized that, as Graeme Turner has recalled, much of the media coverage of the bicentenary was suffused with anxiety that Aboriginal protest would "turn violent." Graeme Turner, *Making It National: Nationalism and Australian Popular Culture* (Sydney: Allen & Unwin, 1994), 84.

34. Broome, *Aboriginal Australians*, 206–43.

35. Inga Clendinnen, "Lecture 4: Inside the Contact Zone Part 1," [Transcript], *True Stories: ABC Boyer Lectures* (1999), http://www.abc.net.au/rn/boyers/stories/s71107.htm (accessed July 28, 2009).

36. Anna Haebich, "'Between Knowing and Not Knowing': Public Knowledge of the Stolen Generations," *Aboriginal History* 25 (2001): 79. For a comprehensive historical account of the various policies and practices of child removal and assimilation, within the context of the survival of Aboriginal families, see Anna Haebich, *Broken Circles: Fragmenting Indigenous Families: 1800–2000* (Fremantle: Fremantle Arts Centre Press, 2000).

37. van Toorn, "Indigenous Australian Life Writing," 1–3.

38. Carmel Bird and Peter Read, eds., *The Lost Children: Thirteen Australians Taken from Their Aboriginal Families Tell of the Struggle to Find Their Natural Parents* (Sydney: Doubleday, 1989).

39. Haebich, "Between Knowing and Not Knowing," 73.
40. Ibid.
41. Healy, *Forgetting Aborigines*, 18.
42. Ibid.
43. Ibid., 5.
44. Morris, *Identity Anecdotes*, 107.
45. Ahmed and Stacey, "Testimonial Cultures," 5.
46. Attwood, "Learning About the Truth," 183.
47. Ibid. Peter Read has been credited with developing the term "stolen generations" in his 1981 report on the history of Indigenous child removal in New South Wales. Peter Read, *The Stolen Generations: The Removal of Aboriginal Children in New South Wales: 1883–1969* (Sydney: Department of Aboriginal Affairs, NSW State Government, 1981).
48. Attwood, "Learning About the Truth," 183.
49. van Toorn, "Indigenous Australian Life Writing," 2–3. See also Penny van Toorn, *Writing Never Arrives Naked: Early Aboriginal Cultures of Writing in Australia* (Canberra: Aboriginal Studies Press, 2006).
50. See Spivak, "Three Women's Texts and Circumfession."
51. Healy, *Forgetting Aborigines*.
52. HREOC, *Bringing Them Home*, 15. For an account of the "Going Home" conference, see Jacqui Katona and Chips Mackinolty, eds., *The Long Road Home . . .: The Going Home Conference, 3–6 October 1994* (Darwin: Karu Aboriginal Child Care Agency, 1996).
53. Linda Briskman, *The Black Grapevine: Aboriginal Activism and the Stolen Generations* (Sydney: The Federation Press, 2003), 101.
54. HREOC, *Bringing Them Home*, 16.
55. Ibid.
56. See Link-Up and Tikka Jan Wilson, *In the Best Interests of the Child?: Stolen Children: Aboriginal Pain/White Shame* (Lawson, NSW: Link-Up (NSW) & Aboriginal History, 1997).
57. HREOC, *Bringing Them Home*, 17.
58. Ibid., 15.
59. Ibid., 17.
60. Ibid., 20.
61. Ibid., 266.
62. Ibid., 37.
63. Much of the conservative criticism of *Bringing them Home* focused on its use of oral evidence. The conservative critical response to the report will be discussed thoroughly in Chapter 5 as a part of the development of a popular culture of "refusing to witness."
64. John Frow, "A Politics of Stolen Time," *Australian Humanities Review* (February 1998), http://www.australianhumanitiesreview.org/archive/Issue-February-1998/ frow1.html (accessed May 5, 2007).
65. Ibid.
66. Oliver, *Witnessing*, 8.
67. On the "politics of recognition" in multicultural societies, more generally, see Charles Taylor, *Multiculturalism and the Politics of Recognition: An Essay with Commentary*, ed. Amy Gutmaan (Princeton, NJ: Princeton University Press, 1992).

68. Frow, "A Politics of Stolen Time." See also Dipesh Chakrabarty, "History and the Politics of Recognition," in *Manifestos for History*, ed. Keith Jenkins, Sue Morgan, and Alun Munslow (London and New York: Routledge, 2007): 77–87.

69. HREOC, *Bringing them Home*, 4.

70. Brigitta Olubas and Lisa Grenwell, "Re-Membering and Taking up an Ethics of Listening: A Response to Loss and the Maternal in 'the Stolen Children,'" *Australian Humanities Review* (July 1999), http://www.lib.latrobe.edu. au/AHR/archive/Issue-July-1999/olubas.html (accessed April 20, 2007).

71. Kennedy and Wilson, "Constructing Shared Histories," 119–39.

72. HREOC, *Bringing Them Home*, 156–57.

73. Ibid., 14, 16, 155, 157.

74. Ibid., 161, 172.

75. Ibid., 266.

76. Frow, "A Politics of Stolen Time."

77. Minow, *Between Vengeance and Forgiveness*; Thompson, *Taking Responsibility for the Past*; Barkan and Karn, eds., *Taking Wrongs Seriously*.

78. Robert I. Rotberg, "Apology, Truth Commissions, and Intrastate Conflict," in *Taking Wrongs Seriously: Apologies and Reconciliation*, ed. Elazar Barkan and Alexander Karn (Stanford, CA: Stanford University Press, 2006), 40.

79. Sarah Nuttall, "Telling 'Free' Stories? Memory and Democracy in South African Autobiography since 1994," in *Negotiating the Past: The Making of Memory in South Africa*, ed. Sarah Nuttall and Carli Coetzee (Oxford: Oxford University Press, 1998), 75–76.

80. Mark R. Amstutz, *The Healing of Nations: The Promise and Limits of Political Forgiveness* (Lanham, MD: Rowman & Littlefield Publishers, 2005), 8. Similarly, Dipesh Chakrabarty has written of the "historical wound" that is addressed through discourses on testimony and healing. Dipesh Chakrabarty, "History and the Politics of Recognition."

81. The work of Cathy Caruth has been central to the critical popularity of trauma theory. See Caruth, ed., *Trauma*; *Unclaimed Experience*.

82. For an overview of relevant criticism, see Susannah Radstone, "Trauma Theory: Contexts, Politics, Ethics," *Paragraph* 30, no. 1 (2007): 9–29. For a critical account of the development of trauma as central to psychotherapy, see Ruth Leys, *Trauma: A Genealogy* (Chicago, IL: University of Chicago Press, 2000).

83. Colvin, "Brothers and Sisters, Do Not Be Afraid of Me," 153.

84. Ibid., 158.

85. Catriona Elder, Angela Pratt, and Cath Ellis, "Running Race: Reconciliation, Nationalism and the Sydney 2000 Olympic Games," *International Review for the Sociology of Sport* 41, no. 2 (2006): 187.

86. Ibid.

87. John Howard cited in Bruce Permezel, "Season 2, Episode 3," in *The Games* (Australia: ABC TV, 1998–2000). For a full transcript of this apology, see John Clarke, "Apology by John Howard, Actor," *Sydney Morning Herald*, February 8, 2008, http://www.smh.com.au/news/general/apology-by-john-howard-actor/2008/02/08/1202234144333.html (accessed October 30, 2010).

88. Elder, Pratt, and Ellis, "Running Race," 188. See also Teresa Heinz Housel, "Australian Nationalism and Globalization: Narratives of the Nation in the 2000 Sydney

Olympics' Opening Ceremony," *Critical Studies in Media Communication* 24, no. 5 (2007): 446–61; John Sinclair, "More Than an Old Flame: National Symbolism and the Media in the Torch Ceremony of the Olympics," *Media International Australia*, no. 97 (November 2000): 35–46.

89. Elder, Pratt, and Ellis, "Running Race," 182–83.

90. James Grubel, "Onwards Reconciliation," *Newcastle Herald*, December 30, 2000, 22.

91. Elder, Pratt, and Ellis, "Running Race," 182.

92. Di Bretherton and David Mellor, "Reconciliation between Aboriginal and Other Australians: The 'Stolen Generations,'" *Journal of Social Issues* 62, no. 1 (2006): 81–98. See also Liz Reed, "'Awakening': The Politics of Indigenous Control and Authenticity at Sydney 2000," *Australasian Music Research* 7, no. 2002 (2003): 95–101.

93. See, for example, Phillip Coorey, "Unfinished Business," *Adelaide Advertiser*, December 30, 2000, 47; Grubel, "Onwards Reconciliation," 22; Marie McInerney, "Australia Set for Federation Party after Big 2000," *Reuters News*, December 30, 2000; Anne Bransdon, "Keeping the Spirit Flowing," *Illawarra Mercury*, December 29, 2000, 29; Fay Burstin, "A United Nation," *Herald Sun*, December 27, 2000, 19; Michael Gordon, "Where Do We Go from Here?" *Age*, December 9, 2000, 4; Kerry Taylor, "The Story So Far. . ." *Age*, December 8, 2000, 4; "Another Party," *Sydney Morning Herald*, November 20, 2000, 14.

94. James Grubel, "New Focus for Reconciliation in Australia's Second Century," *Australian Associated Press*, December 21, 2000.

95. Howard cited in Coorey, "Unfinished Business."

96. Michelle Grattan, "Introduction," in *Reconciliation: Essays on Australian Reconciliation*, ed. Michelle Grattan (Melbourne: Black, 2000), 7.

97. Murray Goot and Tim Rowse, *Divided Nation?: Indigenous Affairs and the Imagined Public* (Melbourne: Melbourne University Press, 2007), 150.

98. Ibid., 154.

99. David Carter, ed., *The Ideas Market: An Alternative Take on Australia's Intellectual Life* (Melbourne: Melbourne University Press, 2004).

100. See Tom Griffiths, "Truth and Fiction: Judith Wright as Historian," *Australian Book Review* (August 2006): 25–30; Bernard Smith, *The Spectre of Truganini* (Sydney: Australian Broadcasting Commission, 1980); W.EH. Stanner, *After the Dreaming* (Crows Nest, NSW: Australian Broadcasting Commission, 1969).

101. Whitlock's work in this area has been extensive. See especially Gillian Whitlock, "Becoming Migloo," in *The Ideas Market*, ed. David Carter (Melbourne: Melbourne University Press, 2004), 236–58; "Active Remembrance: Testimony, Memoir and the Work of Reconciliation," in *Rethinking Settler Colonialism: History and Memory in Australia, Canada, Aotearoa New Zealand and South Africa*, ed. Annie E. Coombes (Manchester and New York: Manchester University Press, 2006), 222–44; "Strategic Remembering: Fabricating Local Subjects," in *Selves Crossing Cultures: Autobiography and Globalisation*, ed. Rosamund Dalziell (Melbourne: Australian Scholarly Publishing, 2002), 162–77; "Consuming Passions: Reconciliation in Women's Intellectual Memoir," *Tulsa Studies in Women's Literature* 23, no. 1 (2004): 13–28.

102. Whitlock, "Becoming Migloo." Key examples of this genre include Henry Reynolds, *Why Weren't We Told: A Personal Search for the Truth About Our History* (Melbourne: Viking, 1999); Inga Clendinnen, *Tiger's Eye: A Memoir* (London: Jonathan Cape, 2001); Peter Read, *Belonging: Australians, Place and Aboriginal Ownership* (Melbourne: Cambridge University Press, 2000); Cassandra Pybus, *Community of Thieves* (Melbourne: Minerva, 1992).

103. Many of Manne's newspaper opinion articles for the *Age*, the *Sydney Morning Herald*, and the *Australian* from his period, along with *In Denial*, have been reprinted in the collection Robert Manne, *Left Right Left: Political Essays 1977–2005* (Melbourne: Black, 2005).

104. Ibid., 10. For a brief overview of the conservative criticism of *Bringing them Home* and the stolen generations, see Macintyre and Clark, *History Wars*, 145–47. This will be elaborated in Chapter 5.

105. On the denial of Aboriginal dispossession more broadly, particularly in the work of Keith Windschuttle, see Tony Taylor, *Denial: History Betrayed* (Melbourne: Melbourne University Press, 2008), 174–209.

106. Robert Manne, "In Denial: The Stolen Generations and the Right," in *Left Right Left: Political Essays 1977–2005*, ed. Robert Manne (Melbourne: Black, 2005), 303.

107. Ibid.

108. Ibid., 304.

109. Ibid., 240.

110. Ibid., 240–42. For a critique of Manne's understanding of genocide, see Patrick Wolfe, "Robert Manne, the Apology and Genocide," *Arena* (April–May 2008): 31–33.

111. Manne, "In Denial," 241.

112. Ibid., 304.

113. Kay Schaffer, "Manne's Generation: White Nation Response to the Stolen Generation Report," *Australian Humanities Review* 24 (June–August 2001), http://www.australianhumanitiesreview.org/archive/Issue-June-2001/schaffer.html (accessed April 24, 2009).

114. See also further criticism of *In Denial* in Bain Attwood, "The Stolen Generations and Genocide: Robert Manne's *in Denial: The Stolen Generations and the Right*," *Aboriginal History* 25 (2001); Melissa Lucashenko, John McLaren, and Jennifer Rose, "Three Responses to Robert Manne's *in Denial*," *Overland*, no. 163 (2001): 15–20.

115. Manne, "In Denial," 305. This is also a key theme of Manne's pre–*In Denial* work around reconciliation. Manne, *Left Right Left: Political Essays 1977–2005*, 201–3.

116. Gaita, "Guilt, Shame and Collective Responsibility," 275–87.

117. Manne, *Left Right Left*, 203.

118. Gaita, "Guilt, Shame and Collective Responsibility," 279.

119. Probyn, *Blush*, ix–x.

120. Ibid., 13–15.

121. Ahmed, "Politics of Bad Feeling," 77.

122. UNESCO, "Sorry Books," *Australian Memory of the World* (2004), http://www.amw.org.au/citation/13 (accessed December 14, 2009).

123. A "snapshot" of Sorry Book messages has been made available online. AIATSIS, "Sorry Book Messages," http://www1.aiatsis.gov.au/exhibitions/ sorrybooks/ sorrybooks_selection.htm (accessed December 14, 2009).
124. Ahmed, "Politics of Bad Feeling," 77.
125. Ibid., 77–78.
126. See especially Caroline Wake, "After Effects: Performing the Ends of Memory: An Introduction to Volume I," *Performance Paradigms* 5, no. 1 (2009), http://www.performanceparadigm.net/journal/issue-51/articles/after-effects-performing-the-ends-of-memory-an-introduction-to-volume-i/ (accessed December 28, 2009); Bryoni Trezise, "Ambivalent Bereavements: Embodying Loss in the Twenty-First Century," *Performance Paradigms* 5, no. 2 (2009), http://www.performanceparadigm.net/journal/issue-52/ articles/ambivalent-bereavements-embodying-loss-in-the-twenty-first-century/ (accessed December 28, 2009).
127. Gay McAuley, ed., *Unstable Ground: Performance and the Politics of Place* (Brussels: P.I.E. Peter Lang, 2006).
128. See ANTaR, "Sea of Hands," http://www.antar.org.au/sea_of_hands (accessed December 14, 2009).
129. Maryrose Casey, "Referendums and Reconciliation Marches: What Bridges Are We Crossing?" *Journal of Australian Studies* 89 (2006): 137.
130. Ibid., 141.
131. Ibid.
132. Ibid., 144.
133. Ibid., 148.
134. Povinelli, *Cunning of Recognition*, 17.
135. Ibid.
136. Ibid. See also Pratt et al. and their conception of reconciliation as a "normative discourse" designed to deflect focus away from substantive change, such as a treaty or compensation for the stolen generations. Angela Pratt, Catriona Elder, and Cath Ellis, "Papering over the Differences: Australian Nationhood and the Normative Discourse of Reconciliation," in *Reconciliation, Multiculturalism, Identities: Difficult Dialogues, Sensible Solutions*, ed. Mary Kalantzis and Bill Cope (Melbourne: Common Ground Publishing, 2001), 135–48.
137. Povinelli, *Cunning of Recognition*, 42.
138. Probyn, *Blush*, 107.
139. Oliver, *Witnessing*, 18.
140. Ibid.
141. Ibid.
142. Ahmed, " Politics of Bad Feeling," 80.
143. Ibid.
144. Probyn-Rapsey, "Complicity, Critique, and Methodology," 65.
145. Ibid., 68.
146. Ibid., 80.

2

"This Is How *I'm* Sorry": Creative Witnessing in Contemporary Australian Historical Fictions

It is the job of art to bear witness.
—Eva Sallis[1]

*Simple truth is not enough to answer to power;
something more like creative events are needed.*
—Stephen Muecke[2]

As Ken Gelder and Paul Salzman have noted, "historical fiction has dominated the Australian literary landscape."[3] The two decades since the bicentenary have seen the publication of numerous historical novels. This has included work by some of Australia's most noted literary writers such as Peter Carey, Richard Flanagan, David Malouf, and Kate Grenville, and authors of best-selling popular fiction, such as Bryce Courtenay and Tim Winton. At the same time, this period has been marked by the release of several historical films that have engaged with Australia's colonial history, including *The Tracker* (2002), *Rabbit-Proof Fence* (2002), *The Proposition* (2005), and, most recently, *Australia* (2008). The overwhelming majority of this historical fiction—in both written and cinematic form—has focused on the frontier and early colonial period. There has, however, been a recent move to explore the impact of the past on contemporary life, as in the work of writers Alex Miller, Andrew McGahan, and Gail Jones.

Critics have deftly explored the use of historical themes by Australian writers, whereas there has been little attention paid to the way in which contemporary historical fictions have articulated with the political and historiographical debates of the history wars.[4] Nor has there been a serious consideration of the contribution of Australian literature and historical film to the collective, postcolonizing process of re-membering.[5] In an effort to address this critical lacuna, this chapter considers the way that fictional work has participated in the broader practice of witnessing to Australia's history of Aboriginal dispossession. To do so is to take seriously the historical work performed by fiction; that is, to understand both the influential role that fiction has played in circulating ideas about the past within the public sphere, and also to affirm its status as "a way of constructing the past with a legitimacy of its own."[6] Consequently, this chapter does not examine historical fiction in terms of its relationship to conventionalized forms of nonfictional representation; it does not compare the novels and films under discussion to other, more "true" versions of the past. Rather, by reading fiction through the concept of witnessing, I explore creative work as a medium for engaging with the legacy of the past in the present, as an imaginative space in which core fantasies of a nation are rehearsed, and, in turn, rearticulated.

To examine the capacity of creative work to witness to Indigenous dispossession, this chapter focuses particularly on Kate Grenville's twinned frontier texts, the novel *The Secret River* (2005) and her writing memoir *Searching for the Secret River* (2006).[7] As a case study, Grenville's texts highlight the dual nature of creative witnessing as both an expression of an individual artist and their desire to engage with the past, and as a medium through which to encourage readers and audiences to perform their own processes of witnessing. Grenville's work has been the most prominent of a recent wave of historical novels, in both popular and critical contexts, and I position her work alongside other contemporary historical fictions, including novels by Gail Jones, Andrew McGahan, and Richard Flanagan. The chapter closes with a brief exploration of two contemporary films centered on the history of the stolen generations: Phillip Noyce's *Rabbit-Proof Fence* (2002) and Baz Luhrmann's *Australia* (2008).[8] If contemporary Australian novelists have largely shied away from engaging with stolen generations' testimony—with the notable exception of Gail Jones' *Sorry* (2007)—these two recent films sought to intervene in the fraught public debate over the implications of *Bringing them Home*.[9] As attempts to witness to the stolen generations, *Rabbit-Proof Fence* and

Australia highlight the powerful role of film as a popular medium of recognition and history making.

Creative Witnessing

Although there has been a willingness, particularly in the areas of Holocaust and memory studies, to consider artistic or creative testimonies, there has been less emphasis on how the work of the secondary witness may be performed through fiction. In fact, Shoshana Felman's foundational work on testimony is drawn from her readings of the modernist literary testimonies of authors such as Primo Levi and Albert Camus.[10] For Felman, modernist literature has been a privileged mode of testimonial expression due to the way in which its aesthetic of fragmentation and elision echoed the partial and incomplete nature of traumatic recall. Alongside this focus on literary testimonies, there has also been a willingness to consider visual art and other creative work as expressive of testimony.[11]

Moreover, though there has been a tendency for critics to view much of the fictional work produced by Australia's Indigenous writers as almost necessarily autobiographical or testimonial, there has not been a concomitant move to understand the creative work produced by settler Australians as a form of witnessing. Aboriginal creative work that has been read as testimonial has included Kim Scott's *Benang* (1999), Larissa Behrendt's *Home* (2004), and Alexis Wright's novels *Plains of Promise* (1997) and *Carpentaria* (2006). Sneja Gunew has criticized the tendency for non-Anglo "minority" writing to be read as autobiographical; whereas Carole Ferrier has argued, with reference to Indigenous women's writing, that although authors such as Wright have begun to employ an almost antirealist aesthetic, their works "still retain . . . a resonance of truth effects in the retelling of history."[12]

To understand creative work as a mode of secondary witnessing is to move the concept beyond a therapeutic context, in which witnessing is understood to occur through the close, dialogic bond forged between the eyewitness and the listener. To see creative work as an extension of the secondary witness' encounter with testimony is to understand that one of the imperatives of witnessing is to extend knowledge of the truth of testimony to others. In this sense, creative witnessing may be seen as a part of Kelly Oliver's notion of witnessing as "response-ability," which acknowledges that the secondary witness occupies a privileged speaking position in relation to the testifier.

To take a broad view of witnessing also acknowledges that a secondary witness may be drawn to witness not from listening to testimony firsthand, but as a response to historical events or social issues more generally. In this way, secondary witnessing could be viewed as a form of advocacy, an attempt to draw attention to injustice on behalf of a subordinated group, as much as an engagement with the demands of testimony itself. Accordingly, the bulk of the creative work to be discussed here should be understood not as a direct response to any individual body of testimony, such as *Bringing them Home,* but as a more diffuse response to the public discourse on reconciliation that circulated during the late 1990s and early twenty-first century. This form of witnessing moves beyond a relationship with an eyewitness to undertake the task of witnessing to the aftermath of colonialism.

Throughout this chapter, I understand the type of witnessing performed by creative work as being twofold. First, creative texts form a part of an artist's own personal response-ability to testimony, and, more broadly, to the public discourse on Aboriginal reconciliation. Moreover, creative work has, for many Australian artists, facilitated a public, extratextual engagement with social issues through their privileged role as public intellectuals. In this way, artists have the capacity to use both their notoriety and their craft to witness to injustice and suffering. Second, creative work can provide a space for audiences and readers to perform the process of witnessing themselves. In this sense, the creative text draws readers and audiences to imagine, in complex and diverse ways, relationships between Indigenous and non-Indigenous Australians. Thus, creative works can be understood simultaneously as the result of the artist's own desire to witness, as well as a medium for opening up spaces for identification, attachment, and recognition within Australian historical consciousness.

Australian Writers as Pubic Intellectuals

In 2005, Australian historian Mark McKenna, author of a highly personalized history of the Eden-Monaro region of New South Wales, spoke out against the increasing role of the personal in contemporary historical culture. "Almost every writer—of fiction and nonfiction—," he argued,

> feels that they cannot understand the country in which they live without first confronting the history of dispossession. The public telling of that personal story of confrontation then

becomes even more important and more powerful than the pages of the text itself.[13]

Although McKenna was apt in his identification of the pervasiveness of personalized engagements with the past, he has overlooked the extent to which this desire to respond personally to history has affected the "pages of the text itself." Australian authors have not only rehearsed their personal connections to history paratextually—in interviews, newspaper articles, and at writers' festivals—but also the desire to witness to Australia's history of dispossession has driven the production of a range of creative texts. What McKenna has viewed as a regrettable trend is, in fact, evidence of the writer's continued presence in the public sphere as a privileged commentator on social, cultural, and moral issues. McKenna has focused only on the comments authors have made outside their texts, whereas this chapter emphasizes the interrelationship between the role of writers as public advocates and their creative work.

Australia's public intellectual culture has been the subject of frequent, circular debates over its relative "health."[14] As David Carter has suggested, these discourses of decline, marked by Edward Said's view of the intellectual as a dissident outsider, have portrayed "the intellectual [as] a romantic hero, summoning the nation's conscience, bearing witness for us all, and embodying the full burden of culture."[15] Against this notion of the autonomous intellectual, bravely "speaking truth to power," Carter has promulgated the view that public intellectuals, and their ideas, are commodities within an "ideas market," standing within rather than outside the logic of the literary marketplace.[16] Extending this analysis, Brigid Rooney has identified these discourses of decline as reflective of deeper anxieties about nationhood and concerns about who defines issues of importance and value to the nation in this period of rapid globalization.[17]

Against a rhetoric of decline, Rooney has argued that the first decade of the twenty-first century has, in fact, "seen the efflorescence of Australian literary activism."[18] In her study of prominent writer-intellectuals, Rooney has highlighted the work of figures as diverse as Judith Wright, Patrick White, Les Murray, David Malouf, and Helen Garner. Rooney has understood the public interventions of these writers, that is, the extratextual work they perform within the public sphere, as "crossings," in which individual writers negotiate the gulf between literature and nation.[19] In understanding these public crossings, Rooney has replaced the homogenous notion of the writer as an intellectual outsider with a spectrum of writerly engagement that encompasses advocacy and activism, as well as more detached or academic intellectual comments.[20] Rooney has emphasized that contemporary public intellectual work might not fit Said's influential definition, whereas Australian public intellectual culture has, nevertheless, been marked by a diverse range of sociopolitical engagements, by writers from a range of ideological positions. In doing so, she has drawn attention to their continued salience within the public sphere, and, especially, their relevance to debates on history and politics.

Recently, the release of anthologies such as 2004's *Authors Take Sides: Iraq and the Gulf War* has demonstrated the desire of authors to reach beyond their own work to make connections with specific counter-publics dedicated to social justice or antiwar activism.[21] In this sense, public intellectual work may be understood as an address to a particular community, or, in other cases, an effort to, in fact, constitute a community of like-minded activists. Moving beyond an Australian context, Mark Sanders has drawn attention to the influential work of public intellectuals who resisted South African apartheid. For Sanders, the public work and activism of writers and intellectuals who resisted the regime was the result of an awareness of their own complicity within structures of dominance. As he has suggested, "the duty to speak out is linked with a will or desire not to be an accomplice."[22] In this way, public intellectual work can be seen to emerge as a form of witnessing, not only to testimony, but also to the writer's complicity and enmeshment in the world beyond their work.

The Writer as Witness

When Kate Grenville's novel *The Secret River* was published in 2005, it quickly became the focal point in a wide-ranging public discussion concerning the relationship between history and fiction.[23] This was not only due to the themes of her novel, which centered on a frontier massacre, but also due to her willingness to discuss, at length, the way she felt that her work performed a broader role though its engagement with the contemporary legacies of the past. As a result, Grenville came under attack from a diverse range of prominent Australian historians, including John Hirst, Mark McKenna, and Inga Clendinnen, for her claims that the novel be read as "truthful."[24] Grenville's proposition was certainly challenging. Unlike history, Grenville claimed that fiction could "actually get inside the experience" of the frontier.[25] The novel, she insisted, sat "up on a ladder, looking down on the history wars," and drew on empathy and "imaginative understanding" to avoid the "polarised positions" of historians.[26]

Grenville's assertions struck at the heart of contemporary anxieties about history writing. Her confident assurance that *The Secret River* offered a "clear-eyed" view of the frontier dovetailed with the widespread public assumption that the historiographic wrangling of the "history wars" amounted to petty, academic in-fighting.[27] It was unsurprising then that some historians, chastened by their experience of the history wars, responded bitterly to Grenville's work.[28] Eager to reclaim the authority they had ceded throughout that period, historians were hardly likely to assent to Grenville's characterization of their discipline as staid and incapable of creative engagement with the past. Indeed, Clendinnen, Hirst, and McKenna each, in strikingly similar ways, chastized Grenville for her empathetic use of historical records. Instead of recognizing the early settlers as fundamentally different from contemporary settler Australians, and seeking to understand the nature of this difference, the historians argued that Grenville's use of empathy had resulted in the creation of a novel populated with characters who thought and acted exactly similar to contemporary, liberal settlers.[29] That is, they argued that *The Secret River* was inhabited by individuals such as Grenville herself, deeply and ahistorically conflicted over frontier violence and the process of colonization.

Although this critique was not without basis, it became the foundation of a broader argument by historians who sought to reaffirm their privileged role as sole arbiters of the nation's past. In this way, historians marginalized the contribution of fiction to historical understanding, with Clendinnen positioning Grenville's "value-added history" as indicative of an alarming trend within Australian culture: the desire of novelists to write the nation's history, "to bump historians off the track."[30] What could have provoked a public discussion over the complexities of employing empathy or creative methods to understand the past instead became an occasion to further entrench the perception that history and fiction, despite some similarities, were radically dissimilar and mutually exclusive. What has been overlooked in analyses of the debate surrounding *The Secret River* is the extent to which Grenville and her critics—especially Clendinnen and McKenna—have been involved in strikingly similar attempts to re-imagine the frontier experience creatively and empathetically, drawing on approaches to writing and using methods that blur conventional generic boundaries.

In other words, Grenville's work is a part of a broader trend among Australian writers, of both history and fiction, to use their work as a forum for witnessing to Australian history.

Here, I use Grenville's work as a starting place to reflect on how non-Indigenous writers have used their work to witness to Australia's history of Indigenous dispossession. While Grenville's 2005 novel, *The Secret River* has been the focus of much critical attention, she has produced two other recent texts that have engaged with frontier history—her so-called "writing memoir" *Searching for the Secret River* (2006) and 2008s *The Lieutenant*, a novel depicting an early colonial cross-cultural friendship.[31] While *The Lieutenant* has been subject to a few early reviews, hitherto there has been a reluctance to consider *Searching* worthy of sustained critical attention. If Grenville's novel has sparked a robust debate, *Searching* has been treated by literary critics as little more than an "exegetical volume."[32] Indeed, though *Searching* did begin life as the exegetical component of Grenville's Creative Writing Ph.D., in its published form, the text needs to be considered a memoir in its own right, rather than as a residue of the production of the novel. A notable exception has been Anica Boulanger-Mashberg's recent work, which has considered *Searching* as a form of "marginalia," though this too has positioned Grenville's memoir as a subordinate parasite text.[33] In contrast, I contend that as a memoir, an act of conscious self-fashioning, *Searching* needs to be read as a part of an emergent body of life writing which details the ethical struggles of settler Australians.

Consequently, I consider Grenville's two *Secret River* texts alongside each other, a parallel reading that illustrates the extent to which the two overlap and are intertwined. *Searching* is not simply a companion piece to *The Secret River.* Together, the texts—a melange of history, genealogy, fiction, and autobiography—bear the mark of Grenville's attempts to witness to the demands of Indigenous testimony. If at first glance *The Secret River* appears to be a conventional historical novel, read alongside *Searching* Grenville's generic struggles emerge; each text registers Grenville's attempts to find the most appropriate technique to witness to the past. At the same time as historians, looking only at her novel, have drawn Grenville into a skirmish over the boundaries between "history" and "fiction," her efforts to witness have blurred these same borders to explore new ways of imagining the frontier.

Contemporary Historical Novels

Grenville is the most visible and commercially successful of a group of contemporary Australian novelists who have experimented with literary and historical techniques in an effort to witness to the legacies of the frontier experience. Throughout the twentieth century, numerous Australian authors have used their work to witness to the colonial experience, including the influential poet-activist Judith Wright, who campaigned around the issues of environmental conservation and Indigenous rights. Recent times have seen the publication of several high-profile literary novels focusing on the violence of the colonial past and its ongoing presence, a list that has included David Malouf's *Remembering Babylon* (1993) and his *The Conversations at Curlow Creek* (1996); Peter Carey's *True History of the Kelly Gang* (2000); Andrew McGahan's *The White Earth* (2004); Richard Flanagan's *Gould's Book of Fish* (2001) and *Wanting* (2008); Roger McDonald's Miles Franklin Prize winning *The Ballad of Desmond Kale* (2005); Gail Jones' *Sorry* (2007); and Alex Miller's cross-cultural romance *Journey to the Stone Country* (2002; another Miles Franklin Prize winner) and his *Landscape of Farewell* (2007), just to name some of the most prominent ones.[34] Most of this work has explored Australia's early history of colonial violence, often focusing on the violence directed toward Indigenous peoples, convicts, and Irish settlers. Other texts, particularly those of Miller and McGahan, have been concerned with tracing the impact of this past violence on contemporary lives, producing novels that attempt to work through this historical legacy.

Australian writers have long drawn on historical themes in their work, whereas the recent explosion in historical fiction has been heavily criticized. Drusilla Modjeska, for example, has trenchantly argued that this work evinces a worrying reluctance to engage with the demands of present life.[35] Yet in the two decades since the bicentenary, the meaning of the colonial past has taken on an unprecedented importance within public culture.[36] Viewed within this context, the popularity of historical themes is not a retreat from the demands of the present, but rather, an urge to return and work through events that are not safely past.[37] In particular, the abundance of work focusing on frontier violence and Aboriginal dispossession has articulated with the broader processes of *fin-de-siècle* reconciliation and settler witnessing. In this way, historical novels have engaged with some of the most debated, present, and urgent historical issues of the last thirty years. The excess of historical fiction can, thus, be seen as a reflection of the desire of writers to personally reassess Australian history and, in doing so, reconceive of their work as a part of their "response-ability" to Indigenous Australians.

The Secret River: "a Pulse of Connectedness"

Kate Grenville's novel *The Secret River* is just one example of an Australian writer responding to contemporary cultural politics through an imaginative engagement with the past.[38] In *The Secret River*, Grenville chronicled the life of William Thornhill, an impoverished English boatman who is transported to New South Wales for "the term of his natural life." Once in the colony, Thornhill quickly earns his freedom and, with his wife Sal and young children, "claims" a section of land on the banks of the Hawkesbury River. While working to cultivate his new life, Thornhill forms a fledgling community with other recently established settlers, and is confronted by the existing owners of his land: the Darug. Thornhill, who comes to hold a deep love for his new country, is positioned by the novel as an "ordinary" family man in sharp contrast to his neighbors: the sadistically violent "Smasher" Sullivan and Thomas Blackwood, a kindly man whose life has become enmeshed with the Darug. Through Thornhill, Grenville achieves a sensitive portrait of a man who, motivated by love for his family and fear of the unknown, participates in a horrifying act of colonial violence. Indeed, the novel turns on a chilling massacre scene and, in doing so, seeks to explore the capacity of ordinary people to perpetrate gruesome acts. This focus on the ordinary individuals within history underscores the extent to which the novel is born of Grenville's attempt to engage with Australia's colonial past on both a personal and familial level.

In the novel's companion text, *Searching for the Secret River,* Grenville explicitly positioned the novel as having developed from her personal engagement with Indigenous testimony and the reconciliation process. For Grenville, the crucial moment came as she participated in the Sydney People's Walk for Reconciliation in 2000. From within the large crowd, Grenville forged a connection and shared a charged look with an elderly Aboriginal woman. In *Searching*, Grenville recounted this experience as transformative: "our eyes met and we shared one of those moments of intensity—a pulse of connectedness."[39] As Grenville recalled, it was a pivotal moment, one that led her to wonder about her family history, in particular the relationship which her ancestor, Solomon Wiseman, had forged with the Aboriginal people of the

Hawkesbury region. "Who might have been living on that land and how he'd persuaded them to leave it," was something that "had never occurred to" her earlier.[40] Grenville's memoir staged this look as a moment of complete transformation: "in that instant of putting my own ancestor together with this woman's ancestor, everything swivelled: the country, the place, my sense of myself in it."[41]

Here, Grenville's confrontation with the contemporary presence of Indigenous people is figured as the motivating force for a journey of self-discovery—a chance to think through her personal connection to Australia's colonial past. For Grenville, this journey began with an exploration of family history. Focusing on the life of her ancestor Wiseman, a Hawkesbury river boatman, Grenville used genealogical research as a method of connecting with the past.[42] As Graeme Davison, who has researched the recent Australian obsession with genealogy, has written, in "family history, Australians may find a clue to a new sense of national becoming."[43] In *Searching* Grenville positioned genealogy as the starting point in a quest to forge a new mode of being Australian.

"More" than History

In order to respond appropriately to Australia's history of dispossession, and explore her own family's complicity in acts of colonial violence, Grenville began to write a nonfictional frontier history to harness the perceived authority of academic historical narratives. For Grenville, the story of her ancestor's relationship with the Darug "drew its power from the fact that it was real. Interposing a layer of invention would defeat my aim: to tell the unvarnished story as truthfully as I could."[44] To abandon nonfiction as the preferred method of writing her story, Grenville would be forced to relinquish the "authoritative voice" of history, and, thus, her work would forfeit any claims to historical truth.[45] Yet in searching for ways to write her history, Grenville quickly considered the need to situate herself within her narrative, possibly through the incorporation of "some elements of memoir," as in the work of Drusilla Modjeska and Helen Garner.[46] The resultant work would be "a wonderful and subtle mix of memoir, history and speculation."[47]

Yet, once beginning her research, Grenville soon abandoned nonfictional writing as limiting, as being somehow unable to access the experiential and emotional realities of the past. Faced with the stubborn opacity of the archives—in which the documents contained "marks on a page, nothing more"—Grenville began to confront the inadequacies of orthodox or traditional historical techniques for understanding the past.[48] As such, *Searching* bears the marks of Grenville's generic oscillation. The work moves from nonfictional history, to genealogy, to memoir as Grenville considers the most appropriate method to witness to the frontier. Here, Grenville performed a dismissal of history that has worked to position her text as authoritative. In this way, her self-conscious appraisal of history writing has served to validate her decision to pursue a highly personalized form of creative history.

In order to understand her own place within national and familial histories of dispossession, Grenville began to explore alternate modes of historical understanding. In particular, Grenville attempted to enter into the experiences of her ancestor through a form of recreation, by attending to the physical and experiential dimensions of history as shaped by the specificities of place. Grenville explored East End London and Wiseman's Ferry in the Hawkesbury region, seeking out those places where Wiseman had lived and worked.

The pivotal moment in Grenville's experiential research occurred when she decided to spend a night in Wiseman's homestead (now a pub), and attempted to imagine what it would have been like for Wiseman and his family to have lived on the frontier in the mid-1800s:

> Suddenly I was claustrophobic in this dark, tree-shaded building, this whole silent little settlement. At this moment I was absolutely certain—as sure as if I'd seen it with my own eyes—that there'd been trouble here on this quiet bend of the river. It might have been trouble with escaped convicts or bushrangers. But in that moment of seeing the place with new eyes, what I saw were spears and guns, and bright blood soaking into the hot dirt. I imagined this fortress being built so that, if any more blood was spilled, Wiseman could be sure it wouldn't be his.[49]

With a repetition of "eyes" and "seeing," Grenville staged an intense phantasmagorical moment where imagination and landscape converge to produce a form of insight or mystical knowledge. Here, Grenville is "absolutely certain" in her knowledge of massacre, yet has literally "seen" nothing, no verifiable evidence of the violence she craves to find. By attempting to enter into the loneliness and fear experienced by her settler ancestors, Grenville believed she, personally (note the constant use of the personal pronoun), had experienced a moment of clarity, a moment of sympathetic recreation that authorizes her imaginings of frontier violence. Though this passage is formally unremarkable, almost cliché, Grenville's emphasis on recreation and imagination perform a crucial rhetorical move. By positioning the personal as a site of authentic historical knowledge, Grenville sought to undercut the authority of more traditional forms of evidence, to stand as witness to the violence of frontier life. This is a truth positioned as beyond the archive, accessible only through the development of a personal connection to place. It is a form of witnessing to what Kelly Oliver has termed the "horrors beyond recognition."[50] For Grenville, it is only through the development of a personal connection to landscape that she can begin to understand the complexities of Wiseman's experience and to probe beyond the absences and inadequacies of the historical record.

Grenville's skeptical view of official records as the true site of historical meaning is repeated in the novel. William Thornhill, the character modeled on Wiseman, is shown to mistrust the version of events provided by colonial officials and media. In *The Secret River*, after the central massacre of Aborigines has taken place, Sal reads to Thornhill from "the *Gazette*." Though Thornhill understood that the paper's report on the slaughter "was not exactly false," it was not "quite the way [he] remembered," and he muses on the numerous things the paper "did not mention."[51] Looking over at the massacre site, Thornhill observed that

> Something had happened to the dirt in that spot so that not as much as a blade of grass had grown there ever since. Nothing was written on the ground. Nor was it written on any page. But the blankness itself might tell the story to anyone who had eyes to see.[52]

Here, Grenville argued that history needs to be read against the grain, for historical meaning to be found beyond the archive. In this way, both *Searching* and *The Secret River* are preoccupied with the exploration of blankness, emptiness, and silence and subsequently figure the frontier as a liminal, unknowable place, marked by absence. Exploring Wiseman's Ferry, Grenville wrote that

> this was an empty place—but empty the way a room was when the people had that minute walked out of it. They left a blank, but the blank held the shape of their presence. I wasn't feeling the emptiness of the place, but the once-fullness of it.[53]

Likewise, for Thornhill, the ultimate meaning of the massacre, and his participation in it, is negotiated in relation to his own conscience, filtered through the landscape. As Thornhill wiles away his evenings "in his favourite spot on the verandah [sic]," he became consumed with scanning the horizon for any signs of a continuing Aboriginal presence: "he strained, squinted through the glass until his eyeballs were dry. Finally he had to recognize that it was no human, just another tree, the size and posture of a man. Each time, it was a new emptiness."[54] In order to perceive the impact of frontier violence, both Grenville and Thornhill adopted a phantasmagoric relationship to the "once-fullness" of the landscape: The only way to perceive the truth of the frontier, Grenville is suggesting, is to develop an imaginative, personalized connection to place attuned to the ongoing presence of the past.

Remaking White Virtue

In both *Searching* and *The Secret River*, Grenville has presented a portrait of settlers struggling to come to terms with their own complicity with acts of frontier violence. The novel has not only functioned as Grenville's creative attempt to bear witness to history, but it has also chronicled Thornhill's own struggle to negotiate the responsibility of secondary witnessing. In the novel, Grenville presented Thornhill's proximity to and involvement in acts of violence ambivalently. During the core massacre scene, Thornhill initially appeared frozen—"he pointed his gun at blacks as they ran but the muzzle was always too slow"; "he could not move, a man in a dream."[55] When he finally did open fire, Grenville presented his action as almost involuntary: "the gun went off with a puff of blue smoke and a pop that sounded puny. . . ."[56] It is the gun here that is figured as the source of action and intentionality, rather than "Thornhill" or "he." Later in the novel, Thornhill is portrayed as a successful and wealthy beneficiary of the massacre, though he is also depicted as engulfed by a mixture of regret and despair, haunted by a "hollow feeling."[57] Lyn McCreddon has described Grenville's portrayal of Thornhill's reaction to his role in the massacre as "richly ambivalent," ascribing his actions to a complicated balance of historical force and personal agency.[58] For historians Hirst and Clendinnen, Thornhill's deliberations on his role in the massacre are a glaring anachronism—the mixed feelings of regret and compassion that could only be felt by a contemporary mind. As Hirst has written of Thornhill, somewhat condescendingly, "he is a very good man, amazingly sensitive for an illiterate waterman brought up in a hard world."[59]

If for Hirst and Clendinnen, Thornhill's conscience is a sign of the novel's inadequacies as a form of history, then for some literary critics, such as Adam Gall, it has indicated the extent to which the novel is implicated in a broader, problematic discourse on reconciliation. Gall has been particularly critical of the extent to which the novel's success indicates that its function is to interpellate the

> "Good" settler and confirm and solidify that position in the consciousness of the reader. Part of being the good settler in this liberal imaginary is the rehearsal of an unflinching examination, and re-evaluation of aspects of the national past.[60]

Indeed, the reader is immersed in Thornhill's interiority, encouraged to sympathize with this hardworking family man, and urged to recoil at the actions of the novel's "bad settler," the grotesque Smasher Sullivan.

However, it is not simply the novel that works to recuperate a white liberal subjectivity. Reading Grenville's novel and her memoir together draws attention to the continuity between Thornhill and Grenville—as represented in both the novel and the memoir—as models of white virtue. In *Searching*, Grenville undertook the task of questioning her assumptions regarding Indigenous peoples and the effects of colonization, and, in doing so, staged the memoir as an attempt to work through her "good intentions" and "high-minded thoughts."[61] Gillian Whitlock has argued, in relation to the white intellectual memoir, that responses to testimony that focus on the ethical virtue of the white witness can actually work to reinforce the authority of the white writer or critic. Accordingly,

> even as they [white writers] seek to exorcise, to expiate, and to invent new ways of belonging, they remain vulnerable to well-intentioned, yet fatally flawed colonizing gestures of sentimentality, benevolence, or humanism that are embedded in powerful traditions in literary, historical, and cultural criticism and scholarship.[62]

Whitlock has been pivotal in drawing attention to the relationship between Indigenous testimony and the white memoir in both contemporary Australian culture and that of other settler nations. Whitlock has written extensively on the recent phenomenon of Australian public intellectuals staging their own self-conscious confrontations with Australia's colonial past, through the production of "becoming migloo" texts.[63] In *Searching*, Grenville staged a confrontation with whiteness through an examination of her own family history; whereas in the novel, the reader is encouraged to consider Australia's foundational violence through an identification with Thornhill. In this way, both texts explore "how complicity with historical injustice lies at the heart of the domestic, the familial and the everyday."[64]

Both texts probe the dilemmas of the white self under colonialism, whereas Thornhill and Grenville occupy distinctly different temporal subject positions in relation to Indigenous peoples and other settlers. Lyn McCredden has pointed to the temporal difference between the colonial space of the novel and our present "post-colonial" milieu, and has pondered that

> it will be interesting to read unfolding scholarly discussion of this novel as Grenville's richly ambivalent, psychic representations of colonial Australia are ideologically measured against post-colonial markers.[65]

To be sure, the novel has attempted to create a nuanced portrait of early colonial life. Despite this, readers are encouraged to view the novel as a form of postcolonial witnessing, as a direct product of contemporary relations between settlers and Indigenous peoples. That is, from the novel's dedication—"to the Aboriginal people of Australia: past, present and future"—to Grenville's numerous outspoken public appearances, readers have been alerted to the text's role in contemporary, postcolonial cultural politics. In one interview, Grenville argued that her novel has been appreciated by Indigenous readers, specifically because "they recognise that the book is my act of acknowledgement, my way of saying: this is how *I'm* sorry."[66] This consistent framing of the novel as an act of apology—a product of postcolonial witnessing—inhibits our ability to read the novel as concerned "only" with the past.

Moreover, the distinct slippage between Thornhill and Grenville (as both author of a novel and subject of a memoir) as figures of white conscience has further complicated the temporal relationship between the texts. The similarity between the two figures, and their twinned reliance on the empathetic imagination as a method for working through the horrors of the frontier, is disruptive of efforts to read

Thornhill and Grenville as occupying distinctly different temporal spaces. This is not simply, as Hirst has asserted, because Grenville is Thornhill, but because the texts are two halves of the same contemporary, personal process of confronting the horrors of the past. The similarities between Thornhill and Grenville alert us to Grenville's struggle to find the right genre for her story: Is hers a story about the past, the present, or their interrelation? On the one hand, this slippage has emphasized the endurance of the past in the present, and, as Fiona Probyn-Rapsey has argued, underscored the continuity of complicity as a structural product of settler colonialism.[67] On the other hand, it has worked to valorize the perspective of the virtuous white settler, essentially "good" yet misguided or uninformed, and, as such, has constituted a fairly limited mode of witnessing.

The extent to which Grenville's work has been oriented toward the refashioning of white settler subjectivity, rather than with an engagement with the demands of testimony, has been most clearly illustrated by the way in which she situated her entire project as motivated by a "look." Though Grenville may have experienced a similar moment of connection, her decision to reify this event as the origin of her project has worked to promote an image of Grenville as a responsible contemporary settler—someone concerned with the impact of the past and eager to engage with the concerns of Indigenous peoples in the present. This figure of the responsible witness has worked to authenticate Grenville's fictional project as both an act of apology and a considered examination of the past. Yet, despite Grenville's efforts to respond to the challenge of Indigenous testimony and protest, her work has served primarily to reinforce the virtue of settler subjectivity.

In *Searching*, the Aboriginal woman that Grenville credits with prompting her family history experiment is mute: The moment is not portrayed as a dialogic exchange but rather as the phantasm of a white liberal imagination. Nevertheless, both Grenville's texts have borne the weight of their attempt to witness to acts "beyond recognition." *The Secret River* moves between genres, from a family romance to a realist historical novel, and, finally, to a form of dramatic tragedy.[68] Grenville's oscillation between history, fiction, and memoir suggests that in order to witness to the horrors of the frontier, something more is required than established modes of historical understanding. Though Grenville's texts have probed the limits of historical knowledge, they have also urged us to consider the role of the personal as a site for an exploration of endurance of the past. In this way, her texts have attested to the capacity of creative work to bear witness, and, in Muecke's terms, have illustrated the extent to which art can "answer to power."[69]

"Sorry Books"

Grenville's use of colonial history as a way of witnessing to the legacies of the past can be contrasted to the work of a range of contemporary Australian novelists.[70] In particular, Grenville's understanding of her novel as an "apology" can be compared with Gail Jones' act of creative witnessing, as in her 2007 novel *Sorry*. As reviewer James Ley has suggested, "the word 'sorry' has become so contentious in recent times that Gail Jones's decision to adopt it as the title of her fourth novel must be interpreted as a political statement."[71] Yet, while Jones has drawn explicitly on contemporary political events, in both her title and the novel's afterward, "A Note On Sorry," the novel is, in fact, a highly complex, allegorical work that has used contemporary debate over an apology as a starting place to explore colonial relationships of the past.[72]

Set during the mid-twentieth century in remote Western Australia, Jones weaved a tale of isolation, exploitation, and cross-cultural friendship focusing on a young settler girl, Perdita and her family's Aboriginal domestic worker, Mary. Neglected by her frail mother and her bitter, eccentric anthropologist father, the novel portrayed the development of a close bond between Perdita and Mary, which forms the heart of the novel. While Jones' work turned on an apology and reconciliation between the girls, the novel's didacticism has been tempered by its literary and theoretical inflection. Jones has borrowed liberally from Shakespeare, especially *A Winter's Tale*, from which the novel's protagonist takes her name, to tell a broader story about the relationships between thought, feeling, and action. As a text of witnessing, *Sorry* is primarily an exercise in mourning, and, as such, has meditated on the meaning of grief and pain. *The Secret River*, too, has been interpreted as a work of mourning though, as Sarah Pinto has argued, it is most appropriately understood as a work of melancholia that positions the white settler as "a melancholic victim," narcissistically attached to his own "sadness and diminished personhood."[73] In contrast, *Sorry* formed a more dialogic, outwardly focused attempt to understand grief: It was, for Jones, "a cautious offering in the process of cultural contrition, and a wish, more personally, to see evident in Australian culture attempts at 'thinking with grief.'"[74]

Though quite different in content and purpose, both *The Secret River* and *Sorry* have presented themselves as "sorry books"—creative works that hope, through their imaginative and empathetic capacities, to further the cause of reconciliation in Australia. For Jones, the task of witnessing has entailed a responsibility to dwell on the experience of grief, to consider how grief may be productive of new ways for Indigenous and non-Indigenous Australians to relate to each other. In contrast, Grenville has sought to cover over the violence of the past, and has been most anxious about the pain experienced by settler Australians. Despite this, the kind of witnessing that both authors have undertaken is also the work of remembering, an attempt to honor contemporary Indigenous testimony through an acknowledgement of Australia's violent history and ongoing settler complicity.

Though Grenville and Jones have been quite explicit in what they see as the aim of their creative witnessing, they are only two of a range of Australian novelists who have used their fiction as a forum to explore the legacies of the past. It is worth noting here that although many novelists have set their work in the past, Andrew McGahan and Alex Miller are two writers who have dealt with Australia's colonial history from the perspective of the present. In Andrew McGahan's 2004 novel *The White Earth*, set during the 1990s in Queensland's Darling Downs region, the past returns to "haunt" and reshape present lives.[75] Similar to *The Secret River*, McGahan has explored the effects of a massacre of Aboriginal people. Yet rather than concentrate only on the perpetrators, McGahan has traced how acts of colonial violence can reverberate across the generations. Set against the backdrop of the *Mabo* decision and the rise of a One Nation-like extreme right political organization, McGahan has chronicled the fortunes of the McIvers, current "possessors" of Kuran Station, and, in doing so, has highlighted the way in which the affects of the past linger to shape present lives. Similarly, Miller has explored history through the present, and in *Journey to the Stone Country* has employed romance to draw Aboriginal and non-Aboriginal characters together.[76] Here, the love story is used redemptively to "heal" present characters who have been marked by colonial violence. Both McGahan and Miller have demonstrated the scope of "historical fiction" to move beyond the frontier scene to witness not only to past horrors but also to the enmeshment of present generations in acts of ongoing violence and dispossession. This body of work has formed a forceful rejoinder to those, such as Howard, who have insisted on divorcing the past—and responsibility for the actions of previous generations—from the present.

Screening the Stolen Generations

In a departure from the nostalgic-period dramas that defined Australia's film "renaissance" in the 1970s, Australian filmmakers have produced a recent "cycle" of history films which have explicitly explored relationships between Indigenous and non-Indigenous Australians.[77] This body of work has included Rolf de Heer's *The Tracker* (2002), Craig Lahiff's *Black and White* (2002), and Ivan Sen's *Beneath Clouds* (2002).[78] Non-Indigenous Australian writers have been reluctant to explore the issue of child removal, preferring to focus instead on the more "distant" colonial past. Crucially, Jones has justified her decision not to represent the stolen generations in *Sorry* on the grounds that it would have been "presumptuous" to do so as a "white Australian."[79] Settler Australian filmmakers, it seems, have been far bolder, choosing to confront viewers with representations of the "colonial" violence of the twentieth century.

In the remainder of this chapter, I will discuss two recent, popular Australian films that have depicted stories of the stolen generations. The first, Phillip Noyce's *Rabbit-Proof Fence* (2002), has adapted Doris Pilkington-Garimara's life narrative about her mother's childhood escape from the Moore River Native Settlement.[80] Set in Western Australia in 1931, the film has chronicled the story of three Indigenous children, Molly Craig (Everlyn Sampi), her sister Daisy (Tianna Sansbury), and their cousin Gracie (Laura Monaghan), as they struggle to return home to Jigalong via the Number 1 *Rabbit-Proof Fence*. Throughout their journey, they are pursued by an Aboriginal tracker (David Gulpilil) and the police, led by "Mr. Devil"—the Western Australian Chief Protector of Aborigines, A.O. Neville, played with menacing restraint by British actor Kenneth Branagh.

The second, Baz Luhrmann's blockbuster romance *Australia* (2008), has centered on the history of the stolen generations as part of an epic retelling of the Australian nation.[81] Set in the late 1930s and during World War II, *Australia* has focused on the Northern Territory cattle trade. The film follows the efforts of a recently widowed British aristocrat, Lady Sarah Ashley (Nicole Kidman), to save her late husband's beloved cattle station, Faraway Downs, from sale to rival station owner "King" Carney (Bryan Brown). The narrative is animated by two love stories: the love that blossoms between the restrained Ashley and

Hugh Jackman's knock-a-bout "Drover," and the maternal bond which develops between Ashley and Nullah (Brandon Walters), an "orphaned" "half-caste" child. This bond is tested by the intervention of Nullah's grandfather, King George (David Gulpilil), who insists that Nullah should "go walkabout" with him; and again, by Nullah's temporary removal by police to the Mission Island children's home.

Though *Rabbit-Proof Fence* and *Australia* have employed divergent generic modes, and have claimed different relationships to historical truth, both have insisted on the importance of telling stories about the stolen generations. In this way, both have contributed to the urgent cultural work of remembering against repeated conservative attempts to deny the truth of stolen generations' narratives.[82] Moreover, as popular films circulating within international networks of cinema distribution and promotion, *Rabbit-Proof Fence* and *Australia* have sought to communicate this history to a global audience. However, more than this, both films have worked to engage their implied settler audiences in a process of witnessing aimed at unsettling their relationship to dominant narratives of Australian identity. Following Felicity Collins and Therese Davis, I consider *Rabbit-Proof Fence* and *Australia* in terms of "back-tracking," and focus on the way both films have created opportunities for audience members to negotiate imaginative connections with historical experience.[83] That is, I am not concerned with critiquing either film in terms of its relationship to a mode of "truthful" historical representation, though both have been subject to heated debates in this fashion. Instead, by employing a notion of spectatorship that foregrounds the heterogeneity of the film image, I examine the way that cinema functions as an ambivalent, fantasy space for the reconsideration of familiar historical narratives.[84]

Over the past two decades, critics have begun to explore historical films as forms of historical representation in their own right. This literature is now large and diverse, with a critical focus that ranges from "Hollywood" film to experimental cinema.[85] The move to consider historical representation in films is especially pronounced in the overlapping areas of Holocaust and memory studies, in which cinematic witnessing to the Shoah has become hotly contested. Accordingly, films, and the visual image more generally, lie at the heart of some of the most fraught discussions of the Holocaust, testimony, and representation.[86] More generally, the work of Robert Rosenstone has been highly influential in prompting an analysis of a genre he has termed the "New History film," a form of film that aims "less to entertain an audience or make profits than to understand the legacy of the past."[87]

Though a commentary on historical films has tended to interrogate its factual basis, as Frances Guerin and Roger Hallas have suggested "within the context of bearing witness, material images do not merely depict the historical world, they participate in its transformation."[88] Moreover, as a medium dependent on audience engagement, films dramatize the relational nature of witnessing, and draw on the audience to affirm or reject the images and ideas they present. In this way,

> the image's role in the process of bearing witness can be seen to rely not upon a faith in the image's technological ability to furnish empirical evidence of the event, but upon a faith in the image's phenomenological capacity to bring the event into iconic presence and to mediate the intersubjective relations that ground the act of bearing witness.[89]

Films may, thus, act to stage a testimonial exchange and draw the audience to affectively connect with their subject.

It is important to stress that both *Rabbit-Proof Fence* and *Australia* have diverged significantly from Rosenstone's model of a commercially detached history film. Both films are firmly embedded within the Hollywood system that privileges the production of audience-driven profit-making features. Moreover, both Noyce and Luhrmann are well-known for their fluency with popular cinematic genres as noted purveyors of action movies and camp romances, respectively. Tony Hughes-d'Aeth has criticized Noyce's positioning of *Rabbit-Proof Fence* as a global, Hollywood film, and Germaine Greer has advanced a similar argument in relation to *Australia*.[90] Both critics have been concerned by the tendency for the filmmakers to "translate" aspects of Indigenous experience into "universal" stories.

In addressing the ability for popular films to engage meaningfully with the past, and with Indigenous testimony specifically, Penny van Toorn's work on the commodification of stolen generation narratives has been instructive. "[T]oo often," van Toorn has written, in discussions of Aboriginal culture, "the term 'commodification' is pronounced as the last word, as though 'commodification' were a dastardly villain who captures and enslaves Indigenous cultures, or a fatal disease whose dire implications for Indigenous cultures were axiomatic."[91] Focusing her discussion on Aboriginal women's life narratives, van Toorn has drawn attention to the fundamental ambivalence of the marketplace and has stressed the way that a commercial publishing context does not occlude the power of Indigenous testimony to provoke diverse reader responses. Van Toorn's rejection of a deterministic anticapitalist stance toward commodification has been adopted by Emily Potter and Kay Schaffer in their thoughtful reading of *Rabbit-Proof Fence*. Drawing on Felix Guattari's model of the "singular event," Potter and Schaffer have argued powerfully that the "film exceeds its own boundaries as a Hollywood product, existing indeterminately in a complex ecology of relations and effects."[92] While remaining sympathetic to arguments about the dangers of commodification, particularly its tendency to reduce cultural specificity to "universal" humanist themes, I share the perspectives of Potter and Schaffer, and Collins and Davis, by affirming the capacity of popular visual media to proffer heterogeneous sites for audience identification.

Translating Testimony

As a text of creative witnessing, *Rabbit-Proof Fence* is itself based on a text of witnessing—Doris Pilkington-Garimara's biographical life narrative *Follow the Rabbit-Proof Fence* (1996).[93] The film, then, is not merely an adaptation. Rather, the movie has formed Noyce and screenwriter Christine Olsen's attempt to witness to Pilkington-Garimara's life narrative and, as such, a part of their response-ability to respond to her story. Both Noyce and Olsen have attested to the "emotional" experience of reading Pilkington-Garimara's work. In her forward to the screenplay, Olsen has stated that reading Pilkington-Garimara's life narrative moved her.[94] Similarly, Noyce has described himself as "overwhelmed by the story. Emotionally overwhelmed."[95] Crucially, both have reflected on their filmmaking process in terms of it being an attempt to isolate which aspect of the story moved them so much, in order to facilitate a similarly emotive process for audience members.

While Pilkington-Garimara worked as a consultant on the film, it is important to emphasize that the end result is less a collaborative life narrative than a translation of Pilkington-Garimara's work.[96] It is this tension that Deborah Cain has argued is highlighted "by the way the film slips seamlessly between a documentary style dealing with a historic event, and the fictionality of a feature film with its narrative more suited to a Hollywood cinema."[97] In one sense, this confirms the film as a text of advocacy. This is not quite the same as speaking for Pilkington-Garimara, but instead indicates the way in which her story has been translated for a general, non-Indigenous, and even non-Australian audience.

Crucial to this process of translation has been the ability to place Molly's story within a broader framework by engaging with what Bain Attwood has described as the archetypal "stolen generations narrative."[98] This has been achieved primarily through the use of didactic titles that bookend the film and provide the viewer with a basic understanding of Australia's history of Indigenous child removal. In particular, the girls are positioned explicitly as members of the stolen generations, and the viewer is introduced to the 1931 Aborigines Act and the figure of A.O. Neville. This broader narrative "framing" is anchored by what Tony Birch has described as the film's "allegoric tone," which "invites an engagement with the wider history of the treatment of Aboriginal people without giving it a direct focus."[99]

Yet, while the film is clearly concerned with a specifically Indigenous experience in Molly's story, Olsen has written of how she felt the narrative, with its central focus on "lost" children, had a more general resonance. Reflecting on her experience of writing the screenplay, Olsen has written that "at first it seemed that this was a classic fairytale: three children stolen away by a wicked witch and taken to her house."[100] Later, Olsen reconceived of Pilkington-Garimara's narrative as "a war story. The country has been invaded and taken over . . . To get back home they must cross through enemy-occupied territory never knowing who their friends are . . ."[101] Finally, Olsen concluded that "my story/Molly's story was about home."[102] Here, the search for a universal narrative framework leads Olsen to settle on a general story about childhood and innocence, about searching for "home." The sense in which the figure of the child formed the filmmakers' key point of identification in their witnessing of Pilkington-Garimara's story is further emphasized by Noyce, who has spoken of how he

> really strongly identified with the three girls, Molly, Daisy and Gracie . . . It was just because they were young children who were powerless and had no redress and seemingly no escape from their destiny. And who, after an almighty effort, triumph. I found myself on their side, in their shoes, massively identifying with them, very soon into the story.[103]

Accordingly, both Noyce and Olsen came to the task of translating Pilkington-Garimara's story from a strong sense of personal identification with the girls.

In her study of autobiographies of childhood, Kate Douglas has emphasized the power of "normative readings" to mediate the reception of stolen generation texts.[104] Douglas has argued that life narratives produced by removed children have been generally interpreted through two key "frames": "the figure of the innocent child, and the successful, resilient, writer who overcomes adversity to author their autobiography."[105] Moreover, as Cath Ellis has argued in relation to stolen children narratives, the central focus is not "indigeneity . . . but the image of the child."[106] By emphasizing the deracinated category of childhood innocence, narratives about child removal have often engaged their readership through the power of empathetic identification with the stolen child. Indeed, it was the affective pull of childhood innocence, with its attendant vulnerability, that allowed Olsen to posit Molly's story as "my story." Most crucially, it was the trope of the innocent child that worked to translate Pilkington-Garimara's narrative to the screen where it was "mainstreamed," to "speak beyond . . . [the] indigenous community to white Australians . . ."[107]

Yet if the affective power of *Rabbit-Proof Fence* can be seen to flow from its decontextualization of Indigenous experience that is, the metamorphosis of a story about the stolen generations into a universal narrative of "lost" children/innocence, at the same time, it is essential to note how the film's ending explicitly reinscribes the Indigenous meanings of the story. The insertion of documentary footage of film's characters—the real life Molly and Daisy—forcefully draws the viewer back into the present. Speaking their language, with English subtitles, the real Molly reaffirms the truth of the film, and extends its narrative by testifying to experiences that take the viewer beyond the film. By allowing the "real" Molly the space to speak directly to the audience, the filmmakers worked to authenticate her narrative and, in doing so, framed the process of viewing the film as an act of witnessing to testimony.

Empathy, Imagination, and Identification

If Olsen's screenwriting technique hinged on her ability to collapse the distance between herself and Molly—by conceiving of the film as my story/Molly's story—the film encouraged audience members to perform a similar overidentification. Throughout *Rabbit-Proof Fence*, the viewer is prompted, through a range of immersive camera techniques, to forge an empathetic identification with Molly that privileges her narrative perspective and draws attention to her encapsulation within the assimilationist polices of the early twentieth-century Australia. The urge to identify with Molly is particularly strong during the scene of her removal from her mother, in which the camera is positioned at child height and much of the action is filmed from Molly's viewpoint. This technique is repeated again during a scene set at Moore River in which A O. Neville inspects the darkness of Molly's skin, the audio track privileging her panicked, muffled breathing.

Noyce's tendency to position the camera so that the audience experiences the film as Molly has been the subject of concern for several critics who are suspicious of the film's sentimental, empathetic agenda. Advancing the trope of the innocent child through immersive techniques in which the viewer is encouraged to inhabit Molly's subjectivity contributes to the universalizing drive of the narrative, what Jane Lydon has described as the "ease with which viewers translate a local, historical event into immediately personal terms."[108] Tony Birch has acknowledged the vital role of empathy in the film, describing "audiences . . . left breathlessly supportive of the girls," whereas Tony Hughes-d'Aeth has been wary of the film's empathetic agenda, arguing that

> the empathetic investment on which the film is so heavily reliant constitutes in my view something of a Trojan Horse. There is no intrinsic thoughtfulness or "thinking into" that is brought about by the use of first-person camera shots or other immersive film techniques. The arrogance of the discourse of assimilation can live just as easily within the polite filmic regimes of Hollywood cinema.[109]

For Hughes-d'Aeth, empathy is inherently problematic, a discourse that elides the incommensurability of difference and encourages a recolonizing of Indigenous experience.

Arguing against this alarmist reading of empathy, Helen Grace has insisted that "the emotional processes involved in this identification [with Molly] locate our own lives within the narrative—even though a key aim of this film is to understand and identify with the point of view of the three girls and their story."[110] For Grace, then, the viewer is certainly drawn into an identificatory relationship with Molly, but, in doing so, is asked to maintain a crucial distance. However, what exactly does it mean for viewers to locate their own lives within *Rabbit-Proof Fence*? While Grace leaves this question largely unexplored, it prompts us to consider alternate ways of viewing the film that are not simply suspicious of its empathetic agenda, nor overly enthusiastic in identifying with Molly. As Collins and Davis, and Potter and Schaffer have suggested, normative readings certainly influence reception, but cannot overdetermine audience reactions. I move now to consider what it might mean for a viewer to maintain a sense of their own subject position during viewing and witness to the film's events by refusing to collapse the distance—temporal and cultural—between the viewer and Molly.

In thinking through how non-Indigenous viewers might resist or complicate the film's core narrative, Susannah Radstone's reading of Marianne Hirsch has been instructive. In her work on postmemory and photography, Marianne Hirsch has employed Kaja Silverman's term "heteropathic identification" to "describe a memorial relation to the experience of others predicated upon both identification and difference."[111] As Hirsch has elaborated, "heteropathic memory (feeling and suffering with the other) means . . . the ability to say 'It could have been me; it was me, also,' and, *at the same time*, 'but it was not me.'"[112] If heteropathy is the ideal mode of identification to be adopted in testimonial witnessing, Hirsch has argued that her subject of inquiry, Holocaust photographs of children, have become so iconic that they are now too open to "trivialization and stereotype . . . which empties them of their particularity, specificity, subjectivity," foreclosing heteropathy.[113]

As with representations of the stolen generations, it is the timeless and universal quality of innocent childhood that has become the focus of widespread Holocaust memorialization. For Radstone, the challenge in witnessing to such images is to move beyond the child, to "struggle to read . . . image[s] in 'the grey zone', that is, in a zone, in which neither 'pure' victimhood, nor 'pure' perpetration hold sway."[114]

Here, Radstone is writing against the tendency within contemporary trauma and memory studies to perform a critical witnessing that is oriented to the experiences of the victim. In contrast, Radstone has argued for a more complex and necessarily conflicted form of witnessing that attends to the possibilities which spectators can identify with figures of perpetration as well as with iconic images of innocence. She has suggested "that scenarios that include the exercise of power and authority arguably prompt a particular identification *with* the wielder of that power, as well as with the object upon whom it is exercised."[115] Although much has been written on how *Rabbit-Proof Fence* promotes empathetic identification with the child, I argue that it simultaneously provides spaces for settler audiences to witness their complicity with acts of colonial violence through a focus on figures of perpetration.

Ambivalence: "Mr. Devil" and Constable Riggs

Several critics have argued that the camera's focus on Molly, Daisy, and Gracie is so forceful that it occludes an engagement with the settler characters. Hughes-d'Aeth's assessment that Branagh plays the role of Neville with a "distancing Britishness" is illustrative of this view. He has argued further, and more "importantly, [that] the Neville of Olsen/Noyce/Branagh . . . embodies the vision of him as a slightly misguided and idiosyncratic fool, rather than as a symptom of an entire culture of indigenous devaluation."[116] Thus, not only are we discouraged from identifying with Neville, but also we are encouraged to view him as a faintly quaint figure, rather than as an agent of colonial violence. Sarah Pinto has argued similarly that the film works to elide the violence of child removal; "Mr. Devil" emerges as a bumbling figure of fun within a hopeful narrative of resistance and overcoming. In fact, the film's plot is so positive that Pinto has contended that "although based on a true story, the film can almost be considered an exercise in counter-factual history."[117] Although such critiques do encapsulate the difficulties that settler viewers may have in identifying with Neville, they fail to take account of the way that *Rabbit-Proof Fence's* narrative of triumph and its representation of Neville as "Mr. Devil" has become important to many members of the stolen generations.[118]

Yet, despite the fact that *Rabbit-Proof Fence* safely maintained its PG classification, for the adult viewer it does contain ample references to the abuse suffered by the Moore River children—as in scenes depicting the punishment of some of the girls via incarceration in a tin shed—and obliquely renders the sexual attacks suffered by Indigenous domestic workers through the character of Mavis (Deborah Mailman). Most importantly, despite the often distancing portrayal of Neville, the film provides an opportunity to engage with notions of perpetration and complicity through the character of Constable Riggs (Jason Clarke). The tendency for critics to focus only on Neville, who, to be fair, does loom large within the film's landscape, has occluded a consideration of the film's representation of other figures of perpetration.

During the scene of the girl's removal, the viewer is given a vital glimpse into the relationships between the local police and the Indigenous community of Jigalong. As Riggs and his colleagues chase the girls and literally tear them from their mother's arms, Riggs screams at the women and, in doing so, provides an insight into his position as an enforcer of WA government policy and his connections with the girls' mothers. Riggs attempts to affirm his authority over the women by asserting that there's "nothing you can do." He goes on to argue that—"I've got no say in it"—in an attempt to distance himself from the scene. He also tells Molly's mother, "I've got the papers Maud," again as a technique of rhetorical distancing and an effort to authorize his actions, but his use of Maud's name signals his ambivalent subject position. Riggs is a figure of the law as well as someone who is familiar with and has a community relationship with the girls and their families. If Neville is a quaint, inscrutable figure, Riggs draws viewers to consider how the perpetrators of child removal were fully embedded within the communities in which these children lived. Through Riggs, Noyce has worked to emphasize the intimacy of colonial violence.

Near the film's close, during the dying stages of Neville's pursuit of Molly and her sister, the ambivalent position of Riggs is again highlighted. When an armed Riggs interrupts the women's business conducted by Molly's mother and grandmother, Riggs is again brought face-to-face with Maud. This time, however, the scene is one of defiance; Maud repels Riggs with her eyes, and the threat of her spear. What is striking here is Riggs' proximity to Maud and his unsuccessful attempts to act as a distant figure of law and authority in the face of Maud's resistance. Although I certainly do not contend that all viewers consider the figure of Riggs in this way, I have found myself drawn to him as an "ordinary" figure of perpetration within the colonial scene. In this way, *Rabbit-Proof Fence* has underscored the radical open-endedness of visual witnessing and affirmed the power of cinema as a medium of historical representation.

Australia

Australia, another recent film centered on the stolen generations' narrative, has been so popular with Australian audiences that it has now outgrossed *Babe* (1995) to become the second-most successful Australian movie after *Crocodile Dundee* (1986).[119] That a film dealing with child removal has become so popular indicates not only the entertainment value of Luhrmann's "outback romance," but also the willingness of Australian audiences to incorporate an understanding of colonial violence into their vision of a nation. In *Australia*, the history of the stolen generations has been interwoven with that of the Second World War. In its focus on the impact of war on Darwin, it has contributed a fresh perspective to popular representations of the home front that are usually focused on the east coast of Australia. The film's emphasis on the Second World War as a theater of national consolidation also offered a counterpoint to dominant cultural myths that position Gallipoli and the First World War as the stage of national becoming. By juxtaposing a story about child removal with a chronicle of war, *Australia* performed a radical repositioning of cultural coordinates, a provisioning of history that "invite[s] the viewer to perform a cinematic kind of backtracking, that is, going over old ground in ways that may lead one to retract or reverse one's opinion."[120]

While Marcia Langton has been effusive in her praise of Luhrmann's film, arguing that it has "given Australians a new past," it is enough to acknowledge that *Australia*, though not without its flaws, has achieved the remarkable feat of integrating some of the most painful aspects of Australian history into a blockbuster historical romance, while retaining a sense of the pain of this past.[121] Against this, Germaine Greer has criticized the film, chiefly on the grounds that it is a "bad" representation. In particular, she has argued that it fails to portray the "truth" of the Northern Territory cattle industry.[122] Here, Greer echoed those critics who have found *Rabbit-Proof Fence* too positive in its portrayal of child removal and frontier life. Although both films have declared distinctly different relationships to historical truth, with *Australia* proudly displaying its kitsch sensibilities, their effect as texts of creative witnessing lay in their common ability to draw viewers not to truth, but to identify with and explore Australia's history, imaginatively and empathetically.

It is important to note that in contrast to *Rabbit-Proof Fence,* Luhrmann does not encourage viewers to identify with the "stolen" child—Nullah—nor, indeed, any of the major characters. They appear as archetypal, mythic figures, particularly in the case of the ludicrously "evil" Neil Fletcher (Nullah's white father), who is played with relish by David Wenham. This is not the space for an extensive discussion of the affect of *Australia's* camp aesthetic *vis-à-vis* the "realist" approach of *Rabbit-Proof Fence*, but it is instructive to consider both styles a part of their respective director's attempts to universalize or "mainstream" the stolen generations' story. Though both approaches are problematic in terms of flattening the specificity of Indigenous peoples' experiences and testimony, they have drawn attention to the power of popular films—in contrast to modernist New History films—to engage spectators in the process of witnessing to the past.

Conclusion

This chapter has considered the way in which creative works—both written and cinematic—have contributed to the broad project of witnessing to the dispossession of Australia's Indigenous peoples. I have suggested that the work of writers, such as Kate Grenville, should be read as both an expression of a personal desire to witness—of "how" individuals are "sorry"—and a space of reflection for readers. Similarly, I have discussed *Rabbit-Proof Fence* and *Australia* as films that engage with Australian history in the mode of "back-tracking"—revisioning the past to explore new possibilities for the future. In doing so, this chapter has augmented Chapter One's analysis of the discourse on reconciliation and settler witnessing, through a close reading of several fictional case studies. The creative texts I have examined both draw on and extend the discourses on witnessing that have emerged in the wake of *Bringing them Home*. All are suffused with a desire to confront the challenge of testimony imaginatively, and, as such, illustrate the extent to which creative witnessing offers a space for critical and empathetic spectatorship. This focus on the affective power of creative work is a necessary corrective to commentary on Indigenous testimony that has focused, almost exclusively, on its circulation within political culture.

Notes

1. Eva Sallis, quoted in Brigid Rooney, *Literary Activists: Writer-Intellectuals and Australian Public Life* (St. Lucia: University of Queensland Press, 2009), 184.
2. Stephen Muecke, *Ancient and Modern: Time, Culture and Indigenous Philosophy* (Sydney: UNSW Press, 2004), 12.
3. Ken Gelder and Paul Salzman, *After the Celebration: Australian Fiction 1989–2007* (Melbourne: Melbourne University Press, 2009), 64.
4. Jo Jones' recent reading of Richard Flanagan's work is a notable exception. Jo Jones, "'Dancing the Old Enlightenment': *Gould's Book of Fish*, the Historical Novel and the Postmodern Sublime," *Journal of the Association for the Study of Australian Literature*, no. Special Issue: The Colonial Present (2008): 114–29.
5. Bob Hodge and Vijay Mishra have, however, considered this issue in Australian literature to 1990. Graham Huggan has recently taken up the question of Australian literature's postcoloniality in a transnational context.

Bob Hodge and Vijay Mishra, *Dark Side of the Dream: Australian Literature and the Postcolonial Mind* (Sydney: Allen & Unwin, 1990); Graham Huggan, *Australian Literature: Postcolonialism, Racism, Transnationalism* (Oxford and New York: Oxford University Press, 2007).

6.   Robert A. Rosenstone, "Introduction," in *Revisioning History: Film and the Construction of a New Past*, ed. Robert A. Rosenstone (Princeton, N.J.: Princeton University Press, 1995), 3.

7.   Kate Grenville, *The Secret River* (Melbourne: Text Publishing, 2005); Kate Grenville, *Searching for the Secret River* (Melbourne: Text, 2006).

8.   Phillip Noyce (dir.), *Rabbit-Proof Fence* (Australia: Magna Pacific Video, 2002); Baz Luhrmann (dir.), *Australia* (Australia: Twentieth Century Fox, 2008).

9.   Gail Jones, *Sorry* (Sydney: Vintage, 2007).

10.   Felman and Laub, *Testimony*.

11.   See Frances Guerin and Roger Hallas, eds., *The Image and the Witness: Trauma, Memory and Visual Culture* (London and New York: Wallflower Press, 2007); Jill Bennett, *Empathic Vision: Affect, Trauma, and Contemporary Art* (Stanford, CA: Stanford University Press, 2005); Apel, *Memory Effects*.

12.   Sneja Gunew, "Against Multiculturalism: Rhetorical Images," in *Multiculturalism, Difference and Postmodernism*, ed. Gordon L. Clark, Dean Forbes, and Roderick Francis (Melbourne: Longman Cheshire, 1993), 50; Carole Ferrier, "'Disappearing Memory' and the Colonial Present in Recent Indigenous Women's Writing," *Journal of the Association for the Study of Australian Literature*, Special Issue: *The Colonial Present Australian Writing for the 21st Century* (2008): 47.

13.   Mark McKenna, "Writing the Past," *The Australian Financial Review*, December 16, 2005, 2.

14.   See Robert Dessaix, ed., *Speaking Their Minds: Intellectuals and the Public Culture in Australia* (Sydney: ABC Books, 1998); Mark Davis, *Gangland: Cultural Elites and the New Generationalism* (Sydney: Allen & Unwin, 1997). To be sure, anxiety over the decline in public intellectual culture has certainly not been restricted to Australia. See, for example, Amitai Etzioni and Alyssa Bowditch, eds., *Public Intellectuals: An Endangered Species?* (Lanham, MD: Rowman & Littlefield Publishers, 2006).

15.   David Carter, "Introduction: Intellectuals and Their Publics," in *The Ideas Market: An Alternative Take on Australia's Intellectual Life*, ed. David Carter (Melbourne: Melbourne University Press, 2004), 3. See also Ned Curthoys and Debjani Ganguly, eds., *Edward Said: The Legacy of a Public Intellectual* (Melbourne: Melbourne University Press, 2007).

16.   Carter, "Introduction," 3.

17.   Rooney, *Literary Activists*, xx–xxii.

18.   Ibid., 181.

19.   Ibid., xxiv.

20.   Ibid., ix–xxxi.

21.   Jean Moorcroft Wilson and Cecil Woolf, eds., *Authors Take Sides: Iraq and the Gulf War* (Melbourne: Melbourne University Press, 2004). See also Bernadette Brennan, ed., *Just Words? Australian Authors Writing for Justice* (St. Lucia: University of Queensland Press, 2008).

22. Mark Sanders, *Complicities: The Intellectual and Apartheid* (Durham, N.C. and London: Duke University Press, 2002), 4.
23. The bulk of this discussion of Grenville's work occurred in the nation's broadsheet newspapers. See especially Stella Clarke, "Havoc in History House," *Australian*, March 4–10, 2006, 8–10; Helen MacDonald, "Novel Views of History," *Australian*, March 25–26, 2006, 14–15; Juliette Hughes, "When the Past Is Always Present," *Age*, August 13, 2005, 8; McKenna, "Writing the Past," 1–2.
24. It was during Grenville's now infamous interview with the ABC's Ramona Koval that she described herself as "up on a ladder, looking down on the history wars," and attracted the ire of several prominent historians. Ramona Koval, "Interview with Kate Grenville," *The Book Show*, July 17, 2005, ABC Radio National, [Transcript], http://www.abc.net.au/ rn/arts/bwriting/stories/s1414510.htm (accessed August 10, 2007). See John Hirst, *Sense and Nonsense in Australian History* (Melbourne: Black Inc. Agenda, 2005), 84–87; McKenna, "Writing the Past"; Inga Clendinnen, *The History Question: Who Owns the Past?*, vol. 23, *Quarterly Essay* (Melbourne: Black, 2006), 16–28; Mark McKenna, "Comfort History," *The Australian*, March 18–19, 2006, 18–19.
25. Kate Grenville cited in Koval, "Interview with Kate Grenville." See also Jane Sullivan, "Skeletons out of the Closet, Review of 'the Secret River,'" *The Age*, July 2, 2005, 1–2.
26. Grenville cited in Koval, "Interview with Kate Grenville."
27. Ann Curthoys and John Docker, *Is History Fiction?* (Sydney: UNSW Press, 2006), 220–37.
28. Although the immediacy of the debate around Grenville's work has passed, it has become almost customary for historians of the frontier, and especially those of colonial NSW, to stake a position *vis-à-vis* her work. See, for example, Grace Karskens, *The Colony: A History of Early Sydney* (Crows Nest, NSW: Allen & Unwin, 2009), 13–14.
29. Hirst, *Sense and Nonsense in Australian History*, 85; McKenna, "Writing the Past"; Clendinnen, *History Question*, 16–23.
30. Clendinnen, *History Question*, 17.
31. Kate Grenville, *The Lieutenant* (Melbourne: Text Publishing, 2008).
32. Adam Gall, "Taking/Taking Up: Recognition and the Frontier in Grenville's *the Secret River*," *Journal of the Association for the Study of Australian Literature* Special Issue: *The Colonial Present Australian Writing for the 21st Century* (2008): 94.
33. Anica Boulanger-Mashberg, "In Her Own Margins: Kate Grenville's *Searching for the Secret River* as Marginalia to *the Secret River*," *Limina* 15 (2009): 1–9.
34. David Malouf, *Remembering Babylon* (Sydney: Random House, 1993); *The Conversations at Curlow Creek* (London: Chatto, 1996); Peter Carey, *True History of the Kelly Gang* (St. Lucia: University of Queensland Press, 2000); Andrew McGahan, *The White Earth* (Crows Nest, NSW: Allen & Unwin, 2004); Richard Flanagan, *Gould's Book of Fish: A Novel in Twelve Fish* (Sydney: Pan Macmillan, 2001); *Wanting* (North Sydney: Knopf, 2008); Roger McDonald, *The Ballad of Desmond Kale* (Milsons Point: Vintage, 2005); Jones, *Sorry*; Alex Miller, *Journey to the Stone Country* (Crows Nest,

NSW: Allen & Unwin, 2002); *Landscape of Farewell* (Crows Nest: Allen & Unwin, 2007).

35. Drusilla Modjeska cited in Delia Falconer, "Historical Novels: Are We Writing Too Many of Them? Is There a Crisis of Relevance in Austlit?," *Eureka Street* 13, no. 2 (March 2003): 31.
36. See Macintyre and Clark, *History Wars*.
37. Rose, *Reports from a Wild Country*.
38. Grenville, *Searching for the Secret River*, 12.
39. Ibid.
40. Ibid., 13.
41. Ibid.
42. Ibid., 31–57.
43. Davison, *Use and Abuse of Australian History*, 109.
44. Grenville, *Searching for the Secret River*, 146.
45. Ibid., 165.
46. Ibid., 147.
47. Ibid.
48. Ibid., 34.
49. Ibid., 104.
50. Oliver, *Witnessing*, 8.
51. Grenville, *Secret River*, 323.
52. Ibid., 325.
53. Ibid., 139.
54. Ibid., 330, 333.
55. Ibid., 305, 307.
56. Ibid., 307.
57. Ibid., 334.
58. Lyn McCredden, "Haunted Identities and the Possible Futures of 'Aust. Lit.,'" *Journal of the Association for the Study of Australian Literature* Special issue: *Spectres, Screens, Shadows, Mirrors* (2007): 23.
59. Hirst, *Sense and Nonsense in Australian History*, 85. See also Clendinnen, *History Question*, 16–23.
60. Gall, "Taking/Taking Up," 101.
61. Grenville, *Searching for the Secret River*, 194.
62. Whitlock, "Consuming Passions," 18.
63. See especially Whitlock, ""Strategic Remembering"; "Becoming Migloo"; "Active Remembrance."
64. Probyn-Rapsey, "Complicity, Critique, and Methodology," 72.
65. McCredden, "Haunted Identities and the Possible Futures of 'Aust. Lit.,'" 23.
66. Grenville cited in Louise Maral, "Warts and All: On Writing *The Secret River*," *University of Sydney News*, August 26, 2006, University of Sydney, [Media release], http://www.usyd.edu.au/news/84.html?newsstoryid=1240 (accessed January 17, 2008).
67. Probyn-Rapsey, "Complicity, Critique, and Methodology," 72.
68. See Eleanor Collins, "Poison in the Flour," *Meanjin* 65, no. 1 (2006): 38–76.
69. Muecke, *Ancient and Modern*, 12.

70. See the excellent summary of contemporary historical novels offered by Gelder and Salzman, *After the Celebration*, 64–94.
71. James Ley, "Review of *Sorry*," *Sydney Morning Herald*, May 4, 2007, http://www.smh.com.au/news/book-reviews/sorry/2007/05/04/1177788377886.html (accessed June 12, 2009).
72. Jones, *Sorry*, 215–16.
73. Sarah Winifred Pinto, "Emotional Histories: Contemporary Australian Historical Fictions," Ph.D. thesis (Department of History, The University of Melbourne, 2007), 102–28.
74. Gail Jones, "Speaking Shadows: Justice and the Poetic," in *Just Words? Australian Authors Writing for Justice*, ed. Bernadette Brennan (St. Lucia: University of Queensland Press, 2008), 85.
75. McGahan, *White Earth*.
76. Miller, *Journey to the Stone Country*.
77. Though the "Revival" films of the 1970s have been understood as "blindly nationalistic visions of unchallenging and mythologised pasts," Sarah Pinto has argued that many of these films, such as *Picnic at Hanging Rock* (1975) and *We of the Never Never* (1982), are, in fact, deeply concerned with the "unsettled" nature of white Australia and, as such, evince a profound sense of alienation from the landscape. Pinto, "Emotional Histories," 62–63. There has been, however, a noticeable shift to an explicit portrayal of colonialism in Australian film; against "nostalgic" period films that merely register, rather than confront or explore, a sense of the uncanny.
78. Rolf de Heer (dir.), *The Tracker* (Australia: Madman Cinema, 2002); Ivan Sen (dir.), *Beneath Clouds* (Australia: Australian Film Finance Corporation & Autumn Films, 2002); Craig Lahiff (dir.), *Black and White* (Australia: Duo/Scala, 2002). See Felicity Collins and Therese Davis, "Disputing History, Remembering Country: *The Tracker* and *Rabbit-Proof Fence*," *Australian Historical Studies* 128 (2006): 36.
79. Jones, "Speaking Shadows," 84.
80. Noyce, *Rabbit-Proof Fence*.
81. Luhrmann, *Australia*.
82. Tony Birch has affirmed the value of *Rabbit-Proof Fence* in precisely these terms. Tony Birch, "'This Is a True Story': *Rabbit-Proof Fence*, 'Mr. Devil' and the Desire to Forget," *Cultural Studies Review* 8, no. 1 (2002): 117–29.
83. Collins and Davis, "Disputing History, Remembering Country," 37.
84. For an overview of the often fraught theorization of spectatorship, see Judith Mayne, *Cinema and Spectatorship* (London and New York: Routledge, 1993).
85. See especially Robert Burgoyne, *Film Nation: Hollywood Looks at U.S. History* (Minneapolis: University of Minnesota Press, 1997); Kenneth M. Cameron, *America on Film: Hollywood and American History* (New York: Continuum, 1997); Deborah Cartmell, I. Q. Hunter, and Imelda Whelehan, eds., *Retrovisions: Reinventing the Past in Film and Fiction* (London: Pluto Press, 2001); Natalie Zemon Davis, *Slaves on Screen: Film and Historical Vision* (Cambridge: Harvard University Press, 2000); Marine Hughes-Warrington, *History Goes to the Movies: Studying History on Film* (New Brunswick: Rutgers University Press, 2007); Robert A. Rosenstone, ed.,

Revisioning History: Film and the Construction of a New Past (Princeton, N.J.: Princeton University Press, 1995); *History on Film/Film on History* (New York: Routledge, 2006).

86. Apel, *Memory Effects*; David Bathrick, Brad Prager, and Michael D. Richardson, eds., *Visualizing the Holocaust: Documents, Aesthetics, Memory* (Rochester, N.Y.: Camden House, 2008); Judith E. Doneson, *The Holocaust in American Film* (Philadelphia: Jewish Publication Society, 1987); Friedlander, ed., *Probing the Limits of Representation*; Toby Haggith and Joanna Newman, *Holocaust and the Moving Image: Representations in Film and Television since 1933* (London: Wallflower Press, 2005); Annette Insdorf, *Indelible Shadows: Film and the Holocaust* (New York: Cambridge University Press, 2002); Stuart Liebman, ed., *Claude Lanzmann's Shoah: Key Essays* (Oxford and New York: Oxford University Press, 2007); Saxton, *Haunted Images*.

87. Rosenstone, "Introduction," 4.

88. Frances Guerin and Roger Hallas, "Introduction," in *The Image and the Witness: Trauma, Memory and Visual Culture*, ed. Frances Guerin and Roger Hallas (London and New York: Wallflower Press, 2007), 4.

89. Ibid., 12.

90. Tony Hughes-d'Aeth, "Which Rabbit-Proof Fence? Empathy, Assimilation, Hollywood," *Australian Humanities Review* 27 (September 2002), http://www.australian humanitiesreview.org/archive/Issue-September-2002/ hughesdaeth.html (accessed May 30, 2009); Germaine Greer, "Once upon a Time in a Land, Far, Far Away," *Guardian*, December 16, 2008, http://www.guardian.co.uk/ film/2008/dec/16/baz-luhrmann-australia (accessed December 20, 2008).

91. van Toorn, "Tactical History Business," 252–66.

92. Emily Potter and Kay Schaffer, "*Rabbit-Proof Fence*, Relational Ecologies and the Commodification of Indigenous Experience," *Australian Humanities Review* 31 (April 2004), http://www.australianhumanitiesreview.org/archive/Issue-April-2004/ schaffer.html (accessed May 2, 2009).

93. Doris Pilkington, *Follow the Rabbit-Proof Fence* (St. Lucia, QLD: University of Queensland Press, 1996).

94. Christine Olsen, *Rabbit-Proof Fence: The Screenplay* (Sydney: Currency Press, 2002), vii.

95. Phillip Noyce cited in Andrew L. Urban, "Noyce, Phillip: Rabbit-Proof Fence," *Urban Cinefile*, February 21, 2002, http://www.urbancinefile.com.au/ home/view.asp?Article_ID=5770 (accessed December 19, 2009).

96. See E. Ann Kaplan on translation as "another modality for sharing trauma." E. Ann Kaplan, *Trauma Culture: The Politics of Terror and Loss in Media and Literature* (New Brunswick, NJ and London: Rutgers University Press, 2005), 101–21.

97. Deborah Cain, "A Fence Too Far? Postcolonial Guilt and the Myth of Distance in *Rabbit Proof Fence*," *Third Text* 18, no. 4 (2004): 297.

98. Attwood, "Learning About the Truth," 183–212.

99. Birch, "This Is a True Story," 121.

100. Olsen, *Rabbit-Proof Fence*, vii.

101. Ibid., vii–viii.

102. Ibid., viii.

103. Noyce cited in Urban, "Noyce, Phillip."
104. Kate Douglas, "The Universal Autobiographer: The Politics of Normative Readings," *Journal of Australian Studies* 72 (2002): 174.
105. Ibid.
106. Ellis, "A Strange Case of Double Vision," 75–79.
107. Douglas, "Universal Autobiographer," 176.
108. Jane Lydon, "A Strange Time Machine: *The Tracker, Black and White,* and *Rabbit-Proof Fence* [Historical Overview]," *Australian Historical Studies* 35, no. 123 (2004): 145–46.
109. Birch, "This Is a True Story," 121; Hughes-d'Aeth, "Which Rabbit-Proof Fence?"
110. Helen Grace, *"Rabbit-Proof Fence*: The Journey of Feeling," *Australian Screen Education* 36 (2004): 143.
111. Radstone, "Social Bonds and Psychical Order: Testimonies," 63. Here, Radstone produces a reading of Hirsch's work in which she draws on Silverman's psychoanalytic reading of love and the visual world. See Kaja Silverman, *The Threshold of the Visible World* (New York: Routledge, 1996).
112. Marianne Hirsch cited in Radstone, "Social Bonds and Psychical Order," 63. Emphasis in original.
113. Ibid.
114. Ibid., 75.
115. Ibid., 65.
116. Hughes-d'Aeth, "Which Rabbit-Proof Fence?"
117. Pinto, "Emotional Histories," 239.
118. See especially Tony Birch's account of the reactions of Indigenous audiences to the film. Birch, "This Is a True Story."
119. Michaela Boland, *"Australia* sets record Down Under," *Variety,* February 26, 2009, http://www.variety.com/article/VR1118000644.html?categoryid=19&cs=1 (accessed December 30, 2009).
120. Collins and Davis, "Disputing History, Remembering Country," 37.
121. Marcia Langton, "Faraway Downs Fantasy Resonates Close to Home," *Sunday Age,* November 23, 2008, 12.
122. Greer, "Once upon a Time in a Land, Far, Far Away."

3

Frontiers of Witnessing: History after Testimony

The future availability of the material contained within the Archive will be restricted to just one person. He will come to us at a time in the future. He will be known as the Professional Historian—or at times by his nomenclature—"The Sophisticated One"... It will be the duty of the Professional Historian to wage a war, a "History War", in defence of the defenceless—the Aborigine—who knows nothing of "history" beyond myths and legends.
                                                              —Tony Birch[1]

In his influential *History and Memory after Auschwitz*, Dominick LaCapra has argued that although "testimony is a crucial source for history," it also "poses special challenges."[2] In particular,

> it raises the issue of the way in which the historian or other analyst becomes a secondary witness, undergoes a transferential relation, and must work out an acceptable subject-position with respect to the witness and his or her testimony.[3]

This chapter explores the "special challenges" that testimony has posed for historians by examining a range of Australian frontier histories that have been written in response to Indigenous testimony. The testimony of Aboriginal peoples has challenged the epistemological basis of "traditional" historical narratives of Australia's past. It has also posed a challenge to the authority of historians as privileged mediators between the past and the present. However, as LaCapra has suggested, it is not simply that Aboriginal testimony has come to provide an important source for historians in the form of oral history, but that an engagement with testimony has driven historians to reconsider the way they produce their histories: "to work out an acceptable subject-position."[4] Here, I examine how the desire to witness has prompted several historians to experiment with elements of autobiography and fiction, in order to respond both historically and empathetically to Australia's history of Indigenous dispossession.

Witnessing to the claims of testimony has irrevocably shaped the way that many historians attempt to hear the voices of the past. Since the late 1980s, both historians and cultural critics have turned increasingly to autobiographical and fictocritical techniques to explore the Australian frontier. Though this can be read as a part of a longer tradition of "experimental" and literary history, I contend that the recent proliferation of this work can be best understood as a response to the affects of Indigenous testimony. For historians, testimony has underscored the limits of "traditional" positivist or objectivist history, prompting not only a reconsideration of the discipline's knowledge claims, but also a critical reassessment of its relationship to the present. In responding to the challenges of testimony, several historians—including the prominent Inga Clendinnen—have adopted witnessing as an integral component of their historical practice. The imperatives of witnessing have been interpreted variously, whereas an inchoate body of work has emerged that privileges the necessity of responding to the voices of the present as the starting point for a study of the past.

This chapter explores the impact of the imperatives of witnessing on academic history making through two case studies: Inga Clendinnen's "Australian" work, especially her frontier monograph *Dancing with Strangers* (2003), and Katrina Schlunke's *Bluff Rock: Autobiography of a Massacre* (2005).[5] At first glance, the work of Clendinnen and Schlunke appears radically dissimilar. Where Clendinnen's work is firmly rooted within the disciplines of history and anthropology and, more specifically, in the ethnohistory movement she helped establish, Schlunke's work has found a home in cultural studies—broadly defined to include creative writing and fictocriticism. Yet despite these divergent academic contexts, both authors bear the weight of witnessing to the present in their approaches to frontier history. Theirs is a history transformed by testimony. Here, testimony is not simply a source: It is the catalyst for a profound reconceptualization of the historian's task and responsibility. For both, a desire to hear Indigenous testimony in the present has necessitated a turn to autobiographical and fictional techniques to render the past. For both authors, testimony has not only disrupted the foundations of history writing, but also complicated the possibility of all forms of realist narrativizing.

This chapter demonstrates how, in differing ways, Clendinnen and Schlunke's desire to witness has reshaped their historical practice. By considering the work of a popular, mainstream historian such as Clendinnen in productive tension with a more clearly academic, marginal writer such as Schlunke, I explore a spectrum of practices that constitute witnessing in contemporary Australian historical writing. In particular, I focus on the turn to the personal and autobiographical; the development of a greater willingness to employ fictional elements within an otherwise nonfictional text; and, most importantly, the construction of empathetic witnessing as a core strand of "ethical" history making.

"Experimental" History

Klaus Neumann has argued recently that notwithstanding the linguistic turn, experimentation in history has been confined to a few "adventurous iconoclasts."[6] Filmmakers, writers, and artists have made startling use of historical materials, whereas the overwhelming majority of historians have continued to write as if the interventions of literary and poststructuralist critics, such as Hayden White, were "a shortlived [sic] fad."[7] Neumann has used the term "experimental history" to encapsulate a broad collection of practices. "Experimental histories are," he has written,

> departures from conventional academic histories in that they do not privilege a single perspective on the past, are not couched within the realist paradigm, do not have a linear narrative structure whose logic is determined by chronology and a series of cause and effect relationships, are not written in the third person, and are not unambiguously non-fiction.[8]

Put more simply, the term "experimental history" can be used to describe any historical work that deviates from a linear, realist narrativization of the past. Yet, crucially, experimental history is not animated by a desire for play or experimentation in and of itself—it is a conscious, necessary response to the material of the past.[9] Experimental approaches have often responded to a particular "difficulty" or challenge posed by a subject, such as a scarcity of archival records, whereas Neumann has noted that experimental history has been most readily adopted by historians attempting to write the history of subaltern or marginalized groups. This has been a driving factor in much of the experimental history focusing on Australia's Indigenous-settler relations, including work by Greg Dening, Deborah Bird Rose, and Stephen Muecke.[10] These writers are, Neumann has argued, "often driven by the urge to take sides and are looking for a form of writing that reflects their anger or despair or grief."[11]

The concept of experimental history has provided a useful framework for considering the relationship between subaltern or "minority" testimony, the historian, and the work of history. As a loose genre or disposition, experimental history has foregrounded the historian's ethical and emotive capacities and their struggle to adopt an appropriate speaking voice for the telling of another's story. Yet, the epithet "experimental" belies the seriousness of this approach to history, and has figured this type of work as the product of the historian's whimsy. This chapter works to privilege the role of testimony as an active, affective force in the making of Australian history. It does so by focusing on how the desire to experiment, to "take sides," is produced by the historian's engagement with Indigenous peoples' testimony. To view "experimental" histories as products of witnessing is to underscore the extent to which contemporary frontier history is a relational history. History, here, is not simply the product of an "experiment," but is rather shaped by the process of witnessing. As such, it is marked by both the historian's attentiveness to testimony and their embeddedness in the present.

Breaking the "Silence"

Recent accounts of the development of Aboriginal history as a discipline have emphasized the role that Indigenous oral history has played in the work of pioneering settler historians. Typically, the importance of Indigenous oral history as a source has been framed by a triumphant narrative in which settler historians have worked to shatter W.E.H. Stanner's "great Australian silence."[12] Accordingly, Bain Attwood has written that

> over the last 25 years or more [Henry] Reynolds and other historians have sought to address the great Australian silence, assuming the function of "remembrancers" by reminding White Australia of what it would prefer to forget. In time they have created . . . the new Australian history.[13]

This version of Aboriginal historiography has privileged the effect of the white voice in breaking through the "silence" cloaking frontier violence and Indigenous dispossession. Lorenzo Veracini has complicated this narrative, however, by emphasizing the role that settler historians, such as Reynolds and Richard Broome, have played in the dissemination of histories of Aboriginal resistance and agency.[14] Despite this, there has been little acknowledgment of the role of testimony—as both a historical source and a motivating force—in the production of frontier histories. Indeed, Veracini has suggested that the major impact of *Bringing them Home* was its introduction of the concept of genocide to Aboriginal historiography, rather than its collection and dissemination of testimony.[15]

Moreover, though both Attwood and Broome have affirmed the importance of oral history, and discussed the way that it has challenged the authority of the historian as "expert," their designation of testimony as "oral history" has worked to limit the affective power of Indigenous speech by positioning it as something professional which historians "choose" to engage with at their discretion.[16] Thus, although historians have been eager to laud Reynolds as a pioneer within the field of Aboriginal history, and to highlight the role his narratives of Indigenous resistance have played in laying the "historical" groundwork for *Mabo* and other land rights battles, there has been little acknowledgment of his role in the development of a culture of historical witnessing.[17]

Listening to the "Other Side"

While Reynolds' histories have evinced a strong interest in oral history as a source for history writing, his intellectual autobiography, *Why Weren't We Told?*, has demonstrated the extent to which Reynolds' historical practice illustrates a commitment to witnessing Indigenous testimony. In the Introduction to the 2006 edition of *The Other Side of the Frontier*, Reynolds described the role that oral history has played in his research, arguing that though oral history provided "compelling evidence," it was "probably less important in itself than the stimulation [it] provided to the imagination and the concurrent growth of empathy."[18] Here, Reynolds highlighted the transformative power of witnessing as a process that engaged his moral faculties. Though he positioned oral history as less important to his narrative than his analysis of European written records, his brief meditation on the power of oral history hinted at the way his engagement with testimony had transformed his approach to history making.

Published in 1999, *Why Weren't We Told?* provided an account of how Reynolds' interest in Aboriginal history and knowledge of contemporary race relations grew from his experiences of living and teaching in remote Australia. Reynolds' work is the paradigmatic personal historical story: It is, according to the subtitle, "a personal search for the truth about our history." It read, at least in part, as a response to conservative criticism that positioned Reynolds' work as a form of "black armband history," irredeemably soiled by political correctness and left-wing bias.[19] It is also a complex, and at times quite intimate, account of one historian's discovery of the violence at the heart of Australian history. Crucially, this is a discovery that is framed as the result of his engagements with Aboriginal and Torres Strait Islanders in the present. *Why Weren't We Told?* is simultaneously a story about the way personal relationships can remake our understanding of the past, and a story of how witnessing can transform the practice of history.

In *Why Weren't We Told?*, Reynolds offered an explanation of how he came to "know" the violence at the core of settler-Indigenous relations. As such, it traced the contours of the Anglo-Australian historical culture that prohibited his "knowing." Throughout the text, Reynolds is positioned not only as an expert, but also as an everyman figure, a typical member of the "Baby Boomer" generation who came of age during an era when it was still possible for an Anglo-Australia to not "remember meeting any non-European people at all during my childhood."[20] Reynolds detailed his upbringing and early education in Tasmania, painting a picture of Anglo-Australia during the "great Australian silence." By doing so, Reynolds worked to develop a point of connection with his assumed white readership: like you, he assured the reader, I just didn't *know.*

For Reynolds, knowledge of Australia's violent, racially divided past—and present—was only acquired through direct personal experience. On moving to Townsville in the 1960s to take up a teaching position, Reynolds found himself in an area "where the traditions, behaviour and attitudes of the frontier era persisted and where race relations were a major cause of friction, a constant topic of discussion and debate."[21] Of particular importance for Reynolds in his "personal search" were the friendships he formed with the local Aboriginal and Torres Straits Islander communities, especially the development of his relationship with Eddie Mabo. It was through Mabo that Reynolds became drawn to the study of frontier history, and the pair began to collect oral histories from Townsville's elderly Aborigines and Islanders during the 1970s.[22] It was this experience of engaging with the testimony of Indigenous peoples, who detailed their experiences with racism and dispossession in their own words, that came to transform Reynolds' historical practice.

"Almost every story we heard," Reynolds explained, "brought the past to life in a way that few written documents could do."[23] Here, Reynolds captured some of the excitement of working with oral sources; their compelling affective quality, and the way in which they seem to draw us closer to the past. However, far from simply being interesting raw source material, the interviews Reynolds conducted in Townsville provided a "history lesson of the most powerful kind, more telling than any amount of research in the archives."[24] Moreover, the interviews not only taught Reynolds about the experiences of some of Townsville's Indigenous peoples, but also prompted Reynolds to reflect on the way in which he, as a settler Australian, was implicated within the history of colonization. In this way, *Why Weren't We Told?* traced how Reynolds' engagement with testimony prompted both his decision to begin researching in the area of Aboriginal history, and a more personal, intimate journey of self-discovery.

Chiefly, *Why Weren't We Told?* foregrounded the importance of self-reflection and conscience in the writing of history. The work is a text of self-analysis that illustrated the power of testimony to transform self-understanding while simultaneously prompting acts of advocacy. By highlighting the role of testimony in his historical practice, Reynolds emphasized the continuity of the past in the present in what Attwood has described as "a liberal or humanitarian tradition."[25] In this way, the text is also an intellectual memoir, a work of self-fashioning implicated in long-standing liberal discourses of sentimentality and benevolence.[26]

Why Weren't We Told? presented a highly flattering self-portrait in which Reynolds is changed by the power of testimony from an "ordinary," blithely ignorant settler Australian, into an empathetic historian who has dedicated his life's work to trying to understand the "other side of the frontier." Here, testimony formed the ground for a profound personal and professional metamorphosis. Though Reynolds' memoir is clearly heartfelt—and led to the production of an important body of historical work—his narrative of moral transformation served to underwrite the authority of his academic work. That is, Reynolds' work acknowledged that testimony posed a challenge to the authority of the historian as "expert," whereas the trope of overcoming ignorance actually functioned to authenticate his text as the product of an enlightened, "knowing" (white) subject.

Writing White Lives

Why Weren't We Told? is, by far, the most visible text within a recent history of an Australian historical memoir, which has included Kate Grenville's aforementioned "writing memoir," *Searching for the Secret River*. Since the bicentenary, there has been an explosion in the publication of personal histories by settler Australians around the themes of reconciliation and Indigenous history. Some of the most prominent, apart from Reynolds' work, have included Cassandra Pybus' *Community of Thieves* (1992); Peter Read's *Belonging* (2000); Inga Clendinnen's *Tigers Eye: A Memoir* (2001); Lynette Russell's *A Little Bird Told Me* (2002); and Martin Flanagan's *In Sunshine or Shadow* (2002).[27] To this list, we may also add Stephen Muecke's *No Road* (1997) and Margaret Sommerville's *Body/Landscape Journals* (1999), though these texts have found a more specialist readership.[28] Though diverse, all these texts have focused on the non-Indigenous self, and have traced the author's contemporary relationship to Indigenous people and their entanglement with the historic process of dispossession.[29] They are narratives that have sought to stage an ethical confrontation with Indigenous testimony as a part of the refashioning of white settler subjectivity. The white self—and in Reynolds' case, the white historian—has been remade through this confrontation.

Whitlock has argued that the emergence of these white memoirs is inextricably linked to the late 1980s explosion of Indigenous testimony; "black testimony," she has noted, "is triggering white memoir."[30] Accordingly,

> by aligning testimony and memoir, we can discern a specific poetics of life narrative in which the power of testimony produces the kind of turbulent and conflicted memoir of belonging and identity that has become a distinctive genre of Australian intellectual work in the recent past, and which sets out to invent a white subject in crisis.[31]

Historians have been prolific writers of such memoirs, and Whitlock has read the work of Read, Reynolds, and Clendinnen not as history, but as memoir. By doing so, she has highlighted the way in which this work has been implicated in a long history of "benevolent" bourgeois autobiography. In her persuasive analysis, Whitlock has examined the emergence of the "becoming migloo" narrative in contemporary intellectual memoir as an ambivalent trope that has interrogated the authority of the white subject while simultaneously recuperating this self as a compassionate moral agent.[32] Although many of the recent white memoirs have been authored by historians, Whitlock has insisted that these texts should be read properly as memoir rather than history, because, as she has contended, "good literature—good memoir—may not necessarily be good history. . . ."[33] In this way, the production of memoir by white historians is an effect of their role as public intellectuals, a task related but not assimilable to their work as historians.

Although "migloo" memoirs have emerged from the 1980s as a response to Indigenous testimony, they are also a part of the small field of historians' autobiographies.[34] As a subgenre of autobiography, these works exist at the conjunction between history and memoir, and explore questions relating both to the construction of the self and to the practice of a discipline.[35] Most often produced in accessible, non-academic language, historians' autobiographies have typically reached a far wider audience than their professional work and, as such, have often made "important contributions to debates with implications that reach well beyond the confines of their professional community."[36]

This has been particularly so in Australia, Jeremy Popkin has argued, due to the proliferation of historians' autobiographies, such as Reynolds', that have explored the professional self within the context of performing the "national" work of confronting the fraught relationship between Indigenous and non-Indigenous Australians.[37] Though historians' autobiographies exist as distinct from both history and autobiography, many historians are increasingly viewing memoir, or at the very least self-conscious introspection, as an essential ingredient in so-called "good history." What is at stake here is an understanding of how testimony has brought not only a "crisis" to white subjectivity, as epitomized by the figure of the white intellectual in crisis, but also a crisis to white historiography.

The "crisis" of testimony in this work is both that of the white subject struggling to belong in post-*Mabo*, post-*Bringing them Home* Australia, as well as the representational and epistemological crisis of white history facing Indigenous oral testimony. Reynolds' work has remained valuable not only as an archetypal white intellectual memoir, but also as a study of the way in which testimony has reshaped the historical practice of many settler historians. In what follows, I consider the Australian work of historian Inga Clendinnen, who became drawn to research in the area of Australian frontier history through an engagement with Indigenous testimony. While I examine Clendinnen's "migloo memoir"—*Tiger's Eye*—I do so within the context of her oeuvre in order to demonstrate that witnessing has come to define not only her autobiographical work, but also her method of history making.

Inga Clendinnen's "Australian" Work

Before 1999, Clendinnen had never written on Australian history and was little known outside academic circles for her work on ancient South American civilizations. In the space of only six years, Clendinnen produced four generically diverse works on Australian subjects, along with numerous opinion articles and reviews, and became one of the nation's most prominent historians. In her twin roles as both an historian and a public intellectual, Clendinnen has been a pivotal contributor to national debates on history, participating both in the former Howard Government's Summit on school history teaching and in the amorphous "history wars."[38] She has played a significant role in contemporary Australian cultural and political life, and while her historical work has won critical praise she has also been lauded as a public figure, winning the 2007 Humanist of the Year award and becoming a companion of the Order of Australia in 2006. Here, I consider Clendinnen's turn to Australian history and explore the centrality of witnessing to her historical project. This body of work includes her ABC Boyer Lecture series *True Stories* (1999), her memoir *Tiger's Eye* (2000), the history *Dancing with Strangers* (2003), and her contribution to the popular *Quarterly Essay* series "The History Question" (2006).[39] By looking beyond Clendinnen's memoir to her "Australian" work as a whole, I demonstrate how her engagements with Australian history are predicated on an ethical confrontation with Indigenous stories.

True Stories

Clendinnen's first foray into Australian history came in 1999, when she was invited to participate in the ABC's prestigious Boyer Lecture Series. For the six lectures, Clendinnen took as her theme "the practical usefulness of good history both morally and politically."[40] Drawing on the ideas of American philosopher Martha Nussbaum, Clendinnen argued that the study of history has a central role to play in the creation of a healthy democracy through the development of civic virtue.[41] For Clendinnen, reflecting on the past experiences of others "liberates" our imagination, exercises our moral faculties, and necessitates critical self-analysis.[42] Here, Clendinnen made a distinction between "good" and "bad" history. So-called "good" history is a history comprising multiple "true stories." These are various, complex, "lumpy," and not easily assimilable to one "national" story. In contrast "bad" history is broad and simple, and, as such, "necessarily false."[43]

Over the course of the six lectures, Clendinnen presented a demonstration of "good" history, which she described as a "cornucopia of true stories."[44] In doing so, she explored several discrete episodes in Australian history. This focus on "episodes" is a hallmark of ethnohistory or ethnographic history. An approach to the past that combines history's focus on temporal change with anthropology's attention to culture, Clendinnen has asserted that ethnohistory "offer[s] the best chance of explaining what we humans do in any particular circumstance, and why we do it."[45] Heavily influenced by anthropologist Clifford Geertz, ethnographic history emerged during the 1970s as a radical challenge to the assumptions of academic history and attempted to rejuvenate the discipline through an embrace of anthropology.[46] Championed by the so-called "Melbourne School," a group that included Clendinnen as well as the prominent historians Greg Dening, Donna Merwick, and Rhys Isaac, ethnographic history has forged an approach to cross-cultural and frontier history that draws on the "thick description" and cultural relativism of anthropology.[47] It rejects grand narratives in order to, in Dening's words, "give back to the past its own present moment."[48]

Clendinnen's lectures faultlessly demonstrated the ethnohistorical technique, whereas her choice of subject matter was far from problematic. In her first lecture, Clendinnen was upfront about her dilemma: "while I am a historian and an Australian, I am not an Australian historian. I have no specialist knowledge of the affairs of this country."[49] In justifying her choice of subject, Clendinnen argued for the urgency of confronting Australia's colonial past. She admitted that initially, she had hoped to avoid discussing so-called "Aboriginal issues." They were, she reasoned, too politicized. She described her knowledge of Aboriginal issues before preparing the lectures as

> the usual confused liberal one: I knew they had been dispossessed, often murderously, and I also suspected that today too many of their wounds . . . were self-inflicted. I did not know what had happened in between. What I have been doing over these last months is curing my ignorance.[50]

Echoing Reynolds, Clendinnen presented a self-portrait of blithe myopia and, in doing so, positioned her preparation of the Boyer Lectures as a period of studied self-reflection and moral transformation.

Broadly, Clendinnen's lectures staged a confrontation with the history of Aboriginal and European relations. In this way, Clendinnen framed her turn to Australian history as a part of her own self-development as an Australian citizen. However, more than simply a personal quest, Clendinnen viewed the study of Australia's Indigenous past as crucial to the development of civic virtue in the present. "Our ignorance of their history, or our denial of it," she wrote, "is a threat to us all, because it is the major impediment in the way of general agreement as to what constitutes justice and decency, which are core issues in any democracy."[51] In this way, Clendinnen participated in the *fin-de-siècle* discourse on reconciliation that positioned witnessing as a core strand in a project of national renewal.

Tellingly, *True Stories* was delivered only two years after the release of *Bringing them Home*, within a wider political milieu preoccupied with the meanings of Indigenous stories and the process of reconciliation. Lecture four of her series—Inside the Contact Zone: Part 1—engaged directly with the issue of the stolen generation. Clendinnen presented the *Bringing them Home* testimonies as a revelation arguing, in a manner similar to Reynolds, that "I didn't know anything about the policy."[52] This confrontation with the history of child removal is central to Clendinnen's project. Eschewing a discussion of the relative guilt or innocence of contemporary settlers in acts of removal, Clendinnen argued instead for the urgency of taking action in the present.[53] For Clendinnen, as a historian, this action centered on the need to produce "true stories" about the nation's past, stories that will assist Australians to engage with Indigenous experience in an empathetic and imaginative way.

Throughout the Boyer Lectures, Clendinnen's engagement with Indigenous stories provided the foundation of her authority as an historian. Though Clendinnen used the lecture series to espouse an ethnohistorical view of the relationship between "good" history and civil society—a view she had advanced in her earlier work on South America and the Holocaust—she justified her ability to speak on Australian topics with reference to her willingness to confront the nation's history of colonization.[54] It was only by curing her own "ignorance" by listening to the "stories" of Aboriginal dispossession that she could accrue the necessary authority to speak of Australia's past. In this way, Clendinnen's transition to Australian history was predicated on the authority of witnessing.

Tiger's Eye

Following on quickly from the Boyer Lecture series, Clendinnen released *Tiger's Eye: A Memoir* in 2000. Unlike the lecture series, which was written quite simply to appeal to a general audience, *Tiger's Eye* is intricate, intimate, and unashamedly literary. Although ostensibly, and in name, "a memoir," the work is generically heterogeneous, and could be more accurately described as a melange of history, fiction, and autobiography. If in *True Stories* Clendinnen staged a relatively uncomplicated transition to Australian history, in *Tiger's Eye* she confronted her own desire to use fiction as a mode of exploring the past.

Broadly, *Tiger's Eye* traced Clendinnen's experience of being critically ill and focused particularly on her feelings of disorientation and powerlessness. While still undergoing hospital treatment, Clendinnen flirted with fiction as an escape from illness. "Only fiction," she reasoned, "can redress the existential ambiguities which stalk the real world."[55] Clendinnen described the seductiveness of fiction as a balm for reality, and much of *Tiger's Eye* is taken up with Clendinnen's lengthy, fictionalized remembrances. The text moved almost seamlessly between autobiography and fiction and, in doing so, offered us a sustained engagement with the unreliability, "the jagged inadequacies" of memory.[56] For Clendinnen, memory was, "an eel, wily, evasive, as hard to hold as any truly vital thing."[57]

Ultimately, Clendinnen rejected both fiction and memory as suitable paths to truth. For the remainder of *Tiger's Eye*, Clendinnen charted her burgeoning interest in Australian history. For Clendinnen, Australian history offered an escape from both the fantasies of fiction and the caprice of memory. Clendinnen completed her first piece of formal writing post-surgery on Tasmanian Chief Protector of Aborigines G. A. Robinson.[58] "After my transplant," she wrote, "and for no clear reason I could fathom, but perhaps a desire for a wider, more stable context, I wanted to learn more," about the Australian past.[59] In Robinson's diaries, Clendinnen argued that she not only rediscovered the joys of primary source research, but also discovered a connection to place. With Robinson as her "guide," Clendinnen confronted directly, for the first time, the fact of white violence in Australian history. Clendinnen produced a close reading of Robinson's diaries, in ethnographic style, in which she focused on Robinson's expeditions and relationships with Indigenous peoples. Juxtaposed with Robinson's diaries is Clendinnen's construction of herself as a historian, slowly piecing together an image of Robinson's life and experiences.

Here, Australian history was figured as the road back to coherent selfhood. By confronting frontier history, Clendinnen is reborn as an historian: the landscape, she declared, was completely "transformed" by her meeting with Robinson.[60] For Whitlock, *Tiger's Eye* "uses auto-biographical writing in pursuit of truth and reconciliation."[61] Crucial to the conciliatory aim of the work is Clendinnen's staging of herself as a white subject in crisis. Clendinnen's reading of Robinson worked to position her as a contemporary (post)colonial subject, able to emphathize with Robinson's humanistic attempts to "assist" Indigenous people, but at the same time, able to achieve a critical distance from this history.

Although *Tiger's Eye* did attempt to explore ways for critics to write with an awareness of their own complicity, it does remain vulnerable to what Whitlock has described as "well-intentioned, yet fatally flawed colonizing gestures of sentimentality, benevolence, or humanism."[62] Chief of these is the way in which the recognition of complicity in *Tiger's Eye* formed the ground for Clendinnen's rebirth as an historian. Witnessing opened Clendinnen to the other, and to the possibilities of unknown stories, only to retreat from the risks involved in relinquishing her authority as an historian.

Dancing with Strangers

Dancing with Strangers (hereafter *Dancing*), Clendinnen's first monograph on Australian history, emerged out of the Robinson sections of *Tiger's Eye*. Thus, although the two texts are quite different in their aims and generic qualities, it is essential to read *Dancing* as intimately connected to the processes of historical reconsideration and self-reflection inaugurated by Clendinnen's memoir. Similar to *Tiger's Eye*, *Dancing* foregrounded the self in the production of historical understanding. Throughout, one can read Clendinnen's construction of her own self as historian alongside her analysis of the life writing of several early British settlers.

Dancing focused on life in the early colony at Sydney Cove and, similar to much ethnohistory, is episodic: a text pieced together from a series of close readings of events and situations. Clendinnen used the diaries of some of the most important administrative figures in the colony, including those of Governor Phillip as well as John Hunter, John White, David Collins, and Watkin Tench. She presented her work quite self-consciously as "a telling of the story" of first contact, immediately alerting the reader to the necessarily partial nature of her narrative. She also represented the major historical personages in her work as "characters," further underscoring her process of narrative construction.[63] At the core of the work are two ethnohistorical episodes: the eponymous "dancing" and the spearing of Governor Phillip. Clendinnen's readings of these events are based on what she terms an "editing out" of her British diary sources—stripping away the commentary of the diarists in order to approach the most unvarnished descriptions of what really happened. Adopting "the silent-film strategy," focusing on actions not words, Clendinnen developed an account of each event by examining the actions described by the diarists for evidence of Aboriginal autonomy and intentionality.[64] Throughout, Clendinnen centered the experience of the Aborigines, whom she referred to as the "Australians," and attempted to read the British sources against the grain to do so. The approach is at once ethnographic and highly imaginative, dependent on the sober moral capacity of the historian and their ability to creatively interpret source materials.[65]

In order to examine the dancing episode, Clendinnen consulted the diary of Lieutenant William Bradley, who, in his journal, described a landing in which "these people mixed with ours and all hands danced together."[66] In her analysis of this episode, Clendinnen engaged the reader explicitly in her quest to imagine the episode: "we can imagine the hair clipping [that accompanied one dancing session], but what can their mysterious 'dancing together' have looked like?"[67] Clendinnen's use of the word "we" here rhetorically invited the reader to collaborate in her creative project and to move beyond the seemingly bizarre or comical qualities to the dancing. In doing so, Clendinnen foregrounded the extent to which ethnohistory, and indeed all history, is dependent on the imagination.

An examination of Clendinnen's reading of the second episode, the spearing of Phillip, is instructive for considering the limitations of Clendinnen's approach to early colonial life. Challenging the conventional reading of Phillip's spearing as "accidental," Clendinnen dismissed the reliability of the British accounts, particularly that of eyewitness Collins. Positioning herself as an "objective" figure, Clendinnen demanded to know "what was really going on?"[68] She proceeded to imagine Baneelon's motivation in inviting Phillip to meet him, and his kinsman's motive in spearing the Governor. Instead of Baneelon emerging as a "buffoon," the Aborigines spoiling a relationship-soothing exchange of gifts with a gratuitous attack, Clendinnen contended that

> Baneelon was pursuing a rapidly evolving political project of his own to establish himself as the crucial hinge-man between the white men and the local tribes, and indeed as the only man capable of eliciting proper compensation for past wrongs from these ignorant intruders . . .[69]

By "editing-out" British comment from the sources and attempting to examine only basic actions, Clendinnen arrived at a startlingly fresh assessment of the event, a ritualistic spearing designed to symbolically avenge British wrongs and clear the way for smooth diplomatic relations. Though Clendinnen's account is imbued with a sense of oversimplification in which the collective force of Aboriginal agency finds its expression in Baneelon alone, with his kinsmen merely pawns in his own political power plays, Clendinnen offered an intriguing way for historians to avoid acquiescing to the cultural myopia of the British source material.

Clendinnen's vision of this incident, and her use of imaginative speculation more generally, has received backhanded criticism from literary critic Deirdre Coleman, who has written that "I think she does an impressive job of imagining (what else can it be?) the 'Australian' side of the encounter . . ."[70] Crucially, not only has Coleman aligned the truth value of Clendinnen's work with that of fiction, but also she has criticized Clendinnen's oblique handling of British violence. When discussing Clendinnen's characterization of one of Phillip's punitive missions as a mere show, rather than a real attack, Coleman has described Clendinnen's interpretation as "nothing less than wishful thinking, an implausible distortion of the record."[71]

Indeed, the picture of first contact, and of Phillip's governorship, that Clendinnen conjures is remarkably rosy. Clendinnen almost hero-worships Phillip, portraying the period of his administration as a time marked by a bumbling friendship and good-natured curiosity. It was, she contended, a "springtime of trust," in which Phillip was "close to visionary in his obstinate dream of integrating these newly discovered people into the British polity."[72] This emphasis on the fundamentally well-intentioned nature of Phillip and his men is also present in Clendinnen's insistence, based on scant evidence, that it was the British who initiated the dancing. For Coleman, this has provided further evidence of Clendinnen's propagation of the erroneous "popular belief that the eighteenth century is a more innocent, more enlightened, less racist period than the nineteenth century."[73]

Unlike the willingness to confront the violent episodes of Australian history, Clendinnen demonstrated in *True Stories* and *Tiger's Eye*, *Dancing* glosses over Phillip's punitive expeditions in favor of elevating an intriguing apocryphal episode—the dancing—to center stage. Despite the appeal of Coleman's explanation of the effect of chivalric discourse, she has failed to account fully for Clendinnen's persistent romanticism, only very obliquely suggesting the presence of a personal and political dimension to Clendinnen's historical imagination.[74] There was surely something other than a lack of research influencing Clendinnen when she wrote that though "nine years is a brief time span," "in my view much of what mattered most in shaping the tone and temper of white-black relations in this country happened during those first few years of contact."[75] Clendinnen's decision to position such an opaque, marginal episode at the heart of her version of the frontier is suggestive of a desire to emphasize, above all else, positive points of early contact.

Clendinnen has written that she hoped that *Dancing* would not be received as a "balm" for the national conscience, yet her ethnohistorical imaginings are clearly tied not only to constructions of herself as a historian, but are also implicated in narratives of national renewal. According to Robert Manne, "no reconciliation [between European settlers and Indigenous people] is . . . possible unless we can discover a version of Australian history that can be shared."[76] For Manne, Clendinnen's work has provided the "most truthful and nourishing" beginning of this shared narrative. In *Dancing*, Clendinnen actively participated in the production of a positive cross-cultural narrative and, in doing so, sought to identify an historical origin for a contemporary, reconciled nation. Yet, for Philip Morrissey, Clendinnen's "baffling" focus on dancing functioned to "render invisible and dematerialise contemporary flesh-and-blood Aborigines."[77] Morrissey has read Clendinnen's work as a part of broader discourses on history that have enacted a "scholarly vanishing" of Aborigines which obscures the presence of sovereign Indigenous peoples in the present.[78] As such, *Dancing's* focus on more "positive" episodes at the expense of an engagement with well-documented frontier violence is suggestive of the desire of some historians to find "useful pasts for people like themselves."[79]

In this way, *Dancing* has registered the limitations of Clendinnen's mode of witnessing. Clendinnen described *Dancing* as "our first shared Australian story . . . [a] tragedy of animated imagination, determined friendship and painfully dying hopes."[80] Similarly, in her introduction, Clendinnen revealed that *Dancing* was animated by a "hope":

> that by retracing the difficulties in the way of understanding people of a different culture we might grasp how taxing and tense a condition "tolerance" is; and how we might achieve social justice between Australia's original immigrants, and those of us who came later.[81]

Here, Clendinnen positioned professional history as the site of renewal for "us"—settler Australians. Though she has couched her work in the rhetoric of reconciliation, she ultimately argued for the primacy of history in this process. "We have," she has argued, "only history to guide us."[82] In this way, though *Dancing* formed the culmination of an historical project that began, in *True Stories*, with an engagement with testimony, it has actually worked to obscure the voices, and demands, of testimony in the present. That is, though Clendinnen's work has been predicated on a willingness to listen to Indigenous stories, as a starting place for a renewed national understanding, *Dancing* reaffirmed the authority of the historian as sole arbiter of the past.

Similar to the diaries with which she works, Clendinnen's history is a work of self-fashioning. As in *True Stories* and *Tiger's Eye*, Clendinnen is eager to portray herself as both professional historian and curious everywoman ready to confront the complexities of Australia's past.[83] Though Clendinnen "invites" her readers to consult the sources alongside her and to challenge her interpretations, her authoritative voice is omnipresent, constantly offering justifications for her highly imaginative enterprise. For Morrissey, her "intimidating magisterial tone" has attempted to "invalidate contrary voices and perspectives."[84] Though framed by the rhetoric of inclusiveness, *Dancing* has served to consolidate Clendinnen's position as an historical authority. It is this issue of authority—the pressing question of who has the right to speak about the past—that has been explored further in "The History Question."

"The History Question"

Clendinnen's 2006 contribution to the *Quarterly Essay* series, "The History Question," took the form of an essay on the current role of history within the public sphere. At its heart lay a critique of Kate Grenville's historical novel *The Secret River.* For Clendinnen, Grenville's use of "empathy" to explore the past was misguided and cannot stand up to the moral imagination of trained historians. She decried the novel for its "opportunistic transpositions and elisions" and, in doing so, created an image of historians and novelists at war—arguing that "novelists have been doing their best to bump historians off the track."[85] In particular, Clendinnen has been concerned that Grenville's use of "Applied Empathy" has inhibited her ability to understand the early settlers as different, in culture and attitude, from contemporary settlers.[86] Accordingly, the novel has been marred by Grenville's "contemporary assumptions and current obsessions," which have been ahistorically projected onto "historical" characters.[87] Yet, as we have seen with *Dancing,* Clendinnen's own work is highly imaginative and has hinged crucially on concepts of historical empathy and moral adjudication. Just as Clendinnen has justified her turn to Australian topics as part of a confrontation with Indigenous stories, Grenville too, as discussed earlier, has described her novel as written in a spirit of witnessing.[88]

The remainder of Clendinnen's *Quarterly Essay* is a justification for the continued authority of historians in the public sphere. The essay is wide ranging, but Clendinnen's insistence on the necessity of historians as guardians of the past hinges on her assertion that although historians use their imaginations just as novelists do, they are "bound" by the historical method and their investments in the past are professional not personal.[89] Yet, Clendinnen's investment in Australian history is personal. What has been consistent across Clendinnen's Australian work is a commitment to Australian history as a part of a broader process of personal self-reflection. Clendinnen has maintained her moral authority, as an historian and an Australian citizen, through her self-conscious engagement with frontier history. Although she has described the novelist's use of empathy and imaginative reconstruction as "opportunistic," as an ethnohistorian her work is fundamentally imaginative. Her eagerness to warn the public about the so-called "dangers" of historical fiction has belied the supposedly "objective" nature of the historian's craft.

Ultimately, "The History Question" presented what Morrissey, borrowing from Marilyn Lake's description of Keith Windschuttle's *The Fabrication of Aboriginal History*, has described as a "self-innocenting narrative."[90] This is not to conflate the work of Clendinnen and Windschuttle, and the divergent impacts that their work has had on Australian historiography. Instead, I emphasize the way in which Clendinnen's history making, predicated on a self-conscious notion of confronting the past, has paradoxically worked to elevate the moral status of her work. Rather than inaugurating a practice of witnessing grounded in dialogic exchange, Clendinnen's confrontation with *Bringing them Home* has resulted in the perpetuation of a liberal narrative of Australian history in which the settler nation is reconciled (to itself). In this schema, the opinions and experiences of Indigenous peoples, as expressed through testimony, are effaced.[91] Clendinnen's has been a form of witnessing in which contemporary settlers are always already "innocent."[92]

From *Why Weren't We Told?* to "I Have Always Known"

When Katrina Schlunke wrote, on the first page of *Bluff Rock*, that she has "always known that Aboriginal people were killed as part of the taking of land in Australia," she signaled both her relationship to and estrangement from the tradition of historical self-reflection enacted by Reynolds and perpetuated by Clendinnen.[93] There is no "becoming migloo" moment in Schlunke's history; here, there are no "skeletons" to be removed from closets, no persuasive "darkness" in the heart. The "migloo" moment has been central to the way settler Australians have witnessed to Indigenous dispossession through the genres of memoir and history. Yet, if part of the appeal of Reynolds and Clendinnen's work has been to prompt a similar coming to knowledge in the reader, Schlunke's work has offered none of the attendant pleasures of coming to know. The kind of moral transformation performed in their work is unavailable to Schlunke's readers. This crucial difference is, at least in part, the result of generational change. If we can understand Reynolds and Clendinnen to have come of age in an era marked by what Anna Haebich has termed a "twilight of knowing," Schlunke, and alongside her other settler Australians born from the late 1960s, were born in a period of "knowledge."[94] Accordingly, Schlunke has written that "it seems" as if the fact of frontier violence "was never a shock."[95]

Bluff Rock has offered an alternative approach to personalized history in which the study of the past works to unravel, rather than reinvent, the white self. Though *Bluff Rock* is a hybrid text, mixing fragments of history, autobiography, and fictocriticism, it is, in essence, an exercise in local history. Focusing on events that occurred during the 1840s at Tenterfield in the NSW Northern Tablelands, *Bluff Rock* has explored the local "legend" that claimed a group of Bundjalung or Ngarabul peoples were chased off the town's eponymous rock by neighboring landowners Edward Irby and Thomas Windeyer.[96] Schlunke set herself the task of investigating these events, though in doing so she disavowed explicitly the position of an expert. For Schlunke, confronting the town's past hinged on having "the courage to say we didn't know . . . [to] displace ourselves from the centre of the moral universe."[97] Schlunke's work then, is an effort to displace the white historian—and by extension, the white self—from the epicenter of history. It also offered a profound challenge to the epistemological sureties of academic history: "The promise of History was that we would know what happened. But there is no single way of 'doing' history, no single way of knowing history."[98]

Though *Bluff Rock* has self-consciously produced a form of history, it has done so not from the context of academic history, but from within the "always inchoate" field of fictocriticism.[99] As a leading exponent of this largely Australian practice, Schlunke, along with Anne Brewster, has described fictocriticism "as a scholarly genre that understands one of its homes to be Cultural Studies."[100] Broadly, fictocriticism has encompassed a set of aesthetic and critical practices that have foregrounded the limits of knowledge and emphasized the importance of interrogating the subject position of the writer.[101] Frequently drawing on feminist and/or poststructural theories, fictocriticism has been adopted readily by authors, such as Stephen Muecke and Anna Gibbs, concerned with representing cross-cultural experience.[102] Blending analysis and storytelling, fictocriticism has made a powerful, albeit marginal, contribution to contemporary criticism.

In the case of *Bluff Rock,* Schlunke has produced a fragmentary text that intersperses a "conventional" non-fictional historical analysis with sections of autobiography, fiction, and theory. She has written with an awareness of queer theory, historiography, and whiteness studies, responding to questions of local history in a voice that is both creative and critical. Schlunke, similar to Clendinnen, has been mistrustful of narrative, and, as such, *Bluff Rock* is a text marked by narrative excess. Describing her style of narrative proliferation and expansion, Schlunke has reflected on the production of "narratives of narratives, narratives on narratives and narrator and narrative co-mingling so that there is no single home for the writing self."[103] For Schlunke, excessive narrativizing not only protects against the false closure and causality of narrative history, thus eschewing the position of omniscient narrator, but has also worked to complicate notions of a unitary self. Schlunke's decision to include fragments written by her partner and research assistant, Susan, has further undermined her role as author and origin of textual meaning.[104] Schlunke's style is clearly the product of her commitment to fictocritical practice, whereas her text has enacted an implicit critique of settler histories that reify the white historian as the moral center of the text.

Instead of working to reconstitute the white self, Schlunke's work has performed an unraveling of the self through a focus on the interactions between self and place. *Bluff Rock* is, according to its subtitle, an "autobiography of massacre." As Schlunke has explained, "this is not an autobiography of a self. It is an autobiography of a past, placed, event. It is an impossibility."[105] In attempting such impossibility, Schlunke has highlighted the complex conjunction between self and place:

> A rock, an event, a past, cannot write itself . . . and yet it does. To claim such a writing as autobiographical shows the ways in which the past is always emerging via someone in particular, writing a particular past, and someone else in particular creates pasts from that writing. We know we can never know all the conditions that make a particular past possible. Here the spectral 'I' of autobiography offers what is understood in musical terms as an irresolvable dissonance. A dissonance that resonates.[106]

Here, Schlunke presented an image of the self as a medium; the self as vessel for the expression of the past in the present. In doing so, she has underscored the way in which stories about the past are shaped by individual, placed, expressions. Thus, in writing the "history" of *Bluff Rock*, Schlunke has also attempted to write something of her own history, and endeavored to understand the perpetrators of massacre, because, she has argued, "I have an investment in knowing them so that I might know myself."[107]

Reviewer Eve Lamborn has expressed ambivalence about Schlunke's use of personal reflection. For Lamborn, "Schlunke's presence is so strong that the book is as much about the story of Bluff Rock as it is about her experiencing Bluff Rock."[108] *Bluff Rock* oscillates between an analysis of historical sources about the massacre—such as the diaries of Irby and a local tourist pamphlet—and digressions about Schlunke's life growing up in Tenterfield. For another reviewer, historian Maria Nugent, this linking of Schlunke's life and the rock is the work's strength. By exploring the interconnections between self and place, *Bluff Rock* "tracks the author's own shifting relationship to what she knows, and what she does not know, via 'The Bluff Rock Massacre Story' about interracial violence in the place she calls home."[109] In this way, Schlunke has used the story of the rock as a starting place for a broader analysis not only of the continuing presence of the past in the present, but also of her role in perpetuating and resisting the "story" of the massacre.

Witnessing/Confessing Whiteness

Unlike the work of Reynolds and Clendinnen, who have positioned their histories as, at least in part, responses to forms of Indigenous testimony, Schlunke's text has attempted a different mode of witnessing to frontier violence. Broadly, Schlunke has framed her work as a response to "the many Aboriginal interventions into hegemonic history."[110] She has suggested, moreover, that "implicitly this book is concerned with the ways in which a non-Aboriginal can write Australian history."[111] In considering the possibility of non-Indigenous history making, Schlunke has worked to witness to the enduring power of whiteness. Drawing on the insights of the interdisciplinary field of whiteness studies, Schlunke focused on the operation of whiteness as an unmarked structuring racial category within colonial New South Wales.[112] In this way, *Bluff Rock* has been concerned not only to make visible the effect of whiteness on historical events and experiences, but also to bear witness to the ways in which whiteness continues to impact on both scholarly work and individual understandings of contemporary race relations. Speculating on her ability to write while being white, Schlunke asks:

> have I reached my own end point, where I simply can't see what he [Irby] does because I do it, or have it, too? Am I writing white? This is the ahistorical threat of whiteness, its all-encompassing power to get me, to give me something I may not even want. I can't see the white except when it is contrasted with its own shadows, but there is often too much light for

shadows to occur. I can't quite believe I *am* white.

Chorus moans: *GET REAL!*[113]

Through a focus on whiteness, Schlunke has worked to witness to the continuity between Irby, and other perpetrators of massacre, and herself. Though Schlunke is careful not to reify whiteness as a fixed, immutable identity, she has, nevertheless, affirmed the enduring power—what she terms the "light"—of whiteness.[114] Ambitiously, Schlunke has framed her fictocritical approach to frontier history as an attempt to begin the "radical fracturing" of whiteness, a process she sees as necessitating "the undoing of 'settlement'—and so also of History as we now know it and do it."[115]

As Fiona Nicoll has argued, identifying one's own whiteness in this way functions as a mode of "coming out," a performance in which the speaker declares their own whiteness and, in doing so, alters their relationship to the self, and to a community of others.[116] To "come out" in this way is, as Robyn Westcott has suggested, "to acknowledge the cumulative force of historical discourse imprinted on the self as subject."[117] In witnessing to her own whiteness, Nicoll has been eager to delineate her work from the genre of confession.[118] She has done so in order to eschew the transformative power of confession—what Radstone has described as "the *becomingness* which constitutes its very heart."[119] For Nicoll, confessing to whiteness would function to reinscribe her position as a "good woman" through the production of conscience and its attendant investment in the display of "good intentions."[120] By refusing to remake herself through witnessing as a "good woman," Nicoll has drawn attention to the centrality of moral virtue to white race privilege and its deployment as a strategy of silencing Indigenous peoples. As Aileen Moreton-Robinson has demonstrated, "whites utilize their race privilege to dismiss the issues and questions being raised [by Indigenous peoples] by recentering themselves through their perceived superior moral or intellectual position."[121]

In the arena of history, the confession of whiteness may be allied to the solidification of the historian's subject position. Though Clendinnen and Reynolds have neither "confessed" their whiteness, nor engaged with the field of whiteness studies, more generally, they have staged their encounters with Indigenous testimony as sites for the examination of their complicity as Anglo subjects. Yet their work has been driven by the "becomingness" of confession and has sought to move teleologically to reaffirm their authority to speak for Australian history. In this way, their confrontation with the white self has functioned as what Westcott has described as "a rhetorical cover for an 'old' metaphysics which masks the presence of the liberal subject who 'knows', and makes truth through self-mastery and authorial intent."[122] In doing so, their work has offered readers the pleasures—"textual and libinal"—of "coming to know" the truth about both Australian history and themselves, as white Australians.[123]

Against the compulsion to confess her whiteness, Schlunke does not attempt to recuperate the white self, or white history, for reconciliation. Rather, *Bluff Rock* has constituted a rejection of liberal history making that works to fracture the certainties of historical authority. For Schlunke, this has meant imagining new connections between people and places—connections that work to collapse the temporal distance between past and present and deny the possibility of arriving at any solid conclusions in relation to the self, the other, and the frontier. In a powerful fictional fragment, Schlunke drew on poet Dorothy Porter's image of the night parrot to "marry" Irby:

> So how do you write 'The Bluff Rock Massacre'? How do you write Irby? Dear Reader, let me marry him. He is my husband; I am his wife. Our unnatural fucking, through insuperable history, makes us both strange. We are the supposedly extinct night parrot . . . [124]

This fictocritical interlude worked to "make strange," or "queer" history, a process of Schlunke connecting herself with Irby that "is both transportive and within the realm of the abject, operating between past and present in a way that denied the stability of either."[125] It is a startling tactic that has sought to disturb the white reader in its refusal to separate contemporary and colonial figures of whiteness.

Ultimately, Schlunke's efforts to open out the "excess" of the past have worked to witness to the impossibility of arriving at a singular truth about the past. Schlunke's thorough analysis of "The Bluff Rock Massacre" has led her to conclude that the local story has functioned as a mythic narrative which conflates a series of violent events. "There are too many massacres," she has written,

> for the single event of "The Bluff Rock Massacre" to be true, and for me to go on being witness to its truth, would be to be a good, educated white. My father (in particular) and mother would have been proud. My grandfather would have

done the Anglo equivalent of spitting in my face. I would be nicely placed as speaking for an injustice to others. I would be a hero of sorts, almost a sort of Judith Wright (without, unfortunately, the poetry). But the truth I found was grubby and unrecognisable.[126]

In this way, Schlunke rejected forcefully the role of the historian as moral authority about the past, "nicely placed" to speak out against injustice. In doing so, her work has performed a profound denunciation of the mode of liberal humanitarian witnessing that has marked the work of authors such as Reynolds and Clendinnen. Schlunke's approach is to write with what Lyn McCredden has termed "self-undoing empathy," "to imagine ourselves not too far from the victims of the past, *but also not too far from the perpetrators.*"[127] It is an approach, to be sure, embedded with risk. However, it is also an approach that embraces the core challenge of historical witnessing: to cede authority.

This notion of ceding or dissolving historical authority has been a key theme within the practice of oral history, though historians within the field have written more typically of "sharing" authority through the telling and recording of stories.[128] Yet, the challenge of Indigenous testimony is more than the call to "share history." It is to begin the messy, almost impossible task of undercutting and undoing the authority of the white historian. Though *Bluff Rock* does, at times, boarder on the self-indulgent, Schlunke's almost forensic examination of the self has begun the task of imagining how witnessing can do more than simply reinscribe the authority of the historian.

Conclusion: Witnessing as Collaboration?

This chapter has highlighted a range of responses by historians and cultural critics to the "crisis" posed by Indigenous testimony for historical understanding. It has concentrated, largely, on academic work, though it has also considered the use of popular genres, such as memoir, by professional historians. The chapter has foregrounded the role Henry Reynolds has played in developing a broadly accepted liberal-humanist mode of historical witnessing, and juxtaposed this model with that suggested by the work of Katrina Schlunke.

Though Schlunke's work is marginal, and has been little discussed within the sphere of academic history, it demonstrates the diversity within practices of historical witnessing and offers just one example of what a rejection of liberal or "mainstream" witnessing might look similar to. Other examples are to be found in the anthropological research of Deborah Bird Rose and Heather Goodall and in the fictocritical practices of Stephen Muecke and Ross Gibson.[129] By way of conclusion, I want to briefly draw attention to the recent, popular television history *First Australians,* as an example of innovative practices of historical witnessing.

Broadcast on SBS over seven parts in 2008, *First Australians* performed a collaborative, dialogic mode of witnessing to the past.[130] Directed by Rachel Perkins and Beck Cole, and produced and largely written by Indigenous filmmakers and writers, *First Australians* brought together a range of Indigenous and non-Indigenous historians to tell a story about the experience of the "First Australians." The entire project operated under the guidelines of Indigenous Cultural and Intellectual Property rights, which ensured that every story told within the program underwent a process whereby it was developed in consultation with the descendents of the peoples featured in each episode.[131] As a work of popular, televisual history, *First Australians* forged links between popular and academic modes of history by featuring the work of professional historians and anthropologists, including Inga Clendinnen, as prominent "talking heads" throughout the program.

First Australians offered a mode of history making that not only centered testimony and the experiences of Indigenous peoples, but also positioned history as a process of negotiation and collaboration. It offered a glimpse of the future of history making in this country, and worked as a powerful counterpoint to the proliferation of Anglo-centered liberal-humanist witnessing. In *First Australians,* there was no single voice of historical authority: in Birch's terms, no "Sophisticated One."[132] Instead, there were myriad voices that challenged, overlapped, and augmented each other. It was a history alive to the endurance of the past in the present.

Notes

1. Tony Birch, "Testimony," *Aboriginal History* 30 (2006): 32.
2. LaCapra, *History and Memory after Auschwitz,* 11.
3. Ibid.
4. Ibid.
5. Inga Clendinnen, *Dancing with Strangers* (Melbourne: Text Publishing, 2003); Katrina Schlunke, *Bluff Rock: Autobiography of a Massacre* (Fremantle: Curtin University Books, 2005).
6. Klaus Neumann, "But Is It History?," *Cultural Studies Review* 14, no. 1 (2008): 21.

143

7.   Ibid.
8.   Ibid. See also Keith Jenkins, Sue Morgan, and Alun Munslow, eds., *Manifestos for History* (London and New York: Routledge, 2007); Alun Munslow, *Deconstructing History*, 2nd ed. (London and New York: Routledge, 2006); Keith Jenkins, *Refiguring History: New Thoughts on an Old Discipline* (London: Routledge, 2003); Stephen Muecke, "Experimental History? The 'Space' of History in Recent Histories of Kimberley Colonialism," *The UTS Review* 2, no. 1 (May 1996): 1–11.
9.   Neumann, "But Is It History?," 24.
10. See especially Greg Dening, *Beach Crossings: Voyaging across Times, Cultures and Self* (Carlton, VIC: The Miegunyah Press, 2004); Deborah Bird Rose, *Dingo Makes Us Human: Life and Land in an Australian Aboriginal Culture* (Oakleigh, VIC: Cambridge University Press, 2000); Stephen Muecke, *No Road (Bitumen All the Way)* (South Fremantle: Fremantle Arts Centre Press, 1997); Greg Dening, *The Death of William Gooch: A History's Anthropology* (Melbourne: Melbourne University Press, 1995); Deborah Bird Rose, *Hidden Histories: Black Stories from Victoria River Downs, Humbert River and Wave Hill Stations* (Canberra: Aboriginal Studies Press, 1991); Greg Dening, *Mr. Bligh's Bad Language: Passion, Power, and Theatre on the Bounty* (Cambridge and New York: Cambridge University Press, 1992); Kim Benterrak et al., *Reading the Country: Introduction to Nomadology* (Fremantle, WA: Fremantle Arts Centre Press, 1984).
11. Neumann, "But Is It History?," 26.
12. Stanner, *After the Dreaming*.
13. Attwood, ed., *In the Age of Mabo*, xv. For a reappraisal of the "great Australian silence," see Healy, *Forgetting Aborigines*; Haebich, *Broken Circles*; "Between Knowing and Not Knowing."
14. Lorenzo Veracini, "A Prehistory of Australia's History Wars: The Evolution of Aboriginal History During the 1970s and 1980s," *Australian Journal of Politics and History* 52, no. 3 (2006): 439–54.
15. Lorenzo Veracini, "Of a 'Contested Ground' and an 'Indelible Stain': A Difficult Reconciliation between Australia and Its Aboriginal History During the 1990s and 2000s," *Aboriginal History* 27 (2003): 225.
16. Bain Attwood and John Arnold, eds., *Power, Knowledge and Aborigines* (Bundoora, VIC: La Trobe University Press, 1992); Attwood, ed., *In the Age of Mabo*; *Telling the Truth About Aboriginal History*; Richard Broome, "Chapter 4: Historians, Aborigines and Australia: Writing the National Past," in *In the Age of Mabo: History, Aborigines and Australia*, ed. Bain Attwood (Sydney: Allen & Unwin, 1996), 54–72.
17. On the role of historians, including Reynolds and Ann McGrath, in the preparation of land rights cases, see Ann Curthoys, Ann Genovese, and Alexander Reilly, *Rights and Redemption: History, Law and Indigenous People* (Sydney: UNSW Press, 2008).
18. Henry Reynolds, *The Other Side of the Frontier: Aboriginal Resistance to the European Invasion of Australia* (Sydney: UNSW Press, 2006), 3.
19. See especially Reynolds, *Why Weren't We Told: A Personal Search for the Truth About Our History*, 243–58.
20. Ibid., 17.

21. Ibid., 29.
22. Ibid., 97, 228.
23. Ibid., 97.
24. Ibid., 40.
25. Attwood, ed., *In the Age of Mabo*, xviii.
26. Whitlock, "Consuming Passions," 18.
27. Lynette Russell, *A Little Bird Told Me: Family Secrets, Necessary Lies* (Crows Nest, NSW: Allen & Unwin, 2002); Martin Flanagan, *In Sunshine or in Shadow* (Sydney: Picador, 2002); Clendinnen, *Tiger's Eye*; Read, *Belonging*; Pybus, *Community of Thieves*.
28. Margaret Somerville, *Body/Landscape Journals* (Melbourne: Spinifex Press, 1999); Muecke, *No Road (Bitumen All the Way)*. For an incisive commentary on these texts, see Probyn, "A Poetics of Failure Is No Bad Thing."
29. Interestingly, in Russell's case, her memoir actually traces a "becoming" Indigenous, in which the white self is remade through a confrontation with hitherto ignored or submerged aspects of family history. Reynolds has explored a similar theme in his recent *Nowhere People*, linking academic inquiry with family history. Though he ultimately declines to identify as Indigenous, despite discovering his own Aboriginal ancestry, he takes prides in "belonging to two families at the same time." Henry Reynolds, *Nowhere People* (Melbourne: Viking, 2005), 239.
30. Whitlock, "Strategic Remembering," 163.
31. Whitlock, "Becoming Migloo," 244.
32. Whitlock, "Consuming Passions," 18.
33. Whitlock, "Strategic Remembering," 175.
34. This form has received attention in two major studies of Australian autobiographical production. Dalziell, *Shameful Autobiographies: Shame in Contemporary Australian Autobiographies and Culture*; David McCooey, *Artful Histories: Modern Australian Autobiography* (Melbourne: Cambridge University Press, 1996).
35. Though this sub-genre of historians' autobiography has its roots in the work of some of the earliest "classical" historians, including Edward Gibbon, it also articulates with the late twentieth-century turn to "personal criticism" across the humanities. Anderson, *Autobiography*, 122. This move to critically analyze the subject position of the critic has been associated most closely with feminist criticism. See, for example, Jane Gallop, *Anecdotal Theory* (Durham, NC: Duke University Press, 2002); Nancy K. Miller, *Getting Personal: Feminist Occasions and Other Autobiographical Acts* (New York: Routledge, 1991); Meaghan Morris, *The Pirate's Fiancée: Feminism, Reading and Postmodernism* (London: Verso, 1988).
36. Jeremy D. Popkin, "*Ego-Histoire* Down Under," *Australian Historical Studies* 129 (2007): 107. See also Popkin's comprehensive book-length study of the form. Jeremy D. Popkin, *History, Historians, and Autobiography* (Chicago, IL: University of Chicago Press, 2005).
37. Popkin, "*Ego-Histoire* Down Under," 119.
38. For Clendinnen's contribution to the national summit on school history teaching, see DEST, "The Australian History Summit: Transcript of

Proceedings." On Clendinnen's participation in the history wars, see Inga Clendinnen, "Dispatches from the History Wars: On the Bitter Battle Being Waged over Our National Past," *Australian Financial Review*, October 31, 2003, 4–5.

39. Inga Clendinnen, *True Stories* (Sydney: ABC Books, 1999); Clendinnen, *Tiger's Eye*; *Dancing with Strangers*; *History Question*.

40. Inga Clendinnen, "Lecture 1: Incident on a Beach," *True Stories*, ABC Boyer Lecture Series, (1999), [Transcript], http://www.abc.net.au/rn/boyers/stories/s66348.htm (accessed July 27, 2009).

41. Nussbaum has been outspoken in her support for the development of the imagination and self-analysis as crucial to the development of a moral, democratic citizenry. See especially Martha Craven Nussbaum, *Cultivating Humanity: A Classical Defense of Reform in Liberal Education* (Cambridge, MA: Harvard University Press, 1997); Martha Craven Nussbaum, *Poetic Justice: The Literary Imagination and Public Life* (Boston, MA: Beacon Press, 1995).

42. Clendinnen, "Lecture 1: Incident on a Beach."

43. Ibid.

44. Inga Clendinnen, "Lecture 6: What Now?," *True Stories*, ABC Boyer Lecture Series, (1999), [Transcript], http://www.abc.net.au/rn/boyers/stories/s74430.htm (accessed July 27, 2009).

45. Clendinnen, *Dancing with Strangers*, 3.

46. Nicholas Thomas, "Ethnographic History," in *The Oxford Companion to Australian History*, ed. Graeme Davison, John Hirst, and Stuart Macintyre (Melbourne: Oxford University Press, 1998), 225–26.

47. See especially Donna Merwick, *Death of a Notary: Conquest and Change in Colonial New York* (Ithaca, N.Y.: Cornell University Press, 1999); Dening, *Death of William Gooch*; Rhys Isaac, *The Transformation of Virginia: 1740-1790* (Chapel Hill: University of North Carolina Press, 1982).

48. Dening, *Beach Crossings*, 22.

49. Clendinnen, "Lecture 1: Incident on a Beach."

50. Ibid.

51. Ibid.

52. Inga Clendinnen, "Lecture 4: Inside the Contact Zone – Part 1," *True Stories*, ABC Boyer Lecture Series, (1999), [Transcript], http://www.abc.net.au/rn/boyers/stories/s71107.htm (accessed July 28, 2009).

53. Inga Clendinnen, "Lecture 5: Inside the Contact Zone – Part 2," *True Stories*, ABC Boyer Lecture Series, (1999), [Transcript], http://www.abc.net.au/rn/boyers/stories/s72763.htm (accessed July 28, 2009).

54. See especially Inga Clendinnen, *Reading the Holocaust* (Cambridge: Cambridge University Press, 1999); *Aztecs: An Interpretation* (Cambridge: Cambridge University Press, 1991). It is important to note here that *Reading the Holocaust* was published in the same year as Clendinnen's Boyer Lectures, and, as such, forms a part of her process of moving outside her area of professional expertise. *Reading the Holocaust* is a more clearly academic work compared with the Lectures, whereas the two projects are united by their aim of "confronting" the violence of the past through a self-conscious "imaginative" engagement.

55. Clendinnen, *Tiger's Eye*, 244.
56. Ibid., 85.
57. Ibid., 243.
58. Inga Clendinnen, "Reading Mr. Robinson," in *Seams of Light: Best Antipodean Essays*, ed. Morag Fraser (Melbourne: Allen & Unwin, 1998), 58–78.
59. Clendinnen, *Tiger's Eye*, 192.
60. Ibid., 218.
61. Whitlock, "Consuming Passions," 17.
62. Ibid., 18.
63. Clendinnen, *Dancing with Strangers*, 18.
64. Ibid., 124.
65. For an elaboration of Clendinnen's view of the historian's moral imagination, see Inga Clendinnen, "Fellow Sufferers: History and Imagination," *Australian Humanities Review* 3 (September 1996), http://www.lib.latrobe.edu.au/AHR/archive/Issue-Sept-1996/clendinnen.html (accessed May 22, 2006).
66. Clendinnen, *Dancing with Strangers*, 8.
67. Ibid., 1, 8–9.
68. Ibid., 111.
69. Ibid., 119.
70. Deirdre Coleman, "Inscrutable History or Incurable Romanticism: Inga Clendinnen's *Dancing with Strangers*," *HEAT* 8 (2004): 207.
71. Ibid., 208.
72. Clendinnen, *Dancing with Strangers*, 23.
73. Coleman, "Inscrutable History or Incurable Romanticism," 206.
74. Coleman has suggested that "the social and personal role of [Clendinnen's] historical imagination is very much in evidence in *Dancing with Strangers*," though it does not develop this observation. Ibid., 212.
75. Clendinnen, *Dancing with Strangers*, 3.
76. Robert Manne, "Shedding New Light on Australia (Review: Dancing with Strangers by Inga Clendinnen)," *Age*, October 6, 2003, 13.
77. Philip Morrissey, "Dancing with Shadows: Erasing Aboriginal Self and Sovereignty," in *Sovereign Subjects: Indigenous Sovereignty Matters*, ed. Aileen Moreton-Robinson (Sydney: Allen & Unwin, 2007), 68–69.
78. Ibid., 69–70.
79. Ann McGrath, "The Rhythm of Strangers (Review: Dancing with Strangers by Inga Clendinnen)," *Age*, November 1, 2003, 4.
80. Clendinnen, *Dancing with Strangers*, 287.
81. Ibid., 5. On Clendinnen's description of Indigenous peoples as immigrants, see Morrissey, "Dancing with Shadows: Erasing Aboriginal Self and Sovereignty," 67.
82. Clendinnen, *Dancing with Strangers*, 287.
83. Ibid., 2–3.
84. Morrissey, "Dancing with Shadows," 68.
85. Clendinnen, *History Question*, 16.
86. Ibid., 28.
87. Ibid.
88. Maral, "Warts and All."

89. Clendinnen, *History Question*, 29–37.
90. Morrissey, "Dancing with Shadows," 68.
91. Clendinnen's unwillingness to engage with the present and political implications of *Bringing them Home* is consistent with the psychoanalytic approach to testimony she developed in *Reading the Holocaust*, in which she sought to "map the silences behind the words." Clendinnen, *Reading the Holocaust*, 30.
92. In particular, Clendinnen has argued, in response to Robert Manne's *Quarterly Essay* "In Denial," that Australians should not be considered "guilty" of genocide. Inga Clendinnen, "First Contact," *Quarterly Essay*, no. 2 (2001): 105–6.
93. Schlunke, *Bluff Rock*, 11.
94. Haebich, "Between Knowing and Not Knowing."
95. Schlunke, *Bluff Rock*, 11. It is interesting to note that Clendinnen has perpetuated Reynolds' "why weren't we told?" refrain in relation to the stolen generations; whereas in her work on the Holocaust, she insisted that "I have known about Nazis for as long as I can remember." Clendinnen, *Reading the Holocaust*, 1. In this way, Clendinnen has positioned the Holocaust as an originary or an a priori site of violence and her project, not as a revelation of the event, but an attempt to know it more fully.
96. Schlunke, *Bluff Rock*, 19–21.
97. Ibid., 13.
98. Ibid., 15.
99. Katrina Schlunke and Anne Brewster, "We Four: Fictocriticism Again," *Continuum: Journal of Media & Cultural Studies* 19, no. 3 (2005): 393.
100. Ibid. For an overview on debates concerning the "origins" and institutional home/s of fictocriticism, see Scott Brook, "Does Anybody Know What Happened to 'Fictocriticism'?: Toward a Fractual Genealogy of Australian Fictocriticism," *Cultural Studies Review* 8, no. 2 (November 2002).
101. Schlunke and Brewster, "We Four," 393–94.
102. See especially Alison Bartlett, "Dear Regina: Formative Conversations About Feminist Writing," *FemTAP: A Journal of Feminist Theory and Practice* (summer 2006), http://www.femtap.com/id14.html (accessed August 14, 2008); Anna Gibbs, "Fictocriticism, Affect, Mimesis: Engendering Differences," *TEXT* 9, no. 1 (2005); Anna Gibbs, "Writing and the Flesh of Others," *Australian Feminist Studies* 18, no. 42 (2003); Heather Kerr, "Fictocritical Empathy and the Work of Mourning," *Cultural Studies Review* 9, no. 1 (May 2003): 180–200; Stephen Muecke, "The Fall: Fictocritical Writing," *Parallax* 8, no. 4 (2002): 108–12; Heather Kerr, "Sympathetic Topographies," *Parallax* 7, no. 2 (2001): 107–26; Heather Kerr and Amanda Nettelbeck, eds., *The Space Between: Australian Women Writing Fictocriticism* (Nedlands: University of Western Australia Press, 1998). Muecke, *No Road (Bitumen All the Way)*.
103. Schlunke, *Bluff Rock*, 16.
104. Ibid., 90.
105. Ibid., 14.
106. Ibid.
107. Ibid., 17.

108. Eve Lamborn, "The Historical Blends with the Personal (Review of *Bluff Rock: Autobiography of a Massacre*)," *Antipodes* 20, no. 2 (2006): 212.
109. Maria Nugent, "Review of *Bluff Rock: Autobiography of a Massacre*," *Australian Historical Studies* 37, no. 128 (2006): 147.
110. Schlunke, *Bluff Rock*, 16.
111. Ibid.
112. On the "invisibility" of whiteness, see particularly Richard Dyer, *White* (New York: Routledge, 1997); Aileen Moreton-Robinson, *Talkin' up to the White Woman: Aboriginal Women and Feminism* (Brisbane: University of Queensland Press, 2000); Ruth Frankenberg, *White Women, Race Matters: The Social Construction of Whiteness* (Minneapolis: University of Minnesota Press, 1993).
113. Schlunke, *Bluff Rock*, 227.
114. Ibid., 235.
115. Ibid.
116. Nicoll, "Indigenous Sovereignty and the Violence of Perspective," 381–82.
117. Westcott, "Witnessing Whiteness," 2.
118. Nicoll, "Indigenous Sovereignty and the Violence of Perspective," 369.
119. Radstone, "Cultures of Confession/Cultures of Testimony," 171. See also Radstone, *Sexual Politics of Time*.
120. Nicoll, "Indigenous Sovereignty and the Violence of Perspective," 279–82.
121. Aileen Moreton-Robinson cited in Ibid., 381.
122. Westcott, "Witnessing Whiteness," 48.
123. Ibid., 1.
124. Schlunke, *Bluff Rock*, 199.
125. Ibid., 205.
126. Ibid., 242.
127. Italics in original. Lyn McCredden, "Writing Authority in Australia," in *The Ideas Market: An Alternative Take on Australia's Intellectual Life*, ed. David Carter (Melbourne: Melbourne University Press, 2004), 94, 92.
128. See especially Robert Perks and Alistair Thomson, eds., *The Oral History Reader* (London and New York: Routledge, 2006); Alistair Thomson, "Sharing Authority: Oral History and the Collaborative Process," *Oral History Review* 30, no. 1 (2003): 23–26; Michael H. Frisch, *A Shared Authority: Essays on the Craft and Meaning of Oral and Public History* (Albany: State University of New York Press, 1990); Lorraine Sitzia, "A Shared Authority: An Impossible Goal?," *Oral History Review* 30, no. 1 (2003): 87–101.
129. Ross Gibson, *Seven Versions of an Australian Badland* (St. Lucia: University of Queensland Press, 2002); Muecke, "The Fall: Fictocritical Writing." Rose, *Dingo Makes Us Human*; Heather Goodall, "Telling Country: Memory, Modernity and Narratives in Rural Australia," *History Workshop Journal* no. 47 (1999): 161–88; Muecke, *No Road (Bitumen All the Way)*; Rose, *Hidden Histories*.
130. Rachel Perkins and Beck Cole (dirs.), *First Australians* (Australia: Special Broadcasting Service Corporation & Madman Entertainment, 2008).

See also the companion book produced alongside the series Rachel Perkins and Marcia Langton, eds., *First Australians: An Illustrated History* (Melbourne: Melbourne University Press, 2008).

131. SBS, "About the Series," *First Australians* (2008), http://www.sbs.com.au/firstaustralians/about (accessed December 12, 2009).
132. Birch, "Testimony," 32.

4

Witnessing UnAustralia: Asylum-Seeker Advocacy and the National Good

In the middle of the night I looked down from the bridge. There's two hatches open and it's hot. Through one I could see 100 people lying there on stretchers; I thought, it's like a slave ship. I thought, Jesus, I thought we were Australians, I thought we were a great, good bloody country . . . If Australia continues down this political path, it will be like apartheid here and people will think that's what we do here but it's not what we should do.

—Anonymous Officer from the HMAS *Tobruk*[1]

UnAustralia—this mean and fearful place—is a country I barely recognise.

—John Frow[2]

In 2004, Australian *Big Brother* contestant Merlin Luck staged a protest in support of asylum seekers during his eviction from the popular reality television program. On leaving the *Big Brother* "compound," Luck refused to participate in the planned live exit interview. Instead, he taped his mouth shut and held up a crudely assembled sign proclaiming "FREE TH REFUGEES."[3] Luck was the first, in both Australian and overseas versions of the program, to successfully subvert the *Big Brother* format for a political end. His "political gimmick" not only worked to counter claims that contemporary "young people" were apolitical and apathetic, but also brought the subject of the mandatory detention of asylum seekers to one of television's highest-rating entertainment programs.[4] Though he was met with jeers from numerous audience members and open hostility from the show's host, Gretel Killeen, Luck's actions were captivating—his determined silence echoing the voicelessness of asylum seekers.

Although Luck refused to speak during his *Big Brother* interview, he later spoke freely about his stunt, confirming that it had been his sole motivation for joining the program.[5] Coming three years after the *Tampa* crisis and the 2001 federal election, Luck's actions sought to refocus public attention on Australia's treatment of asylum seekers and refugees, "to get it back on the political agenda."[6] In doing so, Luck was acutely aware of his role as witness to, and advocate for, asylum seekers, and attuned to the symbolic power of his act. "Honestly," he admitted, "it's been the most powerful moment of my life so far."[7] Luck's comments drew attention to the role of witnessing as both an important method of social and political protest, and a "powerful" instrument of identity formation for the secondary witness.

In sharp contrast to the modes of witnessing that emerged in response to Indigenous testimony, Luck's actions highlighted the extent to which asylum-seeker witnessing developed in response to the paucity of asylum-seeker testimony. As a result, the practice became, largely, a process of speaking on behalf of the voiceless. Luck's actions were paradigmatic of the so-called "new wave" of asylum-seeker advocacy that began in 2001. Thereafter, a diverse range of asylum seeker and refugee support groups "sprang up spontaneously across Australia" to contest the federal government's policy of mandatory detention.[8] While human rights and church organizations had been active in challenging the policy since its inception in 1992, from 2001, "ordinary" Australians became actively and visibly engaged in forms of protest and advocacy on behalf of asylum seekers.

This chapter considers the role of the secondary witness as advocate, "speaking for" and in the place of asylum seekers. Throughout this chapter, I use the terms "advocate" and "witness" interchangeably. Though "advocate" is the most common term used to describe people engaged in material efforts to assist asylum seekers, I understand this behavior, even where it does not bring advocates into direct contact with testimony, as a mode of witnessing. Housed in remote desert and island detention centers, asylum seekers had little access to legal counsel and medical assistance, let alone the media networks that would be essential to disseminating their testimony to the public.[9] Consequently, it was only through the efforts of advocates that asylum-seeker stories were made audible, primarily through letters exchanged with individuals in detention. Advocates served as witnesses to asylum seekers by listening to their experiences—both of detention and of persecution in their home countries—and they also worked as collaborators in the act of testifying. Typically, advocates edited and translated asylum seekers' stories for circulation on the Internet and in anthologies.

Alongside these texts, advocates spoke of their own experiences with asylum seekers, producing a discourse in which witnessing to asylum seekers was figured as a mode of protest against the Howard-led Liberal Coalition Government. However, more than this, advocates frequently described their experiences in terms of protecting so-called "core" Australian values. To work with asylum seekers and to witness their stories was to act in the spirit of the fair go, and enact the values of egalitarianism and decency. This chapter examines the writings of asylum-seeker witnesses—their testimony to the experience of secondary witnessing—particularly the texts collected in the anthology *Acting from the Heart*, and those included as a part of the People's Inquiry into Detention.[10] In doing so, I consider the process of collaboration in the production of asylum-seeker testimony, as well as the use of testimony as a mode of witnessing to the experience of advocacy. In particular, I analyze the way that witnessing to asylum seekers has come to be understood by a vocal minority as a mode of being a "good" Australian.

Witnessing the Settler Nation

While Australian Indigenous peoples and asylum seekers occupy differing structural relationships to the settler nation, the testimony of both groups has unsettled public culture and drawn many to reconsider Australia's treatment of minority groups.[11] Crucially, the testimony and life writing of both groups has intervened in public discourses on history, memory, and social justice, and has served as a prompt to a range of witnessing activities.

In a broader sense, the relationship between both groups and the settler nation lies at the heart of recent debates over citizenship and belonging. This has been particularly evident since 2001, a period that saw the positioning of both the boat arrivals of asylum seekers and Indigenous land rights as infringements on the sovereignty of the settler state.[12] Accordingly, the issues of Aboriginal rights and immigration have been central to competing discourses on contemporary Australian nationalism, and, in fact, have been central to the production of Australian citizenship throughout the nation's history.[13] In particular, both groups have been the focus of the concerns of what Ghassan Hage has termed the "White worrier," the person who attempts to "reassert a sense of governmental power over the nation through their worrying," about migrants, about Indigenous people, *ad infinitum*.[14] However, the converse is also true: Both Indigenous peoples and asylum seekers have been the focus of those settler Australians eager to practice forms of being Australian that have included, and embraced the concerns of, non-Anglo Australians.

This book understands practices of witnessing to Indigenous Australians and asylum seekers as responding to the specificities of distinct and separate testimonies and events. However, at the same time, it underscores the extent to which these practices have overlapped in their concerns with history, nation, and settler belonging. That is, discourse on witnessing as civic virtue has been deployed in relation to both Indigenous and migrant/refugee testimonies and has reproduced the settler listener as "good" through their performance of witnessing. This chapter not only considers asylum-seeker witnessing as a discrete case study, but also works to clarify the problematics of settler witnessing more broadly as a mode of (re)building the liberal-multicultural nation that elides the specificities of "minority" testimony.

2001: The Asylum-Seeker Crises

The year 2001 saw what Mark Davis has described as "a change in the Australian race debate."[15] Though reconciliation and the meanings of Indigenous stories dominated Australian public culture for most of the 1990s, during 2001, a series of immigration "crises" brought refugees and asylum seekers to the forefront of political debate.[16] First, in late August 2001, the Norwegian container ship *MV Tampa* rescued 438 asylum seekers from the dilapidated *Palapa*. The asylum seekers, most fleeing oppression in Afghanistan and Iraq, were headed for Christmas Island, an Australian territory closer to Indonesia than Australia in the Indian Ocean. Determined to prevent the asylum seekers from reaching Christmas Island—and thus making a claim for refuge from an Australian territory—the government hastily devised what became known as the "Pacific Solution," in which some asylum seekers were delivered to New Zealand and the rest were sent to Nauru and other small Pacific nations for detention and "processing" at Australian expense.[17]

The second crisis, the so-called "children overboard" affair, occurred in October during the pre-election period. Despite being in possession of information to the contrary, the government repeatedly asserted that a group of asylum seekers had thrown their children from a boat in a ploy to secure rescue and admittance to the Australian territories.[18] For Philip Ruddock, then minister for immigration, the reported actions formed "some of the most disturbing practices that I have come across in the time I have been involved in public life."[19] As such, the event was leveraged into a broader discussion over the cynicism of "boat people" and the worthiness of asylum seekers of Australian support. The third event, which also occurred during the October election campaign, was the sinking of the so-called SIEVX (Suspected Illegal Entry Vessel X) in international waters between Australia and Indonesia. More than 300 asylum seekers were drowned, many of whom were children.[20] Together these incidents, along with the events of September 11 in the United States, brought asylum seekers, immigration, and security more broadly, decisively into the spotlight.

These three "crises" formed the centerpiece of the 2001 federal election campaign in which border protection and antiterrorism served as the Howard Government's key platforms. For the government, asylum seekers were "illegals" or "queue jumpers" who attempted to circumvent Australia's established immigration practices.[21] The government elided their claims for refugee status by demonizing asylum seekers as privileged individuals who sought not safety from persecution, but a "migration outcome." This was a phrase used especially by Ruddock to refer to those asylum seekers who sought not "temporary protection" but to resettle permanently in Australia. For example, in 2001, Ruddock greeted the possibility of an HREOC inquiry into Australia's treatment of children in detention with the words: "[To stop detaining children] would enable more children to be used by those intent on achieving migration outcomes and getting outcomes to which they might not otherwise be entitled."[22]

Crucially, Howard justified his government's decision to prevent the *Tampa* from entering Australia by drawing on the principles of national sovereignty and humanitarianism:

> We have indicated to the captain that permission to land in Australia will not be granted to this vessel . . . Australia has sought on all occasions to balance against the undoubted right of this country to decide who comes here and in what circumstances, a right that any sovereign nation has, our humanitarian obligations as a warm-hearted, decent international citizen.[23]

Against the claims of refugee activists who beseeched the government to assist asylum seekers as the moral duty of a liberal democratic state, Ruddock too conceptualized the government's refusal to help as a moral act. Speaking about an influx of "boat people" in July 2001, Ruddock argued that

> I could characterise the task for both of us in familiar terms of doing good and fighting evil. The good is extending our compassion and welcome to refugees who have no other option. The fight against evil is against the exploitation by people smugglers of people desirous of a better life and the resultant abuse and distortion of the system that has been set up to support refugees.[24]

Here, both Ruddock and Howard positioned the government's stance on boat arrivals as a part of a broader moral response to the abuse of the immigration system perpetuated by unscrupulous people smugglers. Both worked to affirm a (self)perception of Australia as a "warm-hearted" country, attentive to the claims of refugees, at the same time as they justified the detention and rejection of asylum seekers as a part of the exercise of responsible government.[25]

If the government sought to position their response as the dutiful work of a "good" nation, for many, the re-election of the Howard Government in November was confirmation that the majority of Australians agreed with their government's treatment of asylum seekers.[26] As one MP noted enthusiastically:

> I've never had an issue in my political career . . . which has made so many people come up to me in the street, without any urging whatsoever, and say, "Don't back away". When John Howard put his foot down and said "keep out!", the people of Australia roared their collective approval.[27]

It is the aim of this chapter to trace the work of those Australians whose voices, though small in number, sought to counter this collective roar.

A Vocal Minority: Resistance to Mandatory Detention

Although the mandatory detention of asylum seekers had been introduced by the Keating Labor Government in 1992, as Peter Mares has asserted, after *Tampa*, "the rules of the refugee game in Australia were completely re-cast."[28] The events of 2001 brought several crucial changes to the way asylum seekers were managed by the government.[29] Most important of these were the introduction of offshore detention and "processing" for all unauthorized boat arrivals, and the excision of Christmas, Cartier and the Cocos (Keeling) Islands, and Ashmore Reef, from the Australian migration zone. This entailed a literal "re-mapping" of the nation space and a proliferation of sites that Suvendrini Perera has described as "not Australia."[30]

Not only did these changes embroil the government in complex relationships with several small Pacific nations, but they also marked a "hardening" of immigration policy designed to police Australia's borders with little recourse to avenues of review. These changes attracted the criticism of the United Nations (UN) and human rights organizations that attacked the government's treatment of asylum seekers in detention as deeply inhumane.[31] Crucially, in 2002, UN human rights envoy Prafullachandra Bhagwati found that the detention of children at Woomera in South Australia was "certainly contrary to international standards."[32]

Though he was returned at the 2001 federal election on a "tough" border protection platform, Howard eventually came under criticism even from those within his own party. In June 2005 a selection of self-described "moderates," led by Victorian MP Petro Georgiou, succeeded in securing a "softening" of immigration policy. According to Georgiou, the changes were "a tribute to the persistent and tenacious advocacy of thousands of Australian citizens."[33] Though the Liberal leadership and the majority of Australians supported mandatory detention and the Pacific Solution, Georgiou found allies in a "significant section of the community"; advocates who cared "passionately about the impact of our nation's policies on the individuals most immediately affected by them: asylum seekers and refugees."[34]

In contrast to the issue of reconciliation, which, as demonstrated in Chapter One, attracted solid, albeit fluctuating, levels of support, opinion polling undertaken shortly after the *Tampa* crisis indicated that 77 percent of Australians "agreed or strongly agreed with the government's policy of preventing asylum seeker boats from entering Australian waters."[35] This could be compared with 18 percent who disagreed or strongly disagreed.[36] Murray Goot has undertaken a comprehensive review of opinion polling in the lead-up to the 2001 election.[37] Though polling in early 2001 suggested that it was unlikely that the Howard Government would be returned, polls on the eve of the election indicated the reverse. Goot's work has considered meticulously the numerous polls undertaken throughout 2001, with particular attention to the significant impact of *Tampa* on popular support for the government.

This opposition of Australians to asylum seekers should not be surprising, given the general population's unfamiliarity with refugees. As James Jupp has argued:

> between 1972 and 2000 almost 400 000 [people] arrived under various refugee and humanitarian programs for permanent settlement. With their predecessors and their locally born children, this means that about 5 per cent of Australians have some direct experience of the refugee situation.[38]

By 2004, however, the situation had somewhat changed, with 54.4 percent of those polled strongly agreeing with the policy of "turning back all boats."[39] This sat against a figure of 28 percent who "disagreed or strongly disagreed."[40] Linda Briskman, Susie Latham, and Chris Goddard have argued that this change should be ascribed, at least partly, to the involvement of "ordinary" Australians in various forms of activism and advocacy during the intervening period.[41] This view is echoed by Diane Gosden, though she has been careful to emphasize that despite some changes in public opinion, support for refugees remained a minority view.[42]

Though polling only suggested a small shift in public opinion regarding asylum seekers, the birth of myriad asylum-seeker advocacy groups from 2001 indicated that a general shift in mood took place. In response to the *Tampa* crisis, a range of advocacy groups developed to support asylum seekers, most notably ChilOut: Children Out of Detention, A Just Australia, Rural Australians for Refugees and Spare Rooms for Refugees.[43] Numerous individuals began to visit asylum seekers at detention centers, to offer support and to assist people with their refuge claims. Others wrote letters, engaged in fundraising, and participated in forms of online advocacy. In outlining Australia's opposition to asylum seekers, and immigration more broadly, Jupp argued that

> at the heart of opposition to refugees has been lack of experiences and understanding, rather than racism or even xenophobia. Most of the Australian-born have lived very sheltered lives, including most politicians and public servants.

They cannot be expected to fully understand experiences which they have never witnessed . . . [44]

Here, Jupp signaled the power of witnessing to assist understanding and change opinions. Other commentators have highlighted the authority of witnessing to change public perceptions, with Briskman et al arguing that the Australian public's assent to Howard's treatment of asylum seekers was only sustained because of the lack of information about mandatory detention made available to the public.[45] That is, negative opinions of asylum seekers were formed not only in the almost virtual absence of their voices from the public sphere, but also from a deliberate lack of information about conditions in detention centers.

As I demonstrate through a reading of the testimony of asylum-seeker advocates, the process of witnessing to the experiences of asylum seekers had a profound impact on the lives of many Australians. To be sure, this group remained a minority, but a vocal minority who came to position witnessing as not only a humane response to the suffering of asylum seekers, but also a mode of reinvigorating the nation. This discourse had much in common with the practices of witnessing that supported reconciliation, in both its understanding of witnessing as a mode of "good" Australianness and its privileging of the figure of the Anglo witness as arbiter of national morality.

Asylum-Seeker Testimony

From 2001, a range of texts featuring asylum-seeker testimony began to appear. Hitherto, little information about detention centers was publicly available, and refugee voices were largely absent from the public sphere.[46] Chief among these "new" asylum publications was Heather Tyler's *Asylum* and Julian Burnside's *From Nothing to Zero: Letters from Refugees in Australia's Detention Centres.*[47] These appeared alongside a range of television programs and Web sites designed to highlight the voices of asylum seekers. Most notable among these was the ABC television program *Four Corners'* feature on Shayan Badraie, which aired in August 2001, and follow-up stories on life in detention centers. The story of the then six-year-old Badraie, which depicted the child in a catatonic state in detention, has been oft cited by refugee advocates as a crucial moment in their journey to advocacy.[48]

These texts not only worked to bring asylum-seeker testimony into public circulation but also foregrounded the role of advocates as collaborators in the production of testimony. This collaboration frequently took the form of letter writing, as in Julian Burnside's *From Nothing to Zero*, in which the letters of advocates functioned to elicit the testimony of asylum seekers through the cycle of writing and replying.[49] As a QC and activist, Julian Burnside has performed a range of public intellectual work on behalf of asylum seekers, including editing *From Nothing to Zero*, and providing introductions and forwards to several other anthologies.[50] He has come to be a crucial figure in discourses on asylum-seeker witnessing, performing a similar role to that of Robert Manne in relation to Aboriginal reconciliation.

Only the letters from detainees appear in *From Nothing to Zero*, providing a one-sided record of the letter-writing exchange. These have been heavily edited by Burnside and arranged to illustrate specific "themes" of asylum-seeker experience, such as "Mental Anguish in Detention" and "Children in Detention."[51] Burnside's work demonstrated the role of advocates in establishing a relationship with individual detainees to enable the dissemination of asylum-seeker testimony through broader networks.

The letters not only provide a space for asylum seekers to speak, but they have also highlighted the way that letter writing has acted as a process of self-fashioning for the secondary witness. Letters have served as a forum through which advocates have made contact with asylum seekers, but this experience has also been transformative of the writer's sense of self, remaking the author as a compassionate activist. The role of letter writing in the life of activists has been chronicled by Clara Law's 2004 film *Letters to Ali*, which focused on the relationship forged by Australian doctor Trish Kirby, her family, and a fifteen-year-old Afghani refugee.[52] Prevented from filming "Ali" inside the Port Hedland detention center, Law instead shadowed the family on their road trip to visit Ali, mixing footage of the landscape with interviews. The experience of letter writing is represented as profoundly transforming for Trish and her family, enacting a process of witnessing that remakes "ordinary" Australians as advocates. The absence of footage of Ali not only serves to heighten the audience's connection and identification with Trish as (extra)ordinary citizen(s), but also underscores the role of advocates as a lifeline for detainees with little access to the outside world.

As we have seen in relation to Indigenous peoples' testimony, forms of testimony and life writing are always mediated and edited, and are often the product of highly asymmetrical collaborative relationships. As Kate Douglas has argued, the mediated presence of testimony in the public sphere, particularly its dissemination through edited collections, demonstrates the extent to which the circulation of asylum-seeker voices has been dependent on the work of advocates. While Douglas has noted "that it is the voices of the white Australian witnesses that are heard more often on these issues than those of asylum seekers," she maintains that "these interventions have demonstrably valuable results."[53] For Douglas, the collation of testimony has been an important part of the process of bearing witness to the experience of asylum seekers. In paraphrasing their testimony, or releasing their letters to the public, many advocates have understood their actions as an integral part of their response-ability to asylum seekers. Although the dependence of the asylum seeker on the secondary witness can indeed result in the virtual erasure of the asylum seeker as the subject of asylum-seeker testimony—as in *Letters to Ali*—it has only been through the advocate that asylum-seeker voices, albeit paraphrased and edited, have reached the public sphere.

Parallels can be drawn between the work of asylum-seeker advocates and those Anglo-Australians who assisted several foundational Indigenous women's writers to publish their life stories. Jennifer Jones has examined the relationships forged between three key Indigenous authors—Oodgeroo Noonuccal, Margaret Tucker, and Monica Clare—and their "communities of commitment," typically political or religious groups who supported the women in the writing, editing, and publishing of their life narratives.[54] Jones has chronicled the nuanced relationships formed between these writers and their supporters, but at the same time has drawn attention to the potential pitfalls of these arrangements and their tendency to perpetuate unequal power relationships between writers and editors.[55] Though highly critical of the outcomes of many encounters between Indigenous writers and white editors, Jones has ultimately acknowledged the benefits of cross-racial collaboration in the production of life narrative, with the caveat that more needs to be done to establish "best practice" principles to guide the transmission of life writing.[56]

Refugee advocacy groups similarly formed "communities of commitment" that not only supported asylum seekers emotionally and materially, but also facilitated the transition of their testimony to the public sphere: editing and shaping their words as needed. Tyler, editor of *Asylum*, has understood the role of the secondary witness in these terms. For Tyler, the secondary witness exists to aid the circulation of the asylum seeker's story, and their actions respond to the needs of the asylum seekers accordingly. "What they most wanted was a platform," she has argued, "any platform, to tell their stories and of their treatment within the detention system."[57] Tyler has insisted that most asylum seekers did not "comprehend . . . a book's influences" and were primarily concerned just to express their story to an active listener.[58] Though her testifiers might not have been concerned with her book, Tyler positioned her collection as part of her response-ability as a secondary witness. This ability to pass on and disseminate asylum-seeker stories came to be understood by many advocates as a crucial way to assist the cause of asylum seekers.

The People's Inquiry into Detention

Alongside a range of specific letter writing programs and anthologies of testimony, one group of advocates undertook the task of conducting a large-scale inquiry into the treatment of asylum seekers. This inquiry, convened by a group of social work academics, sought to witness to the experiences of asylum seekers by hearing their evidence in the context of an investigation into the policy of mandatory detention. Though the Howard Government established inquiries into the wrongful deten- tion of Australian resident Cornelia Rau and the unlawful deportation of Vivian Solon, these reviews were focused only on the treatment of specific individuals and not on the affects of the policy of mandatory detention more generally.[59] In 2005, the Australian Council of Heads of Social Work established the People's Inquiry into Detention in re- sponse to the narrow terms of reference given to the Palmer review.[60] The Inquiry was conceived as an act of protest against the Howard Government's treatment of asylum seekers and "based on a view that ordinary Australians have an obligation to act when our government is unwilling to. . . ."[61] It was designed to shed light on processes that had been deliberately hidden from the general public and "shrouded in official secrecy."[62]

This citizen-led inquiry undertook the task of collecting both verbal and written accounts of detention from former detainees, advocates, medical professionals, educators, detention center employees, for- mer government officials, migration agents, and lawyers. The inquiry traveled around Australia to receive evidence, following a template established by major government-run inquiries such as *Bringing them Home* and the Royal Commission into Black Deaths in Custody. The People's Inquiry was also similar to these prior inquiries in its symbolic resonance; it sought to offer the "voiceless" a forum to speak.

The majority of the evidence received by the Inquiry focused on the experiences of asylum seekers who arrived by boat and were detained under the policy of mandatory detention between 1999 and 2002. As the report noted, of the more than 12,000 people detained, more than 11,000 were eventually recognized as refugees.[63] The final report of the Inquiry, *Human Rights Overboard: Seeking Asylum in Australia*, was released in 2008 and was designed to serve as a permanent record of the suffering experienced by asylum seekers under the policy and practice of mandatory detention.

In contrast to the anthologies of Tyler and Burnside, which largely serve as forums for asylum seekers to speak of the persecution they have suffered in their home countries, the Inquiry sought to gather evidence specifically about life in mandatory detention. As such, the report meticulously details life under the policy, with a particular focus on outlining living conditions within the detention centers and the restrictions to medical services and legal counsel imposed by management.[64] Similar to the *Bringing them Home* inquiry, the People's Inquiry positioned the act of testifying as important to the mental health of participants and highlighted the "major therapeutic benefits to those directly affected by the policies."[65] As the first citizen-led inquiry of its type conducted in Australia, the Inquiry represented a remarkable act of "ordinary" witnessing and was undertaken almost entirely by volunteers. In mimicking the mechanics of a Royal Commission or HREOC inquiry, the People's Inquiry functioned as a mode of speaking back to the government. By performing a task that is associated, in democratic nations, with the government—protecting and upholding the principles of human rights—the Inquiry explicitly criticized Howard's administration.

Similar to the work of Tyler and Burnside, who acted as collaborators in the production and circulation of asylum-seeker testimony, the Inquiry understood the task of collecting testimony as empowering the voiceless. The Inquiry explicitly framed its final report in this way, positioning the process as one that "gave voice to many people who had been silenced."[66] Although the aim of the Inquiry was to document the experiences of asylum seekers under detention, the Inquiry also gathered evidence about the experience of asylum-seeker advocates. The Inquiry portrayed advocates as exemplary citizens who defied the Howard Government, individuals who "connected with asylum seekers as human beings through each stage of their journey."[67]

However, in detailing the experiences of asylum-seeker advocates, the Inquiry also underscored their social privilege vis-à-vis asylum seekers and pointed to the inherent asymmetry in their relationships with detainees. Some advocates spoke of their distress at having their own words and acts of protest ignored by government figures. As one advocate despaired:

> I have rung the prime minister's office so many times and I have hit a brick wall. No one has acted and I think that is absolutely disgraceful. When people like me were going into detention and were seeing this damage and were notifying them, they had the power to change that policy, to hear people like me.[68]

Though this advocate vented their frustration at being rebuffed by the government, their awareness of the importance of "people like me" highlighted the extent to which asylum-seeker testimony was facilitated by the work of middle-class "ordinary" Australians, and the social, cultural, and political power that this subject position has accrued. Although advocates were frequently ignored by the government, their ability to access avenues of government complaint and the media highlighted their crucial role in communicating stories about detention to the general public.

Though this relationship is not without its complications, common to all acts of advocacy, the power of advocates to circulate asylum-seeker testimony, when asylum seekers themselves struggled to, affirmed the ongoing necessity of "speaking for" the socially and politically marginalized. The notion of "speaking for" has been a highly contested concept within a range of fields, most particularly within the context of feminist and postcolonial criticism.[69] Gilles Deleuze has drawn attention to what he has described as the "indignity of speaking for others," whereas Spivak has challenged the "self-abnegation" of intellectuals such as Deleuze and Foucault as defeatist, and in fact, a key mode of perpetuating their cultural and political authority in relation to others.[70] Many asylum seeker advocates have reflected on the process of their advocacy through a focus on their own privilege and, in doing so, have sought to ameliorate the colonizing and infantilizing risks of "speaking for."

Many advocates were Australians with a relative sociocultural privilege, and several advocates relayed their own testimony of mental suffering to the Inquiry. As one advocate wrote:

once you've been into Baxter it takes over your life. It's like nothing else is more important. That obligation keeps you going beyond your burnout and I think you'd have to say that that equals a mental-health problem. That's a combination of things-sadness, shame, lack of sleep, anxiety, absolute fear that your friends will be deported and there's nothing you can do.[71]

By providing a space for advocates to speak about their own experiences, rather than simply relaying or paraphrasing the testimony of others, the Inquiry allowed advocates to give voice to the personal costs of advocacy. Some advocates spoke of being exhausted by the process of supporting asylum seekers, whereas others expressed more complex psychological distress produced by their vicarious contact with trauma and acts of violence. For example, when recalling being interviewed about their experience of advocacy, one advocate simply "broke down": "it wasn't until halfway through that interview that I realized maybe I was carrying around an awful, great weight myself, psychologically underneath, because halfway through the interview, I just broke down and cried, and couldn't stop it."[72] In this way, the Inquiry served not only as a space for asylum-seeker stories to be told, but also as a forum for advocates to reflect on the often high personal costs of being involved in advocacy and "recover" themselves.

Acting from the Heart

Although the People's Inquiry drew on the testimony of advocates, it did so, primarily, as a way of gathering information about the conditions of life for asylum seekers in detention. In contrast, *Acting from the Heart*, a collection of advocate testimony released in 2007, foregrounded the experience of the secondary witness. Edited by psychiatrists Sarah Mares and Louise Newman, *Acting from the Heart* included more than fifty stories from asylum-seeker advocates, each detailing the reasons that they became involved in asylum-seeker support networks. The contributions are generically diverse; some take the form of poetry, fictional prose, or cartoons, but the majority are fragmentary, first-person accounts testifying to the contributors' experiences of working as advocates. Based on a number of writing workshops organized by Mares and Newman, the collection was designed to provide advocates with a space to explore "the stresses and vicarious trauma" that they had experienced in their work with asylum seekers.[73] Unlike texts in which the advocate appears as a collaborator or a facilitator in the production of an asylum seeker's testimony, here the secondary witness and their testimony is brought to the fore.

Similar to many of the advocates interviewed for the People's Inquiry, the contributors to *Acting from the Heart* understood the transmission of asylum-seeker testimony as central to their work as advocates. As one contributor, Jessica Perini, wrote, "there are some tales I don't wish to recall because they are too painful [but] I believe that things won't change until the story is told."[74] Here, witnessing to the trauma of others was figured as a vehicle for broader social change. Yet, crucially, this was a social movement comprising the "ordinary" and "suburban."[75] In an effort to counter the government's understanding of advocates as "elite" or "intellectual," disconnected from the concerns (and fears) of the "ordinary people," Mares and Newman positioned their contributors as "everyday people responding to extraordinary circumstances."[76] This was a strategic move that worked to figure advocacy as a vernacular, everyday form of witnessing.

Though contributors are understood as "ordinary" Australians, Mares and Newman have figured their work as explicitly political. They have argued that "to help an asylum seeker who is being harmed by flawed and morally bankrupt government policy is a political act."[77] In particular, contributors wrote of their advocacy as a way of challenging what they viewed as the "erosion" of Australian values by the Howard Government. They sought to reclaim Australia's image as "the land of the fair go."[78] "Individuals came together," wrote Mares and Newman,

> with a common sense of disbelief and outrage that acts of cruelty were undertaken by elected representatives in their name, and that "Australian values" now seemed to include callous self-interest and a disregard for human suffering. The refugee question has essentially become a moral debate and, for some, a way of redefining not just Australian values, but what are essentially human values.[79]

Thus, witnessing to asylum seekers figured not only as an act of political resistance—a way of participating in a subversive discourse on compassion and neighborliness—but also as a way of staying true to the core values of Australian society. If mandatory detention had been justified by the federal government with reference to the protection of "the Australian way of life," the witnesses in *Acting from the Heart* frequently explained their actions in similar terms.[80]

Witnessing UnAustralia

Similar to much refugee activism worldwide, the work of Australian witnesses drew on transnational understandings of human rights. However, at the same time, these rights were positioned within discourses on so-called "Australian values." One contributor to *Acting from the Heart*, Frances Milne, described her advocacy as an extension of her love for Australia: "I love my country and I know what has happened and what is happening to asylum seekers." Similarly, the authors of the People's Inquiry framed their work as an attack on the policy of mandatory detention, which they understood as "diametrically opposed" to the concept of the fair go and other foundational national concepts.[81]

By linking the personal and the national, refugee advocates contextualized the work of witnessing as a process that not only protested the government's actions, but also did so because it understood those actions as contrary to an Australian spirit of generosity and decency. One advocate encapsulated the nexus between human rights and national morality in precisely this way:

> I'm one of the "new wave" of refugee supporters. With a sense of shame, I can say that a few years ago, I knew nothing about refugees. But when you come face to face with them, that was a different experience. And then it's impossible to just forget about it and move on. Because these are real human beings who have come from terrible experiences, but then to get to my country and being treated just unnecessary terribly and unjustly. In some ways it's a sense of duty. Absolute duty.[82]

This advocate framed witnessing to asylum seekers both as a response to the universalized themes of humanity and decency, as well as an action designed to counter the unjust treatment that asylum seekers have experienced in "my country." This sense of personal implication in the government's inhospitable response to asylum seekers illustrated the advocate's ownership over concepts of Australianness.

In this way, witnessing was figured explicitly as an act of citizenship, a "duty" that when performed contributed to the civic virtue of contemporary Australian society. This has been echoed by another advocate cited in *Acting from the Heart*, Lynette Chaikin, who understood her work as a performance of national feeling: "I had to apologise to them and welcome them to my country."[83] In acting to support asylum seekers, many secondary witnesses also acted to change the perception of "my country." In doing so, they demonstrated their ownership over concepts of Australianness, positioning themselves as citizens whose actions could revive the concept of the "fair go" appropriated by the Howard Government.

Crucial to an understanding of asylum-seeker advocacy as an act of civic virtue was the rhetorical positioning of Australia's past as a period of generosity toward outsiders. One advocate explained their work to the People's Inquiry as a response to their realization that Australia was no longer the land of the fair go. "Since 2001," they wrote, "I have had to move from believing that the worst excesses were overseas or back in history, and come to an understanding that Australians are as capable as anyone on earth of bigotry, racism and the ability to ignore injustice."[84] Similarly, Julian Burnside in his introduction to Tyler's *Asylum* wrote that

> This is a timely book, but a discomforting one. It shows what we have become. There was a time when Australia was a good-natured country. There was a time when Australians understood, and responded to, the suffering of others.
>
> Then something went wrong.[85]

Here, Burnside gestured toward a kind of prelapsarian fair go, an imaginary, historical national space in which Australia functioned as a beacon to the wretched. The figure of Malcolm Fraser, the last Liberal prime minister before Howard, and outspoken critic of his government's treatment of asylum seekers and refugees, has been particularly central to the perpetuation of this idea.[86] Fraser's presence in public debate not only provided a stark counterpoint to contemporary Liberal party immigration policy, but also located Australia's lost humanitarianism in the near past as the term of his government, between 1975 and 1983, remained firmly with the living memory of most adult Australians.

Yet, as Klaus Neumann has argued, "the evocation of a golden age when Australians welcomed those fleeing persecution and their government played a key role in alleviating the plight of refugees worldwide, is based on a selective, somewhat inaccurate reading of the past."[87] Through an analysis of Australia's response to asylum seekers in the period before 1973, Neumann demonstrated that Australia has typically admitted refugees as a part of broader nation-building projects; for example, in order to expand the population or to bolster the labor force. Thus, the overriding motivating factor for the government in the selection of refugees has not been their need for assistance, but whether they possessed the qualities, especially the racial qualities, the government desired.[88] By way of conclusion, Neumann asserted that it was not the Howard Government's response to asylum seekers that was unprecedented, rather "what is unprecedented is the willingness of many ordinary Australians in the last few years to assist refugees and asylum seekers—to the extent that some of them are risking a hefty prison sentence by harbouring escapees from detention centres."[89]

Despite its numerous historical elisions, the enduring fantasy of Australia as the land of the fair go was crucial to the framing and circulation of asylum-seeker testimony. All forms of advocacy were understood as a way of performing the values of egalitarianism and decency; whereas the dissemination of asylum-seeker testimony, in particular, was framed as an act of national good. In her preface to *Human Rights Overboard*, Margaret Alston wrote approvingly that, as a result of the People's Inquiry, "the stories of this disturbing era of social policy will be on the record for future generations."[90] This sentiment was reaffirmed throughout the report—by both its authors and witnesses—many of whom "told the organizers they appreciated the opportunity to tell their stories and wanted to ensure that the policies and practices that shamed a nation are not forgotten."[91] Here, asylum-seeker witnessing was positioned as an intervention into future historical discourse. Indeed, as Diane Gosden has argued, "through the dimension of bearing witness to this period, the voices of asylum seekers and their advocates may well be heard not only in the present, but also into the future as part of Australia's historical record."[92] In this schema, the task of the secondary witness is twofold: first, to serve as supporter to individual asylum seekers and second, to gather and circulate their testimony publicly as a way of producing an archive of national shame.

By positioning the collection of asylum-seeker testimony as a national good, some advocates explicitly linked Australia's treatment of asylum seekers with the issue of the stolen generations. As Burnside has asserted with reference to mandatory detention and the Pacific Solution:

This is a scandal which will haunt us for decades. It is quite clear that, as a country, we have learnt nothing at all from the stolen generation. Many people did not know of the stolen generation until years afterwards; this book [of testimony] will show that we know what we are doing to refugees.[93]

Linking the treatment of the stolen generations and asylum seekers not only figured both events as acts of nation shame, events that "haunt" the national conscience, but also underscored the centrality of testimony to the public visibility of both events. If the stolen generations only became prominent within public culture through the circulation of life writing, Burnside has suggested that the work of advocates in collecting testimony will be crucial to preserving a future record of current events. In this way, witnessing to asylum seekers was understood as a noble act of enshrining the present for the future.

Making "Good" Australians

Just as Burnside linked the treatment of asylum seekers and Indigenous peoples as events of national shame, the notion that witnessing is a method of restoring national morality is common to the discourses that have surrounded both asylum seeker and Indigenous testimony. Although asylum seekers and Indigenous peoples have occupied differing structural positions within the national imaginary, the discourses on witnessing to the stories of both groups have been striking similar. Notably, both discourses have hinged on the treatment of children as figures of innocence that deserved the compassion of Australians.[94] Just as the bulk of Indigenous life writing has chronicled the experiences of Aboriginal children, much of the testimony collected by asylum-seeker advocates focused on the plight of children in detention. As such, many of the activities of advocacy organizations have paid attention to children, such as ChilOut, one of the movement's most influential groups. Moreover, just as many Australians were drawn to witness to the stolen generations through stories of child removal, many asylum-seeker advocates were forged through the realization that children were being kept in indefinite detention.

Interestingly, this equation of children with innocence has been extended to encompass the notion that children are exemplary ethical citizens and secondary witnesses. In the case of the Australia IS Refugees! writing program, children and young people were encouraged to perform the role of witnesses by listening to a refugee's story and then writing about it. Instead of reifying the child as the object of witnessing, this project positioned children as secondary witnesses. In doing so, young witnesses were positioned, similar to young testifiers, as custodians of moral innocence and what Eva Sallis has described as "a natural sense of justice."[95]

Importantly, if the figure of the child has been central to the function of humanitarian campaigns, both within Australia and internationally, it has also proved crucial to the operation of (post)colonial discourses on paternalism. This was recently reaffirmed during the Howard Government's Northern Territory Intervention (2007) in which a radical curtailment of Indigenous peoples' land (and civil) rights was underwritten by an insistence that action should be taken in the best interests of "the children."[96] Though the Intervention sought to "save" Indigenous children, in its invocation of the figure of the "lost child," it drew on the salience of the figure of the lost white child, a trope that has been understood, historically, as a marker of settler-colonial guilt.[97] In this way, the figure of the lost or harmed child can be made to serve a range of political and ideological interests; its blank innocence becomes the ground for the reassertion of "goodness," personal, political, and national.

Indeed discourses on both Indigenous and asylum-seeker testimony have hinged on questions of national morality. Over the past two decades, to listen to testimony has been to confront Australia's history—and present—of violence and exclusion. In this way, witnessing has functioned as a broad discourse aimed at rejuvenating the nation; cleansing the body politic of its most destructive and uncaring inclinations. Witnessing to the other, a frequently nonwhite other, has come to form the basis for the performance of "good" Australian citizenship. Yet, if witnessing has come to be associated with a particular mode of liberal multiculturalism, it is also an exclusionary discourse that works to circumscribe who constitutes a "good" Australian.

To ask questions about who might be excluded by practices of witnessing is not to deny that some of the forms of activism and advocacy that have flowed from witnessing have produced real-life gains for many Indigenous peoples and asylum seekers. However, it is, however, to demand that we consider what is at stake in this new form of citizenship. Central to this is an examination of the role of the "good" as a motivating force for the secondary witness. As Elizabeth Povinelli has suggested:

we only approach a true understanding of liberal forms of multiculturalism by inching ever nearer to the good intentions that subjects have, hold, and cherish and to the role these intentions play in solidifying the self-evident good of liberal institutions and procedures.[98]

As discussed in Chapter 1, Sara Ahmed's analysis of the cultural politics of shame is particularly pertinent for a consideration of the role of "good intentions" in contemporary discourse on witnessing. Writing persuasively on the limitations of the politics of "bad feeling" that has emerged in response to Indigenous testimony, Ahmed has argued that much of the rhetoric on Aboriginal reconciliation has been geared toward overcoming shame in the service of rehabilitating the concept of the "good" Australian nation. "Shame," Ahmed has suggested,

"makes" the nation in the very witnessing of past injustice, a witnessing that involves feeling shame, as it exposes the failure of the nation to live up to its ideals. But this exposure is temporary, and becomes the ground for a narrative of national recovery.[99]

As Povinelli has concurred, "mourning a shared shameful past would do no more, and no less, than propel the nation into a new cleansed national form."[100] As a cultural politics of "feeling," then, witnessing has worked to expose settler Australians to the "bad" feelings produced through an engagement with testimony as a stepping-stone on the road to national recovery. Witnessing, on individual, collective, and national scales, has produced affective attachments that bond Australians as "good" citizens within particular national imaginaries. In this way, although Indigenous peoples, asylum seekers, and migrants have been granted a higher level of visibility in public culture, they remain "objects" rather than subjects of feeling—objects in a discourse on good citizenship, rather than good citizens.

In this sense, witnessing can be seen to function as a form of "recognition," a process Povinelli has understood as a "new form of liberal power."[101] For Povinelli, "recognition is at once a formal méconnaissance of a subaltern group's being and of its being worthy of national recognition and, at the same time, a formal moment of being inspected, examined, and investigated."[102] Modes of liberal multicultural witnessing oriented to the needs of the secondary witness, thus, "recognize" and listen to the testimony of liminal groups as a part of the expansion of their own cultural power.[103] This does not nullify the potential cultural or political impact of testimony as an affective force within public culture, but affirms that testimony has functioned as what Whitlock has termed a "soft weapon."[104] Though not without impact, the power of subaltern testimony is highly circumscribed and, as such, has been frequently integrated into unifying and homogenizing accounts of nation and/or humanity. When discourse on witnessing is attached to notions of national goodness, as Suvendrini Perera has suggested, "the desire not only to do good, but to be acknowledged as being good, serves as a form of self-affirmation both in the present and retrospectively, as it is deployed to vindicate whitewashing narratives of national character and history."[105]

Similarly, Jennifer Rutherford has worked to address the centrality of the national good in divergent Australian nationalisms. In doing so, she has been highly critical of what she has termed "the aggressivity of the Ego" in pursuit of the good.[106] Using Lacanian psychoanalysis, Rutherford has drawn attention to "the duplicitous nature of the good, its evasive qualities, and its travelling companion in the history of white Australia—an aggression to both the Other and the self."[107] Though Rutherford's focus has been on the left-liberal antiracism that emerged during the Hanson period, she has argued that the concept of goodness has been crucial to diverse iterations of Australian nationalism, which typically position "neighborliness" and a "fair go" at the heart of an "Australian" value system.[108] As Rutherford has examined, this focus on the good is limiting, and has often worked to conceal Anglo-Australian's defensiveness and aggressiveness toward "outsiders."

The dominant mode of witnessing that has been practiced within contemporary Australian public culture has drawn on testimony in the service of strengthening the liberal multicultural state. Within this schema, there has been little room for ambivalence or ambiguity. Unlike the mode of witnessing proposed by Felman and Laub, and Oliver, this process has rarely been dialogic and, as demonstrated by Povinelli, has typically depended on an assimilative form of recognition.

Oliver has argued powerfully for a reconceptualization of the concept of subjectivity as forged not through recognition, but through witnessing. Fiona Probyn-Rapsey has summarized Oliver's project as an attempt to think through how a dialogic understanding of subjectivity as witnessing "might open up ethical forms of subjectivity not based on normalizing hostility between self/other."[109] "We are," Oliver has argued, by virtue of others. If subjectivity is the process of witnessing sustained through response-ability, then we have a responsibility to response-ability, to the ability to respond. We have an obligation not only to respond but also to respond in a way that opens up rather than closes off the possibility of response by others.[110]

In Oliver's terms, witnessing is an intersubjective exchange between Self and Other, in which the possibility of "response" and continued dialogue always remains open.

Witnessing in these terms is not only mutually transforming, but it can also be risky. It includes the possibility of loss, contradiction, rejection, and misunderstanding—and does not simply incorporate the Other, and their testimony, into (self)serving conceptions of settler identity. Here, the act of witnessing does not "presume that the Other be excluded as threatening or incorporated as same"; it sustains difference.[111]

Contemporary Australian discourse on witnessing has tended to engage with testimony as a stepping-stone to national renewal, and has incorporated difference within an assimilative notion of liberal multiculturalism. Thus, witnessing has typically been a process of engaging with the testimony of Indigenous peoples and migrants, and confronting the painful feelings of complicity, shame, or guilt, as a part of a way of recuperating the "good" white nation. Yet, as Ahmed has argued: "we can stay open to hearing the claims of others, only if we assume that the act of speaking one's shame does not undo the shame of what we speak."[112] For witnessing to support truly democratic social relations, the settler subject cannot always already be the good citizen. To remain open to the testimony of others is to acknowledge that Anglo-Australians are "by virtue" of liminal subjects, and to insist on modes of being Australian that do not collapse difference in the name of a fair go.

To practice witnessing is this form would also necessitate an expansion of the kinds of stories settler Australians "listen" to. This would not only mean a willingness to engage with the testimony of different peoples, but also to develop an openness to hearing stories that present different, and more challenging, versions of Australian history and identity. Writing on the reception of migrant testimony, Sara Wills has lamented the inability of public culture to witness to the loss produced by the experience of migration. This has resulted in the repetition of "positive" migrant success stories and the unwillingness, even inability, to recognize and affirm experiences and narratives that do not emphasize the hospitality of Anglo-Australians or the "contribution" which migrants have made to the nation.[113] As Wills has written, we need to "confront those versions of the multicultural script that serve only to constitute the nation."[114] By remembering the fact of migrancy in Australian history, Wills has suggested that Australians might also be able to witness to the loss and pain experienced by both Indigenous peoples and migrants.[115] Yet, here, witnessing would not assimilate loss as a part of the recovery of a shamed nation, but underscore the extent to which "we live with and beside each other, and yet we are not one."[116]

Indigenous Australians Witness

Though my concern here has been to examine practices of witnessing conducted by Anglo and other non-Indigenous settler Australians, it is instructive to consider the challenge brought to this discourse by the activities of Indigenous witnesses. If the dominant work of witnessing has been to reconstitute the settler nation as good, and decent, the actions of some Indigenous witnesses have forcefully challenged these conceptions of Australian nationalism and their elision of Indigenous sovereignty. In 2001, Gungalidda elder Wadjularbinna released a media statement disputing the Aboriginal and Torres Strait Islander Council's (ATSIC) position on the government's treatment of asylum seekers. Wadjularbinna argued that Howard's policy of refusing hospitality contravened Aboriginal ways of being in this country. "If we as Aboriginal people are true to our culture and spiritual beliefs," she argued, "we should be telling the government that what they are doing to refugees is wrong! Our Aboriginal cultures do not allow us to treat people this way."[117] Here, Wadjularbinna undermined dominant forms of liberal multicultural witnessing. Though her press release was powerfully symbolic, as Perera has argued, "Wadjularbinna's is not some nostalgic invocation of a bygone age. It is an astute recognition of current political realities. She claims responsibility as an indigenous Australian for the treatment of guests in her country."[118] To do so, is to foreground the imbrication of witnessing with discourses on national renewal and goodness. She does this not simply by drawing attention to the ways in which the settler nation is not good—by linking the current mistreatment of asylum seekers with the historical and present oppression of Indigenous peoples—but also by aligning non-Indigenous Australians with boat people as guests in "our country."

As Tony Birch has argued, "it is important that Indigenous people speak on behalf of and with marginalised migrant communities," "not only as an act of moral and political solidarity, but in recognition of the *sovereign* responsibility that they hold."[119] When Indigenous people witness to asylum seekers, and other liminal subjects, they exercise a sovereignty that unmakes the good nation. In doing so, they have paved the way for new iterations of Australianness in which witnessing might serve as the ground for dialogic sociopolitical relations.[120]

Conclusion

In analyzing the forms of witnessing that have occurred in relation to asylum seekers, this chapter has provided only a brief snapshot of the different activities undertaken by secondary witnessing. It has not discussed, for example, the proliferation of creative works of witnessing, such as Eva Sallis' 2005 novel *The Marsh Birds*, nor have I examined the confronting work of performance artist Mike Parr, who has engaged in forms of bodily harm as a way of drawing audiences to witness to the incarceration of asylum seekers.[121]

This chapter has, however, performed two critical moves. First, it has examined the emergence of a discrete discourse on witnessing to asylum seekers in the wake of the *Tampa* incident. Second, and most crucially, it has articulated the enmeshment of discourses on asylum-seeker and Indigenous testimony with the promulgation of ideologies of national goodness.

The figure of the "good" settler witness has become central for an influential, if counter-hegemonic, public of Australians. As I have demonstrated, discourses on witnessing to both Indigenous peoples and asylum seekers have foregrounded the act of witnessing as a per-formance of civic virtue. In doing so, they have reshaped what kinds of stories can be told both within and for the "good" nation. To ana-lyze the affects of secondary witnessing in this way is not to deny the ongoing necessity of "speaking for" others through acts of advocacy, but to question the need for settler witnessing to function only as a mode of reconstituting the hegemony of the white nation. To consider, as I have done, the possibilities of alternate ways of listening is also to question what kinds of stories can be heard within public culture. As Judith Butler has asserted:

The public sphere is constituted in part by what can appear, and the regulation of the sphere of appearance is one way to establish what will count as reality, and what will not. It is also a way of establishing whose lives can be marked as lives, and whose deaths will count as deaths.[122]

In this way, the cultural politics of witnessing is not merely symbolic, but inextricably linked to our capacity to feel for, and to recognize the feelings of, others.

Notes

1. Anonymous HMAS *Tobruk* officer citied in Briskman, Latham, and Goddard, *Human Rights Overboard*, 53–54.
2. John Frow, "UnAustralia: Strangeness and Value," *Cultural Studies Review* 13, no. 2 (2007): 51.
3. At the time of writing, footage of Merlin's eviction protest was available on the Internet. Andi2468, "Merlin's Eviction Protest—Big Brother Australia," *YouTube*, http://www.youtube.com/watch?v=o3N83X0gb_c (accessed October 8, 2009. See also Clare Buttner, "Merlin's Silent Protest," *Sydney Morning Herald*, June 14, 2004, http://www.smh.com.au/articles/2004/06/14/1087065042010.html (accessed October 5, 2009).
4. On the history of political gimmicks and their new role in contemporary "media-tized" politics, see Sean Scalmer, *Dissent Events: Protest, the Media and the Political Gimmick in Australia* (Sydney: UNSW Press, 2002). For a critical analysis of the supposed apathy of the young with reference to Merlin's stunt, see Kate Crawford, *Adult Themes: Rewriting the Rules of Adulthood* (Sydney: Pan Macmillan, 2006), 219–20.
5. Andrea Jackson, "Merlin Luck Speaks Up, Again," *Age*, July 1, 2004, http://www.theage.com.au/articles/2004/06/30/1088488027236.html (accessed on October 5, 2009).
6. Alex Broun, "'Free the Refugees': Merlin Interviewed," *Green Left Weekly*, no. 586, June 23, 2004, http://www.greenleft.org.au/2004/586/32324 (accessed October 5, 2009).
7. Ibid.
8. Diane Gosden, "'What If No One Had Spoken out against This Policy?' the Rise of Asylum Seeker and Refugee Advocacy in Australia," *PORTAL Journal of Multidisciplinary International Studies* 3, no. 1 (2006): 1.
9. Linda Jaivin has outlined both the difficulties experienced by asylum seekers seeking contact with sympathetic "outsiders," and the challenges that journalists and advocates have faced in recording and disseminating their stories. Linda Jaivin, "Truth on the Border: Telling Stories About Asylum Seekers," *Overland*, no. 172 (2008): 8–17.
10. Sarah Mares and Louise Newman, eds., *Acting from the Heart: Australian Advocates for Asylum Seekers Tell Their Stories* (Sydney: Finch Publishing, 2007). The final report of the People's Inquiry into Detention has been published as Briskman, Latham, and Goddard, *Human Rights Overboard*.
11. For an account of the complex relationship between Indigenous Australians and Australian multiculture, see especially Curthoys, "An Uneasy

Conversation: The Multicultural and the Indigenous," 21–36; Hodge and O'Carroll, *Borderwork in Multicultural Australia*.

12. Suvendrini Perera, "Our Patch: Domains of Whiteness, Geographies of Lack and Australia's Racial Horizons in the War on Terror," in *Our Patch: Enacting Australian Sovereignty Post-2001*, ed. Suvendrini Perera (Perth: Network Books, 2007): 119–46.

13. The twinned issues of immigration and land rights were central to the version of nation inaugurated by Pauline Hanson and her One Nation party during the mid-1990s. Michael Leach, Geoffrey Stokes, and Ian Ward, eds., *The Rise and Fall of One Nation* (St. Lucia: University of Queensland Press, 2000); Andrew Markus, *Race: John Howard and the Remaking of Australia* (Crows Nest, NSW: Allen & Unwin, 2001). On the construction of Australian citizenship against both internal and external others, see David Dutton, *One of Us? A Century of Australian Citizenship* (Sydney: UNSW Press, 2002).

14. Hage, *Against Paranoid Nationalism*, 2.

15. Davis, *Land of Plenty*, 217.

16. For an account of these crises and their impact on the 2001 federal election, see Marr and Wilkinson, *Dark Victory*; Mungo MacCallum, "Girt by Sea: Australia, the Refugees and the Politics of Fear," *Quarterly Essay*, no. 5 (2002): 1–73.

17. For an accessible, comprehensive account of the *Tampa* crisis and the Pacific Solution, see Frank Brennan, *Tampering with Asylum: A Universal Humanitarian Problem* (St. Lucia: University of Queensland Press, 2003).

18. Robert Garran, "Navy Scuttles Pm's Story," *Australian*, November 9, 2001, 1. For a critical assessment of this event, see S. J. Odgers, "Report of Independent Assessor to Senate Select Committee on a Certain Maritime Incident," (Sydney: Forbes Chambers, 2002).

19. Philip Ruddock cited in Catherine McGrath, "Children Overboard Scandal: Philip Ruddock," *AM*, February 15, 2002, [Transcript], http://www.abc.net.au/ am/stories/s482040.htm (accessed October 11, 2000).

20. Tony Kevin, *A Certain Maritime Incident: The Sinking of the SIEV X* (Melbourne: Scribe Publications, 2004).

21. For a detailed account of the Howard Government's construction of asylum seekers as "illegal," and the impact of this within public discourse, see Katharine Gelber, "A Fair Queue? Australian Public Discourse on Refugees and Immigration," *Journal of Australian Studies*, no. 77 (2002): 23–30.

22. Ruddock cited in Michael Madigan, "Children 'Used' as an Immigration Loophole," *Courier Mail*, November 29, 2001, 6.

23. Howard cited in Frank Brennan, "Reconciling Our Differences," in *Reconciliation: Essays on Australian Reconciliation*, ed. Michelle Grattan (Melbourne: Black, 2000), 42.

24. Ruddock cited in Robert Manne and David Corlett, "Sending Them Home," in *Left Right Left: Political Essays 1977–2005* (Melbourne: Black, 2005), 398.

25. On the structural conflict between human rights and state sovereignty and the exploitation of this disjunction in debates on national morality, see Robert Dixon, "Citizens and Asylum Seekers: Emotional Literacy,

Rhetorical Leadership and Human Rights," *Cultural Studies Review* 8, no. 2 (2002): 11–26.

26. Manne and Corlett, "Sending Them Home." See also Julian Burnside, *From Nothing to Zero: Letters from Refugees in Australia's Detention Centres* (Melbourne: Lonely Planet Publications, 2003), vii.

27. Ian Causely cited in Peter Mares, *Borderline: Australia's Response to Refugees and Asylum Seekers in the Wake of the Tampa* (Sydney: UNSW Press, 2002), 133.

28. Ibid., 3. For an overview of refugee policy pre-*Tampa* within the context of immigration policy more broadly, see Jupp, *From White Australia to Woomera*; Don McMaster, *Asylum Seekers: Australia's Response to Refugees* (Melbourne: Melbourne University Press, 2001).

29. Jupp, *From White Australia to Woomera*, 185. May Crock and Ben Saul, *Future Seekers: Refugees and the Law in Australia* (Sydney: The Federation Press, 2002), 101.

30. Peta Stephenson, "Typologies of Security: Indigenous and Muslim Australians in the Post-9/11 Imaginary," *Journal of Australian Studies* 33, no. 4 (2009): 476. Suvendrini Perera, "What Is a Camp. . .?," *Borderlands ejournal* 1, no. 1 (2002): 56.

31. It is important to note that criticism of mandatory detention was present from its inception, though it certainly intensified post-*Tampa*. Amnesty International Australia (AIA) was a long-time vociferous critic of Australia's policy of mandatory detention. See AIA, *Australia, a Continuing Shame: The Mandatory Detention of Asylum Seekers*, (Sydney: Amnesty International Australia, 1998); AIA, *The Impact of Indefinite Detention: The Case to Change Australia's Mandatory Detention Regime* (Sydney: AIA Publications, 2005). For criticism of the Pacific Solution, see Oxfam, *Adrift in the Pacific: The Implications of Australia's Pacific Refugee Solution* (Melbourne: Oxfam Community Aid Abroad, 2002). Criticism of the new immigration policies also came from the government's own Human Rights and Equal Opportunity Commission. See HREOC, *A Last Resort?: National Inquiry into Children in Immigration Detention*, (Sydney: Human Rights and Equal Opportunity Commission, 2004).

32. Prafullachandra Bhagwati cited in Megan Saunders, "Woomera Degrades Children—UN Envoy," *Australian*, August 1, 2002, 1.

33. Petro Georgiou cited in Michael Gordon, *Freeing Ali: The Human Face of the Pacific Solution* (Sydney: UNSW, 2005), 10. For a detailed account of the advocacy work of Georgiou and his colleagues, see also Margot O'Neill, *Blind Conscience* (Sydney: UNSW Press, 2008).

34. Gordon, *Freeing Ali*, 10.

35. Gosden, "What If No One Had Spoken Out against This Policy?," 3.

36. Ibid.

37. Murray Goot, "Turning Points: For Whom the Polls Told," in *2001: The Centenary Election*, ed. John Warhurst and Marian Simms (St. Lucia: University of Queensland Press, 2002): 63–92.

38. Jupp, *From White Australia to Woomera*, 177.

39. Gosden, "What If No One Had Spoken Out against This Policy?," 3

40. Ibid.

41. Briskman, Latham, and Goddard, *Human Rights Overboard*, 270.
42. Gosden, "What If No One Had Spoken Out against This Policy?," 2.
43. Gosden provides a concise overview of the growth of these organizations. Ibid., 1–21. See also Anne Coombs' reflection on the foundation of Rural Australians for Refugees, and Junie Ong and Dianne Hiles' work on ChilOut. Anne Coombs, "Mobilising Rural Australia," *Griffith Review* (Autumn 2004); Mares and Newman, eds., *Acting from the Heart: Australian Advocates for Asylum Seekers Tell Their Stories*, 160–67.
44. Jupp, *From White Australia to Woomera*, 177.
45. Briskman, Latham, and Goddard, *Human Rights Overboard*, 15.
46. A notable exception to this was the work of ABC Radio National journalist Peter Mares, whose broadcasts and *Borderline* first appeared in 2001. Mares, *Borderline*.
47. Heather Tyler, *Asylum: Voices Behind the Razor Wire* (Melbourne: Lothian Books, 2003); Burnside, *From Nothing to Zero*. An important later anthology of asylum seeker writings is Rosie Scott and Thomas Keneally, eds., *Another Country* (Broadway, NSW: Sydney Pen & Halstead Press, 2005). For an overview of the emergence of asylum-seeker testimonies as a diverse body of texts, see Douglas, "Lost and Found," 39-58.
48. See the stories of Ngareta Rossell, Junie Ong (cofounder of ChilOut) and Jacquie Everitt in Mares and Newman, eds., *Acting from the Heart: Australian Advocates for Asylum Seekers Tell Their Stories*, 2, 160, 38; Everitt went on to work closely with Badraie and his family and wrote a book detailing her experiences. Jacquie Everitt, *The Bitter Shore* (Sydney: Pan Macmillan, 2008).
49. On the phenomenon of letter writing and web-based advocacy projects, see Kate Douglas, "Witnessing on the Web: Asylum Seekers and Letter-Writing Projects on Australian Activist Websites," *a/b: Auto/Biography Studies* 21, no. 1 (2006): 44–57; Rhys Kelly, "Testimony, Witnessing and Digital Activism," *Southern Review* 40, no. 3 (2008): 7–22.
50. Much of his writing on asylum seekers and the legal ramifications of their incarceration are collected in Julian Burnside, *Watching Brief: Reflections on Human Rights, Law and Justice* (Melbourne: Scribe, 2007).
51. Burnside, *From Nothing to Zero*, 89, 59.
52. Clara Law (dir.), *Letters to Ali* (Australia: Palace Films, 2004).
53. Douglas, "Lost and Found," 44.
54. Jennifer Jones, *Black Writers, White Editors: Episodes of Collaboration and Compromise in Australian Publishing History* (North Melbourne: Australian Scholarly Publishing, 2009).
55. Ibid., 206–36. Issue of collaboration and authority in the production of knowledge about Indigenous peoples has been widely debated, and has typically centered on the relationship between Indigenous women and white feminists. See especially Jackie Huggins and Isabel Tarrago, "Questions of Collaboration," *Hecate* xvi, no. i–ii (1990): 140–47; Moreton-Robinson, *Talkin' up to the White Woman*.
56. Jones, *Black Writers, White Editors*, 233–36.
57. Tyler, *Asylum*, 222.
58. Ibid.

59. Mick Palmer, *Report of the Inquiry into the Immigration Detention of Cornelia Rau* (Canberra: Commonwealth of Australia, 2005). On Vivian Solon, see Jewel Topsfield, "It's a Shameful Episode," *Age*, October 7, 2005, http://www.theage.com.au/ news/immigration/it-is-a-shameful-episode/ 2005/10/06/1128562943594.html (accessed January 10, 2010).
60. Briskman, Latham, and Goddard, *Human Rights Overboard*, 18–19.
61. Ibid., 19.
62. Ibid. The Inquiry's report quotes the then Director-General of Communications Strategies for the Defence Department outlining the policy of restricting access to information and images about asylum seekers: "we got some guidance [from the Prime Minister's office] on ensuring that there were no personalising or humanising images taken of [them]." Briskman, Latham, and Goddard, *Human Rights Overboard*, 5.
63. Briskman, Latham, and Goddard, *Human Rights Overboard*, 20.
64. Ibid., 91. Other investigations have also focused on these aspects of detention, especially the mental health impact of the policy. For example, Diane Barnes, *Asylum Seekers and Refugees in Australia: Issues of Mental Health and Wellbeing* (Parramatta: Transcultural Mental Health Centre, 2003).
65. Briskman, Latham, and Goddard, *Human Rights Overboard*, 10.
66. Ibid.
67. Ibid., 25.
68. Ibid., 266.
69. See, particularly, Judith Roof and Robyn Wiegman, eds., *Who Can Speak? Authority and Critical Identity* (Urbana, IL: University of Illinois Press, 1996). Linda Martin Alcoff, "The Problem of Speaking for Others," *Cultural Critique* (Winter 1991–1992): 5–32, Susan Ostrov Weisser and Jennifer Fleischner, eds., *Feminist Nightmares: Women at Odds—Feminism and the Problem of Sisterhood* (New York: New York University Press, 1994); Trinh T. Minh-ha, *Women, Native, Others: Writing Postcoloniality and Feminism* (Bloomington: Indiana University Press, 1989).
70. Gilles Deleuze cited in Michel Foucault, "Intellectuals and Power," in *Language, Counter-Memory, Practice*, ed. Donald Bouchard (Ithaca, NY: Cornell University Press, 1977), 209; Gayatri Chakravorty Spivak, "Can the Subaltern Speak?," in *Marxism and the Interpretation of Culture*, ed. Cary Nelson and Lawrence Grossberg (Chicago: University of Illinois Press, 1988).
71. Briskman, Latham, and Goddard, *Human Rights Overboard*, 278.
72. Ibid., 279.
73. Mares and Newman, eds., *Acting from the Heart*, xiii.
74. Ibid., 216.
75. Ibid., xii.
76. Ibid., 1.
77. Ibid., xiii.
78. Ibid., xii.
79. Ibid.
80. Ibid., xi.
81. Briskman, Latham, and Goddard, *Human Rights Overboard*, 392.
82. Ibid., 280.
83. Mares and Newmann, eds., *Acting from the Heart*, 78.

84. Briskman, Latham, and Goddard, *Human Rights Overboard*, 280–81.
85. Tyler, *Asylum*, xi.
86. During the Howard period, Fraser became estranged from the Liberal party and criticized Howard throughout his government on issues of mandatory detention, immigration, border control, and the war on terror. For a summary of this tension, see Mike Steketee, "Howard in War Refugee Snub: Fraser," *The Australian*, January 1, 2008, 1.
87. Klaus Neumann, *Refuge Australia: Australia's Humanitarian Record* (Sydney: UNSW Press, 2004), 107.
88. Ibid., 105–11.
89. Ibid., 113.
90. Briskman, Latham, and Goddard, *Human Rights Overboard*, 10.
91. Ibid., 20.
92. Gosden, "What If No One Had Spoken Out against This Policy?," 17.
93. Burnside, *From Nothing to Zero*, vii.
94. Compare, especially, the work of Cath Ellis and Denise Cuthbert with Douglas' reading of child asylum-seeker testimony. Ellis, "A Strange Case of Double Vision," 75–79; Denise Cuthbert, "Holding the Baby: Questions Arising from Research into the Experiences of Non-Aboriginal Adoptive and Foster Mothers of Aboriginal Children," *Journal of Australian Studies*, no. 72 (1998): 39–52; Douglas, "Lost and Found," 39–58.
95. Sonja Dechian, Heather Millar, and Eva Sallis, eds., *Dark Dreams: Australian Refugee Stories by Young Writers Aged 11–20 Years* (Kent Town, SA: Wakefield Press, 2004), 4.
96. Liz Conor, "Howard's Desert Storm," *Overland*, no. 189 (2007): 12–15.
97. Peter Pierce, *The Country of Lost Children: An Australian Anxiety* (Melbourne: Cambridge University Press, 1999).
98. Povinelli, *Cunning of Recognition*, 16.
99. Ahmed, "The Politics of Bad Feeling," 77. See also Ahmed, *Cultural Politics of Emotion*.
100. Povinelli, *Cunning of Recognition*, 42.
101. Ibid., 39.
102. Ibid.
103. For critical readings of multiculturalism—as both policy and cultural practice—see Stephen Castles et al., *Mistaken Identity: Multiculturalism and the Demise of Nationalism in Australia* (Sydney: Pluto Press, 1990); Justin Healey, ed., *Multiculturalism* (Balmain: Spinney Press, 2000).
104. Whitlock, *Soft Weapons*.
105. Suvendrini Perera, "The Good Neighbour: Conspicuous Compassion and the Politics of Proximity," *Borderlands ejournal* 3, no. 3 (2004): 6.
106. Rutherford, *Gauche Intruder*, 27.
107. Ibid.
108. Ibid., 205.
109. Fiona Probyn-Rapsey, "'No Last Word': Postcolonial Witnessing in *Jackson's Track* and *Jackson's Track Revisited*," *Antipodes* (December 2008): 127.
110. Oliver, *Witnessing*, 18.
111. Probyn-Rapsey, "No Last Word," 127.
112. Ahmed, "Politics of Bad Feeling," 80.

113. See especially Sara Wills, "Un-Stitching the Lips of a Migrant Nation," *Australian Historical Studies* 33, no. 118 (2002): 71–89; Sara Wills, "Losing the Right to Country: The Memory of Loss and the Loss of Memory in Claiming the Nation as Space (or Being Cruel to Be Kind in the 'Multicultural' Asylum)," *New Formations* 51 (Winter 2003): 50–65; Sara Wills, "Between the Hostel and the Detention Centre: Possible Trajectories of Migrant Pain and Shame in Australia," ed. William Logan and Keir Reeves (London and New York: Routledge, 2009), 263–80.

114. Wills, "Un-Stitching the Lips of a Migrant Nation," 72.

115. Ibid.

116. Sara Ahmed cited in Wills, "Between the Hostel and the Detention Centre," 276.

117. Wadjularbinna, "A Gungalidda Grassroots Perspective on Refugees and the Recent Events in the Us," *Borderlands ejournal* 1, no. 1 (2002), http://www.borderlands.net.au/ vol1no1_2002/wadjularbinna.html (accessed November 20, 2009).

118. Suvendrini Perera, "A Line in the Sea," *Race & Class* 44, no. 2 (2002): 34–35.

119. Birch, "The Invisible Fire," 116. See also Tony Birch, "The Last Refuge of the 'Un-Australian,'" *UTS Review* 7, no. 1 (2001): 17–22.

120. Irene Watson, "Settled and Unsettled Spaces: Are We Free to Roam?," in *Sovereign Subjects: Indigenous Sovereignty Matters*, ed. Aileen Moreton-Robinson (Crows Nest: Allen & Unwin, 2007), 15–32.

121. Eva Sallis, *The Marsh Birds* (Crows Nest: Allen & Unwin, 2005). On Parr's work see especially Emma Cox, "The Citation of Injury: Regarding the Exceptional Body," *Journal of Australian Studies* 33, no. 4 (2009): 459–72.

122. Judith Butler, *Precarious Life: The Power of Mourning and Violence* (London and New York: Verso, 2004), xx–xxi.

5

"Do You Want the Truth or What I Said?": False Witnessing and the Culture of Denial

Though this book understands witnessing as a widespread practice, it also emphasizes its status as a "minor" nationalism—a way of being Australian not shared by the overwhelming majority of citizens. If, since the mid-1990s, hundreds of thousands of Australians have worked to witness to the claims of Indigenous peoples, and more recently, the plight of asylum seekers, this chapter explores the views of those who remained unmoved by testimony. It considers the attitudes of those who refused to witness to the stories of Indigenous peoples and asylum seekers, those who denied the "truth" and affective power of testimony.

Here, I unravel two twinned phenomena: the specter of the false witness, and the refusal to witness. Cases of false witness, "proved" or implied, perpetuate a climate of doubt, anxiety, and fear in which secondary witnesses become wary of claims based on testimony. This chapter draws on the documentary film *Forbidden Lie$* (2007), based on the Norma Khouri literary hoax, as a starting place to reflect on the role of false witnessing and denial within Australian historical consciousness.[1] I argue that the fear of the false witness—a fear "proven" correct in the case of Norma Khouri—lies at the heart of the refusal to witness.

False witnesses puncture what Philippe Lejeune has termed "the autobiographical pact": the implicit agreement between reader and author that affirms the fidelity of the relationship between an autobiographical text and a real, verifiable individual.[2] The fracturing of the pact between readers/listeners and life narratives not only impacts on the trust of the audience, but also casts doubt on the sociopolitical causes founded on the circulation of "true" life stories. In the case of the stolen generations, instances of supposed unreliable testimony were taken up by conservative commentators as evidence of the broader falsity of *Bringing them Home*. Speculation about the "truth" of stolen generation testimony fueled a "mainstream," popular culture of denial that worked to undermine the moral foundations of the reconciliation process.[3] This discourse articulated with the "history wars," which centered on a series of fraught discussions about the "accuracy" of frontier history, and the broader place of the colonial past in the present.[4] Likewise, the refugee claims of asylum seekers were disrupted through the efforts of Howard Government ministers who positioned them as unreliable sources, and, thus, unworthy of Australian hospitality. The extent to which an attitude of denial and hostility to testimony has thrived in public culture has demonstrated its status as an officially sanctioned response to the claims of life narrative.

In seeking to account for Australians' popular resistance to testimony, this chapter explores a range of interlinked events and issues, including the conjunction of truth, identity, and authority in life narrative; the disruptive power of identity hoaxing; and the legal "failure" of testimony. To do so, I take as my primary focus Anna Broinowski's documentary on the Khouri hoax, *Forbidden Lie$*. Aimed at a Western audience recently battered by the events of September 11, Norma Khouri's life narrative, *Forbidden Love*, worked to confirm readers' antipathy toward the Arab world, and, especially, their fear of Muslim men. Juxtaposing the vulnerability and courage of Jordanian women with a portrayal of the Muslim man as violent oppressor, the Khouri hoax exploited a widespread suspicion of the Muslim Other. Broinowski's film drew attention to the deep-seated prejudices that fueled the popularity of Khouri's work with Western readers, to produce a complex, moving testament to the reader's desire to know the truth and the consequences of breaking this trust.

Alongside an examination of Broinowski's work, I also consider several prominent events of "false" witness in the history of the reception of Indigenous testimony: the long-running Hindmarsh Island Bridge Affair (1994–2001); Andrew Bolt's "exposé" of Lowitja O'Donoghue (2001); and the legal failure of the Cubillo/Gunner stolen generation "test-case" (2000). I read these case studies in productive tension with *Forbidden Lie$*. If the Khouri hoax appears, at first glance, to be an uncomplicated instance of lying, part of a much-vaunted "Australian" tradition of literary hoaxing, its disruption of the public economy of truth, affect, and identity tells us much about the contemporary hunger for, and concomitant suspicion of, "minority" voices.

It has been the case for many public commentators, particularly conservative deniers, that one example of false testimony casts doubt on the veracity of all forms of first-person autobiographical narrative. This has been especially so with regard to testimonial expression deemed affective because of its "minority authority." The tendency to reify hoax testimonies as "proof" of the unreliability of all life narratives has not only contributed to the silencing of minority voices, always already under suspicion as potentially inauthentic, but has also obscured the radical instability of all attempts to fix identity through literary and testimonial representation.

The enthusiastic conservative focus on instances of perceived identity fraud and false testimony that has been a core feature of public culture from the mid-1990s has worked to reinforce a simplistic, "commonsense," alignment between truth, identity, and authorship. This not only chafes against contemporary critical understandings of autobiographical production, but also ignores the way that life narratives are increasingly deployed within a human rights context: as representative of community and collective experience, rather than individual trauma.

While writing against conservative practices of denial, this chapter attends to the fear of the false witness and considers its place within contemporary cultures of history. To do so is to take seriously the implications of false testimony for individual readers, as well as for the human rights and advocacy movements that have depended on the circulation of testimony for the visibility and emotive appeal of their causes. To acknowledge the vulnerability of testimony as a vehicle for social, cultural, and political change, is also to explore the complexities of our desire to learn about the experience of others, particularly those very unlike ourselves.

Affective Voices

To consider a literary hoax such as Khouri's alongside criticism of supposed "false" Indigenous testimony is to examine the relationship between truth, identity, and authorship across a diverse spectrum of life writing. If autobiography, biography, and memoir are often considered more obviously literary, and thus constructed, forms of life expression, testimony has been typically reified as the unvarnished "truth," particularly within popular and legal-judicial discourses.[5] Together, these forms of life narrative have contributed to a heterogeneous "family" of genres used to represent the self. Despite the very real differences between these modes of life writing, and their reception and criticism, differences have generally been elided in popular cultural responses to hoax autobiographies and false testimony. That is, when the truth value of autobiographies and testimonies are questioned within public culture, doubt has tended to hinge on common questions about the relationship between the author or speaker and the real, verifiable experiences of an actual person.

These concerns with authenticity have run counter to contemporary critical inquiry into life narrative in which, as Susanna Egan has suggested, "deliberate imposture barely figures."[6] Questions of identity fraud have been overlooked, perhaps, due to their dependence on the notion that autobiographical expression marks a transparent relationship between the figure of the author and the subject of life narrative. In place of a straightforwardly referential conception of autobiography, critics in the field of life writing have tended to emphasize the performative nature of the autobiographical self. Sidonie Smith and Julia Watson, for example, have argued that all forms of autobiography are performative, maintaining that the self which is often understood as external or before the autobiographical text is, in fact, a product of the text's construction.[7] Moreover, they have differentiated between factual autobiographical claims and the production of autobiographical truth, which is created through an exchange between reader and author. "Of course," they have suggested,

> autobiographical claims such as date of birth can be verified or falsified by recourse to documentation or fact outside the text. But autobiographical truth is a different matter; it is an intersubjective exchange between narrator and reader aimed at producing a shared understanding of the meaning of a life.[8]

Within such a schema, questions about the authenticity of the autobiographical self are intellectually gauche, if not completely superfluous.

Nevertheless, the perceived correspondence between life narratives and actual lives has been crucial to the success of contemporary autobiography and testimony. As Kate Douglas has elaborated:

At a time when two, or perhaps even three generations of literary theorists have primarily been raised on the notion that the biography of the author is almost irrelevant to the text, in the contemporary world of book publication and marketing, the author has if anything become even more crucial to a book's success.[9]

Within this milieu, hoaxes and false testimony not only disrupt faith in autobiographies as a commercial product, but have also precipitated what Egan has understood as "a crisis in autobiographical authenticity."[10] Accordingly, cases that render the autobiographical pact void have had serious implications for "the personal and cultural value of autobiography as a working genre."[11]

If popular responses to autobiography have often hinged on the supposed relationship between text, author, and actual individual, some critics have suggested that a life narrative actually gains its power not from any formal or referential quality, but from its production and transmission of affect. Writing in the wake of the Wilkomirski controversy, Phillip Gourevitch has linked the popularity of the hoax testimony *Fragments* to its affect or emotive power.[12] That is, Gourevitch argued that testimony is read—and valued as authoritative and authentic—because of its ability to transfer different affects to the reader and engage their empathetic capacity.

Binjamin Wilkomirski's memoir *Fragments*, published in German in 1995, presented itself as the recollections of a child Holocaust survivor, before being exposed by journalists as a fabrication.[13] Such was the popularity of *Fragments* that many Holocaust scholars sought to rehabilitate the text as valuable due to the vicarious trauma or "prosthetic" memory which it allowed secondary witnesses to experience.[14] This process of witnessing was deemed to be so valuable, and productive of a profound, experiential relation to the Holocaust among nonsurvivors, that in some discussions, affect was privileged over authenticity. It is a position that has been implicitly supported by the dominant theorizations of testimony within Holocaust studies, particularly in the work of Felman and Laub, who have figured testimony as an expression of trauma, rather than as a representation of actual events.[15]

In their analysis of the critical response to the Wilkomirski hoax, Andrew Gross and Michael Hoffman have argued that *Fragments* remains a troubling text, precisely because it demonstrates that "affect is no guarantee of accuracy."[16] While a hoax testimony may indeed be moving, they have argued that the personal and cultural power of life writing is diminished through a dismissal of referentiality as a marker of authenticity. "If testimony is to mean anything," they have insisted,

> we must be able to assume a direct relation between a particular trauma and a specific narrative. Otherwise, any trauma could produce any narrative—and surely this is the *reductio ad absurdum* of testimony as a critical category.[17]

Similarly, Egan has lamented: "is the impostor, cut loose from reference to the real world, not only able but actually welcome to produce that which was not?"[18]

Further, both Gross and Hoffman, and Egan, have drawn attention to the failures not only of conceiving of autobiography as simplistically referential but also as performative. Referring to the failure of the Helen Demidenko literary hoax, Egan has suggested that Demidenko was "undone" through the excesses of her performance of Ukrainian-ness.[19] Here, "performance became inauthentic, outstripping the requirements of the narrative, unravelling the possibilities of performativity, and strongly suggesting the failure of referentiality."[20] Working to differentiate the concepts of performance and performativity, Egan has argued that a commitment to a complex understanding of life representation does not necessarily entail an abandonment of certain standards of referentiality, on which authenticity ultimately depends.[21]

What, then, do hoaxes demonstrate? For Maggie Nolan and Carrie Dawson, they have functioned as "limit cases in relation to the problematic notion of identity" and emphasize the way in which experiences and understandings of selfhood are "necessarily inseparable from and constituted by language and narrative."[22] Augmenting this perspective is Leigh Gilmore, who has contended that autobiography gains its affective force less from its mimetic correspondence to real personal experience than from the "cultural power of truth telling."[23] This is not to suggest that the veracity of testimony and life narrative does not matter: It palpably does as the critical and popular furore over hoaxes attests. Rather, I suggest it matters not simply because false testimony "fails" to match a verifiable reality, but because testimony's aura of authenticity has underwritten numerous cultural and political claims anchored by first-person stories of injustice, trauma, and suffering. Hoax autobiographies have disrupted not only the claims of specific individuals, but also the power of life narrative as a mode of recognition tied to campaigns for justice and human rights.[24] This, in turn, can and has contributed to a broader climate of suspicion, even denial, inhibiting the ability of minority voices to speak their stories within public culture.

"The Hoax We Had to Have"

In 2003, Random House published Norma Khouri's *Forbidden Love*,[25] her recollections of the honor killing of her best friend, Dahlia.[26] Set in Amman, Jordan during the late 1990s, *Forbidden Love* chronicled the girls' friendship, and their success in opening a unisex hairdressing salon. It also, crucially, told the story of Dahlia's murder at the hands of her father and brothers, who had discovered Dahlia's clandestine, yet chaste, love affair with Michael, a Christian soldier and a customer at the salon. The text followed the fallout of the killing and Khouri detailed how, with Michael's assistance, she fled Jordan and came to write the book in an Athens internet café.

Forbidden Love was clearly marketed as autobiographical nonfiction through the peritexts that Douglas has argued are the hallmarks of life writing publicity: the book cover (and blurb), reviews, and the author's promotional appearances.[27] Alongside a preface assuring readers as to the validity of the narrative, the book is marked by a positive endorsement from author Jean Sasson, who suggested that "this extraordinary true story is well told, worth telling and impossible to put down."[28] Sasson's support placed the work within a well-known and popular "genre of American proto feminist writing about the Middle East."[29] Most troubling, in terms of the texts' status as fraudulent, was the inclusion of an afterword, urging readers to donate their time and money to agitating the Jordanian Government about the cause of honor killings.[30] Here, Whitlock has suggested that

> Khouri is eliciting the empathic response of a secular and humanist readership in the West: those who identify with democracy, feminism, modernity, and who are in these times susceptible to the evangelical desire to promulgate these values across cultures and beyond the West.[31]

The overwhelming popular response to *Forbidden Love* illustrated the widespread resonance of this strategy, and demonstrated the link that Kay Schaffer and Sidonie Smith have traced between testimony and the global politics of human rights.[32]

Forbidden Love sold more than 200,000 copies in Australia before Khouri was exposed in 2004 by journalists Malcolm Knox and Caroline Overington. Presenting his work as the "truth" about the book, Knox revealed that Khouri's real name was Norma Majid Khouri Michael Al-Bagain Toliopoulos, and that "she only lived in Jordan until she was three years old."[33] Khouri had lived in the United States for most of her life and, despite her public statements to the contrary, was married with two children. Based on his own investigations, which included traveling to Chicago to interview relatives, friends, and enemies of Khouri, Knox argued that *Forbidden Love* was false, as Khouri had not lived in Jordan during the period the book covers. Unearthing her involvement in a series of illegal property dealings in Chicago, Knox and Overington declared her a "fugitive not from Jordan but from a life of shady deals and tempestuous family relations."[34] Despite promising to counter Knox's claims, Khouri was unable to convince her publisher that *Forbidden Love* was true, and it was subsequently removed from sale.[35]

Criticism of *Forbidden Love* did not, however, begin with Knox and Overington's research. Both Jordanian human rights advocates and Australian book reviewers had expressed serious reservations about the factual basis of the narrative. Women's and human rights campaigners in Jordan, particularly Amal al-Sabbagh, had written to Khouri's publisher to detail the myriad inaccuracies it contained.[36] The Australian author and Arabic scholar, Eva Sallis, was also disturbed by elements of Khouri's work, particularly her tendency to write with "negative generalizations" about Arab, Muslim men.[37] Indeed, Khouri's text abounded in overblown cliché. Its ominous opening passage sets the tone and acts as a microcosm of Arab stereotyping:

> Jordan is a place where men in sand-coloured business suits hold cell phones to one ear and, in the other, hear the whispers of harsh and ancient laws blowing in from the desert. It is a place where a worldly young queen argues eloquently on CNN for human rights, while a father in a middle-class suburb slits his daughter's throat for committing the most innocent breach of old Bedouin codes of honour.[38]

Though Sallis believed that Khouri's reliance on Orientalist stereo-typing was a "great weakness" of the text, she countered that "Khouri's experiences prevent the reader from engaging critically with the book."[39] Echoing Knox's assertion that Khouri's story "stole readers' hearts," Sallis argued that "we cannot but feel for the author and admire the courage it has taken to write this book and to build a life in exile."[40] Sallis' reluctance to condemn *Forbidden Love*, despite its obvious deficiencies, demonstrated the seductive affect of testimony for the secondary witness; though flawed *Forbidden Love* deserved to be respected as authentic testimony. As Gross and Hoffman have asserted, "when authority is linked to affect, the prescribed reader response is sympathy or personal identification rather than criticism."[41]

This tendency for critics, and readers, to "forgive" *Forbidden Love* its myriad "sins"—which ranged from factual inaccuracies regarding the location of the Jordan River and a profound misunderstanding of the role of Sharia law in Jordan, to its use of unsophisticated language and a reliance on crude Orientalist tropes—affirmed the almost sacred status of testimony as authentic, truthful expression. For Whitlock, it was this foundational connection between testimony and concepts of truth and authority that marked *Forbidden Love* as "a parasite": drawing on the "dominant testimonial current" and through its fraudulence, sapping the power of all testimony.[42]

Although this has been true of all literary and identity hoaxing, the Khouri hoax also exposed something specific about contemporary Australian culture, namely, the susceptibility of reading publics to particular kinds of testimonial fraud. As Whitlock has argued:

> One unpalatable answer to the question of how this particular hoax could be sustained and 'lived out' in the Antipodes is that it is played out in the space created by human rights discourse . . . From the Khouri hoax we can learn, to our embarrassment and shame, that we may be especially vulnerable to propaganda in the form of testimony; and capable of an unquestioning acceptance of certain categories of information about other cultures we know little about if it takes certain generic forms of address.[43]

Here, Whitlock drew attention to the amalgam of affect, genre, and authenticity that coalesced in the reception of Khouri's autobiography, and highlighted the ways in which certain kinds of voices are privileged, at different times, within public culture. Capitalizing on a Western thirst for true stories about life under Islam, Khouri's work both relied on this framework of reception and thoroughly discredited it.[44]

"Australian" Hoaxing

Though the Khouri hoax illustrated what is at stake in the ruptur-
ing of the autobiographical pact, it has also been interpreted within
a distinctly "Australian" tradition of hoaxing.[45] While Khouri is not
Australian—and has never presented herself as such—she was living
in Australia at the time of the publication of *Forbidden Love* and, thus,
conducted the bulk of her initial publicity in Australia. Moreover, it
was in the Australian market that her text proved to be most popular,
even earning a place in a popular reading poll of Australia's "favor-
ite books."[46] As such, *Forbidden Love* has been grouped alongside a
range of divergent hoax events, including the so-called "Ern Malley"
affair, the paradigmatic Australian literary hoax perpetuated by James
McAuley and Harold Stewart, who submitted a "fake" modernist poem
to the avant-garde magazine *Angry Penguins* in 1944; John O'Grady's
imposture of an Italian immigrant in Nino Culotta's *They're a Weird
Mob* (1957); Helen Demidenko/Darville's *The Hand that Signed the
Paper* (1994), an anti-Semitic novelization of her family's supposed
experiences in the Ukraine; and Leon Carmen's invention of stolen
generation testimony in Wanda Koolmatrie's *My Own Sweet Time*
(1997).[47] The proliferation of hoaxes within Australian literary history
has been so marked that it has led some, such as Simon Caterson,
to argue hyperbolically that hoaxing is "inseparable from the wider
Australian narrative."[48]

David Carter has argued that literary critics have customarily differentiated between two types of hoax: "the first works only so long as
it remains undiscovered. The second, by contrast, depends upon being
discovered: only when the hoaxer's cover is blown will the point of the
hoax be revealed."[49] Australia's hoaxing tradition includes both, and
as such, critical discussion of an "Australian" tradition should work to
avoid blurring the effects of different modes of identity fraud. In the
case of Ern Malley, the intended effect of the hoax—an attack on "elite"
faddishness—depended on exposure.[50] In the case of Demidenko, the
imposture was designed to remain hidden in order to authenticate her
text and fraudulent public personae.

By far, the most damaging mode of hoaxing has involved the imposture of ethnic or minority identity: the fraudulent occupation of
subject positions "mainstream" audiences have been eager to learn
about through the circulation of life narrative. This mode of hoaxing has been facilitated by what Sneja Gunew has identified as the

widespread perception that non-English speaking people who write are separated from "any literary signifying systems" and reified as "sociological case studies of authentic victims," incapable of writing in anything other than "plain" language.[51]

Though by no means restricted to Australia, Maggie Nolan and Carrie Dawson have argued that the debates which have surrounded ethnic identity hoaxes, such as that of Helen Demidenko, "tell us about the desire for authenticity in multicultural Australia."[52] Similarly, for Fiona Nicoll, "the Demidenko affair cast a glaring light upon the protocols governing identification and representation within Australian multiculturalism."[53] In particular, it highlighted the thirst of Anglo-Australians for true representations of minority or ethnic experience. For Ivor Indyk, this desire to consume difference has developed in response to a feeling that "the whole notion of Anglo-Australian identity has become emptied of any interest."[54] As such, many, including Robert Manne, lamented the state of contemporary Australian literary culture and insisted that it had become easier for non-Anglo writers to be published than Anglo-Australian ones.[55] Others, such as Edmund Campion, then chairman of the Australia Council's Literature Fund, sought to affirm the benevolence of Anglo-Australians and suggested, "I think all decent minded people want to hear minority voices."[56] For Nicoll, it was precisely this notion of decency and tolerance that the Demidenko hoax had foregrounded; the literary establishment's eager praise of the novel's anti-Semitism demonstrated the apex of Anglo multiculturalism—an ability to tolerate extreme intolerance.[57]

Though Nicoll has been perceptive in her analysis of the role the Demidenko hoax played in exposing, *pace* Hage, the contingency of multicultural tolerance and its desire for authentic otherness, she has not accounted for the effect of ethnic hoaxing on the ability of minority communities to intervene in public culture. To be sure, the intentions of "ethnic" hoaxes have been divergent, ranging from a desire to demonstrate a literary or critical "bias" toward minority or ethnic writing, or a plan to inhabit a fraudulent persona as an attempt to capitalize on the perceived cachet of marginal subject positions. The effects, however, have been strikingly similar: the production of an atmosphere of hostility toward autobiography and testimony, and the affective claims these genres make on the reading public.

The Demidenko hoax not only highlighted the desire of Anglo-Australians to consume narratives of cultural otherness, but also demonstrated how quickly the discursive space produced by minority testimony might be eroded by suspicion. In *Forbidden Lie$*, director Alison Broinowski directly confronted the discomfiture produced by ethnic hoaxing and explored the sense of betrayal felt by readers of Khouri's hoax narrative. In doing so, she considered the space between desire for, and suspicion of, the other, and the effect this has on the power of testimony as a force for social, political, and cultural change.

Forbidden Lie$

In *Forbidden Lie$*, Broinowski set herself the task of "unravelling" the truth about Khouri's life and testimony. Structured almost similar to a "psychological thriller," Broinowski developed Khouri's exposé into a suspenseful plot, employing screen titles creatively to divide the film into a series of "acts" focused on different elements of the hoax: "The Artist," "The Con," "The First Lie."[58] Drawing on extensive interviews with Khouri herself, *Forbidden Lie$* provided an opportunity for Khouri to explain her side of the story while, at the same time, entrapping her by facilitating her enunciation of ever and more elaborate lies. Alongside footage of Khouri, Broinowski presented interviews with those who had been "swindled" by her, particularly former friends and publishers, such as her estranged husband John, and Malcolm Knox and Caroline Overington, the Australian journalists who exposed her. Crucially, Broinowski included interviews with women's rights activists in Jordan—academic Dr. Amal A. Sabbagh and Rana Husseini, journalist for the *Jordanian Times*—and allowed the pair ample space to outline their many and varied objections to Khouri's text.

In seeking to uncover the "truth" of Khouri's book, Broinowski self-consciously explored the mechanics of autobiographical representation. As such, she probed the concepts of "authenticity and [the] attendant fantasies of originary wholeness and certainty" on which testimony rests.[59] *Forbidden Lie$* opened with an address from Khouri explaining the rationale behind her work. Staring directly into the camera, the opening sequence employed the standard tropes of televisual witnessing in order to forge a link between Khouri and the audience. Here, the absence of an on-screen interviewer is crucial in bridging the distance between Khouri and audience members. Recounting her life of oppression in Jordan, Khouri figured Dahlia's murder as profoundly transformative: "it was at that point that I said no more . . . someone has to hear it." Broinowski's use of the rhetorical conventions of testimony worked to interpellate viewers as sympathetic witnesses; this was an important move given the widespread media coverage that had been devoted to Khouri's exposure. Yet, at the same time, Broinowski couched Khouri's opening testimony in a network of Orientalist stereotypes: "Arabic" music, seductive swirls of smoke, and titles presented in a garish burgundy/gold color scheme. In this way, Broinowski drew attention to the tensions inherent in Khouri's work—the strong emotive appeal of her testimony and its transmission through an excessively "authentic," exoticized rhetoric.

This tension between authenticity and performative excess was further underscored by Broinowski's retelling of the plot of *Forbidden Love*. Presenting a series of re-enactments punctuated by Khouri's voice, Broinowski adopted a cheesy, almost camp tone in her replay of Dahlia's love story. Dahlia and Khouri are depicted giggling as they devise ways for Dahlia to meet Michael, and the pair are then stalked through the streets of Amman by Dahlia's hulking, menacing brother. The ironic tone is somewhat disconcertingly carried through to the scene of Dahlia's murder, in which she is depicted cowering in terror while her father stabs her to death. It is not until later in the film—when "Dahlia" rises from her bloodied sheets to laugh along with her "father" and "brothers"—that Broinowski's strategy becomes clear. Khouri's story, she has suggested, was always too "good" to be true.

Despite this tone of playful skepticism, Broinowski seriously explored the seductiveness of Khouri's testimony and considered the betrayal felt by readers who had accepted her story. The autobiographical pact is dramatized through a rapid montage of people intently reading *Forbidden Love* in different locations: on the beach, at a bus stop, on the train. Broinowski juxtaposed this footage with excerpts from interviews with a range of publishers and writers who reflect on their own experience of reading Khouri's story. All commented on how moved they felt when they read *Forbidden Love* for the first time, and affirmed that their connection to the narrative was underwritten by assurances that the "amazing" story was true. Broinowski also included an interview with author Daniel Leser, who had met with Khouri at several Australian writers' festivals, and was shocked by the emotional response of audience members to her presentations. For Leser, Khouri's book fed on Western audiences "fascinated by the Arab man" and played on the fear that a "giant burqua . . . would envelope us if we didn't watch out." This fear was enhanced by Khouri's live testimony to oppression in Jordan, and the highly sympathetic public personae she had developed: the virgin in peril. In this way, the film explored the way that *Forbidden Love* connected to a reading population eager for true stories of life under Islamic regimes, the truth of which was affirmed through the author's public performance of suffering.

Though *Forbidden Lie$* presented a range of critical material about Khouri, relating to both her book and her supposedly criminal actions in the United States, it ultimately acted as a forum for Khouri to attempt to clear her name. For Myke Bartlett, this rendered Broinowski complicit in Khouri's fabulations, as it was Broinowski who edited the film so that Khouri always maintained a right of reply to her critics.[60] Indeed, despite the accusations of myriad interviewees, Khouri is repeatedly offered the opportunity to counter their criticisms, often by adding another layer of explanation to her convoluted story. Crucially, Khouri maintained the book's fidelity throughout the film and, in response to Knox's pleas to come clean, declared that: "I will never call that book a novel." Instead, she argued that *Forbidden Love* was based on the story of a friend who was murdered by her father for falling in love, and becoming pregnant, with a local butcher. She insisted that she had radically changed the settings, dates, and all identifying details of the experience in order to protect both herself and her family from possible retribution from Dahlia's family. Yet these are the very details that her critics claim have robbed her story of authenticity and revealed the text to be the work of an author unfamiliar with life in Jordan. Khouri remained unperturbed by this line of reasoning and, in response to several glaring factual errors identified by Jordanian activists, curtly replied, "I didn't write this as a tourist handbook."

In a spectacular coup, Broinowski convinced Khouri to accompany her to Jordan to gather evidence that would prove both Dahlia's existence and her murder. Yet, despite Khouri's apparent willingness to submit to polygraph testing and tour Jordan, she is ultimately quite open about her propensity for lying. At one point, Khouri responded to a frustrated Broinowski with the cocky, duplicitous question: "do you want the truth or what I said?" Scenes of Khouri anxiously pleading with Jordanian medical officers to confirm Dahlia's death are juxtaposed with one of her bragging to her bodyguard about deceiving Broinowski. Affirming her loyalty to Dahlia, she stated that she "would have spun anything to get her story out there." When confronted by Broinowski with a tape of her mocking the director with her bodyguard, Khouri countered that she did not "trust" Broinowski with the full story. Throughout the film, Khouri argued that she "lied for a reason"; to promote international awareness of honor crimes. However, as Knox has asserted, this lying undercuts the necessary authenticity of her story: "the fact of her being a witness to what she had seen was absolutely essential" to the book's success.

At its core, *Forbidden Lie$* confronts the vexed question of the role of referentiality and affect in the production of popular life narrative. So magnetic was Khouri's personality and so seductive was her storytelling style that several former friends admitted to remaining in thrall to her. Rachel Richardson, Khouri's neighbor on Queensland's Bribie Island, argued that it was John, Khouri's husband, who was behind the deceptions. She maintained this despite being $15,000 poorer for supporting Khouri and her children through the media storm that surrounded *Forbidden Love*. Broinowski employed Richardson as a sympathetic, "everyman" figure in order to illustrate Khouri's irresistible allure. Tellingly, Richardson acknowledged her almost unconscious attraction to Khouri, admitting that, "I worshipped the ground the woman bloody walked on." Broinowski has appeared similarly reverential.

Speaking about the experience of directing *Forbidden Lie$*, Broinowski explained that she was highly skeptical about Khouri before filming, but that "the minute I looked her in the eye I was gone."[61] Though Broinowski goes on to acknowledge the very real damage Khouri has inflicted, to both readers and her former friends, she "can't help but admire her audacity and her spirit . . . She's like your best friend. I really do care about her." Reviewers and audiences, too, have been seduced by Khouri, with the ABC's Margaret Pomeranz describing Khouri's remarkable screen presence as something that we simply "go along with."[62] This stubborn loyalty to Khouri can be compared to the reactions of a school teacher who had invited Khouri to speak to her students on the eve of Khouri's exposé: "Either her story is very, very real or she's a damn fine actress, and I'm fairly astute when it comes to reading people."[63] Accordingly, the film portrayed Khouri as a peculiarly alluring figure, and, in doing so, foregrounded the role of affect in eliciting audience and reader sympathy. In this way, the film lent credence to critical understandings of testimony that emphasize affect over authenticity in the production of the empathetic reaction of secondary witnesses.

However, it is at this point—the point at which the film acknowledged both Khouri's lying and the affective force of her lies—that *Forbidden Lie$* reached an impasse. On the one hand, Khouri is roundly exposed as a con, a woman whom one of Overington's sources described as "the most evil person she had ever met." On the other hand, Khouri emerged as the eternal victim, a courageous survivor of child incest whose testimony and campaign for justice has been unfairly maligned. Ultimately, Broinowski is reluctant to pass final judgment on Khouri. For one reviewer, this refusal to judge has subsequently lent the film a "somewhat postmodern" orientation to truth.[64]

It is certainly the case that the audience is no closer to the "truth" about Khouri than they were at the start of the film. Yet *Forbidden Lie$* does not suggest that the concept of truth does not matter, even if it does underscore the impossibility of ever arriving at one, singular version of Khouri's life. Rather Broinowski, in her stubborn attempt to unravel the "truth" of Khouri's work, has highlighted the delicate balance of truth and affect in the telling of life stories. Even though we come to know Khouri as a "con," we never lose hope that she will prove at least some of her work to be true. In dramatizing the dilemma of the secondary witness, caught between the force of emotion and the desire for a verifiable authenticity, the film stands as a sombre warning about the authority of affect and the vulnerability of our desire to connect through life narrative.

White Aborigines

The Khouri hoax worked to expose the susceptibility of Western readers to anti-Arab testimony, whereas a quite different series of "hoaxes" have occurred to disrupt the testimonial culture of Australian Indigenous peoples. Khouri's fraud, though perpetuated in an Australian context, depended on the transnational reach of human rights discourses for its success. Readers who witnessed to Dahlia's story were encouraged to understand their response as a part of a widespread Western, even feminist, movement against honor crimes in Muslim countries. In contrast, the discourse of witnessing to Indigenous people in Australia has sought to engage witnesses in a specifically national process of confrontation and revitalization.

In 1997, Australians were confronted with two hoaxes drawing on Aboriginal identities: Wanda Koolmatrie/Leon Carmen's *My Own Sweet Time* and the work of "Indigenous" artist Eddie Burrup. Koolmatrie's autobiography, a chronicle of one woman's experience as a part of the stolen generation, was revealed as the work of a white, middle-aged man, Leon Carmen. Published in 1994, Koolmatrie's work had attracted widespread praise and won the Nita May Dobbie Award for a first novel by a female writer. The life narrative told the story of a Pitjantjara girl removed from her mother and raised by white foster parents. In the context of other stolen generation texts, it weaved a resoundingly "positive" narrative that saw Koolmatrie travel to the United States to work as a lyricist and participate in the 1960s counter-culture movement.[65] The exposure of Carmen came barely a week after the revelation of another high-profile Indigenous identity fraud—that Eddie Burrup, Pilbara artist, was, in fact, the "alter ego" of Elizabeth Durack, daughter of a prominent pioneering family.[66]

In their exploitation of stereotyped otherness, both cases resonate with Khouri; both Carmen and Durack exploited "ethnic" difference for commercial gain. The work of Carmen and Durack, however, involved the deliberate imposture of an entirely alternate cultural and ethnic identity, specifically the adoption of Aboriginality by white subjects. If Khouri's fraud was explicable within the context of the global war on terror and a generalized Western fear of Islam, the work of Carmen and Durack pointed to the imbrication of Indigenous life stories and particular conceptions of the Australian nation as multicultural and reconciling. Accordingly, Maggie Nolan has suggested that both the Carmen and Durack cases should be read as a part of a broad spectrum of Anglo-Australian responses to the possessive claims of Indigenous people post-*Mabo*. "Both" hoaxes, she has argued, "have come to be understood as manifestations of white loss of privilege and/or white guilt."[67] In this sense, hoaxing has worked as a form of ventriloquising on behalf of Anglo artists in order to advance, or contest, Australia's postcolonizing.

Crucially, both cases of imposture attracted trenchant criticism from Aboriginal writers and artists. For Vivien Johnson, for example, the Carmen hoax worked to "undermine" the "capacity of Aboriginal art to bear cultural witness: to speak its own truths to mainstream audiences."[68] As *Forbidden Lie$* has demonstrated, faith in life narrative, and its capacity to present new stories to a willing public, is profoundly shaken by cases of hoaxing. As manifestations of a loss of white privilege, the work of Carmen and Durack stood as two particularly pernicious acts of identity fraud, destabilizing the discourses used by Indigenous people to testify to their own experiences and eroding the willingness of white audiences to engage with their stories. In particular, within a wider cultural milieu preoccupied with the legal meanings of Indigenous testimony, Anglo/Aboriginal hoaxes worked to disrupt the evidentiary power of testimony and its use in campaigns for the recognition of Indigenous sovereignty and land rights.

"Inventing" the Stolen Generation

Alongside the actions of Carmen and Durack, the Australian media has been preoccupied not with similarly "clear-cut" cases of hoaxing, but with the capacity of Indigenous witnesses to speak the truth more generally. From the mid-1990s, conservative suspicion of Indigenous testimony coalesced around several prominent events, including the Hindmarsh Island Bridge Royal Commission; the *Cubillo-Gunner* stolen generation "test case"; and, within the context of the release of *Bringing them Home*, with a series of "revelations" about the private lives of prominent Aboriginal leaders, including Lowitja O'Donoghue. If the Hindmarsh Island "affair" served to cast doubt on the validity of Indigenous oral testimony, and by extension, Aboriginal relationships to country, conservative criticism of *Cubillo* and *Bringing them Home* focused on the unreliability of testimony as evidence of a broader "invention" of a stolen generation "myth."[69]

To be clear, I do not understand these events as hoaxes or cases of deliberate imposture. Conservative responses to these events did, however, feed on questions of truth, identity, and affect that, as we have seen, have dominated discussions of hoaxing and debates on the validity of testimony. Any perceived weakness in Aboriginal oral testimony was discounted as evidence of "lying" and an indication that only (white) documentary sources should be used to understand the nation's past. Several conservative columnists have been especially concerned to probe the "truth" of stolen generation testimony; in particular, the Melbourne *Herald Sun's* Andrew Bolt and the Sydney *Daily Telegraph's* Piers Akerman. The work of Bolt and Akerman was augmented by the semiacademic commentary of writers in the journal *Quadrant*, though Bolt and Akerman, and their colleagues in the popular press—Michael Duffy, Frank Devine, and Christopher Pearson—were the most visible proponents of an antitestimony discourse.[70]

Conservative criticism of the stolen generations has often focused on the life histories of specific Indigenous people as a way of casting doubt on the value of *Bringing them Home* as a whole. In 2001, Andrew Bolt reported that contrary to popular belief, Lowitja O'Donoghue had not been stolen from her family; rather, "she was given away" by her father.[71] O'Donoghue, then patron of the National Sorry Day Committee and former ATSIC chairperson, became the center of a media storm focusing on her childhood and the circumstances of her separation from her mother. Drawing on interviews with relatives and communications with O'Donoghue herself, Bolt claimed that O'Donoghue had been voluntarily sent to the missionary-run Colebrook Home in South Australia. Crucially, Bolt claimed that O'Donoghue had "misled Australians" and quoted her as saying, "I don't like the word 'stolen' and it's perhaps true that I've used the word loosely at times."[72] In the face of intense media pressure, O'Donoghue eventually conceded that she was "a removed child, and not necessarily stolen."[73]

Mining the specificities of O'Donoghue's life history, Bolt went on to suggest that his revelation had broader implications for other stolen children and their claims for legal redress and, moreover, for questions of a national apology. It would, he argued, "come as a blow to supporters of the 'stolen generation.'"[74] Accordingly, Bolt argued that the "stolen generations" was a mythic structure promoted by "sanctimonious liberal humanists," and underwritten by the unreliable testimony of Indigenous people, many of whom suffered "false memory syndrome."[75] The accusation that stolen children were the victims of false memory syndrome was argued strongly in the pages of *Quadrant*, where P.P. McGuinness "likened the testimony of the separated children to invented tales of childhood sexual abuse, Satanic possession or alien abduction."[76]

The comments of Bolt and others sparked a media controversy and even drew a response from Howard, who suggested that Australians cease "this navel-gazing about the past":

> It's time we stopped this business about who was to blame for what may or may not have happened in the past. It's time we stopped using excessive . . . outrageous words like genocide and it's time we focused on making things better in the future.[77]

Here, Howard leveraged doubt about the specificities of O'Donoghue's separation from her family to cast aspersions on the concept of a stolen generation as a whole. Moreover, he used anxiety about "what may or may not have happened in the past" as justification for eschewing consideration of settler responsibility for violence committed against Indigenous peoples. Drawing on the life story of only one prominent Indigenous person, both Bolt and Howard sought to extend suspicion of O'Donoghue's testimony to that of all Aboriginal people.

Conservative critics of the stolen generations have typically couched their objection to testimony in "commonsense" understandings of truth and morality. Responding to criticism of his exposé of O'Donoghue, Bolt lamented hyperbolically that "yesterday I learned that telling the truth is a crime against morality in Australia."[78] Similarly, Akerman suggested that "if the Aboriginal industry cannot deal honestly with the issue of the so-called stolen generation then there cannot be any genuine reconciliation."[79] For both Bolt and Akerman, an inability to understand the "truth" about the stolen generation was due not only to the duplicity of Indigenous people, but also the machinations of what Bolt has termed "a moral mafia": a cabal of self-hating white liberals devoted to a black armband view of Australia's past.[80]

In order to overcome these forces, commentators suggested that the emotive or affective dimension of Aboriginal stories needed to be overlooked in favor of a "sober investigation of what did happen."[81] Repeatedly, conservative discussion of the stolen generations has encouraged readers to disengage from the emotive qualities of testimony in order to perceive the facts contained in documentary (colonial) "evidence."[82] Somewhat perversely, the dismissal of testimony has been figured as a way of ascertaining the real facts and, thus, helping to "ease the pain" of those Indigenous people who were separated from their families.[83]

Testimony on Trial

Though published life narratives—and the testimonies recorded as a part of truth and reconciliation commissions—have not been customarily subjected to juridical standards of evidence, conservative commentators have been concerned to track the progress of stolen generation testimony through the courts. Much criticism of *Bringing them Home* focused on its failure to judge testimony according to "the rules of evidence," and, as such, conservatives have fetished court cases involving Indigenous litigants as true tests of authenticity.[84] For some, the court provided the most appropriate space to ascertain the truth of the claims of Indigenous people; conversely, for a range of Aboriginal claimants, the courts served as a forum not to "prove" themselves, but to achieve a tangible form of justice.

By far the most high-profile legal "test" of Indigenous testimony came during *Cubillo v. Commonwealth*.[85] Promoted as a stolen generation "test case" in the media, and noted as highly symbolic by the court itself, the case was brought, in 1999, by the North Australian Aboriginal Legal Aid Service on behalf of Lorna Cubillo and Peter Gunner. Both Cubillo and Gunner had been removed from their Aboriginal families

as children, under powers granted by the *Aboriginals Ordinance 1918*
(NT). Cubillo was eight in 1947 when she was removed to the Retta
Dixon Home in Darwin; whereas Gunner was seven when, in 1956, he
was taken from Utopia Station to St. Mary's Hostel, near Alice Springs.
Their action sought to prove that the government was "vicariously
liable" for their removal as children, and their subsequent detention
and abuse while in care.[86]

Ultimately, Justice O'Loughlin found against Cubillo and Gunner
in his judgment, deciding that the Commonwealth was not liable for
any injury they sustained while in care. Controversially, he also argued,
on the basis of a thumbprint made by Peter Gunner's mother that
she had consented to his removal. The case hinged on O'Loughlin's
interpretation of evidence—both oral and documentary—which he
ultimately found to be "incomplete."[87] With reference to Cubillo,
O'Loughlin accepted her oral evidence regarding the circumstances
of her removal, but claimed that there was a "huge void" with regard
to the reasons that she was removed.[88] In particular, O'Loughlin felt
that the absence of documentary evidence inhibited his ability to rule
on the reasons for her removal; he claimed this in spite of the volumi-
nous material offered by the litigants and their consultant historian,
Ann McGrath, who provided a thorough reading of contemporary
child removal policies. Here, O'Loughlin underscored the court's preference for "official" documentation over both Indigenous testimony
and the historical interpretation of professional historians.[89] For Ann
Curthoys, Ann Genovese, and Alexander Reilly, "the court's preference
for official documentary evidence stands at complete odds with the
notion that Indigenous peoples can 'prove' their own history in the
face of a dominant language, and law."[90] As Trish Luker has concurred,
"Lorna Cubillo failed in her claim because she did not meet the law's
impossible burden of proof."[91]

For historians and legal scholars, *Cubillo* has demonstrated the
incommensurability of the public discourse on reconciliation and redemption, and the evidentiary demands of the Australian legal system.
As Jennifer Clarke has argued, the legal process exposed deficiencies in
stolen generation evidence that were neither apparent, nor especially
important, in the broader public process of "telling our stories" inaugurated by *Bringing them Home*.[92] Accordingly, Luker has argued that
O'Loughlin's failure to witness to the trauma of Cubillo and Gunner,
as demonstrated by their testimony and "in documents which trace a
history of policies intended to erase Indigenous peoples," affirmed "the

law's power to control the way we make sense of traumatic histories and memories."[93] In this way, *Cubillo* served as an "elegy . . . both for a redemptive legal historiography, and for the stolen generations who relied upon it in their quest for justice."[94]

As a "test case," *Cubillo* underscored the complexities of seeking justice within the courts and traced the limits of testimony within this context. It did not, however, serve to disprove the existence of a stolen generation and, in the case of Cubillo herself, it actually affirmed the horrific circumstances of her removal.[95] Nevertheless, for conservative commentators, *Cubillo* was highly significant and cast doubt on all forms of Indigenous testimony.[96] In response to their "failure," Bolt concluded that "the 'stolen generation' can no longer expect us to believe them without question."[97] For Bolt, *Cubillo* was the latest in a long line of supposedly false stolen generation testimony, which included Charles Perkins, Cathy Freeman's grandmother, and Lowitja O'Donoghue as false "stolen" children. In this way, conservative critics underscored the authority of the (colonial) law to adjudicate Indigenous testimony and reified the legal process as the only assurance of its truthfulness. In doing so, they eroded the discursive space available for the sympathetic dissemination and reception of stolen generation testimony.

If the controversies surrounding *Cubillo* and O'Donoghue linked "faulty" Aboriginal testimony to the truthfulness of the stolen generations as an historical process, the earlier "Hindmarsh Island affair" highlighted tensions between testimony and the law in the context of land rights and heritage protection. During the 1990s, Ngarrindjeri women rose to national prominence as a result of their efforts to prevent the construction of a bridge connecting *Kumarangk* (Hindmarsh Island) in the lower Murray River, with Goolwa on mainland South Australia, areas they considered to be of crucial spiritual importance. Within a broader post-*Mabo* political milieu preoccupied with the meanings of Aboriginal stories and their implications for land rights, the Hindmarsh controversy captivated the Australian media's imagination and became a conservative *cause célèbre*. The long-running "affair" began in 1994 and centered on a group of Ngarrindjeri women clustered around Doreen Kartinyeri, who argued that the *Kumarangk* area was significant in terms of their fertility.[98] They claimed that since the significance of the Coorong was classified as restricted knowledge within their culture, they could not elaborate publicly as to the area's importance.

At its core, the "affair" hinged on a dispute between two groups of Ngarrindjeri women: those allied with Kartinyeri and a group of self-described "dissident" women who questioned the existence of restricted knowledge about the Coorong.[99] The subsequent Hindmarsh Island Royal Commission found that several Ngarrindjeri women had colluded in the "fabrication" of secret knowledge, and ruled that construction could proceed.[100] The Ngarrindjeri women involved were branded "liars"—despite the fact that they had refused to provide evidence to the Commission—and the phrase "secret women's business" became a conservative byword for lying Aborigines.[101]

In 2001, Tom and Wendy Chapman, the couple behind the bridge development, brought action against a range of parties they believed contributed to costly delays in the construction of the bridge, including anthropologists involved in the preparation of the Ngarrindjeri's heritage case and former Aboriginal Affairs Minister, Robert Tickner who had initially blocked construction. While Justice von Doussa found against the Chapmans in his judgment, he crucially reassessed the genuineness of Ngarrindjeri belief regarding the area covered by the bridge, exonerating the women.[102] Though Kartinyeri lived to hear von Doussa's verdict, the affair had already succeeded in mocking Indigenous relationships to country and working to discredit testimony. Accordingly, Irene Watson has suggested that when the Ngarrindjeri women presented "another way of knowing the world" that threatened "white privilege," "white 'truth' prevailed."[103]

Within the context of subsequent land rights campaigns, the event set a precedent for the dismissal of applications to heritage protection based on cultural knowledge not freely available to settlers. It also, in a post-*Mabo* climate, worked to destabilize Indigenous being in place and refigured Anglo-Australians as superior guardians of normative relations to the country. This was particularly demonstrated in the affair's reliance on white anthropological expertise and its use by the law.[104] In this way, Hindmarsh Island set the scene for the development of a popular culture of denial of Indigenous testimony, which, as we have seen, took on renewed force in the late 1990s in response to the challenge of *Bringing them Home*.

Conclusion: Failed Witnesses

Popular commentary about the truthfulness of Indigenous testimony produced a climate of doubt in which the words of Aboriginal people were continually under suspicion. However, more than this, widespread criticism of the truth value of oral testimony was productive of a contemporary culture of historical denial. With regard to the stolen generations, both Bolt and Howard used cases of supposed lying to cast doubt on all testimony to child removal. On this foundation, they built the case that stolen generation testimony had inappropriately maligned the nation's history, smearing "too much dirt ... on our past."[105] Here, conservatives doubted not only the "truth" of the testimony of individuals, but also the broader role that Indigenous testimony had played in intervening in public memory about Australian history. For Tony Taylor, denial is something more than a descriptive term; it is a "pathology" and an "historical genre in its own right."[106] To consider conservative criticism of Aboriginal testimony in this way is to examine how it operated as a pervasive discourse on historical truth employing "exaggerated language, exaggerated argument and exaggerated external threat."[107] While Taylor has traced these techniques in the work of Keith Windschuttle and his stubborn denial of colonial violence, they are also evident in the popular conservative journalism of Bolt and Akerman in their insistence on the existence of a pernicious "Aboriginal industry."[108]

Robert Manne, in his polemic "In Denial: The Stolen Generations and the Right," has also examined the mechanics of conservative denial. Manne has demonstrated how conservative writers sought to discredit the stolen generations through an exaggeratedly forensic focus on the stories of key individuals, and has explained these denialist tendencies as "part of a larger culture war—over the meaning of Aboriginal dispossession."[109] Speculating on why conservative denial has been so fierce, Manne positioned these writers as failed witnesses. "Some," he argued, "have so little capacity for empathy that they genuinely cannot imagine the harm inflicted on a child taken from the warmth of a family to a loveless institution where their skin colour is regarded as a cause for shame . . ."[110] Here, Manne drew attention to the centrality of affect in the reception of testimony and the necessity for secondary witnesses to empathize with marginalized subjects. In refusing to respond affectively to testimony, conservative writers failed to understand testimony as a mode of speech dependent on the existence of a willing witness to activate its truth.

As theorists of testimony have affirmed, the "truth" of testimony is confirmed only through the exchange of witnessing.[111] This is not to argue that authenticity or referentiality is not important in assessing the truth value of testimony, but to emphasize the extent to which testimony is dependent on the willingness of a listener to engage. Truth, then, in autobiographical and testimonial terms is contingent: on the vagaries of memory and the complexities of subjective experiences and, most crucially, on the capacity of the secondary witness to engage in dialogue. Testimony cannot perform its cultural and political work without secondary witnesses. The refusal to witness, then, is, in the first instance, to do violence to an individual or a group, to deny the truth of their experiences of suffering or injustice, and to fail to recognize the mark of their survival.

The refusal to witness is also, at its core, the refusal to engage in a broader discourse of remaking Australianness. As Manne has identified, the conservative attack on stolen generation testimony was also, at the same time, an attack on broader ways of understanding the past in the present. Throughout the 1990s and into the twenty-first century, the testimony of marginalized subjects has been attached to processes of national revitalization that have hinged on the recognition of the other's story as Australia's story. The cultural politics of witnessing is, as I have stressed throughout, ambivalent. It has advanced only "baby steps," in Lauren Berlant's terms, toward the amelioration of the suffering of subaltern and marginalized peoples.[112] Indeed, as I have argued, witnessing has frequently underwritten the renewed authority of settler subjects to speak of and for the (good) nation. However, to ignore testimony is to elide the possibilities of witnessing as an active force for change: both symbolic and actual. It is to preclude what Deborah Bird Rose has understood as "a moral engagement of the past in the present," an approach that

> resists closure, whether that closure aims to decree that the violence in the past (or even in the present) is finished, or whether it claims more specifically to outlaw or ridicule historians and others who seek to remember violence.[113]

Ultimately, conservative criticism of testimony as faulty evidence has worked to obscure a key value of testimony, which is its ability to activate the process of witnessing, a form of memory work that opens the possibility of remaking the past in the present.

Testimony is not only an important form of oral history, and, as such, a challenge to narratives of the past that are dependent solely on (colonial) documentary evidence, but it is also a mode of affective engagement which exceeds the circumstances and requirements of positivist historiography. It is not simply that, *pace* Cubillo, a greater burden of proof was placed on Indigenous testimony, but also that it remained the colonial law/subject which adjudicated between different versions of the past.

For some, particularly Berlant and Attwood, the rise of a cultural politics of personal testimony has been deeply troubling, evincing a contraction of the public sphere and of the ability to mount an analysis of the authenticity and affect of personal speech. Accordingly, Bain Attwood has cautioned that testimony collapses the distance between the past and the present, eroding critical distance.[114] To be sure, the rise of personal testimony has troubled legalistic understandings of testimony as "proof" and has underscored the ethical urgency of viewing the present as a site of possible restitution, or, at the very least, working through for the traumatized and the victims of historical injustice. Failure to acknowledge testimony as a legitimate mode of relating to the past is, thus, also a failure to conceive of alternative modes of knowing the past. To embrace the affective power of testimony—and to attempt to witness to its truth—is also, necessarily, to "risk" what Dipesh Chakrabarty has described as "the disorder that could also be democracy."[115]

To be clear, I have not argued that concepts of referentiality are unimportant when considering life narrative and testimony, but I have complicated this through an awareness of the process of witnessing. The secondary witness is vulnerable to hoax testimony, and, as such, may often hold quite legitimate concerns about the meanings of life narratives. Yet this suspicion often exceeds the circumstances of a particular hoax, destabilizing the broader cultural work performed by testimony. Since the early 1990s, hoaxing, deliberate imposture, and conservative denial combined to contribute to a climate of doubt, in which the voices of minority subjects were always, already, under suspicion. This is my chief concern: It is not simply that the cultural politics of testimony reifies personal experience over critical distance, but that this culture and the culture of denial are oriented toward Anglo-Australians as arbiters of both individual truth and the national past. To accept the challenge—and risks—of a more ambivalent form of witnessing testimony is to work toward the ceding of this privilege and a remaking of Australianness as a paradigm in which all voices are worthy of attention and belief.

Notes

1. Alison Broinowski (dir.), *Forbidden Lie$* (Australia: Palace Films, 2007).
2. Philippe Lejeune, *On Autobiography*, ed. Paul John Eakin, trans. Katherine Leary (Minneapolis: University of Minnesota Press, 1989).
3. Robert Manne delivers an excellent précis of this culture of denial in Manne, "In Denial," 217–305.
4. This was particularly the case in the debate surrounding the work of Keith Windschuttle, who sought to demonstrate that several prominent historians had "fabricated" the truth about frontier history. Windschuttle, *Fabrication of Aboriginal History Volume 1*; Manne, ed., *Whitewash*.
5. For a comprehensive guide to the differences between genres of life writing, see Smith and Watson, *Reading Autobiography*.
6. Susanna Egan, "The Company She Keeps: Demidenko and the Problems of Imposture in Autobiography," *Australian Literary Studies* 21, no. 4 (2004): 15.
7. Smith and Watson, *Reading Autobiography*, 12–14.
8. Ibid., 13.
9. Kate Douglas, "'Blurbing' Autobiographical: Authorship and Autobiography," *Biography* 24, no. 4 (2001): 806.
10. Egan, "Company She Keeps," 15.
11. Ibid., 25.
12. Phillip Gourevitch cited in Andrew S. Gross and Michael J. Hoffman, "Memory, Authority, and Identity: Holocaust Studies in Light of the Wilkomirski Debate," *Biography* 27, no. 1 (2004): 33.
13. Stefan Maechler, *The Wilkomirski Affair: A Study in Biographical Truth* (New York: Schocken, 2001).
14. See especially the invocation of the notion of "secondhand witnessing" in Michael Bernard-Donals, "Beyond the Question of Authenticity: Witness and Testimony in the *Fragments* Controversy," *PMLA* 116, no. 5 (2001): 1302–15. Compare with the concept of "prosthetic memory," a product the transferential relationship between testifier and witness in Alison Landsberg, "America, the Holocaust, and the Mass Culture of Memory: Toward a Radical Politics of Empathy," *New German Critique: An Interdisciplinary Journal of German Studies* 71 (Spring–Summer 1997): 63–87.
15. Felman and Laub, *Testimony*, 5.
16. Gross and Hoffman, "Memory, Authority, and Identity," 35.
17. Ibid., 37.
18. Egan, "Company She Keeps," 21.
19. Ibid., 22.
20. Ibid., 24.
21. Ibid.
22. Maggie Nolan and Carrie Dawson, "Who's Who? Mapping Hoaxes and Imposture in Australian Literary History," *Australian Literary Studies* 21, no. 4 (2004): xiii.
23. Gilmore, *Limits of Autobiography*, 3.
24. See Gillian Whitlock, "Tainted Testimony: The Khouri Affair," *Australian Literary Studies* 21, no. 4 (2004): 165–77.
25. Ibid., 167.

26. Norma Khouri, *Forbidden Love* (London: Doubleday, 2003). The text was published in America under the title *Honor Lost*.
27. Kate Douglas, "'Blurbing' Autobiographical."
28. Khouri, *Forbidden Love*.
29. Whitlock, "Tainted Testimony," 169.
30. Cited in Ibid. It should be noted that this afterward did not appear in all versions of *Forbidden Love*.
31. Ibid., 169.
32. Schaffer and Smith, *Human Rights and Narrated Lives*.
33. Malcolm Knox, "Her Life as a Fake: Bestseller's Lies Exposed," *Sydney Morning Herald*, July 24, 2004, 1. See also Malcolm Knox, "Word of Honour? The Plot Thickens in Khouri Saga," *Age*, July 27, 2004, 1.
34. Malcolm Knox and Caroline Overington, "Khouri—the Troubled Life of a Fake," *Age*, July 31, 2004, 3.
35. Dan Silkstone, "Forbidden Love Off the Shelves," *Age*, July 27, 2004.
36. This early criticism of *Forbidden Love* is mentioned by Knox and Overington, "Khouri—the Troubled Life of a Fake."
37. Eva Sallis, "The Blinkers of an Unspeakable Horror," *Sydney Morning Herald*, March 1, 2003, 14.
38. Khouri, *Forbidden Love*, 1.
39. Sallis, "The Blinkers of an Unspeakable Horror," 4.
40. Knox, "Her Life as a Fake"; Sallis, "Blinkers of an Unspeakable Horror."
41. Gross and Hoffman, "Memory, Authority, and Identity," 34.
42. Whitlock, "Tainted Testimony," 171.
43. Ibid., 173.
44. On the proliferation of Arab stereotypes post-September 11, particularly in Australia, see Scott Poynting et al., *Bin Laden in the Suburbs: Criminalising the Arab Other* (Sydney: Sydney Institute of Criminology, 2004).
45. The hoax was discussed in this mode from the moment of its exposure. See Knox, "Her Life as a Fake."
46. Ibid.
47. A large body of work has developed around "Australian" hoaxing. See especially Melissa Katsoulis, *Telling Tales: A History of Literary Hoaxes* (Melbourne: Hardie Grant Books, 2010); Simon Caterson, *Hoax Nation: Australian Fakes and Frauds, from Plato to Norma Khouri* (Melbourne: Arcade Publications, 2009); Iain McIntyre, *How to Make Trouble and Influence People: Pranks, Hoaxes, Graffiti and Political Mischief-Making* (Sydney: Breakdown Press, 2009); Maggie Nolan, "In His Own Sweet Time: Carmen's Coming Out," *Australian Literary Studies* 21, no. 4 (2004): 134–48; David Carter, "O' Grady, John *See* 'Culotta, Nino': Popular Authorship, Duplicity and Celebrity," *Australian Literary Studies* 21, no. 4 (2004): 56–73; Michael Heyward, *The Ern Malley Affair* (St. Lucia: University of Queensland Press, 1993). On Helen Demidenko, see Sonia Mycak, "Demidenko/Darville: A Ukrainian-Australian Point of View," *Australian Literary Studies* 21, no. 4 (2004): 111–33; Robert Manne, *The Culture of Forgetting: Helen Demidenko and the Holocaust* (Melbourne: Text Publishing, 1996); John Jost, Gianna Totaro, and Christine Tyshing, eds., *The Demidenko File* (Ringwood: Penguin, 1996); A.P. Riemer, *The Demidenko Debate* (St. Leonard's, NSW: Allen & Unwin, 1996). For a critical reappraisal of the role

of the Demidenko affair in the contemporary Australian media, see Davis, *Gangland*.

48. Simon Caterson cited in Katherine Wilson, "Playing Us for Suckers," *Age*, January 1–2, 2010, 16.

49. Carter, "O' Grady, John *See* 'Culotta, Nino," 56–58. Carter has complicated this division through his reading of O'Grady's work, arguing that although O'Grady did not seek to be discovered, *They're a Weird Mob* contained a "built-in obsolescence."

50. This mode of hoax, in which the object is to criticize literary or cultural institutions, includes the American Alan Sokal hoax and the more recent Australian Sharon Gould/*Quadrant* hoax. On the latter, see Justine Ferrari and Samantha Maiden, "Keith Windschuttle caught in *Quadrant* hoax," *Australian*, January 7, 2009, http://www.theaustralian.com.au/business/media/windschuttle-caught-in-quadrant-hoax/story-e6frg996-1111118495607 (accessed November 19, 2009).

51. Gunew, "Against Multiculturalism," 50.

52. Nolan and Dawson, "Who's Who? Mapping Hoaxes and Imposture in Australian Literary History," vi. While many critics are eager to ascribe hoaxing to some peculiarly Australian condition, Laura Browder's study of ethnic imposture in American literary provides a much-needed corrective Laura Browder, *Slippery Characters: Ethnic Impersonators and American Identities* (Chapel Hill: University of North Carolina Press, 2000).

53. Nicoll, "Pseudo-Hyphens and Barbaric/Binaries," 79.

54. Ivor Indyk cited in Luke Slattery and Bill Leak, "Identity Crisis," *Australian*, March 15, 1997, 21.

55. Robert Manne cited in Ibid. Throughout the Demidenko affair, this claim was frequently deployed, without any supporting statistical evidence, as a part of a broader lament about a supposed lack of interest in "Australian" culture.

56. Edmund Campion cited in Ibid.

57. Nicoll, "Pseudo-Hyphens and Barbaric/Binaries," 79–83.

58. Marguerite O'Hara, "Stranger Than Non-Fiction: The Slippery Truth in *Forbidden Lie$*," *Metro Magazine*, no. 114 (2007): 20–25.

59. Nolan and Dawson, "Who's Who? Mapping Hoaxes and Imposture in Australian Literary History," xi.

60. Myke Bartlett, "The Unbelievable Truth of *Forbidden Lie$*," *Screen Education*, no. 48 (2007): 36.

61. Alison Broinowski cited in Richard Fidler, "In Conversation with Director Alison Broinowski," ABC *Local Radio*, September 10, 2007, [Transcript], http://www.abc.net.au/queensland/conversations/stories/s2028619.htm?nsw (accessed December 14, 2009).

62. Margaret Pomeranz, "Forbidden Lies," *At the Movies*, ABC TV, September 5, 2007, http://www.abc.net.au/atthemovies/txt/s2007185.htm (accessed November 25, 2009).

63. Kate Legge, "Hoaxer So Hard to Read," *Australian*, July 31, 2004, 1–2.

64. Bartlett, "The Unbelievable Truth of *Forbidden Lie$*," 36.

65. Nolan, "In His Own Sweet Time," 142.

66. Both hoaxes attracted a deluge of media coverage in both Australia and overseas. See, for example, Debra Jopson and Kelly Burke, "Painting Hoax

Has Art World Divided," *Sydney Morning Herald*, March 8, 1997, 5; Clyde H. Farnsworth, "Two Artists, Neither Aboriginal (nor Original) after All," *New York Times*, April 2, 1997, 9.

67. Nolan and Dawson, "Who's Who? Mapping Hoaxes and Imposture in Australian Literary History," ix.

68. Vivien Johnson cited in Nolan, "In His Own Sweet Time," 138–39.

69. *Herald Sun* columnist Andrew Bolt is particularly known for his characterization of the stolen generations as a "myth." See, for example Andrew Bolt, "Straight Talking Seen as a Crime," *Herald Sun*, February 24, 2001, 3; Andrew Bolt, "A Moral Mafia," *Herald Sun*, April 13, 2000, 18.

70. In Robert Manne's terms, Bolt et al. formed "the troops" in a conservative campaign against *Bringing them Home*. Manne, "In Denial," 272–73.

71. Bolt, "Straight Talking Seen as a Crime," 3.

72. Andrew Bolt, "Sorry, but I Wasn't 'Stolen'—Leader Admits She Lied," *Daily Telegraph*, February 23, 2001, 3.

73. Ibid.

74. Ibid.

75. Bolt, "Moral Mafia," 18.

76. P.P. McGuinness cited in Manne, "In Denial," 272. A public discourse on false memory syndrome developed in the West during the early 1990s in response to a spate of high-profile "false" accusations of rape and "satanic" sexual abuse, and allegations of the misuse of "recovered memory" therapies. For analysis of this phenomenon in the United States, see Jane Kilby, *Violence and the Cultural Politics of Trauma* (Edinburgh: Edinburgh University Press, 2007); Terence W. Campbell, *Smoke and Mirrors: The Devastating Effect of False Sexual Abuse Claims* (New York: Insight Books, 1998); Claudette Wassil-Grimm, *Diagnosis for Disaster: The Devastating Truth About False Memory Syndrome and Its Impact on Accusers and Families* (Woodstock, N.Y.: Overlook Press, 1995). With reference to the stolen generations, see Bryoni Trezise, "Recovering Memories: Versions of a Misremembered Australian Body," *Australian Feminist Law Journal* 29 (December 2008): 155–75.

77. John Howard cited in Emma Macdonald, "Stolen Claim Backfires on O'Donoghue," *Canberra Times*, February 24, 2001, 1.

78. Bolt, "Straight Talking Seen as a Crime," 3.

79. Piers Akerman, "Sorry, It's the Truth," *Courier Mail*, March 2, 2001, 13.

80. Bolt, "Moral Mafia," 18.

81. Editorial, "The Healing Value of the Truth," *Courier Mail*, February 24, 2001, 22.

82. See especially Akerman, "Sorry, It's the Truth," 13.

83. Ibid. See also, Piers Akerman, "Embracing the Lie Prolongs the Pain," *Daily Telegraph*, April 6, 2000, 23.

84. On criticism of *Bringing them Home* for failing to cross-examine witnesses, see Ron Brunton, "Betraying the Victims: The 'Stolen Generations' Report," *IPA Backgrounder* 10, no. 1 (1998).

85. *Cubillo v. Commonwealth*: (1999) 89 FCR 528; (2000) 103 FCR 1; (2001) 112 FCR 171. It is instructive, though beyond the scope of this chapter, to compare the "failure'" of Cubillo-Gunner and its treatment of Indigenous testimony to other cases, particularly the first stolen generation case,

Kruger v. The Commonwealth (1997) 190 CLR 1; the land rights case *Yorta Yorta Aboriginal Community v. State of Victoria* [1998] 1606 FA; and the first successful stolen generation compensation case *Trevorrow v. State of South Australia (No 5)* [2007] SASC 285. For a detailed analysis of these cases and their significance for the legal status of Aboriginal testimony, see Curthoys, Genovese, and Reilly, *Rights and Redemption*.

86. Ibid., 134. For a detailed summary of the case, see Jennifer Clarke, "Case note: *Cubillo v. The Commonwealth*," *Melbourne University Law Review* 25, (2001), http://www.austlii.edu.au/au/journals/MULR/2001/7.html#Heading68 (accessed November 22, 2009).

87. O'Loughlin J. cited in Trish Luker, "Postcolonising Amnesia in the Discourse of Reconciliation: The Void in the Law's Response to the Stolen Generations," *Australian Feminist Law Journal* 22 (June 2005): 82.

88. O'Loughlin cited in Ibid.

89. A small body of critical material has emerged to analyze the disjunction between law's history and that of professional historians. See especially Curthoys, Genovese, and Reilly, *Rights and Redemption*; Iain McCalman and Ann McGrath, eds., *Proof & Truth: The Humanist as Expert* (Canberra: The Australian Academy of Humanities, 2003); Peter Read, "The Stolen Generations, the Historian and the Court Room," *Aboriginal History* 26 (2002): 51–61.

90. Curthoys, Genovese, and Reilly, *Rights and Redemption*, 136. See also Alisoun Neville, "*Cubillo v. Commonwealth*: Classifying Text and the Violence of Exclusion," *Macquarie Law Journal* 5 (2005): 31–55; Trish Luker, "Intention and Iterability in *Cubillo v. Commonwealth*," *Journal of Australian Studies* 84 (2005): 35–42.

91. Luker, "Postcolonising Amnesia in the Discourse of Reconciliation," 85.

92. Clarke, "Case note: *Cubillo v. The Commonwealth*."

93. Luker, "Postcolonising Amnesia in the Discourse of Reconciliation," 87. See also Trish Luker, "Ineffaceable Memories: The Truth of Testimony," *Australian Feminist Law Journal* 29 (December 2008): 133–54.

94. Curthoys, Genovese, and Reilly, *Rights and Redemption*, 137.

95. Lorna Cubillo's testimony of her removal included descriptions of "a lot of people crying" and "hitting themselves with hunting sticks so that blood was pouring down their faces." Lorna Cubillo cited in Luker, "Postcolonising Amnesia in the Discourse of Reconciliation," 85.

96. See, for example, Akerman, "Sorry, It's the Truth," 13; Mark Metherell and Debra Jopson, "Stolen Children Ruling Vindicates Stance: Pm," *Sydney Morning Herald*, August 12, 2000, 2; Michael Duffy, "Myths Perpetuate a Stake in Victimhood," *Daily Telegraph*, August 12, 2000, 23.

97. Andrew Bolt, "Confusing Emotion with Facts Won't Help the Aboriginal Cause," *Herald Sun*, August 14, 2000, 18.

98. Though the planning process and application for the bridge began as early as 1989, the "affair" did not become public until 1994 when the Aboriginal Legal Rights Movement, acting on behalf of a group of Ngarrindjeri people, sought to protect the area under the Commonwealth's *Aboriginal and Torres Strait Islander Heritage Protection Act 1984*. For a summary of events, see Curthoys, Genovese, and Reilly, *Rights and Redemption*, 167–90. See also

Margaret Simons, *The Meeting of the Waters: The Hindmarsh Island Affair* (Sydney: Hodder, 2003).

99. For an account of this dispute from Kartinyeri's perspective, see Doreen Kartinyeri and Sue Anderson, *Doreen Kartinyeri: My Ngarindjeri Calling* (Canberra: Aboriginal Studies Press, 2008).

100. Hindmarsh Island Bridge Royal Commission, *Report of the Hindmarsh Island Bridge Royal Commission* (Adelaide: The Royal Commission, 1995). The bridge was completed in 2001.

101. Bolt referred to the affair as a "nonsense case," whereas Akerman described the "secret women's business" as "ideological hogwash cooked up by feminist anthropologists." Bolt, "Confusing Emotion with Facts Won't Help the Aboriginal Cause," 18. Piers Akerman, "Truth and the Black Armband Brigade," *Daily Telegraph*, March 1, 2001, 19.

102. *Chapman v. Luminis Pty Lt (No 4)* (2001) 123 FCR 62. See also Curthoys, Genovese, and Reilly, *Rights and Redemption*, 167–90.

103. Watson, "Settled and Unsettled Spaces: Are We Free to Roam?," 16. On the intersectionality of gender and race in the law's treatment of the Ngarrindjeri women, see Joanna Bourke, "Women's Business: Sex, Secrets and the Hindmarsh Island Affair," *UNSW Law Journal* 20, no. 2 (1997): 333–51.

104. Curthoys, Genovese, and Reilly, *Rights and Redemption*, 168.

105. Bolt, "Confusing Emotion with Facts Won't Help the Aboriginal Cause," 18. For more on Bolt's claims regarding Charles Perkins, see Andrew Bolt, "Stolen? No, Helped in Education," *Herald Sun*, April 10, 2000, 20.

106. Taylor, *Denial*, ix.

107. Ibid., 182.

108. Akerman, "Sorry, Its the Truth," 13.

109. Manne, "In Denial," 303.

110. Ibid.

111. This, as demonstrated earlier, has been particularly so in the work of Felman and Laub. Felman and Laub, *Testimony*.

112. Berlant, " Subject of True Feeling: Pain, Privacy, and Politics," 85.

113. Rose, *Reports from a Wild Country*, 14.

114. See especially Attwood, *Telling the Truth About Aboriginal History*; and Attwood, "In the Age of Testimony: The Stolen Generations Narrative, 'Distance', and Public History," 75–95.

115. Bain Attwood and Dipesh Chakrabarty, "Risky Histories," *Meanjin* 65, no. 1 (2006): 207.

6

Witnessing (Dis)possession: Victims, Battlers, and "Ordinary" Australians

Over the past two decades, testimony has complicated Australia's self-image as the egalitarian land of the fair go. It has emphasized the ongoing struggles of many Indigenous peoples, recent migrants, and asylum seekers, while highlighting the privilege of "ordinary" settler Australians. Throughout this book, I have been concerned, primarily, with tracing the response of settler Australians to the testimonies of Indigenous peoples and asylum seekers. As a form of public memory work, this mode of witnessing has sought to bring "minority" stories within a national framework, and, by doing so, to remake understandings of which stories—and whose voices—matter within contemporary culture. In contrast, this chapter examines some of the ways that settler Australians have witnessed to their own experiences. This constitutes a form of witnessing oriented not toward the Other, but to the concerns of the dominant cultural group.

As a way of opening a discussion of settler testimony, this chapter examines the 2007 surf-documentary *Bra Boys*.[1] In particular, it explores the way *Bra Boys* has used the battler trope to witness to an old story of Anglo-Australian victimhood. It traces the persistence of the battler trope and examines the potential pleasures this narrative has held for settler Australians in the context of the contemporary explosion of "minority" testimony. In doing so, I consider the role of testimony as the preeminent genre of contemporary identity politics—shared by "mainstream" and subaltern subjects alike—and discuss the ambivalence of witnessing as a liberal practice of recognition and social justice.

This chapter also considers the relationship between testimonies of suffering and trauma, and more "positive" stories of battler triumph,

217

by examining the long-running Australian Broadcasting Commission (ABC) television program *Australian Story*. It focuses on the program as a vehicle of positive or "feel-good" testimony, contextualizing it with reference to broader questions concerning the proliferation of "ordinary" voices within the public sphere. I argue that *Australian Story* has highlighted the desire of Australians to connect with each other through the sharing of testimony, to produce a sense of Australianness from a fabric of "true stories."[2] At the same time, it has affirmed the power of dominant cultural narratives to shape the kinds of stories "we" tell each other.

Set against the *fin-de-siècle* explosion of "minority" testimony, settler stories have maintained their valency within the public sphere. In differing ways, both *Bra Boys* and *Australian Story* have demanded that we listen, once again, to the voice of the "struggling," white battler. These texts have, in differing ways, invited their viewers to take pleasure in the reproduction of Anglo-Australian victimhood and reposition the white, socially disadvantaged male at the center of national narratives of belonging. This is not to suggest that Anglo subjects have appropriated the mechanics of witnessing for their own narratives. On the contrary, I highlight the extent to which genres of testimony and autobiographical representation are attractive forms of public communication for all. "Minority" testimony has challenged settler Australians to reimagine a vision of good citizenship against the revelation that Australia is not only a nation founded on the colonial dispossession of Indigenous peoples, but also a nation which perpetuates the disadvantage of a range of social and cultural groups. At the same time, the continued presence of the Anglo battler narrative has highlighted the power of testimonial expression to exist, not as a force for change, but to reinforce prevailing relations of power.

Unsettling Stories

Released in 2007, *Bra Boys* chronicled the struggles of the Abberton brothers—Sunny, Jai, Koby, and Dakota—core members of the eponymous surf gang.[3] Based at Maroubra beach in Sydney's southeastern suburbs, the Bra Boys are Australia's most infamous and internationally recognized surf gang, an amorphous "tribe" including hundreds of "members." Directed and cowritten by Sunny Abberton, the documentary focused on his siblings as the nucleus of the group. The film described the Abbertons' impoverished, violent childhoods, and offered a redemptive battler narrative in which the brothers find salvation through surfing. The Boys have attracted considerable negative media attention due to their frequent involvement in conflicts with rival surfers and the law.[4] As a documentary produced by its own subject, *Bra Boys* is a performance of defiance, an attempt to proudly tell "their story" in the face of ongoing scrutiny. In this way, *Bra Boys* has functioned as a form of testimony, drawing on the iconic battler trope to express "the truth" of the Boys' experience.

Generically, *Bra Boys* is a surf movie. Through its portrayal of the exhilaration of surfing, the film participated in a long-standing international tradition of films produced by and for surfers. While the surf has been a subject for filmmakers since the earliest days of cinema, surf movies emerged during the first half of the twentieth century as a distinct genre and, despite a spike in popularity during the 1960s, have always maintained a niche audience.[5] Yet, within Australia, *Bra Boys* has attracted an outstandingly large general audience. In fact, *Bra Boys* has become something of a phenomenon, breaking all existing box office records—and surpassing previous record-holder *Cane Toads* (1988)—to become the country's highest grossing documentary.[6] The wide appeal of *Bra Boys* has demonstrated the way it engages with a broader process of national storytelling. In this sense, *Bra Boys* is not simply a surf movie; but it has also actively participated in struggles over history, identity, and belonging within public culture.

Central to *Bra Boys'* success has been its use of the iconic battler narrative as a mode of testimony. The "battler" has figured within Australian cultural history as the embodiment of the national values of hard work, egalitarianism, and perseverance. Although the battler is closely related to the pioneer myth, it was consolidated during the labor struggles of the nineteenth century to become a celebrated radical nationalist archetype.[7] In essence, the battler is an underdog figure, someone who has struggled to succeed against the odds. The battler has reappeared frequently in Australian public culture, most recently as the key theme of the 1997 film *The Castle*, the focus of Pauline Hanson's One Nation Party during the 1990s, and as former Prime Minister John Howard's target constituency.[8] *Bra Boys* has employed the battler narrative as a way of authenticating the film as a type of victim testimony. In drawing on such a powerful cultural myth, *Bra Boys* has placed the Abberton brothers within a familiar history of white struggle, inviting the audience to identify with the Boys and to understand their story as the "truth." As such, *Bra Boys* has served as an intervention into contemporary testimonial culture.

Produced in the wake of the 2005 Cronulla riots, *Bra Boys* has complicated ideas about the ways testimonial expression circulates in the public sphere. Both *Bra Boys* and the riots—a series of violent clashes between Anglo and Lebanese Australians at south Sydney's Cronulla beach—hinged on a resurgent identity politics that emphasized the proprietary rights of white, masculine, and "mainstream" subjects. If the voices of marginalized Australians have received focused attention over the past decade, *Bra Boys* works within an older, foundational discourse that asserts the primacy of narratives of white, male struggle. As a form of testimony, I argue that *Bra Boys* has worked to interpellate the audience as active participants in storytelling, calling on them to witness to the truth of the Boys' experiences. In doing so, *Bra Boys* has employed the iconic battler trope to retell an old story about settler belonging in Australian spaces.

If the *fin-de-siècle* explosion in testimony has been crucial in the development of a national politics of recognition and reconciliation for the subaltern, *Bra Boys* has reanimated an older discourse in which the white, male citizen has figured as the only "authentic" subject of victimhood. *Bra Boys* is not only proof, in the words of the film's narrator, Russell Crowe, that "their culture has survived," but it is also a reminder of the shifting ways we hear the voices of the "dispossessed." In using the battler narrative as a form of testimony, *Bra Boys* has participated in an enduring discourse of white belonging that legitimates settler possession as the "reward" for historic suffering. It is a powerful cultural narrative fueled by a blithe amnesia that claims moral virtue as it elides the sovereign claims of Indigenous Australians. As Clifton Evers, cultural critic and surfer, was once warned by "Max," the Indigenous custodian of his local surf spot, settler Australians "forget the power [they] have to ignore our stories while furthering [their] own."[9]

It is within the wider context of the explosion of "minority" testimony that I read *Bra Boys*. To do so is not to argue that *Bra Boys* constitutes a form of appropriation. If the most obvious use of testimony within Australia has been by Indigenous peoples and, to a lesser extent other disenfranchised groups, *Bra Boys* demonstrates the contemporary shift from testimony as a subaltern genre to a pervasive mode of self-expression. The rise of testimony and the formation of a cultural politics of "intimacy" are global phenomena; and *Bra Boys* has circulated within worldwide commercial surfing networks.[10] Yet *Bra Boys* has remained concerned with expressing a narrative of identity connected to specifically Australian places. In particular, *Bra Boys* has engaged with a network of national storytelling in which Indigenous testimony, and its implications for settler belonging, has been prominent. *Bra Boys*, with its unambiguous assertion of ownership over Maroubra beach, has implicitly challenged Indigenous testimony as a reassertion of sovereignty.

To consider *Bra Boys* as a form of testimony is to recognize that the rise of first-person speech as a mode of authenticity has fueled the proliferation of new testimonial forms. Directed and cowritten by Sunny Abberton, the film departed from a conventional documentary framework in being produced by its own subject. This "lack" of objectivity has troubled some reviewers, in particular ABC TV's *At the Movies'* David Stratton, who has bemoaned the film's lack of "balance," as "all a bit self-serving."[11] Here, film theorist Michael Renov's consideration of "first-person" or autobiographical documentary is instructive.[12] First-person documentaries, Renov has argued, have functioned as acts of self-definition, the means by which individuals and groups can harness the medium of visual self-inscription to intervene in public discourses about themselves. As such, first-person documentaries have constituted a departure from so-called "objective" or "distant" schools of documentary filmmaking to participate in the "diversity of autobiographical practices that engage with and perform subjectivity."[13] In doing so, first-person documentaries have registered the "collision" of autobiographical and documentary forms and test the perimeters of foundational concepts of "truth" and "self." In what follows, I consider *Bra Boys* as a controlled exercise in self-fashioning, an attempt to testify to the truth of a collective experience.

Setting the Scene

Bra Boys opens with a frenetic five-minute montage that works to establish the Boys as "survivors" within the harsh suburban landscape of Maroubra. Amateur film clips of the Boys surfing and hanging out are spliced with police footage of altercations between the Boys and the local establishment. Here, *Bra Boys* uses the trope of suburbia as a wasteland to set up what Evers has aptly described as "a ghetto imaginary of Maroubra."[14] This is sustained throughout the film via shots of Long Bay Gaol, dilapidated Housing Commission flats, and graffitied streetscapes. The sense that Maroubra is a suburb "under siege" is further emphasized through the use of footage of hovering police helicopters and the piercing sound of sirens. Scored by Bra Boy Jamie Holt with a mixture of acoustic guitar and faux "gangsta" rap,

Maroubra emerged unequivocally as a place where, in the words of one the film's interviewees, "heavy shit" happens.

Against this backdrop of suburban disintegration, *Bra Boys* has advanced its core narrative of struggle and triumph. In essence, the film tells the story of how the Abberton brothers rose to surfing stardom from a childhood of poverty and neglect. With their fathers absent and their mother addicted to heroin, the brothers sought the company of older boys and friends in the surf. There, they formed the "Bra Boys," a surfing "brotherhood" and second family. However, surfing not only provided a way to escape domestic troubles, but it also ultimately became the brothers' main focus in life and eventually, a way to secure their financial futures. This overarching narrative of triumph pivoted around three main episodes in the development of the gang. First, the events surrounding the Boys' violent clash with off-duty police at the Coogee-Randwick RSL Club on December 22, 2002; second, the death of local "standover man" Anthony Hines in August 2003 and the subsequent arrest and murder trial of Jai Abberton; and lastly, the Boys' role as community mediators in the aftermath of the 2005 Cronulla riots.

The core episode is the "death" of Anthony Hines, for which Jai was charged with murder, and Koby with attempting to pervert the course of justice. While the Boys are presented as essentially good-natured, the film is not shy in depicting their aggression. In this sense, the film has acted as an attempt to "clear" the Boys' name and make the violent aspects of their life understandable. The film does not attempt to deny Jai's actions and, in fact, actually confirms, quite casually, that he did shoot Hines and dump his naked body over a cliff, and Hines is portrayed as a vicious standover man who terrorized the community and attempted to rape Jai's girlfriend. Here, Jai is exonerated as masculine protector.[15] More broadly, the film has attempted to provide a context and a host of mitigating circumstances to account for the propensity of the Boys to engage in acts of violence and intimidation.

Crucial to the status of *Bra Boys* is its focus on the individual Abberton brothers and their struggle to succeed. The movie has adopted this classical survival narrative—a key testimonial trope—and has anchored it through footage in which the Boys speak directly to the camera about the difficulties they have faced. The bulk of the film comprises "talking heads"-style interviews in which the audience sees the Abberton brothers and other members of the gang talking about their experiences. Further, the film has worked to sustain a direct relationship between the Boys and the audience through an emphasis on the physicality of the Abbertons, particularly Koby, the most talented surfer and "star" of the film. The camera lingers on the Boys' bare, tattooed torsos; a nakedness that signals their intimidating physical strength at the same time as it figures an embodied vulnerability. Koby is most often shot, naked from the waist up, against a darkened studio background: The sparseness of these images serve not only to reinforce a sense of immediacy in his connection to the viewer, but also to present Koby's words as the unvarnished "truth." In other instances, the Abberton brothers are shot against the beach, or, most notably, inside a burnt-out, vandalized building. The contrast between the urban decay of Maroubra and the vivid surf is stark; the beach emerges as the Boys' only escape.

Bra Boys is an extremely slick production. It is fast-paced, melodramatic, and peppered with stunning footage of the Boys surfing. Accordingly, Evers has described it as a "film [that] sucks you in."[16] For Evers, the audience is drawn into "quite an ugly world of surfing, localism, violence, mateship and masculinity."[17] The film is certainly appealing, though it is not simply that surfing and violence are inherently exciting. The "success" of *Bra Boys* as a form of testimony lies in the way it consciously works to "suck" you in, to establish an emotional connection, and to interpellate audience members as sympathetic witnesses. When Crowe, in his opening narration, uttered the words "this is their story," he invited the audience to witness to the truth of *Bra Boys*. In this way, the audience is drawn to actively participate as witnesses to the Boys' story. However, to function as testimony, *Bra Boys* has needed to elicit the affective response of the audience. Its primary mode of achieving this has been through the reproduction of the iconic Australian battler narrative.

Witnessing the Battler

Drawing on the nationalist iconography of the surfer, the film placed the Boys firmly within an Australian history of antiauthoritarianism. This narrative has been crucially foregrounded by the deployment of larrikin icon and Academy Award winning actor Russell Crowe as narrator.[18] Best noted for his hypermasculine performances, Crowe has also played a role in a real-life battler struggle: that of the working-class South Sydney Rabbitohs Rugby League Club.[19] Central to the film's appeal is the way the Boys are established as marginalized "outsider" figures who have struggled to succeed. Crowe positioned the Boys as having overcome the establishment's historic antagonism toward surfers: "over the years," he intoned, "authorities have battled to disperse the surf tribes." In this way, *Bra Boys* has merged the "surfer," a more marginal, subcultural figure, with the image of the hardworking, struggling, "battler."

During the twentieth century, the surfer emerged alongside the lifesaver as a key figure in Australia's national imaginary, as heir apparent in a lineage of "battler" icons, including the bushman and the digger—the "continuing image of Australian masculinity—able-bodiedness, heroic sacrifice and racial purity."[20] The figure of the battler has endured as the embodiment of the so-called "Australian values" of hard work and persistence. The battler is, according to Sean Scalmer, "the protagonist of the Australian legend."[21] The surfer has been, however, a far more ambivalent figure, often coded as the hedonistic other to the lifesaver. Against the community-minded discipline of the lifesaver, a figure devoted to hard work and public service, the surfer has been demonized as unruly and apathetic.[22] In *Bra Boys*, the surfer is transformed into the noble battler through an emphasis on hard work and mateship. Surfing is indeed a leisure activity, the pastime of choice for "bludgers," whereas professional surfing has been the means by which the Boys have escaped the poverty and neglect of their childhoods.

Bra Boys has explicitly drawn on the notion of the battler through its emphasis on the efforts of the Boys to work hard to escape poverty. Theirs is a brotherhood forged through the experience of violent neglect. Life could be hard, but as Koby argued, "it was good, it turned us into what we are." This experience of disadvantage not only cemented the strength of fraternal bonds, but also solidified familial connections. This is illustrated in the film's focus on the close relationship between the Boys and their grandmother, Mavis Abberton, the family matriarch who raised the brothers in the absence of their parents. The film's depiction of this filial connection is crucial not only to its attempt to soften the more violent elements of the Boys' personae, but also to the film's emotional appeal to the audience. The relationship between the Boys and their grandmother is anchored through a montage of family "happy snaps" that show the Boys playing at creating surf gangs named in her honor. It is the now-adult members of one of these infant gangs—Ma's Hell Team—that serve as her disconsolate pallbearers in a funeral scene which has provided this otherwise tightly controlled film with a core of unvarnished emotion.

The funeral scene, in which the Boys struggle to contain their tears, enacts the masculine ideals of stoicism and loyalty and, in doing so, has drawn attention to the extent to which this film is, ultimately, about bonds between men. Apart from Ma, women are barely present in *Bra Boys*. As such, it is important to emphasize that the battler, here, is marked as explicitly masculine. However, more than this, as self-styled battlers, the Boys have portrayed themselves as violent men, positioning them within a lineage of violent, yet heroic, male struggle that has included figures such as Ned Kelly.

In their work on Gregor Jordan's 2003 film *Ned Kelly*, Sarah Pinto and Leigh Boucher have linked the resurgence of the Kelly legend to *fin-de-siècle* anxieties over the legitimacy of "a violent fraternal speaking voice."[23] Though, as Katherine Biber has argued, "violent white men are the backbone of [Australian] culture," Pinto and Boucher have read *Ned Kelly* as responding to widespread contemporary concern that the white, working-class man has "borne the brunt of the social, political, and economic changes of late twentieth century capitalism."[24] As such, Jordan's turn to Kelly has represented an attempt to "resuscitate" the political legitimacy of a white male speaking voice in response to its recently "weakened" status.[25]

Bra Boys has been similarly concerned to "revive" the affective power of the voice of the battler and to privilege its suffering. Here, *Bra Boys*, similar to *Ned Kelly*, has engaged with what Ghassan Hage has termed "a sense of white decline," whereby Anglo-Australians have perceived themselves to no longer have the "national privileges or opportunities or promises that are perceived to have existed in a previous era."[26] This anxiety is particularly evident in the film's aggressive promulgation of the notion of the Boys as people who have been profoundly disadvantaged and who have turned to violence as a mode of protection and self-preservation. Yet, while *Bra Boys* has worked to "revive" an historic sense of the battler to underwrite the Boys' testimonial claims, it has also evinced the nuanced class connotations of contemporary usage of the battler trope, in particular responding to its strategic deployment by John Howard.

The battler is related to the long-standing nationalist archetypes of the digger and bushman, whereas the battler has figured in recent cultural memory as a key trope within former Prime Minister John Howard's neoliberal ideology. In 2004, Howard indicated the diffuse nature of the battler label:

It's not an exclusive definition, the battler is somebody who finds in life that they have to work hard for everything they get . . . normally you then look at it in terms of somebody who's not earning a huge income but somebody who is trying to better themselves, and I've always been attracted to people who try to better themselves.[27]

Here, the battler has been defined through a self-perception of struggle; the image is cross-class or aspirational. The "battler" is an historic term, with distinctly working-class and union resonances; whereas during the Howard era, the "battler" came to apply to an amorphous group: "the ordinary, struggling people."[28] As Nick Dyrenfurth has argued, within Howard's battler discourse, the notion of "the working class is made obsolete not only due to its material wants but also by its aspiration to middle-class membership."[29]

Even though Howard's use of the battler trope succeeded in interpellating a broad range of people, it is important to note that his elision of the term's historic class-specificity was felt as a loss by some people who had previously self-identified as battlers. As Mark Peel has noted in his oral history of disadvantage, many of the impoverished were dissatisfied by Howard's broad use of the term. They were, he has noted, "growing suspicious of a term that had been twisted by conservatives to mean people with much more than they had."[30] This sense of disenfranchisement from members of the old working classes can be compared with Judith Brett's discussion of the appeal of Howard's politics for so-called "ordinary people." Brett has demonstrated that for Howard, the effect of the battler narrative lay in its ability to engage a broad group of Australians who imagined themselves as "struggling."[31]

Crucially, the Abbertons have embodied the ambiguous class identity of the Howard-style battler. On the eve of his final court appearance on charges of perverting the course of justice, Koby spoke with Sunny about his ambitions. "I want," he asserted, to "try to do good things for my family, make money, buy houses and you know, sell them, and get my little brother a good education and help out my family with money." It is a striking scene in which Koby, obviously terrified of a conviction, struggled to articulate the greater purpose of surfing professionally.

The film does not detail the Boys' income from surfing competitions and endorsements; so, it is difficult to gauge whether Koby's fears about lack of money are based on a poor financial situation. Yet, this is beside the point. In expressing love for his family and desire to care for them, Koby has actually asserted, repeatedly, his need for ever more money. In the quest to provide for his family, Koby illustrated the extent to which the contemporary, aspirational battler should "battle" to attain a mythic state of ultimate financial security.

The film portrayed Maroubra as a site of dysfunction and did so by eliding the area's recent gentrification and the Boys' own participation in an aspirational lifestyle. The Boys, however, do display an awareness of their comparative privilege, as Koby has demonstrated in expressing the sentiment that his family were "lucky" to be living near the beach, compared with those who were assigned housing commission accommodation, "out in fucking Liverpool." As residents of Sydney's beachside Eastern suburbs, they occupied a position of relative privilege compared with that of the "westie," the quintessential "internal Other" in Sydney's suburban imaginary. In this sense, though the Boys presented themselves as disadvantaged, they did not draw on the discourse of "white trash."[32]

Evers has been particularly critical of the film's tendency to gloss the recent gentrification of Maroubra.[33] I agree that it is essential to emphasize that the levels of socioeconomic disadvantage—and ethnic diversity—experienced by Maroubra locals are more uneven than the *Bra Boys* has suggested.[34] Yet, while the film's portrayal of Maroubra might be unrealistic, the audience is drawn to identify with the brothers as self-proclaimed battlers. The strength of the narrative lies not in its relationship to reality, but in its attachment to long-standing Australian myths about virtue and victimhood. If it is easy to decry the film for its heavy-handed tone and its exaggerations, it is another thing entirely to address the film's seductiveness and to explore the enduring appeal of narratives of white victimhood.

The most striking way in which *Bra Boys* has offered the viewer the opportunity to indulge in the pleasures of identifying with white victimhood is through its presentation of Koby's murder trial. While the film, as a whole, advanced a generic battler narrative of triumph, the events surrounding Koby's trial form a suspenseful subplot in which the viewer is invited to join the Boys on their journey to support their brother. The film strategically extends this subplot, frequently digressing to present more general material about the Boys' lives. The tension around Koby's fate is reinforced through a series of interviews with all his brothers who expressed anxiety about the pending outcome; so, it is not until quite late in the film that we witness Koby's acquittal.

The emotional "reward" for investing in this subplot is large, as the joyous party that follows is the film's affective highpoint. The party scene, in which Koby's lawyers are lauded with a drunken guard of honor, echoed the ending of another iconic battler movie *The Castle*, in which the QC and everyone toast the white battler's final defeat of adversity. The pull to invest emotionally in Koby's trial is reinforced when it is revealed that members of the jury who acquitted Koby lingered after the end of proceedings to comfort and hug him in an exuberant, public affirmation of his innocence. It is, moreover, crucial that Koby's testimony—his insistence that Hines was shot during an attempt to protect his girlfriend—is seen to be validated by the legal process. As a viewer, it is difficult to resist the cumulative pleasures of identifying with Koby's struggle; it not only formed the heart of the narrative, but also offered an affective release that drew on the enduring power of narratives in which the "little Aussie battler" triumphs.

White Virtue

In drawing on the authority of testimony to authenticate a story of white struggle, *Bra Boys* should be read as a part of what Ann Curthoys has described as the "white victim narrative" of Australian history.[35] This narrative has emphasized the character-forming difficulties experienced by Anglo-Australians since settlement, such as the harsh pioneer experience and the defeat at Gallipoli. For Curthoys, the legitimacy of the white nation has hinged on its self-perception of victimhood.[36] Through their experiences of struggle and suffering, white settler Australians have earned the right to claim the nation as their own. To be sure, this is a narrative that not only excludes virtue but also a narrative which claims virtue. To speak from the position of the victim is to claim a highly affective, authoritative voice. Testimony, as a mode of speech, has drawn much of its power from this nexus between victimhood, virtue, and "truth."

In this way, we can read *Bra Boys'* invocation of the battler as a part of a broader, legitimating white victim narrative. Yet as James Jupp has suggested, the experiences of the majority of recent non-Anglo migrants to Australia fit clearly within the bounds of a battler narrative of struggle.[37] The battler could, thus, be seen to encompass a broad range of individuals and experiences—particularly those of Indigenous peoples and migrants who have often struggled to "succeed" within Australian society. The broad "neutrality" of the battler has signaled both its malleability as a cultural concept, and its intrinsic, unmarked "whiteness." Accordingly, Sean Scalmer has argued that

> the battler is the key actor in the drama of white Australian history; the key exponent of the 'Australian' values of egalitarianism and mateship. The whiteness of the battler is amplified by the historical resonance of the term—its very mustiness harks back to an earlier time when inequalities of income were not strongly associated with ethnicity, and when non-whites did not struggle economically (because they were politically invisible).[38]

To understand the extent to which the battler, particularly Howard's aspirational battler, has figured as white allows us to recognize the way *Bra Boys* has engaged with and perpetuated a broader narrative of white victimhood. It is crucial to explore the way this victim narrative has continued both to play a central role in the marginalization of nonwhite voices within public culture, and to underwrite white Australian possession. At the same time, it is essential to confront how the endurance of the battler narrative has been inextricable from the pleasures it has provided white Australians through its dissemination in popular cultural forms such as *Bra Boys*.

Within the context of a post-Cronulla and now, post-Apology Australia, *Bra Boys* is an ambivalent text. If Prime Minister Kevin Rudd's Apology to Australia's Indigenous peoples was designed to mark a symbolic break from a past deaf to the testimony of the dispossessed, the popularity of *Bra Boys* has demonstrated the ongoing role narratives that white victimhood have played in the maintenance of prevailing structures of power. *Bra Boys* exists within a wider milieu in which the valorization of the voice of the white battler has become central to an often aggressively racist cultural politics. Indeed, it is difficult to read *Bra Boys* without some reference to the complex politics of race, space, and national identity that has coalesced in the wake of September 11, the Bali bombings, and, most recently, the Cronulla riots.

Although the Abberton brothers were not themselves directly involved in the Cronulla riots, they did position themselves as mediators in its aftermath. The film depicted their efforts to engage Lebanese and Anglo youth in productive dialogue. Yet, other scenes portrayed their perpetuation of a highly exclusionary, violent localism. Commentators writing on the riots have emphasized localism as one of the key causal factors.[39] Evers has described localism as a way of "carving up space": It is often described by surfers as the flow-on effect of "being proud of your beach," and although it may entail violence, directed toward outsiders as well as "insiders," it is, nevertheless, a form of care and bonding between men.[40] Bra Boys emphasized the often violent process of initiation that individuals should go through to become "locals." Once a member, many of the Boys tattoo Maroubra's postcode 2035 on their bodies, cementing physically their "tribal" claims.

Bra Boys' depiction of localism can be read as an expression of what Aileen Moreton-Robinson and Fiona Nicoll have called "patriarchal white sovereignty," a regime of power that has manifested itself historically in acts of white possession.[41] In the film, we see the Boys not only enforce their "local's rights" at Maroubra, but they also take the viewer to Cape Solander, at nearby Kurnell, a surf break they have taken possession of exclusively, dubbing it "Ours."[42] "Ours" has not only been the site of violence between Bra Boys and nonlocal surfers, but it is also the site of the nation's original act of possession. Cape Solander, located at the mouth of Botany Bay, was first colonized in 1770 by Captain Cook.[43] Here, Bra Boys' imbrication with dominant, nationally oriented narratives of possession is marked by its erasure. The casual amnesia of white victimhood asserts that "Ours" simply is; this is not an overt challenge to Indigenous sovereignty, rather, the everyday, naturalized effects of a white possessive logic.

Despite Bra Boys' portrayal of localism and its reproduction of a white battler narrative, the film has worked to defend the group as inclusive. This is illustrated through a particularly striking scene in which some of the Boys assist a surfer with dwarfism to climb into a cave. The extent to which the group is multiethnic is reinforced during the film's self-congratulatory conclusion in which Sunny described Maroubra as "one of the most multicultural beaches in Australia." The film is concluded with a rapid sequence in which members of the Bra Boys stare defiantly at the camera and state their nationality: "Australian," "Half Australian—Half Nigerian," "Aboriginal, Half Aboriginal—Half Danish," and so on. It is difficult to know whether this multicultural sentiment is simply a way to avoid criticism in the wake of Cronulla. In any case, the effect is uplifting, promoting the gang's "locals only" ethos as the epitome of mateship. However, tellingly, when describing the reprisal attacks the Boys faced after the riots, Sunny has insisted that "half the people who defended the beach that night were ethnics and three couldn't even speak English." There are certainly some prominent Indigenous and non-Anglo members of the Bra Boys, yet the inclusiveness of the "tribe" has been firmly grounded in an implicitly racialized localism in which all nonwhites are, in the words of Sunny, "ethnics," who use the beach at the Boys' discretion.[44]

This possessive logic is, similar to the discourse on whiteness itself, so firmly naturalized as to become invisible. Cape Solander is simply "Ours," the history of colonization glossed over as a surfer slides through the waves. As Sunny declared without irony, "we think the beach belongs to everyone," but people coming to the beach need to recognize that "there might be a whole history and a culture there spanning for generations and that should be respected." It is a strikingly possessive claim that gains its power from its very casualness. This uncomplicated and taken-for-granted assertion of non-Indigenous belonging is advanced by the affective force of *Bra Boys'* victim testimony in which historic disadvantage is used to justify the right to control use of "their" beach. Sunny's assertion that the Bra Boys' surf culture is the *only* local culture of significance at Maroubra signaled the power of his testimony to obscure multiple other "local" stories.

Anxious Voices

Although *Bra Boys* has illustrated the extent to which narratives of white victimhood are naturalized within popular culture, it is a film that has also displayed a profound anxiety regarding the legitimacy of settler belonging. As we have seen, this is evident in the way the film has drawn on the battler trope to assuage a sense of Anglo decline. It is also present in the way the film has underscored the tenuous nature of the Boys' claims to "possess" Maroubra by explicitly linking the story of the Boys with the local Aboriginal people, the Eora. Crowe's opening narration provided a history of Maroubra in which the Boys' conflict with local authorities is said to have originated in "colonial times" when Aborigines were banned from ocean swimming. Moreover, Crowe linked the Eora and settlers on the basis of social class, arguing that early twentieth-century poverty "saw the poor forced to live among the Aborigines in the bays and caves." In emphasizing the extent to which the Boys' story, and the history of Maroubra itself, is entangled with the experiences of the Eora, *Bra Boys* attempted to reinforce the group's possessive attachment to the beach by co-opting the sovereign claims of the area's Indigenous owners. In doing so, the film has elided anxiety about the legitimacy of the Boys' possession

231

through an aggressive assertion of their experience as "ordinary" and naturally in place.[45]

In essence, *Bra Boys* is a declaration of identity that has registered a contemporary crisis of the very concepts of testimony and identity. As Ahmed and Stacey have attested, "if testimony is bound up with truth and justice, then it's coming into being also registers the crisis in both of these concepts; for one testifies when the truth is in doubt; [the] 'truth' itself has become subject to appeal."[46] Similarly, Shoshana Felman has argued that "testimony is called for in a situation where the truth is not clear, where there is already a 'crisis of truth.'"[47] The sense that *Bra Boys* has worked hard to establish a coherent group identity has foregrounded the way that testimony has functioned to contest and assert, rather than simply express "truth." Though the Boys have been most obviously concerned to counter the negative images of them produced by the police and nonlocals, their desire to anchor their narrative with a connection to the Eora suggested that the implications of Indigenous sovereignty do unsettle the group, albeit in a muted, even unconscious way.

In his account of first-person documentary, Renov, following Foucault, has argued that autobiographical films illustrate how subjectivity has become the "current site of struggle" for groups "massively separated from the engines of representation."[48] Within this context, the attempt to fix selfhood through testimonial expression has served as "a vital expression of agency."[49] The film has projected an image of Maroubra as an area besieged, and of a people quite literally the subject of the authorities' panoptic gaze; the beach shadowed by Long Bay Gaol that "from its hilltop location served as a constant warning to the community below." In this sense, the film has not only been an attempt to control the kinds of images and stories that are produced about the Boys, but it has also, implicitly, participated in a broader struggle over whose stories get heard, and validated, within public culture.

"Ordinary" Voices

Though *Bra Boys* has operated as a highly successful vehicle of self-representation—both in terms of box-office success and in the level of control the Boys maintained throughout its production—it was not the first time the Abbertons had sought to tell their story. In 2005, the ABC's *Australian Story* produced an episode focusing on Koby Abberton.[50] Titled "Sons of Beaches," the episode followed Koby as he awaited the outcome of his charge for perverting the course of justice. Covering much of the same ground as *Bra Boys*, the episode also employed the strategy of contextualizing Koby's story with reference to the battler narrative. In her introduction, Caroline Jones, noted journalist and long-time *Australian Story* presenter, described Koby's life story in terms of struggle and triumph:

> A young man escapes a troubled childhood to become one of the world's most successful big-wave surfers. But when one of his brothers is charged with murder his past catches up with him again.[51]

This narrative was reinforced by Koby's testimony in which his surfing success was firmly positioned as a momentous achievement for a boy from "the backstreets of Maroubra."[52] Though ostensibly about Koby, the *Australian Story* episode included interviews with his brothers and friends, and, as such, served to produce a loosely collective narrative about the Boys, as in the later film.

Bra Boys has stood alone, whereas "Sons of Beaches" formed just one episode of a long-running series. As such, the use of the battler trope within "Sons of Beaches" should be read alongside its use within *Australian Story* as a series. In what follows, I examine *Australian Story* as a vehicle of televisual witnessing that has encouraged Australians to witness to "ourselves." More specifically, *Australian Story* draws on the battler narrative as a framework through which to tell stories about the experiences of both "ordinary" and extraordinary Australians.

In a recent companion text to *Australian Story*, Jones explained the show's "personal" approach to storytelling. "In a just and humane society," she argued that

> there should be a place for everyone's story to be heard. The sharing of each other's stories is the beginning of community. It is how we begin to know each other: through an interest and curiosity in points of difference as well as our common ground. It is the sharing of these stories that can diminish misunderstanding and conflict . . . The telling and the hearing create a bond.[53]

The process Jones described here—this exchange of stories between a teller and a listener—is one of witnessing. By foregrounding the personal voice, *Australian Story* draws audiences to identify with and witness to the experiences of its subjects. This process of witnessing has worked to produce a loose form of national community through the affirmation of shared stories.

Since 1996, the ABC's *Australia Story* has delivered a weekly, half-hour segment devoted to one individual's story. Produced from Brisbane, with a special mandate for rural and regional coverage, *Australian Story* was developed during a restructuring of the ABC's current affairs programming.[54] The program has provided a platform for interviewees to "narrate" their own stories, and, in doing so, has sought to portray the diversity of Australians and their experiences. As such, the individuals selected to appear have been heterogeneous, and have ranged from politicians and prominent sportspeople to so-called "ordinary" Australians. This "personal approach" has been highly successful, with some episodes attracting more than 1 million viewers.[55] Currently broadcast at 8 pm on Mondays, recent episodes have included profiles on the former Liberal Opposition Leader Malcolm Turnbull; on John Rogers and Brian McDermott, survivors of a yachting accident on the *Excalibur*; and on entertainer Ian Rogerson and his autistic son.[56] Though each episode may be viewed on its own, as a series, *Australian Story* has worked to produce an accumulative archive of stories—a contemporary record of Australian lives.

Televisual Witnessing

As a genre of television, *Australian Story* has borrowed from both current affairs and cinematic documentary to form what Frances Bonner and Susan McKay have called "a variant type of documentary television."[57] In its emphasis on the personal and "human interest," it has also formed a part of John Langer's loose category of the "other news," a term he has employed to describe news content that has often been derided as "soft" or "tabloid," content which glories in the "triumphs of celebrities and ordinary people."[58] Yet, *Australian Story* has contrasted sharply with other testimony-led programs such as chat shows, and profile-driven interview programs. Its distance from the more sensationalist forms of human interest television is particularly evident in the seriousness with which it approaches the "everyday" experiences of its subjects. *Australian Story* is further differentiated by rendering the interviewing process largely invisible on air, and by its avoidance of the confrontational style of other current affairs programs such as *A Current Affair* and *Today Tonight*.[59] Its unusually positive, even indulgent, engagement with its subjects has seen the program drawn into debates about the tabloidization of Australian current affairs and the supposed decline of "serious" news.[60] Bonner and McKay have worked to recuperate *Australian Story* from this context in order to consider its contribution to the Australian mediascape as a "rich site of working through."[61]

A typical episode of *Australian Story* focuses on one individual's story, and largely comprises testimonial fragments in which the subject appears to address the audience directly. This material is typically supplemented with talking-heads-style comments from the subject's relatives or colleagues, and reenactment or news footage of relevant events. The episodes are always introduced with a short preamble from a more well-known or "celebrity" figure who, as Bonner has argued, "testifies to [the subject's story as] deserving attention."[62] Apart from this introduction, the intimate connection between viewer and subject is reinforced by the on-screen absence of an interviewer or other mediating presence. In this way, *Australian Story* is positioned as a text of witnessing that hinges on the relationship between viewer and subject. *Australian Story's* use of testimony is contrasted with confessional modes of television, such as chat programs and those that focus on celebrity scandal. In these programs, the subject discloses or "confesses" to an audience for judgment; in *Australian Story*, the subject provides testimony of their experiences of particular events in which they typically occupy the position of "victim."[63] This emphasis on testimony as a way of approaching the "truth" of personal experience has placed the program firmly within a broader cultural context in which testimony has come to be understood as a privileged mode of expression.

Television has played a central role in the development of a global culture of testimony and intimacy. It has been, according to John Ellis, "one of the technologies of the audio-visual which have introduced a new modality of perception into the world, that of witness."[64] Formally, television has produced a form of copresence in which the distance between the viewer and the subject is simultaneously sustained and collapsed. The practice of televisual witnessing, then, has been highly dependent on the notion of audience response, and an understanding of spectatorship as driven by processes of identification and empathetic attachment.[65] In the realm of television, it is the audience that has functioned as the second person, connecting with and validating on-screen testimony.

Within media studies, there has been an emphasis on the way television communicates the testimony of so-called "distant sufferers" to Western audiences.[66] Although testimony has been a global force, and television has certainly become central not only to the reportage of atrocity and violence, but also to campaigns for its amelioration, my interest throughout this book has been on the persistent circulation of testimony within discourses on the nation. It is through the process of testimonial exchange that forms of public memory are reproduced and interrogated. Television has occupied a particularly important role in the production of public memory through its omnipresence as a technology of "publicness."[67] Accordingly, John Hartley has argued that "television, popular newspapers, magazines and photography, the popular media of the modern period, are the public domain, the place where and the means by which the public is created and has its being."[68] Though media critics have been eager to laud the emergence of a postbroadcast age of television and an era of global or transnational viewing practices, as Graeme Turner has recently affirmed, the nation continues to "matter" within television studies.[69] It is within this context that I read *Australian Story* as a vehicle for the telling—and witnessing—of peculiarly "Australian" stories. Here, television is not simply a space of representing the nation, but of calling forth national communities and specific publics through the circulation and witnessing of testimony.

Telling Australian Stories

In many ways, it is difficult to argue that *Australian Story* has worked to produce any specific understanding of Australian identity, or any particular image of who constitutes an Australian. Though its basic format has remained unchanged since its inception, it is the openness of this format—and its ability to accommodate and communicate such a diverse range of stories—that has inhibited attempts to understand the program as working to "fix" any homogenous sense of national identity. Yet, as Bonner and McKay have demonstrated, a range of core "themes" are clearly discernible. They have argued that

> through its coverage of the lives and experiences of both ordinary and celebrity Australians, [the show] provides a set of examples of how those Australians live their lives, and through their stories it portrays the personal qualities that are valued in Australia today.[70]

These values, they have suggested, include perseverance, the importance of family, and altruism.[71] Though Bonner and McKay have resisted an understanding of these values as imbricated with battler mythology, I argue that these values are integral to the Anglo battler narrative. This is particularly so of perseverance, which has articulated strongly with the battler figure's struggle to succeed against the odds. To be sure, the program has rarely featured so-called "working-class" subjects, but it has overwhelmingly showcased Anglo-Australian narratives of struggle and triumph.

The battlers of *Australian Story* are typically "ordinary" in a solidly middle-class fashion, but their stories are framed as exemplars of the iconic Australian values of perseverance, hard work, and mateship. Tracing the program from its beginning in 1996, it is clear that the program has engaged with a broader political and cultural process in which notions of the working class were superseded by Howard's "classless" conception of the nonelite, "ordinary" Australian.[72] In this way, the program has served as testament to both the endurance of foundational myths of Anglo-Australian culture and the contemporary instability of these concepts.

In order to draw out the ambivalent role of *Australian Story* within public memory, I briefly examine an episode that focused on the Black Saturday bushfires. The episode—titled "Her Beauty and Her Terror"—first aired on September 28, 2009.[73] The piece focused on the stories of twin brother and sister, Patrick and Bronwyn O'Gorman, whose parents and younger brother perished in the fires at their home in Humevale, near Kinglake, on Black Saturday, February 7, 2009. The episode exists as a part of the *Australian Story* series, but crucially, at the same time within broader networks of media commentary on the bushfires.[74]

The program was introduced by Drew Ambrose, a documentary filmmaker who had been compiling an online Web site about the fires. Ambrose positioned the twins explicitly as survivors: "Bron and Pat aren't victims, they're survivors, with a steely resolve to live life."[75] He concluded this introduction with the words that are common to most episodes, "This is their story." These words work to rhetorically signify the status of the program as unvarnished testimony, and to interpellate the audience as a part of the witnessing exchange. Similar to many of the episodes that have focused on family death, the episode functioned in a memorial mode, working to record the achievements of those who have died, particularly those of the O'Gorman's younger brother. It also provided a forum for an outpouring of grief, though this was expressed in quite a controlled way by the twins. For example, when describing her feelings after the event Bronwyn underscored her confusion: "I think it's just been a continual feeling of numbness and shock, that we lost our mum and our dad and our brother . . . And our way of life."[76] Though the piece did give voice to the twin's experiences of suffering, their story was placed firmly within an overarching narrative of overcoming, which showcased their resilience and their ability to move on with their lives.

The *Australian Story* online guestbook provided a forum for viewers to respond to each episode, and served as a way to test their ideas about the possibilities of television as a technology of witnessing. Most of the responses to "Her Beauty and Her Terror" have emphasized the excess of feeling experienced by viewers.[77] Jac05 wrote, "I felt incredible sadness hearing about your family." Similarly, Wxtx responded with "seeing how massive this tragedy was and still is brought overflowing tears to my eyes." Wxtx contributed by validating the testimony of the O'Gormans: "I know words will never change anything but I just wanted you both to know how sorry i [sic] am for your loss and for the fact your parents and younger brother were not warned of the magnitude of the fire." Here, Wxtx contributed to the discourse on warnings and the failure of fire warning systems that have come to surround the event.[78] Other commenters echoed these empathetic responses, with some, such as TheresaP, adding that they found the twins "hope and determination, and . . . [their] courage and strength . . . an inspiration."

Here, viewers were engaged in a mode of witnessing that sought to recognize the experience and suffering of the other, and to reconsider their own lives within this context. The guestbook illustrated that one of the strengths of the *Australian Story* format is its emphasis on the specificities of the personal which has sought to break up monolithic media coverage of current events. That said, the tendency for *Australian Story* to select stories and frame testimonies positively, and with reference to iconic tropes of triumph and struggle, has limited the ability of the program to offer viewers the chance to witness to testimonies that challenge key concepts within Australian cultural memory. In the case of the O'Gorman's, their story was placed firmly within the context of a battler narrative and, subsequently, affirmed in this fashion by commenters. In this way, testimony to personal tragedy is muted by the program's relentless emphasis on the "positive" aspects of the O'Gorman's story, such as their resilience and the loyalty they have demonstrated by supporting each other.

Australia Story's core narrative template is one of struggle and overcoming. This has been used to frame episodes that focus on personal tragedy and disaster such as the O'Gorman's and the feature on the *Excalibur* yachting accident; episodes on more generalized hardship such as "Sons of Beaches"; and, in episodes focusing on disease, as in the recent profile on Yothu Yindi lead singer Mandawuy Yunupingu's struggle with kidney disease. Though one of *Australian Story's* rare non-Anglo subjects, the extent to which Yunupingu's testimony was framed within the battler narrative is telling. While Yunupingu's life story could have been presented in a myriad ways, drawing on themes potentially disruptive to white viewers, an overwhelming emphasis was placed on his personal struggle with disease, a universal struggle that has defined him as "no different from any other person you know."[79]

At its heart, *Australian Story* presents testimony of triumph. Thus, although the program does not actively work to present a rigid account of national identity, its reliance on the battler trope has occluded an engagement with stories that undermine this powerful cultural script. *Australian Story*, then, is testament to both the diversity of Australian stories and the enduring power of the battler narrative as the national story. It has highlighted the desire of Australians to connect with each other through the sharing of testimony, at the same time as it has affirmed the power of dominant cultural narratives to shape the kinds of stories "we" tell each other.

Conclusion

Both *Australian Story* and *Bra Boys* are divergent texts—in medium, genre, and implied audience—and these programs have anchored settler testimony through the deployment of the historic battler trope. In doing so, both texts have underwritten what Hage has termed the discourse on "Anglo decline," and, as such, have forcefully recentered narratives of (white) settler disadvantage.[80] If *Australian Story* has offered a more heterogeneous range of "Australian" stories, albeit relentlessly positive in tone, *Bra Boys* has illustrated the extent to which narratives of white victimhood continue to exclude: spatially, culturally, and historically. The film's possessive logic is underpinned by a narrative of disadvantage that has challenged the white viewer to identify with the Boys as battlers. In *Australian Story*, the battler is both declassed and thoroughly naturalized as a figure that epitomizes

Australian ordinariness. Nevertheless, in its presentation of narratives of triumph and overcoming, the program has drawn on the status of the battler trope as a key structuring narrative within Australian cultural history. Here, the audience, as secondary witness, has been crucial to sustaining the meaning of both texts. Thus, to adopt a questioning mode as a viewer goes some way to blunting the affective power of narratives of settler triumph.

However, to appreciate the enduring appeal of white victim narratives within a broader national context is to consider the ambivalence of contemporary discourses on citizenship and multiculturalism that have called on white Australians to witness to the testimony of the socially and politically marginalized. This is not to argue that either *Bra Boys* or *Australian Story* have appropriated the affective power of minority testimony. Rather, I have emphasized the extent to which both evince the proliferation of testimonial forms as a part of a broader, global turn to a public politics of intimacy and emotion. Yet at the same time, I have demonstrated the extent to which the testimonial voice, the affective voice that stakes a claim for truth and authenticity, can continue to be used to reinforce existing relations of power on peculiarly local, regional, and national scales. Both *Bra Boys* and *Australian Story* have stood as testament to the enduring, seductive power of white testimony, the continued resonance of stories that luxuriate in the "struggle"—and success—of the white, socially disadvantaged male. As such, they have drawn attention to the instability of witnessing as a politics of recognition that has promised to secure the stories of minority subjects within public memory. Most troublingly, as texts of settler witnessing, *Bra Boys* and *Australian Story* have served as challenging reminders of the way so-called "ordinary" Australians hear the voices of the "dispossessed."

Notes

1. Sunny Abberton (dir.), *Bra Boys* (Australia: Bradahood Productions, 2007).
2. Clendinnen, *True Stories*.
3. Abberton, *Bra Boys*.
4. Preceding the film's release, the group attracted a large volume of negative media scrutiny; see especially Les Kennedy, "Night the Thin Blue Line Ran into the Maroubra Stomp," *Sydney Morning Herald*, December 24, 2002, 1. Since Jai's 2005 acquittal for the murder of Anthony Hines, coverage has tended to be far more positive, often focusing on the charitable activities of the Boys. See Angela Cuming, "Freed Bra Boys Happy but Beach Visit Falls Flat," *Sydney Morning Herald*, March 12, 2006, http://www.smh.com.

au/news/national/freed-bra-boys-happy-but-beach-visit-falls-flat/2006/
03/11/1141701732478.html (accessed January 20, 2009); Angela Cuming
and Catherine Munro, "Rage over 7000 Meters for Beaches," *Sun Herald*,
August 7, 2005, 13.

5.   Thoms Albie, *Surfmovies: The History of the Surf Film in Australia* (Noosa
     Heads: Shore Thing Publishing, 2000), 3.

6.   "Bra Boys Breaks Box Office Record," *ABC Online*, March 27, 2007, http://
     www.abc.net.au/news/newsitems/200703/s1882217.htm (accessed January
     12, 2009).

7.   For a succinct overview of the "battler" in Australian history, see Sean
     Scalmer, "The Battlers Versus the Elites," *Overland*, no. 154 (1999): 9–13.

8.   Rob Sitch (dir.), *The Castle* (Australia: Working Dog, 1997).

9.   Clifton Evers, "Rethinking Gubbah Localism," *Kurungabaa: A Journal of
     the History, Literature and Ideas for Surfers* 1, no. 1 (2008): 4.

10. Berlant, "Subject of True Feeling," 49–84.

11. David Stratton, "Bra Boys," *At the Movies*, ABC TV, March 14, 2007, [Tran-
     script], http://www.abc.net.au/atthemovies/txt/s1864026.htm (accessed
     January 11, 2009).

12. Michael Renov, "First-Person Films: Some Theses on Self-Inscription," in
     Rethinking Documentary: New Perspectives, New Practices, ed. Thomas
     Austin and Wilma de Jong (New York: Open University Press, 2008),
     39–41.

13. Michael Renov, *The Subject of Documentary* (Minneapolis and London:
     University of Minnesota Press, 2004), xii.

14. Clifton Evers, "My Brother's Keeper or My Brother's Problem?" *OnLine
     Opinion: Australia's Ejournal of Social and Political Debate*, March 14,
     2007, http://www.onlineopinion.com.au/view.asp?article=5607 (accessed
     February 4, 2009).

15. Natasha Wallace, "Surf Gang Member Cleared of Standover Man's Murder,"
     Sydney Morning Herald, May 6, 2005, http://www.smh.com.au/news/
     National/Surf-gang-member-cleared-of-standover-mans-murder/2005/0
     5/05/1115092629172.html (accessed February 15, 2009).

16. Evers, "My Brother's Keeper or My Brother's Problem?"

17. Ibid.

18. Russell Crowe has been an outspoken supporter of the Bra Boys and is now
     slated to make his directorial debut with a fictionalized version of their story.
     See Dianne Garrett, "Crow to Direct 'Bra Boys," *Variety*, March 21, 2007,
     http://www.variety.com/ article/VR1117961590.html?categoryid=13&cs=1
     (accessed February 15, 2009).

19. Crowe purchased a large stake in the club to save it from imminent financial
     collapse. "Crowe in Bid to Buy Beloved Rabbitohs Club," *Age*, September
     18, 2005, http://www.theage.com.au/news/league/crowe-in-bid-to-buy-
     beloved-rabbitohs-club/2005/ 09/17/1126750170627.html (accessed
     February 15, 2009).

20. Kay Saunders cited in Clifton Evers, "Locals Only!," in *Everyday Multicul-
     turalism Conference Proceedings*, ed. Selaraj Velayutham and Amanda Wise
     (Sydney: Centre for Research on Social Inclusion, Macquarie University,
     2007), 2. For a broader discussion of the gendered and racialized meanings
     of the surfer and the beach, see Meaghan Morris, "On the Beach," in *Too*

Soon Too Late: History in Popular Culture (Bloomington: Indiana University Press, 1998), 93–112; Isobel Crombie, "Laughing Gobs in Bathing Costumes," in *Body Culture: Max Dupain, Photography and Australian Culture 1919–1939* (Melbourne: Peleus Press/NGV, 2004), 176–91.

21. Scalmer, "Battlers Versus the Elites," 12.

22. See Richard White, *Inventing Australia: Images and Identity 1788–1980* (Sydney: George Allen & Unwin, 1981), 154–57; John Fiske, Bob Hodge, and Graeme Turner, *Myths of Oz: Reading Australian Popular Culture* (Sydney: Allen & Unwin, 1987).

23. Sarah Pinto and Leigh Boucher, "Fighting for Legitimacy: Masculinity, Political Voice and *Ned Kelly," Journal of Interdisciplinary Gender Studies* 10, no. 1 (2006): 13.

24. Katherine Biber cited in Ibid., 1.

25. Ibid., 20.

26. Hage, *Against Paranoid Nationalism*, 64; See also Hage, *White Nation*.

27. John Howard cited in Brendan Nicholson and Jason Koutsoukis, "Howard's Battlers a Broad Church," *Age*, May 19, 2004, http://www.theage.com. au/articles/ 2004/05/18/1084783513331.html?from=storylhs (accessed February 15, 2009).

28. Scalmer, "Battlers Versus the Elites," 9.

29. Nick Dyrenfurth, "Battlers, Refugees and the Republic: John Howard's Language of Citizenship," *Journal of Australian Studies* 84 (2005): 188. On the changing nature of class and the perceptions of class within Australia, see Davis, *Land of Plenty*, 78–104.

30. Mark Peel, *The Lowest Rung: Voices of Australian Poverty* (Cambridge: Cambridge University Press, 2003), xi.

31. Judith Brett, "Relaxed and Comfortable: The Liberal Party's Australia," *Quarterly Essay*, no. 19 (2005): 1–79.

32. See Matt Wray and Annalee Mewitz, "Introduction," in *White Trash: Race and Class in America*, ed. Matt Wray and Annalee Mewitz (New York and London: Routledge, 1997). On the microgeography of Sydney, see Zora Simic, "Were Westies White? Negotiating Race and Place in the Western Suburbs of Sydney," in *Historicising Whiteness: Transnational Perspective on the Construction of an Identity*, ed. Leigh Boucher, Jane Carey, and Katherine Ellinghaus (Melbourne: RMIT Publishing in association with the School of Historical Studies, University of Melbourne, 2007), 63–70; Jock Collins and Scott Poynting, eds., *The Other Sydney: Communities, Identities and Inequalities in Western Sydney* (Melbourne: Common Ground Publishing, 2006).

33. Evers, "My Brother's Keeper or My Brother's Problem?" See also Samantha Selinger-Morris, "Bra Boys Do Drink Latte," *Sydney Morning Herald*, January 13, 2010, 3.

34. Figures from the 2006 Census demonstrate that 52.7 percent of Maroubra residents were born in Australia, followed by 3.4 percent born in Indonesia and 3 percent born in England. Fifty-seven percent of Maroubra residents reported English as the only language spoken at home, compared with a national figure of 83 percent, which suggests that Maroubra experiences an above-average level of ethnic and linguistic diversity. On the issue of

income, Maroubra residents reported a median weekly family income of $1,404, compared with the lower Australia-wide average of $1,171. See "2006 Census Quick Stats: Maroubra (State Suburb)" and "Cultural Diversity Overview," 2006 Census, *Australian Bureau of Statistics*, http://www.abs.gov.au (accessed February 15, 2009).

35. Ann Curthoys, "Whose Home? Expulsion, Exodus, and Exile in White Australian Historical Mythology," *Journal of Australian Studies*, no. 61(1999): 1–19.

36. Ibid.

37. James Jupp, "An Anxious Society Fears the Worst," *Journal of Australian Studies* 55 (1997): 3.

38. Scalmer, " Battlers Versus the Elites," 11.

39. Scott Poynting, "What Caused the Cronulla Riot?," *Race and Class* 48 (2006): 85–92. For a discussion of the role of racialized concepts in the riots, see Suvendrini Perera, "Race Terror, Sydney, December 2005," *Borderlands ejournal* 5, no. 1 (2006), http://www.borderlands.net.au/vol5no1_2006/perera_raceterror.htm (accessed January 20, 2009).

40. Evers, "Locals Only!," 1.

41. Aileen Moreton-Robinson and Fiona Nicoll, "We Shall Fight Them on the Beaches: Protesting Cultures of White Possession," *Journal of Australian Studies* 30, no. 89 (2006): 150.

42. Heath Gilmore, "Bra Boys Say It's Ours and We'll Fight for It," *Sydney Morning Herald*, July 15, 2007, http://www.smh.com.au/news/national/bra-boys-say-its-ours/2007/ 07/14/1183833835467.html (accessed January 20, 2009).

43. On the endurance of Cook within the white possessive imaginary, see Katrina Schlunke, "Historicising Whiteness: Captain Cook Possesses Australia," in *Historicising Whiteness*, 41–50.

44. Moreton-Robinson and Nicoll, "We Shall Fight Them on the Beaches," 150.

45. Hage, *Against Paranoid Nationalism*, 64–66.

46. Ahmed and Stacey, "Testimonial Cultures," 2.

47. Shoshana Felman cited in Anderson, *Autobiography*, 127.

48. Renov, "First-Person Films," 47.

49. Ibid.

50. "Sons of Beaches," *Australian Story*, ABC TV, November 7, 2005, [Transcript], http://www.abc.net.au/austory/content/2005/s1500406.htm (accessed December 25, 2009).

51. Caroline Jones cited in Ibid.

52. Koby Abberton cited in Ibid.

53. Caroline Jones, *Australian Story: Off the Record* (Sydney: ABC Books, 2007), 1.

54. For an outline of the genesis of *Australia Story*, see Frances Bonner, "Testimonial Current Affairs: The *Australian Story* Approach to Celebrity," *Media International Australia*, no. 121 (November 2006): 29–30.

55. Ibid., 29.

56. This snapshot of subjects refers to programs shown between August and October 2009.

57. Frances Bonner and Susan McKay, "Personalizing Current Affairs without Becoming Tabloid: The Case of *Australian Story*," *Journalism* 8 (2007): 644.

58. John Langer, *Tabloid Television: Popular Journalism and the "Other News"* (London and New York: Routledge, 1998), 8, 35.

59. For a detailed analysis of the storytelling style of *Today Tonight*, see Damian McIver, "Representing Australianness: Our National Identity Brought to You by *Today Tonight*," *Media International Australia*, no. 131 (May 2009): 46–56.

60. On the tabloidization of Australian media, see especially Graeme Turner, *Ending the Affair: The Decline of Current Affairs in Australia* (Sydney: UNSW Press, 2005); Graeme Turner, "'Popularising Politics': *This Day Tonight* and Australian Television Current Affairs," *Media International Australia*, no. 106 (February 2003): 137–50; Catharine Lumby, *Gotcha: Life in a Tabloid World* (St. Leonard, NSW: Allen & Unwin, 1999).

61. Bonner and McKay, "Personalizing Current Affairs without Becoming Tabloid," 640.

62. Bonner, "Testimonial Current Affairs," 35.

63. See especially Jon Dovey, *Freakshow: First Person Media and Factual Television* (London: Pluto Press, 2000); Kevin Glynn, *Tabloid Culture: Trash Taste, Popular Power, and the Transformation of American Television* (Durham, NC London: Duke University Press, 2000); Langer, *Tabloid Television*.

64. John Ellis, *Seeing Things: Television in the Age of Uncertainty* (London and New York: I B Tauris Publishers, 2000), 1.

65. There is a large literature on spectatorship that focuses, primarily, on film. For a comprehensive overview of developments in this field, see Mayne, *Cinema and Spectatorship*. For a useful analysis of spectatorship and the production of meaning with regard to television, see Anne O'Keeffe, *Investigating Media Discourse* (London and New York: Routledge, 2006).

66. See Paul Frosh and Amit Pinchevski, *Media Witnessing: Testimony in the Age of Mass Communication* (London: Palgrave Macmillan, 2009); Lilie Chouliaraki, *The Spectatorship of Suffering* (London: SAGE Publications, 2006); and Luc Boltanski, *Distant Suffering: Morality, Media and Politics* (Cambridge: Cambridge University Press, 1999).

67. See, for example, John Hartley, *The Politics of Pictures: The Creation of the Public in the Age of Popular Media* (London and New York: Routledge, 1992); John Hartley, *Uses of Television* (London: Routledge, 1999); Nick Couldry, *Place of Media Power: Pilgrims and Witnesses of the Media Age* (London: Routledge, 2000).

68. Hartley, *Politics of Pictures*, 1.

69. Graeme Turner, "Television and the Nation: Does This Matter Any More?," in *Television Studies After TV: Understanding Television in the Post-Broadcast Era*, ed. Graeme Turner and Jinna Tay (London and New York: Routledge, 2009).

70. Bonner and McKay, "Personalizing Current Affairs without Becoming Tabloid," 652.

71. Ibid., 646.
72. See Brett, "Relaxed and Comfortable," 1–79.
73. "Her Beauty and Her Terror," *Australian Story*, ABC TV, September 28, 2009, [Transcript], http://www.abc.net.au/austory/content/2007/s2698824. htm (accessed October 20, 2009).
74. It is not within my focus but a comprehensive analysis of the memorialization of Black Saturday would contextualize the work of *Australian Story* with reference to a range of emergent testimonial texts, including the National Day of Mourning, held on February 22, 2009, and anthologies of survivor testimony. See, for example, John McGourty, ed., *Black Saturday: Stories of Love, Loss and Courage from the Victorian Bushfires* (Pymble, NSW: HarperCollins, 2009).
75. Drew Ambrose cited in "Her Beauty and Her Terror."
76. Bronwyn O'Gorman cited in Ibid.
77. The *Australian Story* guestbook for "Her Beauty and Her Terror" is available at http://www2b.abc.net.au/tmb/Client/MessageList. aspx?b=55&t=127&te=True. The quotes cited later were gathered on October 4, 2009.
78. See especially Robert Manne, "Why We weren't Warned," *The Monthly* 47 (July 2009), http://www.themonthly.com.au/monthly-essays-robert-manne-why-we-weren-t-warned-victorian-bushfires-and-royal-commission-1780 (accessed September 20, 2009); Tom Griffiths, "'An Unnatural Disaster'? Remembering and Forgetting Bushfire," *History Australia* 6, no. 2 (2009).
79. Mandawuy Yunupingu cited in "Message from Mandawuy," *Australian Story*, ABC TV, October 19, 2009, [Transcript], http://www.abc.net.au/austory/ content/2007/s2719125.htm (accessed December 30, 2009).
80. Hage, *White Nation*.

Conclusion: Witnessing Australian Stories

In late 2009, then Prime Minister Kevin Rudd delivered another national apology.[1] This time, the recipients of Rudd's words were the so-called "Forgotten Australians." Though its origins are unclear, the term was adopted by the federal government to refer to the childhood experiences of two distinct groups.[2] The first, and largest, comprise individuals who had been in institutional and out-of-home care as children. It has been estimated that over the course of the twentieth century, more than 500,000 Australian children spent time in some form of out-of-home care, many in government institutions and church-run orphanages.[3] Though *Bringing them Home* had demonstrated that many Indigenous children had been subject to enforced institutional care during this period, the forgotten Australians have been positioned as an explicitly Anglo-Australian group.[4] The second group number between 7000 and 10,000, and include former British child migrants who had been sent to Australia unaccompanied between 1947 and 1967. Children were transported to Australia by a range of church and nongovernment organizations as a part of a British government Commonwealth population scheme; a total of approximately 150,000 British children emigrated under the postwar *Children's Act 1948*, the majority to Canada.[5] Once in Australia, child migrants were not adopted but rather, sent to nongovernment institutions in which they were often subjected to harsh work regimes.[6]

The reasons that children were taken into government and church care are complex and include both cases of parental abandonment and state intervention.[7] Likewise, the circumstances under which children emigrated were diverse; some were orphans, whereas others were sent by parents who were hopeful that their children would find a better life in Australia.[8] Since the late 1980s, both groups have testified to their experiences of institutional care, with many describing how they suffered from ill-treatment and abuse by their "carers." These revelations are a part of a global phenomenon in which the now adult have began to reflect, and agitate for compensation, over childhood neglect and exploitation. In this context, by far the most prominent testimony of child mistreatment has been of sex abuse perpetrated by church groups.[9]

The experiences of former child migrants came to prominence in Australian public culture chiefly through the publication of Philip Bean and Joy Melville's 1989 history *Lost Children of the Empire*—which was quickly followed by stories about the ill-treatment of nonmigrant children in religious and government-run "care" homes.[10] The emergence of these testimonies led the federal government to instigate a series of inquiries into the experiences of both child migrants and Australian-born children who had been in out-of-home care. In 2001, the Senate Community Affairs References Committee released *Lost Innocents*, its report into child migration, which was followed in 2004 and 2005 by reports on the forgotten Australians.[11] Though these inquires were not funded to the level of *Bringing them Home*, they each called for and received hundreds of written personal testimonies of childhood ill-treatment. Rudd's apology was formulated in response to these enquiries, which had recommended that both groups be recognized in a manner similar to the stolen generations.[12] The decision to adhere to these recommendations and grant another apology was highly symbolic, and positioned the ill-treatment of all children as a matter of national concern.

Similar to his first apology to Australia's Indigenous peoples, Rudd figured the apology to the forgotten Australians as "a turning point in our nation's story."[13] It was necessary, he suggested, to confront this "shameful" period in Australian history in order to consider "how this was all possible in this country of the fair go."[14] Throughout the apology, Rudd borrowed heavily on the template established by the apology to the stolen generations. Here, the need to witness to the testimony of former child migrants and care leavers was portrayed as necessary not only to honor the experience of individuals, but also to cleanse the nation so that we can "go forward with confidence into the future."[15] As in the first apology, Rudd highlighted the testimony of individuals—Gary, Gus, Robyn, and Judy—and affirmed the need to validate their stories. This process of collective witnessing sought to grant "closure" to individuals at the same time as it performed an intervention into public memory.

The link between individual suffering and collective, national memory was further underscored by the government's decision to develop a repository of the testimony of the forgotten Australians, along the same line as the National Library of Australia's *Bringing them Home* Oral History Project.[16] "This can," Rudd suggested, "assist the nation to learn from your experiences." Here, witnessing to histories and memories of child abuse would guard against its future repetition—for, as Rudd insisted, "a nation that forgets its past is condemned to relive it."[17] In this way, Rudd implicitly connected the experiences of the forgotten Australians and the stolen generations through the notion of childhood innocence.

However, in linking the forgotten Australians with the stolen generations, the specifities of the experiences of these groups was elided. The claims that members of the stolen generations have made for national recognition, through *Bringing them Home* and myriad other life writings, have rested not only on accounts of childhood neglect or violence, but also on an understanding that these experiences were the product of a range of national and state government-level policies of racial assimilation, segregation, and genocide. The experiences of care leaves, while certainly personally distressing and reflective of a serious failure of child protection systems, is the result of a less obviously national history. Yet if the apology to the stolen generations came at the end of a period in which debate over the meaning of Indigenous testimony was prominent and fraught, the "truth" of the stories of the forgotten Australians has been uncontested. In stark contrast to the reception of stolen generation and asylum-seeker testimony, no one suggested that we should not believe the memories of former child migrants and care leavers. There has, in fact, hitherto been little commentary on this second national apology.

Journalists have, however, drawn on the apology in order to discuss the present "crisis" in child protective services.[18] Andrew Bolt has criticized the apology to the forgotten Australians in these terms, arguing that the government should not apologize for "saving" children from parental neglect and abuse.[19] Yet, this form of criticism has been rare. Indeed, the first apology attracted innumerable column inches and a conservative outcry, whereas the apology to the forgotten Australians has passed almost without comment.

Despite this, some of the forgotten Australians have felt overlooked compared to the stolen generations. "I've been waiting for years for this," argued former child migrant Dorothy Chernikov. "When Kevin

Rudd said sorry to the Stolen Generation, tears came to my eyes because I thought What about us? We came from the other side of the world."[20] Here, Chernikov recalled the apology to the stolen generations as an affront to her suffering, and, in doing so, positioned child migrants as an almost abject group. Joanna Penglase, founder of the Care Leavers Australia Network (CLAN), has also been concerned with the attention granted to the stolen generations over former children in care. "We number hundreds of thousands across Australia," Penglase has argued, "more than the Aboriginal Stolen Generations, more than the adoptees who have services in every state, more than the child migrants who numbered at most ten thousand people."[21] Although Penglase has been eager to draw attention to the neglect of care leavers, she has asserted that doing so is not intended as a reflection on other groups. It is not, she has suggested, "to deny in any way the significance of those tragic histories or the right of those groups to recognition and to services."[22] Yet if it is not to deny recognition to these other groups, it is to set care leavers apart as a unique group, whose suffering and size has defined them as different from others and, by extension, as more worthy of attention and recompense.

Larissa Behrendt, prominent Indigenous legal scholar and activist, has drawn attention to the way that different constituencies of suffering have jostled for attention within Australian public culture. While not criticizing the apology to the forgotten Australians per se, Behrendt's opinion piece used the second apology as leverage for a discussion about the way in which the Rudd Government has failed to follow through on the promise of their first apology to the stolen generations.[23] How can the government apologize to the forgotten Australians, Behrendt has implied, without displacing the urgent and ongoing claims of the stolen generations? To link the apologies in this way is to emphasize the extent to which the practice of official apologies has been deployed to foreclose, rather than facilitate engagement with "victims" of injustice. It is also to highlight the cultural power that has coalesced around the status of victimhood, drawing attention to its privileged place within contemporary cultural politics.

It is clear that the stories of the forgotten Australians have drawn on the testimonial context which has accrued around the testimony of the stolen generations. As Kay Schaffer and Sidonie Smith have argued, "at any historical moment, only certain stories are tellable [sic] and intelligible to a broader audience."[24] The ability of the forgotten Australians to be transformed, in Rudd's terms, to the "Remembered Australians," has been dependent on the emergence of a specifically national culture of witnessing in which listening to testimony has figured as a form of civic virtue.[25] Within contemporary Australian culture, the discourse of apology has been thoroughly mainstreamed as a way of managing potentially disruptive memories and experiences, through inclusion in a positive narrative of national progress and redemption. In this sense, the rhetoric of witnessing and a template of national apology are now firmly entrenched within Australian public culture. Society is primed to hear the voices of the marginalized, to interpret their stories within the context of a broader national story, and to respond to testimony through particular generic forms of address, such as an apology. The extent to which this discourse on witnessing has become normative was illustrated by the scant attention paid to the apology to the forgotten Australians.

The term "Forgotten Australians" is a powerful label and one that has sought to make a significant intervention into Australian historical consciousness. It is a term that has attempted to set a group of (white) Australians apart from others as especially neglected and overlooked by the mainstream. It has implicitly done so against the recent attention given to stolen generations' testimony. In this sense, though the forgotten Australians have been dependent on the stolen generations for their cultural visibility, the term is also a reaction to the attention that Indigenous peoples have received. The label forgotten Australians has echoed—albeit unintentionally—former Prime Minister Robert Menzies' designation "the forgotten people". Menzies employed the term to rally the "ordinary" middle classes, a group united by a self-perception of being overlooked.[26] Crucially, to be forgotten is to have your experiences and suffering dismissed, to be rendered insignificant on the national stage. However, as Chris Healy has reminded us, forgetting is a necessary process, for both individuals and nations. "Without forgetting," Healy has suggested, "there is only an endless present overwhelmed by the flow of everything all at once."[27] As Susan Sontag has elaborated, "to make peace is to forget. To reconcile, it is necessary that memory be faulty and limited."[28]

Although I do not suggest that the stories of former child migrants and care leavers are unworthy of attention, and should be promptly "forgotten," the politics of national forgetting and remembering is far from neutral. In particular, I am troubled by the adoption of the label "Forgotten Australians" to, once again, highlight the suffering of settler Australians. The links forged in the second apology between the suffering of white children—whose experiences of institutional care have varied widely—and national history has illustrated the extent to which the cultural politics of witnessing has become key to contemporary nation building. It is not simply that child migrants and care leavers have been treated unjustly or abused, but that they have been ignored by national history and it is for national history that their suffering should be recognized. As argued throughout this book, witnessing has come to function as a form of memory work oriented to the stories of marginalized peoples, who have sought to use personal testimony as a vehicle for national recognition and reparation. However, as the recent apology to the forgotten Australians makes explicit, the cultural politics of witnessing is also, at the same time, the ground of a fierce contestation over whose stories get to count as "Australian."

*****

Throughout this book, I have taken a national approach to what has become a global politics of personal testimony. Although transnational and global analyses have been illuminating, this book has examined how witnessing has emerged within Australia as a form of memory work linked to the reproduction of a specifically national community. In the West, the turn to an ethics of the personal has signaled a profound transformation of political language and contemporary public culture. However, the rise of testimony has not heralded the emergence of the "pathological public sphere."[29] As Joy Damousi has argued, "the expression of these [personal] memories is often a political act; it invariably exposes the perpetuation of 'states of injury' by individuals, governments, the state, and nations."[30] Accordingly, even with its profound limits, witnessing remains important. The chance to speak your story in public, and to be believed, has continued to matter to a diverse range of individuals, groups, and communities.

This book has argued that from the late 1980s, a widespread and broadly popular public discourse on witnessing emerged in Australian public culture. Each chapter examined the nuances of witnessing through a focus on particular texts as case studies: from Kate Grenville's frontier novel *The Secret River*, through to the People's Inquiry into Detention and the surf documentary *Bra Boys*. The phenomenon of historical denial and the refusal to witness were also considered through an analysis of the conservative criticism of *Bringing them Home* and the recent film *Forbidden Lie$*, a documentary that chronicled the Khouri literary hoax. This grounding in literary–historical textual analysis has been crucial to illustrating the extent to which forms of testimony and witnessing have been shaped by—and have, in turn, influenced—their various contexts of expression, circulation, and reception. The breadth of texts selected has, moreover, illustrated the omnipresence of witnessing in contemporary Australian culture—the extent to which it has permeated both popular and academic contexts.

The analysis of specific case studies has been augmented by a central focus on the relationship between individual stories and public memory. Witnessing names an exchange that moves beyond the individual and their testimony. As such, processes of witnessing have functioned as forms of representation that have been crucial to reproducing both individual and group identity. In particular, witnessing played a key role in anchoring the formation of a counter-public of Australians committed to listening to testimony and, as such, worked to articulate a distinct mode of Australianness. Through an examination of the way that specific settler Australians—such as Robert Manne, Inga Clendinnen, and Julian Burnside—have witnessed to both asylum seekers and Indigenous peoples, I have demonstrated some of the ways in which witnessing has become linked to notions of "good" Australian citizenship. As we have seen, the act of witnessing became central to the way that a large minority of Australians understood themselves as (white) national citizens. As such, this book has analyzed the relationship between witnessing and ideas of national goodness and renewal. As a form of memory work, witnessing has come to influence whose stories and whose histories "matter" to the nation. Most frequently, testimony of historic injustice and suffering has been expressed by marginalized groups, only to be subsumed within a redemptive narrative of national renewal, in which settler Australians witness to demonstrate their—and their nation's—benevolent goodness.

While underscoring the extent to which witnessing has become a global phenomenon, this book is testament to the continued benefits of a nationally oriented approach to both memory studies and cultural history. Through a focus on the specifities of witnessing in Australia, I have demonstrated the way that witnessing is entangled with discourses on national history, virtue, identity, and citizenship. Even as witnessing draws on transnational understandings of human rights or childhood innocence, it is anchored within and actively participates in the formation of a distinctly national memorial community. This is, of course, not to argue that witnessing constitutes a homogenous or static set of cultural practices. As demonstrated, witnessing has been highly criticized within Australia, mostly notably as an "elite" practice by the Howard federal government. Nevertheless, it has emerged as a prominent practice that has worked to constitute a diverse community of Australians who understand witnessing as the apotheosis of a fair go.

*****

Ultimately, this book has been a history of a shifting present. It has been shaped, necessarily, by the specificities of this historical moment, and steered by the concerns of its author. Crucially, as a white settler Australian, I have attempted to work with a sense of my own complicity in the perpetuation of injustice toward Indigenous peoples and asylum seekers. In doing so, I have been keen to avoid, as far as anyone can, what Patricia Yaeger has called "the pleasures of academic melancholy."[31] Yet, at the same time, I have felt a sense of distance from the mode of historical witnessing inaugurated by Reynolds and Clendinnen, and largely perpetuated in contemporary historical practice today. This distance is, of course, primarily generational: It has been impossible for me, as it was for Schlunke, to say "I didn't know."

Testimony has typically been discussed, and theorized, as a tool of the subaltern. It has been identified as a mode of resisting rather than sustaining the cultural and political status quo. Yet, as Chapter Six demonstrated, testimony has become a preeminent form of representation, as likely to be deployed by a minority racial group or class as it is to be adopted by celebrities and "ordinary" citizens. Exploring the imbrication of testimony with the maintenance of settler hegemony has been crucial to my examination of both the limits and potential benefits of witnessing as a cultural politics. In particular, confronting the pleasures of witnessing for Anglo-Australians is an important step in exploring the investment settler Australians have in occupying the status of privileged victimhood.

In navigating the specifities of settler witnessing as a settler Australian, I have been most heartened by the urging of Fiona Nicoll's work to forgo the pleasures of being a "good woman."[32] This is not to say that I seek to be "bad," and to revel in the kind of haughty academic pose that phrase might imply. Rather, it is to keep in view the extent to which witnessing, along with generic forms of left-liberal critique, continue to dominate the high moral ground of public debate. It is in this spirit that I present this book not as a defence of my ethical credentials, but as a contribution to a conversation which I hope will never end.

As a form of memory work, witnessing has served to broaden who can speak, and be believed, within public culture. Yet as a mode of recognition, linked to the perpetuation of liberal multiculturalism, witnessing has reified "minority" citizens as objects of national feeling, rather than active citizens. As a left-liberal response to Australia's twinned narratives—migration and the Indigenous—witnessing has tended to privilege settler Australians as the arbiters of truth and national history. To offer a critique of a liberal discourse on witnessing in this way is not to erode the value of symbolic collective action, or to deny that settler Australians have witnessed to testimony in complex and diverse ways, many of them intimate and personal, rather than public. I do, however, question the imbrication of witnessing with teleological processes of national recovery, and caution against discourses that figure history as something to be "overcome." To speak in these terms is to perpetuate a cycle of forgetfulness in which injustice is perpetually "overcome," and a reconciled future consistently called forth, but never present.

To do otherwise is to remain open to the possibilities of witnessing—a more ambivalent kind of witnessing in which settler Australians forgo the solipsistic pleasures of being "good citizens" in order to engage with the implications of testimony not simply for the past or the future, but for present ways of being. As the former Rudd government's apology to the forgotten Australians demonstrated so clearly, witnessing will continue to be a key battleground in contemporary Australian nationalism for some time.[33] It not only shapes the circulation and reception of testimony, but also serves as a space of contestation over whose stories—and whose suffering—will be remembered in public culture. It is paramount that critics continue to question the operation of the cultural politics of emotion, both globally and in specific national theatres, and examine the political stakes in the mainstreaming of witnessing as a mode of managing, rather than engaging with, the other. In doing so, we should remain open to the dialogic possibilities of witnessing and understand, as Deborah Bird Rose has reminded us, that it is the present, not the future, that remains "the real site of action in the world."[34]

Notes

1. Kevin Rudd, "Address at the Apology to the Forgotten Australians and Former Child Migrants," November 16, 2009; Great Hall, Parliament House, *Prime Minister of Australia: Speeches*, http://www.pm.gov.au/node/6321 (accessed January 9, 2010.

2. Former child migrants have been previously referred to as "lost innocents," and care leavers have been described as "the forgotten Australians." Yet, a 2009 Senate progress report on investigations into the testimony of both groups have merged their experiences under the term "Forgotten Australians," and this usage was adopted by Rudd's apology. Senate Community Affairs References Committee, *Lost Innocents and Forgotten Australians Revisited: Report on the Progress with the Implementation of the Recommendations of the Lost Innocents and Forgotten Australians Reports* (Canberra: Senate Community Affairs References Committee, 2009).

3. Community Affairs References Committee, *Forgotten Australians: A Report on Australians Who Experienced Institutional or out-of-Home Care as Children* (Canberra: Community Affairs References Committee, 2004), xv.

4. The terms of reference for the 2004 Senate report on the forgotten Australians specifically exclude Indigenous peoples from this category. Ibid., 2. The extent to which Indigenous and non-Indigenous children were subject to similar forms of institutionalization is dramatically illustrated by Alana Valentine's play about the experiences of the "inmates" of the Parramatta Girls' Home. Alana Valentine, *Parramatta Girls* (Sydney: Currency Press, 2007).

5. Coral Dow and Janet Phillips, "Background Note: 'Forgotten Australians' and 'Lost Innocents': Child Migrants and Children in Institutional Care in Australia," *Parliamentary Library*, November 11, 2009, http://www.aph. gov.au/library/pubs/ bn/sp/childmigrants.htm#_ftn1 (accessed January 26, 2010).

6. Senate Community Affairs References Committee, *Lost Innocents: Righting the Record—Report on Child Migration* (Canberra: Senate Community Affairs References Committee Secretariat, 2001).

7. Community Affairs References Committee, *Forgotten Australians*, 65–84.

8. Senate Community Affairs References Committee, *Lost Innocents*, 11–45.

9. See, for example, the furore of the recent inquiry into child abuse by the Irish clergy. Henry McDonald, "Irish Church and Police Covered by Child Sex Abuse, Report Says," *Guardian*, November 26, 2009, http://www. guardian.co.uk/world/2009/nov/26/ireland-church-sex-abuse (accessed January 26, 2010).

10. Philip Bean and Joy Melville, *Lost Children of the Empire* (London and Sydney: Unwin Hyman, 1989). See also Margaret Humphreys, *Empty Cradles* (London and Sydney: Doubleday, 1994); Alan Gill, *Orphans of Empire: The Shocking True Story of Child Migration to Australia* (Sydney: Random House, 1997); David Hill, *The Forgotten Children: Fairbridge Farm School and Its Betrayal of Australia's Child Migrants* (North Sydney: Random House Australia, 2007); Michael Jenkins (dir.), *The Leaving of Liverpool* (Australia: Roadshow Entertainment, 2005); Valentine, *Parramatta Girls*.

11. The Australian enquiry into child migration followed a British investigation into the use of child migration programs throughout the Commonwealth. Select Committee on Health Great Britain House of Commons, *The Welfare of Former British Child Migrants* (London: House of Commons, 1998); Senate Community Affairs References Committee, *Lost Innocents*; Community Affairs References Committee, *Forgotten Australians*; Community Affairs References Committee, *Protecting Vulnerable Children: A National*

Challenge: Second Report on the Inquiry into Children in Institutional or out-of-Home Care (Canberra: Community Affairs References Committee, 2005); Senate Community Affairs References Committee, *Lost Innocents and Forgotten Australians Revisited.*

12. Community Affairs References Committee, *Forgotten Australians*, 187–96; Senate Community Affairs References Committee, *Lost Innocents*, 227.

13. Rudd, "Address at the Apology to the Forgotten Australians and Former Child Migrants."

14. Ibid.

15. Ibid.

16. See, for example, Doreen Mellor and Anna Haebich's work with the National Library of Australia's stolen generation testimonies. Doreen Mellor and Anna Haebich, *Many Voices: Reflections on Experiences of Indigenous Child Separation* (Canberra: National Library of Australia, 2002).

17. Ibid.

18. For example, Chris Goddard and Joe Tucco, "In Victoria, Another Forgotten Generation in the Making," *Australian*, December 7, 2009, 16.

19. Andrew Bolt, "Time to Save Our Children," *Herald Sun*, December 18, 2009, 1.

20. Dorothy Chernikov cited in Ari Sharp, "Apology for 'Forgotten Australians,'" *Sydney Morning Herald*, November 16, 2009, 6.

21. Joanna Penglase, "'Wardies and Homies': The Forgotten Australians," *Care Leavers Australia Network*, n. d., http://www.clan.org.au/page.php?pageID=23 (accessed January 9, 2010). See also Joanna Penglase, *Orphans of the Living: Growing Up in 'Care' in Twentieth-Century Australia* (Fremantle: Curtin University Books, 2005).

22. Ibid.

23. Larissa Behrendt, "Show Us the Money for the First Apology," *Sydney Morning Herald*, November 19, 2009, 17.

24. Kay Schaffer and Sidonie Smith, "Conjunctions: Life Narratives in the Field of Human Rights," *Biography* 27, no. 1 (Winter 2004): 19.

25. Rudd, "Address at the Apology to the Forgotten Australians."

26. See Judith Brett, *Robert Menzies' Forgotten People* (Chippendale, NSW: Macmillan Australia, 1992).

27. Healy, *Forgetting Aborigines*, 9.

28. Susan Sontag, *Regarding the Pain of Others* (New York: Farrar, Straus and Giroux, 2003), 115.

29. Mark Seltzer, "Wound Culture: Trauma in the Pathological Public Sphere," *October* 80 (Spring 1997): 3–26.

30. Joy Damousi, "History Matters: The Politics of Grief and Injury in Australian History," *Australian Historical Studies* 118 (2002): 112.

31. Patricia Yaeger, "Consuming Trauma; or, the Pleasures of Merely Circulating," in *Extremities: Trauma, Testimony, and Community*, ed. Nancy K. Miller and Jason Tougaw (Urbana and Chicago: University of Illinois Press, 2002), 29.

32. Nicoll, "Indigenous Sovereignty and the Violence of Perspective," 369–85.

33. At the time of writing, Australia is undergoing a period of government change. In June 2010, Prime Minister Rudd was replaced by a member of his own Labor party—Julia Gillard—a change that was narrowly endorsed

by the electorate at the August federal election. While it remains to be seen whether the shift to Gillard will substantially alter the direction of the Labor government, early action with regard to asylum seekers suggests that the politics of witnessing and national virtue will endure for some time. In October 2010, Prime Minister Gillard announced a major change to the government's policy on asylum seekers by responding to public pressure to remove children and their families from detention. Announcing the shift to community housing, Gillard explained that "I don't think it's the Australian way to have kids behind razor wire." Julia Gillard cited in Patricia Karvelas and Paul Maley, "P.M. Julia Gillard Softens Detention Stance," *Australian*, October 19, 2010, 1.

34.   Rose, *Reports from a Wild Country*, 10.

Bibliography

The section on key texts includes those works which are used as primary sources and form the basis of the major case studies throughout the book. Some of these sources are, of course, also drawn upon as secondary source material. For clarity, the remainder of the bibliography is arranged by genre or type of source.

Key Texts

Abberton, Sunny (dir.). *Bra Boys*. Australia: Bradahood Productions, 2007.

Australian Story. Australia: ABC TV, 1996–present.

Briskman, Linda, Susie Latham, and Chris Goddard. *Human Rights Overboard: Seeking Asylum in Australia*. Carlton North: Scribe, 2008.

Broinowski, Alison (dir.). *Forbidden Lie$*. Australia: Palace Films, 2007.

Clendinnen, Inga. *Dancing with Strangers*. Melbourne: Text Publishing, 2003.

———. *The History Question: Who Owns the Past?* Vol. 23, *Quarterly Essay*. Melbourne: Black, 2006.

———. *Tiger's Eye: A Memoir*. London: Jonathan Cape, 2001.

———. *True Stories*. Sydney: ABC Books, 1999. http://www.abc.net.au/rn/boyers/index/BoyersChronoIdx.htm#1999 (accessed July 27, 2009).

Grenville, Kate. *Searching for the Secret River*. Melbourne: Text, 2006.

———. *The Secret River*. Melbourne: Text Publishing, 2005.

Human Rights and Equal Opportunity Commission. *Bringing Them Home: Report of the National Inquiry into the Separation of Aboriginal and Torres Strait Islander Children from Their Families*. Sydney: Human Rights and Equal Opportunity Commission, 1997.

Khouri, Norma. *Forbidden Love*. London: Doubleday, 2003.

Luhrmann, Baz (dir.). *Australia*. Australia: Twentieth Century Fox, 2008.

Manne, Robert. "In Denial: The Stolen Generations and the Right." In *Left Right Left: Political Essays 1977-2005*, edited by Robert Manne, 217–305. Melbourne: Black, 2005.

Mares, Sarah, and Louise Newman, eds. *Acting from the Heart: Australian Advocates for Asylum Seekers Tell Their Stories*. Sydney: Finch Publishing, 2007.

Noyce, Phillip (dir.). *Rabbit-Proof Fence*. Australia: Magna Pacific Video, 2002.

Perkins, Rachel, and Beck Cole (dirs.). *First Australians*. Australia: Special Broadcasting Service Corporation & Madman Entertainment, 2008.

Reynolds, Henry. *Why Weren't We Told: A Personal Search for the Truth About Our History*. Melbourne: Viking, 1999.

Rudd, Kevin, "Address at the Apology to the Forgotten Australians and Former Child Migrants." November 16, 2009, Great Hall, Parliament House. *Prime Minister of Australia: Speeches.* http://www.pm.gov.au/node/6321 (accessed January 9, 2010).
———. "Apology to Australia's Indigenous Peoples." February 13, 2008, Parliament House, Canberra. *Prime Minister of Australia: Speeches.* http://www.pm.gov. au/node/5952 (accessed January 23, 2010).
Schlunke, Katrina. *Bluff Rock: Autobiography of a Massacre.* Fremantle: Curtin University Books, 2005.

Autobiographies and Life Writing

Clendinnen, Inga. *Tiger's Eye: A Memoir.* London: Jonathan Cape, 2001.
Flanagan, Martin. *In Sunshine or in Shadow.* Sydney: Picador, 2002.
Grenville, Kate. *Searching for the Secret River.* Melbourne: Text, 2006.
Morgan, Sally. *My Place.* Fremantle: Fremantle Arts Centre Press, 1987.
Pybus, Cassandra. *Community of Thieves.* Melbourne: Minerva, 1992.
Read, Peter. *Belonging: Australians, Place and Aboriginal Ownership.* Melbourne: Cambridge University Press, 2000.
Reynolds, Henry. *Nowhere People.* Melbourne: Viking, 2005.
———. *Why Weren't We Told: A Personal Search for the Truth About Our History.* Melbourne: Viking, 1999.
Russell, Lynette. *A Little Bird Told Me: Family Secrets, Necessary Lies.* Crows Nest, NSW: Allen & Unwin, 2002.

Films and Television Programs

Abberton, Sunny (dir.). *Bra Boys.* Australia: Bradahood Productions, 2007.
Australian Story. Australia: ABC TV, 1996–present.
Broinowski, Alison (dir.). *Forbidden Lie$.* Australia: Palace Films, 2007.
de Heer, Rolf (dir.). *The Tracker.* Australia: Madman Cinema, 2002.
Jenkins, Michael (dir.). *The Leaving of Liverpool.* Australia: Roadshow Entertainment, 2005.
Lahiff, Craig (dir.). *Black and White.* Australia: Duo/Scala, 2002.
Law, Clara (dir.). *Letters to Ali.* Australia: Palace Films, 2004.
Luhrmann, Baz (dir.). *Australia.* Australia: Twentieth Century Fox, 2008.
Noyce, Phillip (dir.). *Rabbit-Proof Fence.* Australia: Magna Pacific Video, 2002.
Perkins, Rachel, and Beck Cole (dirs.). *First Australians.* Australia: Special Broadcasting Service Corporation & Madman Entertainment, 2008.
Permezel, Bruce (dir.). *The Games.* Australia: ABC TV, 1998–2000.
Sen, Ivan (dir.). *Beneath Clouds.* Australia: Australian Film Finance Corporation & Autumn Films, 2002.
Sitch, Rob (dir.). *The Castle.* Australia: Working Dog, 1997.

Newspapers (Print and Online)

ABC Online
Adelaide Advertiser
Age
Australian

Bibliography

Australian Associated Press
Australian Financial Review
Canberra Times
Courier Mail
Daily Telegraph
Green Left Weekly
Guardian
Herald Sun
Illawarra Mercury
Newcastle Herald
New York Times
Reuters News
Sunday Age
Sun Herald
Sydney Morning Herald

Novels

Carey, Peter. *True History of the Kelly Gang*. St. Lucia: University of Queensland Press, 2000.
Flanagan, Richard. *Gould's Book of Fish: A Novel in Twelve Fish*. Sydney: Pan Macmillan, 2001.
———. *Wanting*. North Sydney: Knopf, 2008.
Grenville, Kate. *The Lieutenant*. Melbourne: Text Publishing, 2008.
———. *The Secret River*. Melbourne: Text Publishing, 2005.
Jones, Gail. *Sorry*. Sydney: Vintage, 2007.
Malouf, David. *The Conversations at Curlow Creek*. London: Chatto, 1996.
———. *Remembering Babylon*. Sydney: Random House, 1993.
McDonald, Roger. *The Ballad of Desmond Kale*. Milsons Point: Vintage, 2005.
McGahan, Andrew. *The White Earth*. Crows Nest, NSW: Allen & Unwin, 2004.
Miller, Alex. *Journey to the Stone Country*. Crows Nest, NSW: Allen & Unwin, 2002.
———. *Landscape of Farewell*. Crows Nest: Allen & Unwin, 2007.
Sallis, Eva. *The Marsh Birds*. Crows Nest: Allen & Unwin, 2005.

Reports

Briskman, Linda, Susie Latham, and Chris Goddard. *Human Rights Overboard: Seeking Asylum in Australia*. Carlton North: Scribe, 2008.
Community Affairs References Committee. *Forgotten Australians: A Report on Australians Who Experienced Institutional or out-of-Home Care as Children*. Canberra: Community Affairs References Committee, 2004.
———. *Protecting Vulnerable Children: A National Challenge: Second Report on the Inquiry into Children in Institutional or out-of-Home Care*. Canberra: Community Affairs References Committee, 2005.
Hindmarsh Island Bridge Royal Commission. *Report of the Hindmarsh Island Bridge Royal Commission*. Adelaide: The Royal Commission, 1995.
Human Rights and Equal Opportunity Commission. *Bringing Them Home: Report of the National Inquiry into the Separation of Aboriginal and Torres Strait Islander Children from Their Families*. Sydney: Human Rights and Equal Opportunity Commission, 1997.

261

———. "A Last Resort?: National Inquiry into Children in Immigration Detention." Sydney: Human Rights and Equal Opportunity Commission, 2004.

Katona, Jacqui, and Chips Mackinolty, eds. *The Long Road Home . . . : The Going Home Conference, 3-6 October 1994*. Darwin: Karu Aboriginal Child Care Agency, 1996.

Link-Up, and Tikka Jan Wilson. *In the Best Interests of the Child?: Stolen Children: Aboriginal Pain/White Shame*. Lawson, NSW: Link-Up (NSW) & Aboriginal History, 1997.

Odgers, S. J. *Report of Independent Assessor to Senate Select Committee on a Certain Maritime Incident*. Sydney: Forbes Chambers, 2002.

Oxfam. *Adrift in the Pacific: The Implications of Australia's Pacific Refugee Solution*. Melbourne: Oxfam Community Aid Abroad, 2002.

Palmer, Mick. *Report of the Inquiry into the Immigration Detention of Cornelia Rau*. Canberra: Commonwealth of Australia, 2005.

Royal Commission into Aboriginal Deaths in Custody. *National Report of the Royal Commission into Aboriginal Deaths in Custody, Vol. 1*. Canberra: Australian Government Publishing Service, 1991.

Royal Commission into British Nuclear Tests in Australia. *Report of the Royal Commission into British Nuclear Tests in Australia*. Canberra: Australian Government Publishing Service, 1985.

Select Committee on Health, Great Britain House of Commons. *The Welfare of Former British Child Migrants*. London: House of Commons, 1998.

Senate Community Affairs References Committee. *Lost Innocents and Forgotten Australians Revisited: Report on the Progress with the Implementation of the Recommendations of the Lost Innocents and Forgotten Australians Reports*. Canberra: Senate Community Affairs References Committee, 2009.

———. *Lost Innocents: Righting the Record - Report on Child Migration*. Canberra: Senate Community Affairs References Committee Secretariat, 2001.

Websites

Australian Bureau of Statistics, http://www.abs.gov.au/
Australians for Native Title and Reconciliation, http://www.antar.org.au/
Australian Story, http://www.abc.net.au/austory/
First Australians, http://www.sbs.com.au/firstaustralians/
UNESCO, *Australian Memory of the World*, http://www.amw.org.au/
YouTube, http://www.youtube.com/

Books, Chapters, and Articles

Agamben, Giorgio. *Remnants of Auschwitz: The Witness and the Archive*. New York: Zone Books, 1999.

Ahmed, Sara. *The Cultural Politics of Emotion*. New York: Routledge, 2004.

———. "The Politics of Bad Feeling." *Australian Critical Race and Whiteness Studies Association Journal* 1 (2005): 72–85.

Ahmed, Sara, and Jackie Stacey. "Testimonial Cultures: An Introduction." *Cultural Values* 5, no. 1 (2001): 1–6.

Albie, Thoms. *Surfmovies: The History of the Surf Film in Australia*. Noosa Heads: Shore Thing Publishing, 2000.

Albrechsten, Janet. "The History Wars." *Sydney Papers* 15, no. 3/4 (Winter/Spring 2003): 84–92.

Alcoff, Linda Martin. "The Problem of Speaking for Others." *Cultural Critique* (Winter 1991–1992): 5–32.

Amstutz, Mark R. *The Healing of Nations: The Promise and Limits of Political Forgiveness*. Lanham: Rowman & Littlefield Publishers, 2005.

Anderson, Benedict. *Imagined Communities: Reflections on the Origin and Spread of Nationalism*. London: Verso, 1983.

Anderson, Linda. *Autobiography*. London and New York: Routledge, 2001.

Antze, Paul, and Michael Lambek, eds. *Tense Past: Cultural Essay in Trauma and Memory*. New York: Routledge, 1996.

Apel, Dora. *Memory Effects: The Holocaust and the Art of Secondary Witnessing*. New Brunswick, NJ and London: Rutgers University Press, 2002.

Atkinson, Paul, and Anna Poletti. "The Limits of Testimony." *Southern Review* 40, no. 3 (2008): 1–6.

Attwood, Bain, ed. *In the Age of Mabo: History, Aborigines and Australia*. Sydney: Allen & Unwin, 1996.

———. "In the Age of Testimony: The Stolen Generations Narrative, 'Distance,' and Public History." *Public Culture* 20, no. 1 (2008): 75–95.

———. "'Learning About the Truth': The Stolen Generations Narrative." In *Telling Stories: Indigenous History and Memory in Australia and New Zealand*, edited by Bain Attwood and Fiona Magowan, 183–212. Sydney: Allen & Unwin, 2001.

———. "Portrait of an Aboriginal as an Artist: Sally Morgan and the Construction of Aboriginality." *Australian Historical Studies* 25, no. 99 (1992): 302–18.

———. "The Stolen Generations and Genocide: Robert Manne's in *Denial: The Stolen Generations and the Right*." *Aboriginal History* 25 (2001): 163–72.

———. *Telling the Truth About Aboriginal History*. Sydney: Allen & Unwin, 2005.

———. "Whose Dreaming? Reviewing the *Review of the National Museum of Australia*." *History Australia* 1, no. 2 (July 2004): 279–94.

Attwood, Bain, and Dipesh Chakrabarty. "Risky Histories." *Meanjin* 65, no. 1 (2006): 200–207.

Attwood, Bain, and John Arnold, eds. *Power, Knowledge and Aborigines*. Bundoora, VIC: La Trobe University Press, 1992.

Back, Les. *The Art of Listening*. London: Berg, 2007.

Bal, Mieke, Jonathan Crewe, and Leo Spitzer, eds. *Acts of Memory: Cultural Recall in the Present*. Hanover, NH: Dartmouth College & University Press of New England, 1999.

Barkan, Elazar, and Alexander Karn, eds. *Taking Wrongs Seriously: Apologies and Reconciliation*. Stanford, CA: Stanford University Press, 2006.

Barnes, Diane. *Asylum Seekers and Refugees in Australia: Issues of Mental Health and Wellbeing*. Parramatta: Transcultural Mental Health Centre, 2003.

Bartlett, Alison. "Dear Regina: Formative Conversations About Feminist Writing." *FemTAP: A Journal of Feminist Theory and Practice* (Summer 2006). http://www.femtap.com/id14.html (accessed August 14, 2008).

Bartlett, Myke. "The Unbelievable Truth of *Forbidden Lie$*." *Screen Education*, no. 48 (2007): 30–36.

Bathrick, David, Brad Prager, and Michael D. Richardson, eds. *Visualizing the Holocaust: Documents, Aesthetics, Memory*. Rochester, N.Y.: Camden House, 2008.

Baum, Steven K. *The Psychology of Genocide: Perpetrators, Bystanders, and Rescuers*. Cambridge: Cambridge University Press, 2008.

Bean, Philip, and Joy Melville. *Lost Children of the Empire*. London and Sydney: Unwin Hyman, 1989.

Bennett, Jill. *Empathic Vision: Affect, Trauma, and Contemporary Art*. Stanford, CA: Stanford University Press, 2005.

Bennett, Jill, and Rosanne Kennedy. "Introduction." In *World Memory: Personal Trajectories in Global Time*, edited by Jill Bennett and Rosanne Kennedy, 1–15. London and New York: Palgrave Macmillan, 2003.

——, eds. *World Memory: Personal Trajectories in Global Time*. London and New York: Palgrave Macmillan, 2003.

Bennett, Tony, Pat Buckridge, David Carter, and Colin Mercer, eds. *Celebrating the Nation: A Critical Study of Australia's Bicentenary*. Sydney: Allen and Unwin, 1992.

Benterrak, Kim, Stephen Muecke, Paddy Roe, and Ray Keogh. *Reading the Country: Introduction to Nomadology*. Fremantle, WA: Fremantle Arts Centre Press, 1984.

Berlant, Lauren, ed. *Compassion: The Culture and Politics of an Emotion*. London: Routledge, 2004.

——. "The Subject of True Feeling: Pain, Privacy, and Politics." In *Cultural Pluralism, Identity Politics, and the Law*, edited by Austin Sarat and Thomas R. Kearns, 49–84. Ann Arbor: University of Michigan Press, 1999.

Bernard-Donals, Michael. "Beyond the Question of Authenticity: Witness and Testimony in the *Fragments* Controversy." *PMLA* 116, no. 5 (2001): 1302–15.

Beverley, John. *Testimonio: On the Politics of Truth*. Minneapolis and London: University of Minnesota Press, 2004.

Bhabha, Homi K., ed. *Nation and Narration*. London: Routledge, 1990.

Bickford, Susan. *The Dissonance of Democracy: Listening, Conflict, and Citizenship*. Ithaca, N.Y.: Cornell University Press, 1996.

Birch, Tony. "'The Invisible Fire': Indigenous Sovereignty, History and Responsibility." In *Sovereign Subjects: Indigenous Sovereignty Matters*, edited by Aileen Moreton-Robinson, 105–17. Crows Nest, NSW: Allen & Unwin, 2007.

——. "Testimony." *Aboriginal History* 30 (2006): 29–32.

——. "'History Is Never Bloodless': Getting It Wrong after One Hundred Years of Federation." *Australian Historical Studies* 33, no. 118 (2002): 42–53.

——. "'This Is a True Story': *Rabbit-Proof Fence*, 'Mr. Devil' and the Desire to Forget." *Cultural Studies Review* 8, no. 1 (2002): 117–29.

——. "The Last Refuge of the 'Un-Australian.'" *UTS Review* 7, no. 1 (2001): 17–22.

——. "Half-Caste." *Australian Historical Studies* 25, no. 100 (1993): 458.

Bird, Carmel, and Peter Read, eds. *The Lost Children: Thirteen Australians Taken from Their Aboriginal Families Tell of the Struggle to Find Their Natural Parents*. Sydney: Doubleday, 1989.

Boland, Michaela. "*Australia* sets record Down Under." *Variety*, February 26, 2009. http://www.variety.com/article/VR1118000644 .html?categoryid=19&cs=1 (accessed December 30, 2009).

Boltanski, Luc. *Distant Suffering: Morality, Media and Politics*. Cambridge: Cambridge University Press, 1999.

Bonner, Frances. "Testimonial Current Affairs: The *Australian Story* Approach to Celebrity." *Media International Australia*, no. 121 (November 2006): 29–40.

Bonner, Frances, and Susan McKay. "Personalizing Current Affairs without Becoming Tabloid: The Case of *Australian Story.*" *Journalism* 8 (2007): 640–56.

Boucher, Leigh, Jane Carey, and Katherine Ellinghaus, eds. *Historicising Whiteness: Transnational Perspectives on the Construction of an Identity.* Melbourne: RMIT Publishing in association with the School of Historical Studies, University of Melbourne, 2007.

Boulanger-Mashberg, Anica. "In Her Own Margins: Kate Grenville's *Searching for the Secret River* as Marginalia to *the Secret River.*" *Limina* 15 (2009): 1–9.

Bourke, Joanna. "Women's Business: Sex, Secrets and the Hindmarsh Island Affair." *UNSW Law Journal* 20, no. 2 (1997): 333–51.

Brennan, Bernadette, ed. *Just Words? Australian Authors Writing for Justice.* St. Lucia: University of Queensland Press, 2008.

Brennan, Frank. *Tampering with Asylum: A Universal Humanitarian Problem.* St. Lucia: University of Queensland Press, 2003.

———. "Reconciling Our Differences." In *Reconciliation: Essays on Australian Reconciliation*, edited by Michelle Grattan, 25–32. Melbourne: Black, 2000.

Bretherton, Di, and David Mellor. "Reconciliation between Aboriginal and Other Australians: The 'Stolen Generations.'" *Journal of Social Issues* 62, no. 1 (2006): 81–98.

Brett, Judith. "Relaxed and Comfortable: The Liberal Party's Australia." *Quarterly Essay*, no. 19 (2005): 1–79.

———. *Robert Menzies' Forgotten People.* Chippendale, NSW: Macmillan Australia, 1992.

Brewster, Anne. "Writing Whiteness: The Personal Turn." *Australian Humanities Review*, no. 35 (June 2005). http://www.lib.latrobe.edu.au/AHR/archive/Issue-June-2005/brewster.html (accessed April 13, 2008).

———. *Reading Aboriginal Women's Autobiography.* Sydney: Sydney University Press, 1996.

Brewster, Anne, and Hazel Smith. "Affections: Friendship, Community, Bodies." *TEXT* 7, no. 2 (2003). http://www.textjournal.com.au/oct03/brewstersmith. htm (accessed April 13, 2008).

Briskman, Linda. *The Black Grapevine: Aboriginal Activism and the Stolen Generations.* Sydney: The Federation Press, 2003.

Briskman, Linda, Susie Latham, and Chris Goddard. *Human Rights Overboard: Seeking Asylum in Australia.* Carlton North: Scribe, 2008.

Brook, Scott. "'Does Anybody Know What Happened to "Fictocriticism"?': Toward a Fractual Genealogy of Australian Fictocriticism." *Cultural Studies Review* 8, no. 2 (November 2002): 104–18.

Broome, Richard. *Aboriginal Australians.* Sydney: Allen & Unwin, 2001.

———. "Chapter 4: Historians, Aborigines and Australia: Writing the National Past." In *In the Age of Mabo: History, Aborigines and Australia*, edited by Bain Attwood, 54–72. Sydney: Allen & Unwin, 1996.

Brophy, Sarah. *Witnessing AIDS: Writing, Testimony and the Work of Mourning.* Toronto: University of Toronto Press, 2004.

Browder, Laura. *Slippery Characters: Ethnic Impersonators and American Identities.* Chapel Hill: University of North Carolina Press, 2000.

Brunton, Ron. "Betraying the Victims: The 'Stolen Generations' Report." *IPA Backgrounder* 10, no. 1 (1998): 1–24.

Burgoyne, Robert. *Film Nation: Hollywood Looks at U.S. History*. Minneapolis: University of Minnesota Press, 1997.

Burnside, Julian. *Watching Brief: Reflections on Human Rights, Law and Justice*. Melbourne: Scribe, 2007.

———. *From Nothing to Zero: Letters from Refugees in Australia's Detention Centres*. Melbourne: Lonely Planet Publications, 2003.

Butler, Judith. *Precarious Life: The Power of Mourning and Violence*. London and New York: Verso, 2004.

Cain, Deborah. "A Fence Too Far? Postcolonial Guilt and the Myth of Distance in *Rabbit Proof Fence*." *Third Text* 18, no. 4 (2004): 297–303.

Cameron, Kenneth M. *America on Film: Hollywood and American History*. New York: Continuum, 1997.

Campbell, Terence W. *Smoke and Mirrors: The Devastating Effect of False Sexual Abuse Claims*. New York: Insight Books, 1998.

Carey, Jane, and Claire McLisky, eds. *Creating White Australia*. Sydney: Sydney University Press, 2009.

Carter, David. "Introduction: Intellectuals and Their Publics." In *The Ideas Market: An Alternative Take on Australia's Intellectual Life*, edited by David Carter, 1–11. Melbourne: Melbourne University Press, 2004.

———. "'O' Grady, John *See* "Culotta, Nino': Popular Authorship, Duplicity and Celebrity." *Australian Literary Studies* 21, no. 4 (2004): 56–73.

———, ed. *The Ideas Market: An Alternative Take on Australia's Intellectual Life*. Melbourne: Melbourne University Press, 2004.

Cartmell, Deborah, I. Q. Hunter, and Imelda Whelehan, eds. *Retrovisions: Reinventing the Past in Film and Fiction*. London: Pluto Press, 2001.

Caruth, Cathy. *Unclaimed Experience: Trauma, Narrative, and History*. Baltimore, MD: John Hopkins University Press, 1996.

———, ed. *Trauma: Explorations in Memory*. Baltimore, MD: John Hopkins University Press, 1995.

Casey, Dawn. "Culture Wars: Museums, Politics and Controversy." *Open Museum Journal* 6 (September 2003): 1–23.

Casey, Maryrose. "Referendums and Reconciliation Marches: What Bridges Are We Crossing?" *Journal of Australian Studies* 89 (2006): 137–52.

Castles, Stephen, Mary Kalantzis, Bill Cope, and Michael Morrissey. *Mistaken Identity: Multiculturalism and the Demise of Nationalism in Australia*. Sydney: Pluto Press, 1990.

———. *The Bicentenary and the Failure of Australian Nationalism*. Annandale, NSW: Common Ground, 1987.

Caterson, Simon. *Hoax Nation: Australian Fakes and Frauds, from Plato to Norma Khouri*. Melbourne: Arcade Publications, 2009.

Chakrabarty, Dipesh. "History and the Politics of Recognition." In *Manifestos for History*, edited by Keith Jenkins, Sue Morgan and Alun Munslow, 77–87. London and New York: Routledge, 2007.

Chouliaraki, Lilie. *The Spectatorship of Suffering*. London: SAGE Publications, 2006.

Chun, Wendy Hui Kyong. "Unbearable Witness: Toward a Politics of Listening." *Differences: A Journal of Feminist Cultural Studies* 11, no. 1 (1999): 112–49.

Clarke, Jennifer. "Case note: *Cubillo v. The Commonwealth.*" *Melbourne University Law Review* 25, (2001). http://www.austlii.edu.au/au/journals/MULR/2001/7. html#Heading68 (accessed November 22, 2009).

Clendinnen, Inga. *The History Question: Who Owns the Past?* Vol. 23, *Quarterly Essay.* Melbourne: Black, 2006.

——. *Dancing with Strangers.* Melbourne: Text Publishing, 2003.

——. "Dispatches from the History Wars: On the Bitter Battle Being Waged over Our National Past." *Australian Financial Review*, October 31, 2003, Review 4–5.

——. "First Contact." *Quarterly Essay*, no. 2 (2001): 98–108.

——. *Reading the Holocaust.* Cambridge: Cambridge University Press, 1999.

——. *True Stories.* Sydney: ABC Books, 1999. http://www.abc.net.au/rn/boyers/index/BoyersChronoIdx.htm#1999 (accessed July 27, 2009).

——. "Reading Mr. Robinson." In *Seams of Light: Best Antipodean Essays*, edited by Morag Fraser, 58–78. Melbourne: Allen & Unwin, 1998.

——. "Fellow Sufferers: History and Imagination." *Australian Humanities Review* 3 (September 1996). http://www.lib.latrobe.edu.au/AHR archive/Issue-Sept-1996/clendinnen.html (accessed May 22, 2006).

——. *Aztecs: An Interpretation.* Cambridge: Cambridge University Press, 1991.

Coady, C. A. J. *Testimony: A Philosophical Study.* Oxford: Clarendon Press, 1992.

Coleman, Deirdre. "Inscrutable History or Incurable Romanticism: Inga Clendinnen's *Dancing with Strangers.*" *HEAT* 8 (2004): 201–13.

Collins, Eleanor. "Poison in the Flour." *Meanjin* 65, no. 1 (2006): 38–76.

Collins, Felicity, and Therese Davis. "Disputing History, Remembering Country: *The Tracker* and *Rabbit-Proof Fence.*" *Australian Historical Studies* 128 (2006): 35–54.

——. *Australian Cinema after Mabo.* Cambridge: Cambridge University Press, 2004.

Collins, Jock, and Scott Poynting, eds. *The Other Sydney: Communities, Identities and Inequalities in Western Sydney.* Melbourne: Common Ground Publishing, 2006.

Colvin, Christopher J. "'Brothers and Sisters, Do Not Be Afraid of Me': Trauma, History and the Therapeutic Imagination in the New South Africa." In *Contested Pasts: The Politics of Memory*, edited by Katharine Hodgkin and Susannah Radstone, 153–67. London: Routledge, 2003.

Confino, Alon. "Collective Memory and Cultural History: Problems of Method." *American Historical Review* 102, no. 5 (December 1997): 1386–403.

Conor, Liz. "Howard's Desert Storm." *Overland*, no. 189 (2007): 12–15.

Coombs, Anne. "Mobilising Rural Australia." *Griffith Review* (Autumn 2004): 123–35.

Coombes, Annie E., ed. *Rethinking Settler Colonialism: History and Memory in Australia, Canada, Aotearoa New Zealand and South Africa.* Manchester & New York: Manchester University Press, 2006.

Corbett, Helen, and Tony Vinson. "Black Deaths in Custody: Instigating the Royal Commission." In *Actions Speak: Strategies and Lessons from Australian Social and Community Action*, edited by Eileen Baldry and Tony Vinson, 95–104. Melbourne: Longman Cheshire, 1991.

Couldry, Nick. *The Place of Media Power: Pilgrims and Witnesses of the Media Age*. London: Routledge, 2000.

Council for Aboriginal Reconciliation. "Australian Declaration Towards Reconciliation." *Reconciliation Australia* (2000). http://www.austlii.edu.au/au/other/IndigLRes/car/2000/12/pg3.htm (accessed April 15, 2009).

Cox, Emma. "The Citation of Injury: Regarding the Exceptional Body." *Journal of Australian Studies* 33, no. 4 (2009): 459–72.

Crawford, Kate. *Adult Themes: Rewriting the Rules of Adulthood*. Sydney: Pan Macmillan, 2006.

Crock, May, and Ben Saul. *Future Seekers: Refugees and the Law in Australia*. Sydney: The Federation Press, 2002.

Crombie, Isobel. "Laughing Gobs in Bathing Costumes." In *Body Culture: Max Dupain, Photography and Australian Culture 1919-1939*, 176–91. Melbourne: Peleus Press/NGV, 2004.

Cunningham, Stuart. "Popular Media as Public 'Sphericules' for Diasporic Communities." *International Journal of Cultural Studies* 4 (2001): 131–47.

Curthoys, Ann. "An Uneasy Conversation: The Multicultural and the Indigenous." In *Race, Colour and Identity in Australia and New Zealand*, edited by John Docker and Gerhard Fischer, 21–36. Sydney: UNSW Press, 2000.

——. "Whose Home? Expulsion, Exodus, and Exile in White Australian Historical Mythology." *Journal of Australian Studies* 61, no. 1–19 (1999).

Curthoys, Ann, and John Docker. *Is History Fiction?* Sydney: UNSW Press, 2006.

Curthoys, Ann, Ann Genovese, and Alexander Reilly. *Rights and Redemption: History, Law and Indigenous People*. Sydney: UNSW Press, 2008.

Curthoys, Ned, and Debjani Ganguly, eds. *Edward Said: The Legacy of a Public Intellectual*. Melbourne: Melbourne University Press, 2007.

Cuthbert, Denise. "Holding the Baby: Questions Arising from Research into the Experiences of Non-Aboriginal Adoptive and Foster Mothers of Aboriginal Children." *Journal of Australian Studies*, no. 72 (1998): 39–52.

Dalziell, Rosamund. *Shameful Autobiographies: Shame in Contemporary Australian Autobiographies and Culture*. Melbourne: Melbourne University Press, 1999.

Damousi, Joy. "History Matters: The Politics of Grief and Injury in Australian History." *Australian Historical Studies* 118 (2002): 100–12.

——. *Living with the Aftermath: Trauma, Nostalgia and Grief in Post-War Australia*. Cambridge and Melbourne: Cambridge University Press, 2001.

——. Joy. *The Labour of Loss: Mourning, Memory and Wartime Bereavement in Australia*. Cambridge and Melbourne: Cambridge University Press, 1999.

Darian-Smith, Kate, and Paula Hamilton. *Memory and History in Twentieth Century Australia*. Melbourne: Oxford University Press, 1994.

Davis, Mark. *The Land of Plenty: Australia in the 2000s*. Melbourne: Melbourne University Press, 2008.

——. *Gangland: Cultural Elites and the New Generationalism*. Sydney: Allen & Unwin, 1997.

Davis, Natalie Zemon. *Slaves on Screen: Film and Historical Vision*. Cambridge: Harvard University Press, 2000.

Davison, Graeme. *The Use and Abuse of Australian History*. Sydney: Allen & Unwin, 2000.

Dechian, Sonja, Heather Millar, and Eva Sallis, eds. *Dark Dreams: Australian Refugee Stories by Young Writers Aged 11-20 Years*. Kent Town, SA: Wakefield Press, 2004.

Deleuze, Gilles, and Felix Guattari. *Kafka: Toward a Minor Literature*. Translated by Dana Polan. Minneapolis: University of Minnesota Press, 1986.

Dening, Greg. *Beach Crossings: Voyaging across Times, Cultures and Self*. Carlton, Victoria: The Miegunyah Press, 2004.

———. *The Death of William Gooch: A History's Anthropology*. Melbourne: Melbourne University Press, 1995.

———. *Mr. Bligh's Bad Language: Passion, Power, and Theatre on the Bounty*. Cambridge and New York: Cambridge University Press, 1992.

Department of Education, Science and Training. "The Australian History Summit: Transcript of Proceedings." Canberra: Department of Education, Science and Training, 2006.

Dessaix, Robert, ed. *Speaking Their Minds: Intellectuals and the Public Culture in Australia*. Sydney: ABC Books, 1998.

Dixon, Robert. "Citizens and Asylum Seekers: Emotional Literacy, Rhetorical Leadership and Human Rights." *Cultural Studies Review* 8, no. 2 (2002): 11–26.

Docker, John, and Gerhard Fischer. *Race, Colour and Identity in Australia and New Zealand*. Sydney: UNSW Press, 2000.

Doneson, Judith E. *The Holocaust in American Film*. Philadelphia, PA: Jewish Publication Society, 1987.

Douglas, Kate. "'Lost and Found': The Life Narratives of Child Asylum." *Life Writing* 3, no. 1 (2006): 39–58.

———. "Witnessing on the Web: Asylum Seekers and Letter-Writing Projects on Australian Activist Websites." *a/b: Auto/Biography Studies* 21, no. 1 (2006): 44–57.

———. "The Universal Autobiographer: The Politics of Normative Readings." *Journal of Australian Studies* 72 (2002): 173–79.

———. "'Blurbing' Autobiographical: Authorship and Autobiography." *Biography* 24, no. 4 (2001): 806–26.

Dovey, Jon. *Freakshow: First Person Media and Factual Television*. London: Pluto Press, 2000.

Dow, Coral and Janet Phillips. "Background Note: 'Forgotten Australians' and 'Lost Innocents': Child Migrants and Children in Institutional Care in Australia". *Parliamentary Library*. November 11, 2009. http://www.aph.gov.au/library/pubs/bn/sp/childmigrants.htm#_ftn1 (accessed January 26, 2010).

Dreher, Tanja. "Listening across Difference: Media and Multiculturalism Beyond the Politics of Voice." *Continuum: Journal of Media & Cultural Studies* 23, no. 4 (2009): 445–58.

Dutton, David. *One of Us? A Century of Australian Citizenship*. Sydney: UNSW Press, 2002.

Dyer, Richard. *White*. New York: Routledge, 1997.

Dyrenfurth, Nick. "Battlers, Refugees and the Republic: John Howard's Language of Citizenship." *Journal of Australian Studies* 84 (2005): 183–96.

Egan, Susanna. "The Company She Keeps: Demidenko and the Problems of Imposture in Autobiography." *Australian Literary Studies* 21, no. 4 (2004): 14–27.

Elder, Catriona. *Being Australian: Narratives of National Identity*. Sydney: Allen & Unwin, 2007.

Elder, Catriona, Angela Pratt, and Cath Ellis. "Running Race: Reconciliation, Nationalism and the Sydney 2000 Olympic Games." *International Review for the Sociology of Sport* 41, no. 2 (2006): 181–200.

Ellis, Cath. "A Strange Case of Double Vision: Reading Carmel Bird's *Stolen Children: Their Stories*." *Overland* 158 (2000): 75–79.

Ellis, John. *Seeing Things: Television in the Age of Uncertainty*. London and New York: I B Tauris Publishers, 2000.

Etzioni, Amitai, and Alyssa Bowditch, eds. *Public Intellectuals: An Endangered Species?* Lanham, MD: Rowman & Littlefield Publishers, 2006.

Everitt, Jacquie. *The Bitter Shore*. Sydney: Pan Macmillan, 2008.

Evers, Clifton. "Rethinking Gubbah Localism." *Kurungabaa: A Journal of the History, Literature and Ideas for Surfers* 1, no. 1 (2008): 1–4.

———. "Locals Only!" In *Everyday Multiculturalism Conference Proceedings*, edited by Selaraj Velayutham and Amanda Wise, 1–9. Sydney: Centre for Research on Social Inclusion, Macquarie University, 2007.

———. "My brother's keeper or my brother's problem?" *OnLine Opinion: Australia's Ejournal of Social and Political Debate*, March 14, 2007. http://www.online-opinion.com.au/view.asp?article=5607 (accessed February 4, 2009).

Falconer, Delia. "Historical Novels: Are We Writing Too Many of Them? Is There a Crisis of Relevance in Austlit?" *Eureka Street* 13, no. 2 (March 2003): 31–34.

Felman, Shoshana. "Introduction." In *Testimony: Crises of Witnessing in Literature, Psychoanalysis, and History*, edited by Shoshana Felman and Dori Laub. New York and London: Routledge, 1992.

Felman, Shoshana, and Dori Laub. *Testimony: Crises of Witnessing in Literature, Psychoanalysis, and History*. New York and London: Routledge, 1992.

Ferrier, Carole. "'Disappearing Memory" and the Colonial Present in Recent Indigenous Women's Writing." *Journal of the Association for the Study of Australian Literature*, Special Issue: *The Colonial Present Australian Writing for the 21st Century* (2008): 37–55.

Fidler, Richard. "In Conversation with Director Alison Broinowski," ABC *Local Radio*, September 10, 2007, [Transcript]. http://www.abc.net.au/queensland/conversations/stories/s2028619.htm?nsw (accessed December 14, 2009).

Fiske, John, Bob Hodge, and Graeme Turner. *Myths of Oz: Reading Australian Popular Culture*. Sydney: Allen & Unwin, 1987.

Foucault, Michel. "Intellectuals and Power." In *Language, Counter-Memory, Practice*, edited by Donald Bouchard. Ithaca, NY: Cornell University Press, 1977.

Frankenberg, Ruth. *White Women, Race Matters: The Social Construction of Whiteness*. Minneapolis: University of Minnesota Press, 1993.

Fraser, Nancy. "Rethinking the Public Sphere: A Contribution To the Critique of Actually Existing Democracy." In *Habermas and the Public Sphere*, edited by Craig Calhoun, 109–42. Cambridge, MA: MIT Press, 1992.

Friedlander, Saul, ed. *Probing the Limits of Representation: Nazism and the "Final Solution"*. Cambridge, MA and London: Harvard University Press, 1992.

Frisch, Michael H. *A Shared Authority: Essays on the Craft and Meaning of Oral and Public History*. Albany: State University of New York Press, 1990.

Frosh, Paul, and Amit Pinchevski. *Media Witnessing: Testimony in the Age of Mass Communication*. London: Palgrave Macmillan, 2009.

Frow, John. "UnAustralia: Strangeness and Value." *Cultural Studies Review* 13, no. 2 (2007): 38–52.

———. "A Politics of Stolen Time". *Australian Humanities Review* (February 1998). http://www.australianhumanitiesreview.org/ archive/Issue-February-1998/ frow1.html (accessed May 5, 2007).

Gaita, Raimond. "Guilt, Shame and Collective Responsibility." In *Reconciliation: Essays on Australian Reconciliation*, edited by Michelle Grattan, 275–87. Melbourne: Black, 2000.

Gall, Adam. "Taking/Taking Up: Recognition and the Frontier in Grenville's *the Secret River*." *Journal of the Association for the Study of Australian Literature* Special Issue: *The Colonial Present Australian Writing for the 21st Century* (2008): 94–104.

Gallop, Jane. *Anecdotal Theory*. Durham, NC: Duke University Press, 2002.

Garrett, Dianne. "Crow to Direct 'Bra Boys.'" *Variety*, March 21, 2007. http://www.variety.com/article/VR1117961590.html?categoryid=13&cs=1 (accessed February 15, 2009).

Gelber, Katharine. "A Fair Queue? Australian Public Discourse on Refugees and Immigration." *Journal of Australian Studies*, no. 77 (2002): 23–30.

Gelder, Ken, and Paul Salzman. *After the Celebration: Australian Fiction 1989-2007*. Melbourne: Melbourne University Press, 2009.

Gemes, Juno. "Witnessing the Apology." *Australian Aboriginal Studies*, no. 1 (2008): 115–23.

Gibbs, Anna. "Fictocriticism, Affect, Mimesis: Engendering Differences." *TEXT* 9, no. 1 (2005).

———. "Writing and the Flesh of Others." *Australian Feminist Studies* 18, no. 42 (2003): 309–19.

Gibson, Mark. "Noel Pearson and the 'Cultural Left': Between Listening and Deaf Opposition." *Continuum: Journal of Media & Cultural Studies* 23, no. 4 (2009): 465–76.

Gibson, Ross. *Seven Versions of an Australian Badland*. St. Lucia: University of Queensland Press, 2002.

Gigliotti, Simone. "Unspeakable Pasts as Limit Events: The Holocaust, Genocide, and the Stolen Generations." *Australian Journal of Politics and History* 49, no. 2 (2003): 164–81.

Gill, Alan. *Orphans of Empire: The Shocking True Story of Child Migration to Australia*. Sydney: Random House, 1997.

Gilmore, Leigh. *The Limits of Autobiography: Trauma and Testimony*. Ithaca, NY and London: Cornell University Press, 2001.

Gitlin, Todd. "Public Sphere or Public Sphericules?" In *Media, Ritual and Identity*, edited by Tamar Liebes and James Curran, 175–202. London: Routledge, 1998.

Glynn, Kevin. *Tabloid Culture: Trash Taste, Popular Power, and the Transformation of American Television*. Durham, NC and London: Duke University Press, 2000.

Goodall, Heather. "Challenging Voices: Tracing the Problematic Role of Testimony in Political Change." *Australian Literary Studies* 22, no. 4 (2006): 513–18.

———. "Telling Country: Memory, Modernity and Narratives in Rural Australia." *History Workshop Journal*, no. 47 (1999): 161–88.

———. "Colonialism and Catastrophe: Contested Memories of Nuclear Testing and Measles Epidemics at Ernabella." In *Memory and History in Twentieth-Century*

Australia, edited by Kate Darian-Smith and Paula Hamilton, 55–76. Melbourne: Oxford University Press, 1994.

Gooder, Haydie, and Jane M. Jacobs. "'On the Border of the Unsayable': The Apology in Postcolonizing Australia." *Interventions* 2, no. 2 (2000): 229–47.

Goot, Murray. "Turning Points: For Whom the Polls Told." In *2001: The Centenary Election*, edited by John Warhurst and Marian Simms. St. Lucia: University of Queensland Press, 2002.

Goot, Murray, and Tim Rowse. *Divided Nation?: Indigenous Affairs and the Imagined Public*. Melbourne: Melbourne University Press, 2007.

——, eds. *Make a Better Offer: The Politics of Mabo*. Leichhardt, NSW: Pluto Press, 1994.

Gordon, Michael. *Freeing Ali: The Human Face of the Pacific Solution*. Sydney: UNSW, 2005.

Gore, James. "The Idea of a National Museum for Australia." *Museum History Journal* 1, no. 1 (2008): 75–102.

Gosden, Diane. "'What If No One Had Spoken out against This Policy?' the Rise of Asylum Seeker and Refugee Advocacy in Australia." *PORTAL Journal of Multidisciplinary International Studies* 3, no. 1 (2006): 1–21.

Grace, Helen. "*Rabbit-Proof Fence*: The Journey of Feeling." *Australian Screen Education* 36 (2004): 143–49.

Grattan, Michelle. "Introduction." In *Reconciliation: Essays on Australian Reconciliation*, edited by Michelle Grattan, 3–8. Melbourne: Black, 2000.

Gregg, Melissa. "Affect." *M/C Journal* 8, no. 6 (2005): 1–13.

——. *Cultural Studies' Affective Voices*. London: Palgrave Macmillan, 2006.

Gregory, Jenny. "At the Australian History Summit." *History Australia* 4, no. 1 (June 2007): 10.1–10.5.

Griffiths, Tom. "'An Unnatural Disaster'? Remembering and Forgetting Bushfire." *History Australia* 6, no. 2 (2009): 35.1–35.7.

——. "Truth and Fiction: Judith Wright as Historian." *Australian Book Review* (August 2006): 25–30.

Gross, Andrew S., and Michael J. Hoffman. "Memory, Authority, and Identity: Holocaust Studies in Light of the Wilkomirski Debate." *Biography* 27, no. 1 (2004): 25–47.

Guerin, Frances, and Roger Hallas. "Introduction." In *The Image and the Witness: Trauma, Memory and Visual Culture*, edited by Frances Guerin and Roger Hallas, 1–20. London and New York: Wallflower Press, 2007.

——, eds. *The Image and the Witness: Trauma, Memory and Visual Culture*. London and New York: Wallflower Press, 2007.

Gunew, Sneja. *Haunted Nations: The Colonial Dimensions of Multiculturalisms*. London: Routledge, 2004.

——. "Against Multiculturalism: Rhetorical Images." In *Multiculturalism, Difference and Postmodernism*, edited by Gordon L. Clark, Dean Forbes and Roderick Francis, 38–53. Melbourne: Longman Cheshire, 1993.

Habermas, Jürgen. *The Structural Transformation of the Public Sphere: An Inquiry into a Category of Bourgeois Society*. Translated by Frederick Lawrence. Cambridge, MA: MIT Press, 1989.

Haebich, Anna. "'Between Knowing and Not Knowing': Public Knowledge of the Stolen Generations." *Aboriginal History* 25 (2001): 71–90.

———. *Broken Circles: Fragmenting Indigenous Families: 1800-2000*. Fremantle: Fremantle Arts Centre Press, 2000.

Hage, Ghassan. *Against Paranoid Nationalism: Searching for Hope in a Shrinking Society*. Annandale, NSW: Pluto Press, 2003.

———. *White Nation: Fantasies of White Supremacy in a Multicultural Society*. Annandale, NSW: Pluto Press, 2000.

Haggith, Toby, and Joanna Newman. *Holocaust and the Moving Image: Representations in Film and Television since 1933*. London: Wallflower Press, 2005.

Hamilton, Paula. "Memory Studies and Cultural History." In *Cultural History in Australia*, edited by Hsu-Ming Teo and Richard White, 81–97. Sydney: UNSW Press, 2003.

———. "Sale of the Century?: Memory and Historical Consciousness in Australia." In *Contested Pasts: The Politics of Memory*, edited by Katharine Hodgkin and Susannah Radstone, 136–52. London: Routledge, 2003.

Hamilton, Paula, and Linda Shopes. "Introduction: Building Partnerships between Oral History and Memory Studies." In *Oral History and Public Memories*, edited by Paula Hamilton and Linda Shopes, vii–xvii. Philadelphia, PA: Temple University Press, 2008.

Hansen, Guy. "White Hot History: The Review of the National Museum of Australia." *Public History Review* 11 (2004): 39–50.

Hartley, John. *Uses of Television*. London: Routledge, 1999.

———. *The Politics of Pictures: The Creation of the Public in the Age of Popular Media*. London and New York: Routledge, 1992.

Hartley, John, and Alan McKee. *The Indigenous Public Sphere: The Reporting and Reception of Aboriginal Issues in the Australian Media*. Oxford: Oxford University Press, 2000.

Hatley, James. *Suffering Witness: The Quandary of Responsibility after the Irreparable*. Albany, N.Y.: State University of New York Press, 2000.

Healey, Justin, ed. *Multiculturalism*. Balmain: Spinney Press, 2000.

Healy, Chris. *Forgetting Aborigines*. Sydney: UNSW Press, 2008.

———. *From the Ruins of Colonialism: History as Social Memory*. Cambridge: Cambridge University Press, 1997.

Heyward, Michael. *The Ern Malley Affair*. St. Lucia: University of Queensland Press, 1993.

Hill, David. *The Forgotten Children: Fairbridge Farm School and Its Betrayal of Australia's Child Migrants*. North Sydney: Random House Australia, 2007.

Hirsch, Marianne, and Leo Spitzer. "The Witness in the Archive: Holocaust Studies/Memory Studies." *Memory Studies* 2, no. 2 (2009): 151–70.

Hirst, John. *Sense and Nonsense in Australian History*. Melbourne: Black. Agenda, 2005.

Hodge, Bob, and Vijay Mishra. *Dark Side of the Dream: Australian Literature and the Postcolonial Mind*. Sydney: Allen & Unwin, 1990.

Hodge, Bob, and John O'Carroll. *Borderwork in Multicultural Australia*. Sydney: Allen & Unwin, 2006.

Hodgkin, Katharine, and Susannah Radstone, eds. *Contested Pasts: The Politics of Memory*. London: Routledge, 2003.

Housel, Teresa Heinz. "Australian Nationalism and Globalization: Narratives of the Nation in the 2000 Sydney Olympics' Opening Ceremony." *Critical Studies in Media Communication* 24, no. 5 (2007): 446–61.

Howard, John. "Address to the National Press Club." Great Hall, Parliament House, January 25, 2006. http://pandora.nla.gov.au/pan/10052/200603210000/www.pm.gov.au/news/speeches/speech1754.html (accessed January 30, 2009).

———. "Opening Address to the Australian Reconciliation Convention – Melbourne, 1997." *Australian Legal Information Institute.* http://www.austlii.edu.au/au/other/IndigLRes/car/1997/4/pmspoken.html (accessed January 25, 2009).

Huggan, Graham. *Australian Literature: Postcolonialism, Racism, Transnationalism.* Oxford and New York: Oxford University Press, 2007.

Huggins, Jackie. "Always Was Always Will Be." *Australian Historical Studies* 25, no. 100 (1993): 459–64.

Huggins, Jackie, and Isabel Tarrago. "Questions of Collaboration." *Hecate* xvi, no. i–ii (1990): 140–47.

Hughes-d'Aeth, Tony. "Which Rabbit-Proof Fence? Empathy, Assimilation, Hollywood." *Australian Humanities Review* 27 (September 2002). http://www.australianhumanitiesreview.org/archive/ Issue-September-2002/hughesdaeth.html (accessed May 30, 2009).

Hughes-Warrington, Marine. *History Goes to the Movies: Studying History on Film.* New Brunswick: Rutgers University Press, 2007.

Humphreys, Margaret. *Empty Cradles.* London and Sydney: Doubleday, 1994.

Husband, Charles. "Between Listening and Understanding." *Continuum: Journal of Media & Cultural Studies* 23, no. 4 (2009): 441–43.

———. "Differentiated Citizenship and the Multi-Ethnic Public Sphere." *Journal of International Communication* 5, no. 1/2 (1998): 134–48.

Huyssen, Andreas. "Trauma and Memory: A New Imaginary of Temporality." In *World Memory: Personal Trajectories in Global Time,* edited by Jill Bennett and Rosanne Kennedy, 16–29. London and New York: Palgrave Macmillan, 2003.

———. "Present Pasts: Media, Politics, Amnesia." In *Globalization,* edited by Arjun Appadurai, 57–77. Durham, NC and London: Duke University Press, 2001.

Insdorf, Annette. *Indelible Shadows: Film and the Holocaust.* New York: Cambridge University Press, 2002.

Irving, Helen. *To Constitute a Nation: A Cultural History of Australia's Constitution.* Melbourne: Cambridge University Press, 1999.

Isaac, Rhys. *The Transformation of Virginia: 1740-1790.* Chapel Hill: University of North Carolina Press, 1982.

Jackson, Liz. "Interview with John Howard, 19 February 1996." *Four Corners,* ABC, [Transcript]. http://www.abc.net.au/4corners/ content/2004/s1212701.htm (accessed January 28, 2009).

Jaivin, Linda. "Truth on the Border: Telling Stories About Asylum Seekers." *Overland,* no. 172 (2008): 8–17.

James, Wilmot, and Linda van de Vijver, eds. *After the TRC: Reflections on Truth and Reconciliation in South Africa.* Cape Town: David Philip Publishers, 2000.

Janson, Susan, and Stuart Macintyre, eds. *Making the Bicentenary: Special Issue of Australian Historical Studies.* Parkville, VIC: University of Melbourne, 1988.

Jenkins, Keith. *Refiguring History: New Thoughts on an Old Discipline*. London: Routledge, 2003.

Jenkins, Keith, Sue Morgan, and Alun Munslow, eds. *Manifestos for History*. London and New York: Routledge, 2007.

Johnson, Carol. "John Howard's 'Values' and Australian Identity." *Australian Journal of Political Science* 42, no. 2 (June 2007): 195–209.

Jones, Caroline. *Australian Story: Off the Record*. Sydney: ABC Books, 2007.

Jones, Gail. "Speaking Shadows: Justice and the Poetic." In *Just Words? Australian Authors Writing for Justice*, edited by Bernadette Brennan, 76–86. St. Lucia: University of Queensland Press, 2008.

Jones, Jennifer. *Black Writers, White Editors: Episodes of Collaboration and Compromise in Australian Publishing History*. North Melbourne: Australian Scholarly Publishing, 2009.

———. "Why Weren't We Listening? Oodgeroo and Judith Wright." *Overland* 171 (2003): 44–49.

Jones, Jo. "'Dancing the Old Enlightenment': *Gould's Book of Fish*, the Historical Novel and the Postmodern Sublime." *Journal of the Association for the Study of Australian Literature*, Special Issue: *The Colonial Present Australian Writing for the 21st Century* (2008): 114–29.

Jost, John, Gianna Totaro, and Christine Tyshing, eds. *The Demidenko File*. Ringwood: Penguin, 1996.

Jupp, James. *From White Australia to Woomera: The Story of Australian Immigration*. 2nd ed. Melbourne: Cambridge University Press, 2007.

———. "An Anxious Society Fears the Worst." *Journal of Australian Studies* 55 (1997): 1–11.

Kaplan, E. Ann. *Trauma Culture: The Politics of Terror and Loss in Media and Literature*. New Brunswick, NJ and London: Rutgers University Press, 2005.

Karskens, Grace. *The Colony: A History of Early Sydney*. Crows Nest, NSW: Allen & Unwin, 2009.

Kartinyeri, Doreen, and Sue Anderson. *Doreen Kartinyeri: My Ngarindjeri Calling*. Canberra: Aboriginal Studies Press, 2008.

Katsoulis, Melissa. *Telling Tales: A History of Literary Hoaxes*. Melbourne: Hardie Grant Books, 2010.

Keating, Paul. "The Redfern Address, 1992." In *Stirring Australian Speeches: The Definitive Collection from Botany to Bali*, edited by Michael Cathcart and Kate Darian-Smith, 317–22. Melbourne: Melbourne University Press, 2004.

Kelly, Rhys. "Testimony, Witnessing and Digital Activism." *Southern Review* 40, no. 3 (2008): 7–22.

Kennedy, Rosanne. "Stolen Generations Testimony: Trauma, Historiography, and the Question of 'Truth.'" *Aboriginal History* 25 (2001): 116–31.

———. "The Narrator as Witness: Testimony, Trauma and Narrative Form in *My Place*." *Meridian* 16, no. 2 (1997): 235–60.

Kennedy, Rosanne, and Tikka Jan Wilson. "Constructing Shared Histories: Stolen Generations Testimony, Narrative Therapy and Address." In *World Memory: Personal Trajectories in Global Time*, 119–39. London and New York: Palgrave Macmillan, 2003.

Kerr, Heather. "Fictocritical Empathy and the Work of Mourning." *Cultural Studies Review* 9, no. 1 (May 2003): 180–200.

——. "Sympathetic Topographies." *Parallax* 7, no. 2 (2001): 107–26.

Kerr, Heather, and Amanda Nettelbeck, eds. *The Space Between: Australian Women Writing Fictocriticism.* Nedlands: University of Western Australia Press, 1998.

Kevin, Tony. *A Certain Maritime Incident: The Sinking of the SIEV X.* Melbourne: Scribe Publications, 2004.

Khouri, Norma. *Forbidden Love.* London: Doubleday, 2003.

Kilby, Jane. *Violence and the Cultural Politics of Trauma.* Edinburgh: Edinburgh University Press, 2007.

Klein, Kerwin Lee. "On the Emergence of Memory in Historical Discourse." *Representations* 69 (2000): 127–50.

Knudsen, Eva Rask. *The Circle & the Spiral: A Study of Australian Aboriginal and New Zealand Maori Literature.* Amsterdam and New York: Rodopi, 2004.

Koval, Ramona. "Interview with Kate Grenville." *The Book Show.* July 17, 2005. ABC Radio National, [Transcript]. http://www.abc.net.au/rn/arts/bwriting/stories/s1414510.htm (accessed August 10, 2007).

Kuhn, Annette. *Family Secrets: Acts of Memory and Imagination.* London and New York: Verso, 2002.

LaCapra, Dominick. "Resisting Apocalypse and Rethinking History." In *Manifestos for History,* edited by Keith Jenkins, Sue Morgan and Alun Munslow, 160–78. London and New York: Routledge, 2007.

——. *History in Transit: Experience, Identity, Critical Theory.* Ithaca, N.Y. and London: Cornell University Press, 2004.

——. *Writing History, Writing Trauma.* Baltimore, M.D. and London: The John Hopkins Press, 2001.

——. *History and Memory after Auschwitz.* Ithaca, N.Y. and London: Cornell University Press, 1998.

Lackey, Jennifer, and Ernest Sosa, eds. *The Epistemology of Testimony.* Oxford: Clarendon Press, 2006.

Lamborn, Eve. "The Historical Blends with the Personal (Review of *Bluff Rock: Autobiography of a Massacre)." Antipodes* 20, no. 2 (2006): 212.

Landsberg, Alison. "America, the Holocaust, and the Mass Culture of Memory: Toward a Radical Politics of Empathy." *New German Critique: An Interdisciplinary Journal of German Studies* 71 (Spring–Summer 1997): 63–87.

Langer, John. *Tabloid Television: Popular Journalism and the 'Other News'.* London and New York: Routledge, 1998.

Langer, Lawrence L. *Holocaust Testimonies: The Ruins of Memory.* New Haven, CT: Yale University Press, 1991.

Laub, Dori. "Bearing Witness, or the Vicissitudes of Listening." In *Testimony: Crises of Witnessing in Literature, Psychoanalysis, and History,* edited by Shoshana Felman and Dori Laub, 57–74. New York and London: Routledge, 1992.

Leach, Michael, Geoffrey Stokes, and Ian Ward, eds. *The Rise and Fall of One Nation.* St. Lucia: University of Queensland Press, 2000.

Lejeune, Philippe. *On Autobiography.* Translated by Katherine Leary. Edited by Paul John Eakin. Minneapolis: University of Minnesota Press, 1989.

Lewis, John. "The History Wars from a Logical Perspective." *Quadrant* 48, no. 1–2 (January–February 2004): 54–57.

Leys, Ruth. *Trauma: A Genealogy.* Chicago, I.L.: University of Chicago Press, 2000.

Liebman, Stuart, ed. *Claude Lanzmann's Shoah: Key Essays*. Oxford and New York: Oxford University Press, 2007.

Lloyd, Justin. "The Listening Cure." *Continuum: Journal of Media & Cultural Studies* 23, no. 4 (2009): 447–87.

Lucashenko, Melissa, John McLaren, and Jennifer Rose. "Three Responses to Robert Manne's *in Denial.*" *Overland*, no. 163 (2001): 15–20.

Luker, Trish. "Ineffaceable Memories: The Truth of Testimony." *Australian Feminist Law Journal* 29 (December 2008): 133–54.

———. "Intention and Iterability in *Cubillo v. Commonwealth.*" *Journal of Australian Studies* 84 (2005): 35–42.

———. "'Postcolonising Amnesia in the Discourse of Reconciliation: The Void in the Law's Response to the Stolen Generations.'" *Australian Feminist Law Journal* 22 (June 2005): 67–88.

Lumby, Catharine. *Gotcha: Life in a Tabloid World*. St. Leonard, NSW: Allen & Unwin, 1999.

Lydon, Jane. "A Strange Time Machine: *The Tracker, Black and White*, and *Rabbit-Proof Fence* [Historical Overview]." *Australian Historical Studies* 35, no. 123 (2004): 137–48.

McAuley, Gay, ed. *Unstable Ground: Performance and the Politics of Place*. Brussels: P.I.E. Peter Lang, 2006.

MacCallum, Mungo. "Girt by Sea: Australia, the Refugees and the Politics of Fear." *Quarterly Essay*, no. 5 (2002): 1–73.

McCalman, Iain, and Ann McGrath, eds. *Proof & Truth: The Humanist as Expert*. Canberra: The Australian Academy of Humanities, 2003.

McCooey, David. *Artful Histories: Modern Australian Autobiography*. Melbourne: Cambridge University Press, 1996.

McCredden, Lyn. "Haunted Identities and the Possible Futures of 'Aust. Lit.'" *Journal of the Association for the Study of Australian Literature* Special issue: Spectres, Screens, Shadows, Mirrors (2007): 12–22.

———. "Writing Authority in Australia." In *The Ideas Market: An Alternative Take on Australia's Intellectual Life*, edited by David Carter, 80–94. Melbourne: Melbourne University Press, 2004.

McDonald, David, and Chris Cunneen. "Aboriginal Incarceration and Deaths in Custody: Looking Back and Looking Forward." *Current Issues in Criminal Justice* 9, no. 1 (1997): 5–20.

McGourty, John, ed. *Black Saturday: Stories of Love, Loss and Courage from the Victorian Bushfires*. Pymble, NSW: HarperCollins, 2009.

McGrath, Shane. "Compassionate Refugee Politics." *M/C Journal* 8, no. 6 (2005).

McIntyre, Iain. *How to Make Trouble and Influence People: Pranks, Hoaxes, Graffiti and Political Mischief-Making*. Sydney: Breakdown Press, 2009.

Macintyre, Stuart, and Anna Clark. *The History Wars*. Melbourne: Melbourne University Press, 2003.

McIver, Damian. "Representing Australianness: Our National Identity Brought to You by *Today Tonight.*" *Media International Australia*, no. 131 (May 2009): 46–56.

McKenna, Mark. "Metaphors of Lights and Darkness: The Politics of 'Black Armband' History." *Melbourne Journal of Politics* 25 (1998): 67–84.

McMaster, Don. *Asylum Seekers: Australia's Response to Refugees.* Melbourne: Melbourne University Press, 2001.

Maechler, Stefan. *The Wilkomirski Affair: A Study in Biographical Truth.* New York: Schocken, 2001.

Manne, Robert. "Why we weren't warned." *The Monthly* 47 (July 2009). http://www.themonthly.com.au/monthly-essays-robert-manne-why-we-weren-t-warned-victorian-bushfires-and-royal-commission-1780 (accessed September 20, 2009).

———. "In Denial: The Stolen Generations and the Right." In *Left Right Left: Political Essays 1977-2005,* edited by Robert Manne, 217–305. Melbourne: Black, 2005.

———. *Left Right Left: Political Essays 1977-2005.* Melbourne: Black, 2005.

———, ed. *Whitewash: On Keith Windschuttle's Fabrication of Aboriginal History.* Melbourne: Black Inc. Agenda, 2003.

———. *The Culture of Forgetting: Helen Demidenko and the Holocaust.* Melbourne: Text Publishing, 1996.

Manne, Robert, and David Corlett. "Sending Them Home." In *Left Right Left: Political Essays 1977-2005,* 392–467. Melbourne: Black, 2005.

Maral, Louise. "Warts and All: On Writing *The Secret River.*" *University of Sydney News.* August 26, 2006. University of Sydney, [Media release]. http://www.usyd.edu.au/news/84.html?newsstoryid=1240 (accessed January 17, 2008.

Marchetti, Elena. "The Deep Colonizing Practices of the Australian Royal Commission into Aboriginal Deaths in Custody." *Journal of Law and Society* 33, no. 3 (2006): 451–74.

———. "Critical Reflections Upon Australia's Royal Commission into Aboriginal Deaths in Custody." *Macquarie Law Journal* 5 (2005): 103–25.

Mares, Peter. *Borderline: Australia's Response to Refugees and Asylum Seekers in the Wake of the Tampa.* Sydney: UNSW Press, 2002.

Mares, Sarah, and Louise Newman, eds. *Acting from the Heart: Australian Advocates for Asylum Seekers Tell Their Stories.* Sydney: Finch Publishing, 2007.

Markus, Andrew. *Race: John Howard and the Remaking of Australia.* Crows Nest, NSW: Allen & Unwin, 2001.

Marr, David, and Marian Wilkinson. *Dark Victory.* Sydney: Allen & Unwin, 2003.

Mayne, Judith. *Cinema and Spectatorship.* London and New York: Routledge, 1993.

Merwick, Donna. *Death of a Notary: Conquest and Change in Colonial New York.* Ithaca, N.Y.: Cornell University Press, 1999.

Miller, Nancy K. *Getting Personal: Feminist Occasions and Other Autobiographical Acts.* New York: Routledge, 1991.

Miller, Nancy K., and Jason Tougaw. "Introduction: Extremities." In *Extremities: Trauma, Testimony, and Community,* edited by Nancy K. Miller and Jason Tougaw, 1–24. Urbana and Chicago: University of Illinois Press, 2002.

Minh-ha, Trinh T. *Women, Native, Others: Writing Postcoloniality and Feminism.* Bloomington: Indiana University Press, 1989.

Minow, Martha L. *Between Vengeance and Forgiveness: Facing History after Genocide and Mass Violence.* Boston, MA: Beacon Press, 1998.

Moran, Anthony. "What Settler Australians Talk About When They Talk About Aborigines: Reflections on an in-Depth Interview Study." *Ethnic and Racial Studies* 32, no. 5 (2009): 781–801.

Moreton-Robinson, Aileen. "Indigenous History Wars and the Virtue of the White Nation." In *The Ideas Market: An Alternative Take on Australia's Intellectual Life*, edited by David Carter, 219–35. Melbourne: Melbourne University Press, 2004.

———, ed. *Whitening Race: Essays in Social and Cultural Criticism*. Canberra: Aboriginal Studies Press, 2004.

———. Aileen. *Talkin' up to the White Woman: Aboriginal Women and Feminism*. Brisbane: University of Queensland Press, 2000.

Moreton-Robinson, Aileen, and Fiona Nicoll. "We Shall Fight Them on the Beaches: Protesting Cultures of White Possession." *Journal of Australian Studies* 30, no. 89 (2006): 149–60.

Morris, Meaghan. *Identity Anecdotes: Translation and Mass Culture*. London: Sage, 2006.

———. "On the Beach." In *Too Soon Too Late: History in Popular Culture*, 93–112. Bloomington: Indiana University Press, 1998.

———. "Panorama: The Live, the Dead and the Living." In *Island in the Stream: Myths of Place in Australian Culture*, edited by Paul Foss, 160–87. Pluto Press, 1988.

———. *The Pirate's Fiancée: Feminism, Reading and Postmodernism*. London: Verso, 1988.

Morrissey, Philip. "Dancing with Shadows: Erasing Aboriginal Self and Sovereignty." In *Sovereign Subjects: Indigenous Sovereignty Matters*, edited by Aileen Moreton-Robinson, 65–75. Sydney: Allen & Unwin, 2007.

Mudrooroo. *The Indigenous Literature of Australia: Milli Milli Wangka*. Melbourne: Hyland House, 1997.

Muecke, Stephen. *Ancient and Modern: Time, Culture and Indigenous Philosophy*. Sydney: UNSW Press, 2004.

———. "The Fall: Fictocritical Writing." *Parallax* 8, no. 4 (2002): 108–12.

———. *No Road (Bitumen All the Way)*. South Fremantle: Fremantle Arts Centre Press, 1997.

———. "Experimental History? The 'Space' of History in Recent Histories of Kimberley Colonialism." *The UTS Review* 2, no. 1 (May 1996): 1–11.

———. "Aboriginal Literature and the Repressive Hypothesis." *Southerly* 48, no. 4 (December 1988): 405–18.

Munslow, Alun. *Deconstructing History*. 2nd ed. London and New York: Routledge, 2006.

Mycak, Sonia. "Demidenko/Darville: A Ukrainian-Australian Point of View." *Australian Literary Studies* 21, no. 4 (2004): 111–33.

Neumann, Klaus. "But Is It History?" *Cultural Studies Review* 14, no. 1 (2008): 19–32.

———. *Refuge Australia: Australia's Humanitarian Record*. Sydney: UNSW Press, 2004.

Neville, Alisoun. "*Cubillo v. Commonwealth*: Classifying Text and the Violence of Exclusion." *Macquarie Law Journal* 5 (2005): 31–55.

Newman, Joan. "Race, Gender and Identity: *My Place* as Autobiography." In *Whose Place?: A Study of Sally Morgan's My Place*, edited by Delys Bird and Dennis Haskell, 66–74. Sydney: Angus & Robertson, 1992.

Nicoll, Fiona. "Indigenous Sovereignty and the Violence of Perspective: A White Woman's Coming out Story." *Australian Feminist Studies* 15, no. 33 (2000): 369–85.

——. "Pseudo-Hyphens and Barbaric/Binaries: Anglo-Celticity and the Cultural Politics of Tolerance." *Queensland Review* 6, no. 1 (1999): 77–84.

Nolan, Maggie. "In His Own Sweet Time: Carmen's Coming Out." *Australian Literary Studies* 21, no. 4 (2004): 134–48.

Nolan, Maggie, and Carrie Dawson. "Who's Who? Mapping Hoaxes and Imposture in Australian Literary History." *Australian Literary Studies* 21, no. 4 (2004): v–xx.

Nora, Pierre. "Reasons for the Current Upsurge in Memory." *Eurozine*. April 19, 2002. http://www.eurozine.com/articles/2002-04-19-nora-en.html (accessed August 3, 2007).

Nugent, Maria. "Review of *Bluff Rock: Autobiography of a Massacre*." *Australian Historical Studies* 37, no. 128 (2006): 146–48.

Nussbaum, Martha Craven. *Cultivating Humanity: A Classical Defense of Reform in Liberal Education*. Cambridge, MA: Harvard University Press, 1997.

——. *Poetic Justice: The Literary Imagination and Public Life*. Boston, MA: Beacon Press, 1995.

Nuttall, Sarah. "Telling 'Free' Stories? Memory and Democracy in South African Autobiography since 1994." In *Negotiating the Past: The Making of Memory in South Africa*, edited by Sarah Nuttall and Carli Coetzee, 75–88. Oxford: Oxford University Press, 1998.

Nuttall, Sarah, and Carli Coetzee, eds. *Negotiating the Past: The Making of Memory in South Africa*. Oxford: Oxford University Press, 1998.

O'Hara, Marguerite. "Stranger Than Non-Fiction: The Slippery Truth in *Forbidden Lie$*." *Metro Magazine*, no. 114 (2007): 20–25.

O'Keeffe, Anne. *Investigating Media Discourse*. London and New York: Routledge, 2006.

Olick, Jeffrey K. *The Politics of Regret: Collective Memory in the Age of Atrocity*. New York: Routledge, 2007.

Oliver, Kelly. *Witnessing: Beyond Recognition*. Minneapolis and London: University of Minnesota Press, 2001.

Olsen, Christine. *Rabbit-Proof Fence: The Screenplay*. Sydney: Currency Press, 2002.

Olubas, Brigitta, and Lisa Grenwell. "Re-Membering and Taking up an Ethics of Listening: A Response to Loss and the Maternal in 'the Stolen Children.'" *Australian Humanities Review* (July 1999). http://www.lib.latrobe.edu.au/AHR/archive/Issue-July-1999/olubas.html (accessed on April 20, 2007).

O'Neill, Margot. *Blind Conscience*. Sydney: UNSW Press, 2008.

Peel, Mark. *The Lowest Rung: Voices of Australian Poverty*. Cambridge: Cambridge University Press, 2003.

Penglase, Joanna. "'Wardies and Homies': The Forgotten Australians." *Care Leavers Australia Network*. n. d. http://www.clan.org.au/ page.php?pageID=23 (accessed January 9, 2010).

——. *Orphans of the Living: Growing up in 'Care' in Twentieth-Century Australia*. Fremantle: Curtin University Books, 2005.

Perera, Suvendrini, ed. *Our Patch: Enacting Australian Sovereignty Post-2001*. Perth: API Network, 2007.

——. "Our Patch: Domains of Whiteness, Geographies of Lack and Australia's Racial Horizons in the War on Terror." In *Our Patch: Enacting Australian*

Sovereignty Post-2001, edited by Suvendrini Perera, 119–46. Perth: Network Books, 2007.

———. "Race Terror, Sydney, December 2005." *Borderlands ejournal* 5, no. 1 (2006). http://www.borderlands.net.au/ vol5no1_2006/ perera_raceterror. htm (accessed January 20, 2009).

———. "The Good Neighbour: Conspicuous Compassion and the Politics of Proximity." *Borderlands ejournal* 3, no. 3 (2004).

———. "A Line in the Sea." *Race & Class* 44, no. 2 (2002): 23–39.

———. "What Is a Camp...?" *Borderlands ejournal* 1, no. 1 (2002): 1–63.

Perks, Robert, and Alistair Thomson, eds. *The Oral History Reader*. London and New York: Routledge, 2006.

Pierce, Peter. *The Country of Lost Children: An Australian Anxiety*. Melbourne: Cambridge University Press, 1999.

Pilkington, Doris. *Follow the Rabbit-Proof Fence*. St. Lucia, QLD: University of Queensland Press, 1996.

Pinto, Sarah, and Leigh Boucher. "Fighting for Legitimacy: Masculinity, Political Voice and *Ned Kelly.*" *Journal of Interdisciplinary Gender Studies* 10, no. 1 (2006): 1–29.

Pomeranz, Margaret. "Forbidden Lies," *At the Movies*, ABC TV, September 5, 2007, http://www.abc.net.au/atthemovies/txt/ s2007185.htm (accessed November 25, 2009).

Popkin, Jeremy D. *"Ego-Histoire* Down Under." *Australian Historical Studies* 129 (2007): 106–23.

———. *History, Historians, and Autobiography*. Chicago, I.L.: University of Chicago Press, 2005.

Potter, Emily and Kay Schaffer, *"Rabbit-Proof Fence*, Relational Ecologies and the Commodification of Indigenous Experience." *Australian Humanities Review* 31 (April 2004). http://www.australian humanitiesreview.org/archive/ Issue-April-2004/schaffer.html (accessed May 2, 2009).

Povinelli, Elizabeth A. *The Cunning of Recognition: Indigenous Alterities and the Making of Australian Multiculturalism*. Durham, N.C. and London: Duke University Press, 2002.

Poynting, Scott. "What Caused the Cronulla Riot?" *Race and Class* 48 (2006): 85–92.

Poynting, Scott, Greg Noble, Paul Tabar, and Jock Collins. *Bin Laden in the Suburbs: Criminalising the Arab Other*. Sydney: Sydney Institute of Criminology, 2004.

Pratt, Angela. *Practising Reconciliation?: The Politics of Reconciliation in the Australian Parliament, 1991-2000*. Canberra: Department of Parliamentary Services, 2005.

Pratt, Angela, Catriona Elder, and Cath Ellis. "Papering over the Differences: Australian Nationhood and the Normative Discourse of Reconciliation." In *Reconciliation, Multiculturalism, Identities: Difficult Dialogues, Sensible Solutions*, edited by Mary Kalantzis and Bill Cope, 135–48. Melbourne: Common Ground Publishing, 2001.

Probyn, Elspeth. *Blush: Faces of Shame*. Minneapolis and London: University of Minnesota Press, 2005.

———. "A-ffect: Let Her Rip." *M/C Journal* 8, no. 6 (2005): 1–18.

Probyn, Fiona. "Playing Chicken at the Intersection: The White Critic in/of Critical Whiteness Studies." *Borderlands ejournal* 13, no. 2 (2004). http://www.border-lands.net.au/vol3no2_2004/ probyn_ playing.htm (accessed April 4, 2009).
———. "A Poetics of Failure Is No Bad Thing: Stephen Muecke and Margaret Somerville's White Writing." *Journal of Australian Studies* 75 (2002): 17–26.
Probyn-Rapsey, Fiona. "Complicity, Critique, and Methodology." *ARIEL: A Review of International English Literature* 38, no. 2 (2008): 65–82.
———. "'No Last Word': Postcolonial Witnessing in *Jackson's Track* and *Jackson's Track Revisited.*" *Antipodes* (December 2008): 123–28.
Purdy, Jeannie. "Royal Commissions and Omissions: What Was Left out of the Report on the Death of John Pat." *Australian Journal of Law and Society* 10 (1994): 37–66.
Pybus, Cassandra. *Community of Thieves.* Melbourne: Minerva, 1992.
Radstone, Susannah. "Memory Studies: For and Against." *Memory Studies* 1, no. 1 (2007): 27–35.
———. *The Sexual Politics of Time: Confession, Nostalgia, Memory.* London and New York: Routledge, 2007.
———. "Trauma Theory: Contexts, Politics, Ethics." *Paragraph* 30, no. 1 (2007): 9–29.
———. "Cultures of Confession/Cultures of Testimony: Turning the Subject inside Out." In *Modern Confessional Writing: New Critical Essays,* edited by Jo Gill, 166–79. London and New York: Routledge, 2006.
———. "Reconceiving Binaries: The Limits of Memory." *History Workshop Journal* 59 (2005): 134–50.
———. "Social Bonds and Psychical Order: Testimonies." *Cultural Values* 5, no. 1 (2001): 59–78.
Read, Peter. "The Stolen Generations, the Historian and the Court Room." *Aboriginal History* 26 (2002): 51–61.
———. *The Stolen Generations: The Removal of Aboriginal Children in New South Wales: 1883–1969.* Sydney: Department of Aboriginal Affairs, NSW State Government, 1981.
Reed, Liz. "'Awakening': The Politics of Indigenous Control and Authenticity at Sydney 2000." *Australasian Music Research* 7, no. 2002 (2003): 95–101.
Renov, Michael. "First-Person Films: Some Theses on Self-Inscription." In *Rethinking Documentary: New Perspectives, New Practices,* edited by Thomas Austin and Wilma de Jong, 39–50. New York: Open University Press, 2008.
———. *The Subject of Documentary.* Minneapolis and London: University of Minnesota Press, 2004.
Reynolds, Henry. *The Other Side of the Frontier: Aboriginal Resistance to the European Invasion of Australia.* Sydney: UNSW Press, 2006.
Riemer, A.P. *The Demidenko Debate.* St. Leonards, NSW: Allen & Unwin, 1996.
Robbins, Jane. "The Howard Government and Indigenous Rights: An Imposed National Unity?" *Australian Journal of Political Science* 42, no. 2 (June 2007): 315–28.
Roof, Judith, and Robyn Wiegman, eds. *Who Can Speak? Authority and Critical Identity.* Urbana, I.L.: University of Illinois Press, 1996.
Rooney, Brigid. *Literary Activists: Writer-Intellectuals and Australian Public Life.* St. Lucia: University of Queensland Press, 2009.

Rose, Deborah Bird. *Reports from a Wild Country: Ethics for Decolonisation.* Sydney: UNSW Press, 2004.

———. *Dingo Makes Us Human: Life and Land in an Australian Aboriginal Culture.* Oakleigh, VIC: Cambridge University Press, 2000.

———. *Hidden Histories: Black Stories from Victoria River Downs, Humbert River and Wave Hill Stations.* Canberra: Aboriginal Studies Press, 1991.

Rosenstone, Robert A., ed. *Revisioning History: Film and the Construction of a New Past.* Princeton: Princeton University Press, 1995.

———. "Introduction." In *Revisioning History: Film and the Construction of a New Past,* edited by Robert A. Rosenstone, 3–14. Princeton: Princeton University Press, 1995.

———. *History on Film/Film on History.* New York: Routledge, 2006.

Rotberg, Robert I. "Apology, Truth Commissions, and Intrastate Conflict." In *Taking Wrongs Seriously: Apologies and Reconciliation,* edited by Elazar Barkan and Alexander Karn, 33–49. Stanford, C.A.: Stanford University Press, 2006.

Roth, Michael S. *The Ironist's Cage: Memory, Trauma and the Construction of History.* New York: Columbia University Press, 1995.

Roth, Michael S., and Charles G. Salas, eds. *Disturbing Remains: Memory, History and Crisis in the Twentieth Century.* Los Angeles, C.A.: Getty Research Institute, 2001.

Rowse, Tim. *After Mabo: Interpreting Indigenous Traditions.* Carlton: Melbourne University Press, 1993.

———. "Sally Morgan's Kaftan." *Australian Historical Studies* 25, no. 100 (1993): 465–68.

Rudd, Kevin, "Address at the Apology to the Forgotten Australians and Former Child Migrants." November 16, 2009, Great Hall, Parliament House. *Prime Minister of Australia: Speeches.* http://www.pm.gov.au/node/6321 (accessed January 9, 2010).

———. "Apology to Australia's Indigenous Peoples." February 13, 2008, Parliament House, Canberra. *Prime Minister of Australia: Speeches.* http://www.pm.gov.au/node/5952 (accessed January 23, 2010).

Rutherford, Jennifer. *The Gauche Intruder: Freud, Lacan and the White Australian Fantasy.* Melbourne: Melbourne University Press, 2000.

Sanders, Mark. *Complicities: The Intellectual and Apartheid.* Durham, N.C. and London: Duke University Press, 2002.

Saxton, Libby. *Haunted Images: Film, Ethics, Testimony and the Holocaust.* London and New York: Wallflower Press, 2008.

Scalmer, Sean. *Dissent Events: Protest, the Media and the Political Gimmick in Australia.* Sydney: UNSW Press, 2002.

———. "The Battlers Versus the Elites." *Overland,* no. 154 (1999): 9–13.

Schaffer, Kay. "Legitimating the Personal Voice: Shame and the Stolen Generation Testimony." In *Resistance and Reconciliations: Writing in the Commonwealth,* edited by Bruce Bennett, Susan Cowan, Jacqueline Lo, Satendra Nandan and Jennifer Webb, 47–62. Canberra: The Association for Commonwealth Literature and Language Studies, 2003.

———. "Manne's Generation: White Nation Response to the Stolen Generation Report." *Australian Humanities Review* 24 (June–August 2001). http://www.australianhumanitiesreview.org/archive/Issue-June-2001/ schaffer.html (accessed April 24, 2009).

Schaffer, Kay, and Sidonie Smith. "Conjunctions: Life Narratives in the Field of Human Rights." *Biography* 27, no. 1 (Winter 2004): 1–24.

――――. *Human Rights and Narrated Lives: The Ethics of Recognition*. New York: Palgrave Macmillan, 2004.

Schlunke, Katrina. "Historicising Whiteness: Captain Cook Possesses Australia." In *Historicising Whiteness: Transnational Perspectives on the Construction of an Identity*, edited by Leigh Boucher, Jane Carey and Katherine Ellinghaus, 41–50. Melbourne: RMIT Publishing/School of Historical Studies, University of Melbourne, 2007.

――――. *Bluff Rock: Autobiography of a Massacre*. Fremantle: Curtin University Books, 2005.

Schlunke, Katrina, and Anne Brewster. "We Four: Fictocriticism Again." *Continuum: Journal of Media & Cultural Studies* 19, no. 3 (2005): 393–95.

Scott, Joan W. "The Evidence of Experience." *Critical Inquiry* 17, no. 4 (Summer 1991): 773–97.

Scott, Rosie, and Thomas Keneally, eds. *Another Country*. Broadway, NSW: Sydney Pen & Halstead Press, 2005.

Sedgwick, Eve Kosofsky, and Adam Frank, eds. *Shame and Its Sisters: A Silvan Tomkins Reader*. Durham, N.C. and London: Duke University Press, 1995.

Seltzer, Mark. "Wound Culture: Trauma in the Pathological Public Sphere." *October* 80 (Spring 1997): 3–26.

Sheridan, Susan. "Different Lives: Two Aboriginal Women's Stories." *Antipodes* 2, no. 1 (1989): 20–23.

Silverman, Kaja. *The Threshold of the Visible World*. New York: Routledge, 1996.

Simic, Zora. "Were Westies White? Negotiating Race and Place in the Western Suburbs of Sydney." In *Historicising Whiteness: Transnational Perspective on the Construction of an Identity*, edited by Leigh Boucher, Jane Carey and Katherine Ellinghaus, 63–70. Melbourne: RMIT Publishing in association with the School of Historical Studies, University of Melbourne, 2007.

Simons, Margaret. *The Meeting of the Waters: The Hindmarsh Island Affair*. Sydney: Hodder, 2003.

Sinclair, John. "More Than an Old Flame: National Symbolism and the Media in the Torch Ceremony of the Olympics." *Media International Australia*, no. 97 (November 2000): 35–46.

Sitzia, Lorraine. "A Shared Authority: An Impossible Goal?" *Oral History Review* 30, no. 1 (2003): 87–101.

Smith, Bernard. *The Spectre of Truganini*. Sydney: Australian Broadcasting Commission, 1980.

Smith, Sidonie, and Julia Watson. *Reading Autobiography: A Guide for Interpreting Life Narratives*. Minneapolis and London: University of Minnesota Press, 2001.

Sobchack, Vivian, ed. *The Persistence of History: Cinema, Television, and the Modern Event*. New York and London: Routledge, 1996.

Somerville, Margaret. *Body/Landscape Journals*. Melbourne: Spinifex Press, 1999.

Sontag, Susan. *Regarding the Pain of Others*. New York: Farrar, Straus and Giroux, 2003.

Spillman, Lyn. *Nation and Commemoration: Creating National Identities in the United States and Australia*. Cambridge and New York: Cambridge University Press, 1997.

Spivak, Gayatri Chakravorty. "Three Women's Texts and Circumfession." In *Postcolonialism & Autobiography*, edited by Alfred Hornung and Enrstpeter Ruhe, 7–24. Amsterdam: Rodopi, 1998.

———. "Can the Subaltern Speak?" In *Marxism and the Interpretation of Culture*, edited by Cary Nelson and Lawrence Grossberg, 271–313. Chicago: University of Illinois Press, 1988.

Stanner, W.E.H. *After the Dreaming*. Crows Nest, NSW: Australian Broadcasting Commission, 1969.

Stephenson, Peta. "Typologies of Security: Indigenous and Muslim Australians in the Post-9/11 Imaginary." *Journal of Australian Studies* 33, no. 4 (2009): 473–88.

Stratton, David. "Bra Boys," *At the Movies*, ABC TV, March 14, 2007, [Transcript]. http://www.abc.net.au/atthemovies/txt/s1864026.htm (accessed January 11, 2009).

Sturken, Marita. *Tangled Memories: The Vietnam War, the AIDS Epidemic, and the Politics of Remembering*. Berkeley: University of California Press, 1997.

Tatz, Colin. *With Intent to Destroy: Reflecting on Genocide*. London: Verso, 2003.

———. "The Reconciliation Bargain." *Melbourne Journal of Politics* 25 (1998): 1–5.

Taylor, Charles. *Multiculturalism and "the Politics of Recognition": An Essay with Commentary*. Edited by Amy Gutmaan. Princeton, N.J.: Princeton University Press, 1992.

Taylor, Tony. *Denial: History Betrayed*. Melbourne: Melbourne University Press, 2008.

Tebbutt, John. "The Object of Listening." *Continuum: Journal of Media & Cultural Studies* 23, no. 4 (2009): 549–59.

Thill, Cate. "Courageous Listening, Responsibility for the Other and the Northern Territory Intervention." *Continuum: Journal of Media & Cultural Studies* 23, no. 4 (2009): 537–48.

Thomas, Nicholas. "Ethnographic History." In *The Oxford Companion to Australian History*, edited by Graeme Davison, John Hirst and Stuart Macintyre, 225–26. Melbourne: Oxford University Press, 1998.

Thompson, Janna. *Taking Responsibility for the Past: Reparation and Historical Injustice*. Cambridge: Polity Press, 2002.

Thomson, Alistair. "Sharing Authority: Oral History and the Collaborative Process." *Oral History Review* 30, no. 1 (2003): 23–26.

Trezise, Bryoni. "Ambivalent Bereavements: Embodying Loss in the Twenty-First Century." *Performance Paradigms* 5, no. 2 (2009). http://www.performanceparadigm.net/journal/issue2/articles/ambivalent-bereavements-embodying-loss-in-the-twenty-first-century/ (accessed December 28, 2009).

———. "Recovering Memories: Versions of a Misremembered Australian Body." *Australian Feminist Law Journal* 29 (December 2008): 155–75.

Tumarkin, Maria. *Traumascapes: The Power and Fate of Places Transformed by Tragedy*. Carlton: Melbourne University Press, 2005.

Turner, Graeme. "Television and the Nation: Does This Matter Any More?" in *Television Studies After TV: Understanding Television in the Post-Broadcast Era*, edited by Graeme Turner and Jinna Tay, 54–64. London and New York: Routledge, 2009.

———. *Ending the Affair: The Decline of Current Affairs in Australia.* Sydney: UNSW Press, 2005.

———. "'Popularising Politics': *This Day Tonight* and Australian Television Current Affairs." *Media International Australia*, no. 106 (February 2003): 137–50.

———. "'Why Does Cultural Studies Want History,'" *Australian Historical Studies* 33, no. 118 (2002): 113–20.

———. *Making It National: Nationalism and Australian Popular Culture.* Sydney: Allen & Unwin, 1994.

Tyler, Heather. *Asylum: Voices Behind the Razor Wire.* Melbourne: Lothian Books, 2003.

Urban, Andrew L. "Noyce, Phillip: Rabbit-Proof Fence." *Urban Cinefile*, February 21, 2002. http://www.urbancinefile.com.au/ home/view.asp?Article_ID=5770 (accessed December 19, 2009).

Valentine, Alana. *Parramatta Girls.* Sydney: Currency Press, 2007.

van Toorn, Penny. *Writing Never Arrives Naked: Early Aboriginal Cultures of Writing in Australia.* Canberra: Aboriginal Studies Press, 2006.

———. "Indigenous Australian Life Writing: Tactics and Transformations." In *Telling Stories: Indigenous History and Memory in Australia and New Zealand*, edited by Bain Attwood and Fiona Magowan, 1–20. Sydney: Allen & Unwin, 2001.

———. "Indigenous Texts and Narratives." In *The Cambridge Companion to Australian Literature*, edited by Elizabeth Webby, 19–49. Cambridge: Cambridge University Press, 2000.

———. "Tactical History Business: The Ambivalent Politics of Commodifying the Stolen Generations Stories." *Southerly* (Spring–Summer 1999): 252–66.

Veracini, Lorenzo. "A Prehistory of Australia's History Wars: The Evolution of Aboriginal History During the 1970s and 1980s." *Australian Journal of Politics and History* 52, no. 3 (2006): 439–54.

———. "Of a 'Contested Ground' and an 'Indelible Stain': A Difficult Reconciliation between Australia and Its Aboriginal History During the 1990s and 2000s." *Aboriginal History* 27 (2003): 224–39.

Wadjularbinna, "A Gungalidda Grassroots Perspective on Refugees and the Recent Events in the Us," *Borderlands ejournal* 1, no. 1 (2002). http://www.borderlands. net.au/vol1no1_2002/wadjularbinna.html (accessed November 20, 2009).

Wake, Caroline. "After Effects: Performing the Ends of Memory: An Introduction to Volume I." *Performance Paradigms* 5, no. 1 (2009). http://www.performan-ceparadigm.net/journal/issue-51/ articles/after-effects-performing-the-ends-of-memory-an-introduction-to-volume-i/ (accessed December 28, 2009).

Warner, Michael. "Publics and Counterpublics." *Public Culture* 14, no. 1 (2002): 49–90.

Wassil-Grimm, Claudette. *Diagnosis for Disaster: The Devastating Truth About False Memory Syndrome and Its Impact on Accusers and Families.* Woodstock, N.Y.: Overlook Press, 1995.

Watson, Christine. "'Believe Me': Acts of Witnessing in Aboriginal Women's Autobiographical Narratives." *Journal of Australian Studies* 64 (2000): 142–52.

Watson, Irene. "Settled and Unsettled Spaces: Are We Free to Roam?" In *Sovereign Subjects: Indigenous Sovereignty Matters*, edited by Aileen Moreton-Robinson, 15–32. Crows Nest: Allen & Unwin, 2007.

Weine, Stevan. *Testimony after Catastrophe: Narrating the Traumas of Political Violence.* Evanston, I.L.: Northwestern University Press, 2006.

Weisser, Susan Ostrov, and Jennifer Fleischner, eds. *Feminist Nightmares: Women at Odds - Feminism and the Problem of Sisterhood.* New York: New York University Press, 1994.

Westcott, Robyn. "Witnessing Whiteness: Articulating Race and the 'Politics of Style.'" *Borderlands ejournal* 3, no. 2 (2004). http://www.borderlands.net. au/vol3no2_2004/westcott_witnessing.html (accessed June 6, 2009).

White, Richard. *Inventing Australia: Images and Identity 1788-1980.* Sydney: George Allen & Unwin, 1981.

Whitlock, Gillian. *Soft Weapons: Autobiography in Transit.* Chicago, I.L.: Chicago University Press, 2007.

———. "Active Remembrance: Testimony, Memoir and the Work of Reconciliation." In *Rethinking Settler Colonialism: History and Memory in Australia, Canada, Aotearoa New Zealand and South Africa,* edited by Annie E. Coombes. 24–44. Manchester and New York: Manchester University Press, 2006.

———. "Becoming Migloo." In *The Ideas Market,* edited by David Carter, 236–58. Melbourne: Melbourne University Press, 2004.

———. "Consuming Passions: Reconciliation in Women's Intellectual Memoir." *Tulsa Studies in Women's Literature* 23, no. 1 (2004): 13–28.

———. "Tainted Testimony: The Khouri Affair." *Australian Literary Studies* 21, no. 4 (2004): 165–77.

———. "Strategic Remembering: Fabricating Local Subjects." In *Selves Crossing Cultures: Autobiography and Globalisation,* edited by Rosamund Dalziell, 162–77. Melbourne: Australian Scholarly Publishing, 2002.

———. "In the Second Person: Narrative Transactions in Stolen Generations Testimony." *Biography* 21, no. 1 (Winter 2001): 197–214.

———. "From Biography to Autobiography." In *The Cambridge Companion to Australian Literature,* edited by Elizabeth Webby, 232–57. Cambridge: Cambridge University Press, 2000.

Wieviorka, Annette. *The Era of the Witness.* Translated by Jared Stark. Ithaca, N.Y.: Cornell University Press, 2006.

Wills, Sara. "Between the Hostel and the Detention Centre: Possible Trajectories of Migrant Pain and Shame in Australia." Edited by William Logan and Keir Reeves, 263–80. London and New York: Routledge, 2009.

———. "Losing the Right to Country: The Memory of Loss and the Loss of Memory in Claiming the Nation as Space (or Being Cruel to Be Kind in the 'Multicultural' Asylum)." *New Formations* 51 (Winter 2003): 50–65.

———. "Un-Stitching the Lips of a Migrant Nation." *Australian Historical Studies* 33, no. 118 (2002): 71–89.

Wilson, Jean Moorcroft, and Cecil Woolf, eds. *Authors Take Sides: Iraq and the Gulf War.* Melbourne: Melbourne University Press, 2004.

Wilson, Tikka Jan. "Racism, Moral Community, and Australian Aboriginal Testimony." *Biography* 27, no. 1 (Winter 2004): 78–103.

Wimmer, Adi. "Why We Need Black Armbands." *Journal of Australian Studies* 75 (2002): 13–16, 176.

Windschuttle, Keith. *The Fabrication of Aboriginal History Volume 1: Van Dieman's Land 1803-1847.* Vol. 1. Sydney: Macleay Press, 2002.

Winter, J.M., ed. *Remembering War: The Great War between Memory and History in the Twentieth Century.* New Haven, C.T.: Yale University Press, 2006.

———. *Sites of Memory, Sites of Mourning: The Great War in European Cultural History.* Cambridge and New York: Cambridge University Press, 1995.

Wolfe, Patrick. "Robert Manne, the Apology and Genocide." *Arena* (April–May 2008): 31–33.

Wray, Matt, and Annalee Mewitz. "Introduction." In *White Trash: Race and Class in America,* edited by Matt Wray and Annalee Mewitz, 1–14. New York and London: Routledge, 1997.

Yaeger, Patricia. "Consuming Trauma; or, the Pleasures of Merely Circulating." In *Extremities: Trauma, Testimony, and Community,* edited by Nancy K. Miller and Jason Tougaw, 25–51. Urbana and Chicago: University of Illinois Press, 2002.

Yonetani, Julia. "The 'History Wars' in Comparative Perspective." *Cultural Studies Review* 10, no. 2 (September 2004): 33–50.

Young, James. *The Texture of Memory: Holocaust Memorials and Meaning.* New Haven, C.T. and London: Yale University Press, 1993.

Theses

Pinto, Sarah Winifred. "Emotional Histories: Contemporary Australian Historical Fictions." Ph.D. Thesis, Department of History, The University of Melbourne, 2007.

Index